CHRISTIAN ANTIOCH

CHRISTIAN ANTIOCH

A study of
early Christian thought
in the East

D. S. WALLACE-HADRILL

CAMBRIDGE UNIVERSITY PRESS

CAMBRIDGE
LONDON   NEW YORK   NEW ROCHELLE
MELBOURNE   SYDNEY

Published by the Press Syndicate of the University of Cambridge
The Pitt Building, Trumpington Street, Cambridge CB2 1RP
32 East 57th Street, New York, NY 10022, USA
296 Beaconsfield Parade, Middle Park, Melbourne 3206, Australia

First published 1982

Printed in Great Britain at
the University Press, Cambridge

Library of Congress catalogue card number: 81-17100

British Library Cataloguing in Publication Data
Wallace-Hadrill, D. S.
    Christian Antioch: a study of early Christian
    thought in the East.
    1. Antiochian school
    I. Title
    230'.1'3   BR205

ISBN 0 521 23425 5

Contents

Foreword	*page* vii
Abbreviations	viii
Introduction: survey of the history of Antioch	1
1 The religious background to Antiochene Christianity: pagan, jewish, gnostic	14
2 The interpretation of the biblical record	27
3 Historiography in the Eastern Church	52
4 The doctrine of the nature of God	67
5 The use of Greek philosophy by the Eastern Church	96
6 The human experience of Christ and the salvation of man	117
7 Antiochene theology and the religious life	151
Appendix 1. Eastern representation at Nicaea	165
Appendix 2. The feminine element in Syrian Christianity	167
Notes	169
Bibliography	207
Index	215

Foreword

This book had its beginning, I think, on a day early in the second World War when I asked Professor Thomas Walter Manson to recommend a book which would give me a general view of all that was meant by the term 'Antiochene'. He replied, 'There isn't such a book', and then with the twinkle of the eye which endeared him to so many, he added, 'so you had better write it.' The present book, thirty-nine years later, is far from being the book which that greatest of scholars may have had in mind, but I have tried to make it one which might have been useful to me in my youth.

I have been fortunate in the generous understanding of my wife; in the scholarship of my friend, Mr J. K. Waddell, who many times saved me from my own ignorance; in my surgeon, Mr Robert Ryall, who gave me that very great gift, time in which to finish what I had begun; and in the constant support of my brother, Professor J. M. Wallace-Hadrill, to whom I dedicate a book which would have been better if I had more often acted on his advice.

MICHAELI, FRATRI ET SOCIO

Aldenham, Hertfordshire   D. S. W.-H.

Abbreviations

A.C.O.	*Acta Conciliorum Oecumenicorum*, ed. E. Schwartz (Berlin, 1914ff.)
C.S.C.O.	Corpus Scriptorum Christianorum Orientalium (Louvain, 1903ff.)
C.S.E.L.	Corpus Scriptorum Ecclesiasticorum Latinorum (Vienna, 1866ff.)
G.C.S.	Die griechischen christlichen Schriftsteller der ersten drei Jahrhunderte (Leipzig and Berlin, 1897ff.)
H.T.R.	*Harvard Theological Review* (New York, 1908ff.; Cambridge, Mass., 1910ff.)
J.R.S.	*Journal of Roman Studies* (London, 1911ff.)
J.T.S.	*Journal of Theological Studies* (London, 1900–5; Oxford, 1906–49; N.S., Oxford, 1950ff.)
P.G.	Patrologia Graeca, ed. J. P. Migne (162 vols., Paris, 1857–66)
P.L.	Patrologia Latina, ed. J. P. Migne (221 vols., Paris, 1844–64)
Pat. Or.	Patrologia Orientalis, ed. R. Graffin and F. Nau (Paris, 1903ff.)
Pat. Syr.	Patrologia Syriaca (Paris, 1894–1926)
S.C.	*Sources chrétiennes* (Paris, 1941ff.)
T.U.	Texte und Untersuchungen (Leipzig)
Z.A.T.W.	*Zeitschrift für die alttestamentliche Wissenschaft*
Z.N.T.W.	*Zeitschrift für die neutestamentliche Wissenschaft*

Introduction: survey of the history of Antioch

The name 'Antioch' can denote three different areas: the walled city; the administrative region, comprising the surrounding countryside and its villages, extending perhaps as far as fifty miles from the city; the ecclesiastical diocese, whose vast extent is shown on the map.[1] This brief introductory survey is confined largely to the city. Succeeding chapters will spread wider to embrace cultural centres elsewhere in the diocese. The administrative region surrounding the city is not directly treated at all.

The geographical location of Antioch was in part the cause of its wealth and importance and was in part the cause of its eclipse. It was built in a fertile, well-watered region which controlled an important network of roads linking east with west and north with south. It was, however, situated on a geological formation which made it prone to severe earthquakes and the eventual southward extension of the city up the slopes of Mount Silpius rendered it dangerously vulnerable to attack from above. The combination of repeated destruction by earthquakes and the skilful use of the higher slopes of the mountain by the Persian invaders in the sixth century A.D. and the Arab invaders in the seventh ensured that despite its great commercial and military importance the rôle of Antioch as the key city of the eastern empire could not survive indefinitely.

The founding of Antioch shortly after the death of Alexander the Great in 323 B.C. formed part of a plan to secure north western Syria in the control of Seleucus Nicator, into whose hands this part of Alexander's immense territories fell. Seleucus had obtained Syria by force of arms, defeating Antigonus at Ipsus in 301 B.C. Antigonus had already begun to build a city in a strong position between the River Orontes and the Lake of Antioch, but Seleucus chose a new site about five miles to the south east, between the river and the north western slopes of Mount Silpius, named it after his father Antiochus, and brought to it a population composed of Athenians from the abortive city of Antigonia, some descendants of earlier settlers in the district and a large number of his own Macedonian soldiers with their wives and children. Within a century the male nucleus of the population is said to have comprised 6,000 men.[2] A great attraction of this site was the proximity of Daphne, less than ten miles down river to the south west, an

1

area of remarkable natural beauty, endowed with springs and groves of
trees and associated in local mythology with Herakles, Apollo, the maiden
Daphne and the judgement of Paris. Daphne became a flourishing suburb
of Antioch, eventually containing a stadium for Olympic games which
rivalled those held in Greece.

Antioch had not originally been intended to be the capital of Syria. It
took over this function from Seleucia on the Mediterranean coast at an
unknown date and became the administrative and military centre of the
region for the remainder of its history, excluding brief periods of disgrace
in Roman times when it was stripped of its dignity after particularly bad
displays of civil insubordination. Its rapidly-growing importance is indicated
by the expansion of the city by Seleucus II during the mid-third century
B.C., when it overflowed on to the island in the Orontes. As the river
approaches Antioch from the north east it divides to enclose the island,
which is rather less than a mile in length and half a mile in width. The river
provided a good defensive boundary to the west of the city.

The growing influence of Rome in the eastern Mediterranean during the
early second century B.C. was felt in Antioch when it received migrants
from Greece, possibly refugees from Roman rule. Antiochus III (223–
187 B.C.) supported Hannibal against Rome and paid for his support by
being defeated by Roman forces in 190 B.C. and being subjected to the
payment of heavy annual tribute. The influx of Greek migrants necessi-
tated further expansion of the city, this time eastwards up the foothills
of Mount Silpius. Under the Hellenizing zeal of Antiochus IV, Epiphanes
(175–163 B.C.) Antioch began to earn the reputation for luxury and magnificence which later caused Ammianus Marcellinus to call the city 'the
fair crown of the Orient'. The eastward extension of the city was given its
own name, Epiphania, and was equipped with its own *agora* and public
buildings. The first steps were at the same time taken to control the flow
of the variable torrent named Parmenius, which in flood rushed down
Mount Silpius through the city into the Orontes. Epiphanes built an aque-
duct to carry this unpredictable stream through his new district of Epiphania to storage cisterns on the mountainside, before it was allowed to
descend to the river. It is probable that the great half-finished Charonion
bust carved in the stone of the mountainside was begun and abandoned at
this period, possibly during a time of plague. The failure of Epiphanes'
policy of Hellenization to integrate the Jews into his scheme to unite the
Mediterranean seaboard gave rise to outbreaks of anti-Jewish rioting in
Antioch, the earliest recorded instance of a phenomenon that was to
persist for the next seven centuries. The increasing dominance of Rome
brought with it a corresponding decline in the power of the Seleucid kings,
to the point at which Antiochus VII (138–129 B.C.) was defeated by the
Parthians on his eastern frontier. There followed a period of intrigue be-

tween contenders for the throne during which Antioch could only decline further. Although Cicero described the city as renowned and populous and praised its reputation for scholarship and the arts, this cannot have amounted to much in comparison with what was to come during the Christian era. There were commercial links with the west through the port of Delos as an intermediary, but the political instability of the first century B.C. rendered commerce a risky venture. The uncertainties of life at Antioch during this period lends probability to the report that, when Tigranes of Armenia occupied Syria in 83 B.C., he did so at the invitation of Syrians who wanted security. But Tigranes' rule, whether begun peacefully or by force of arms, gradually lost its initial Hellenic character and resembled more and more that of an eastern despot. The removal of Tigranes with Roman help in 69 B.C. and a further brief period of intrigue and disorder in the city opened the way for Rome to take charge of an increasingly troubled region and bring it to order. The Seleucid era ended ignominiously.

Pompey entered Antioch in 64 B.C., taking Syria under Roman control while leaving to the Syrian cities a certain measure of freedom in their internal affairs. The council building at Antioch was repaired to fulfil this purpose, and the land held by the sacred grove at Daphne was extended. Taking advantage of the proximity of the Mediterranean seaport of Seleucia, of the network of great roads at the centre of which Antioch stood, and of the position of the city midway between east and west, Roman commercial activity soon flourished. The province of Syria was placed under the control of a proconsul. Antioch had not yet attained the immense military importance that it was to enjoy, but was already strong enough to withstand a siege in 51 B.C. by the Parthians, who had followed up a successful engagement with Roman forces three years earlier and had invaded Syria. The city supported Caesar against Pompey in 48 B.C. and was rewarded by notable additions to its public buildings, including the Kaisarion basilica at its centre. Caesar's aim was the Romanization of Antioch to succeed the older Hellenistic culture upon which the city had been founded. Symbolic of this was the erection of statues depicting the Fortune of Rome and Caesar himself. After Caesar's murder and the assumption of power by the triumvirate, Antony resided for a time in Syria with the object of raising money, and during his absence at Alexandria in 40 B.C., Syria was over-run by the Parthians, perhaps not with too great difficulty, for the Syrians welcomed Parthian rule as being more generous than that to which they had been accustomed. Antioch surrendered to the invaders and remained under their control for a year, until Antony's forces again gained the upper hand in Syria. Parthia continued to be a stumbling block to Antony's ambition to emulate the conquests of Alexander. After his marriage to Cleopatra, which probably took place in Antioch, Antony followed Alexander's footsteps eastwards, to be defeated by the Parthians in 39 B.C.

The collapse of Antony's rule in the east and his suicide in 30 B.C. opened up new possibilities of prosperity in Antioch, as in the rest of the Roman world, now entering upon the *Pax Romana* of Augustus. During this period, Syria became an imperial province under a legate and a procurator resident in Antioch, with two or three legions stationed at this strategically-important point. The gift of new buildings, begun by Augustus and continued by Agrippa and Tiberius, proclaimed the dignity and magnificence of the city as one of the greatest in the empire. A main street running through the centre of Antioch, approximately from south west to north east, was constructed during the reigns of Augustus and Tiberius, adorned richly with colonnades and vaulted mosaic coverings over the crossings. Temples were built or restored, new theatres, baths and gates were provided, new statues set up, and works taken in hand to protect the city further from the Parmenius torrent descending Mount Silpius. In addition to this lavish expenditure on enriching the buildings of the city, Augustus instituted the Olympic games at Antioch, endowed to be held every four years, though this interval would vary in years to follow. At times the games would lapse altogether, as in A.D. 41, when financial maladministration caused their closure, until Claudius permitted their reinstatement thirteen years later. By the opening of the Christian era, Antioch was not only a city of architectural splendour and the major military centre of the eastern empire, but also the hub of the diplomatic balance which, throughout the Augustan age, maintained peaceful relations with Armenia and Parthia and with Rome's tributary states in the east. The effect of close contact with the east upon the religious and cultural life of the city will be noticed in later chapters.

Like every ancient city, Antioch was subject to severe damage by fire. During the period of Tiberius' enrichment of the city, great destruction was caused by fire in the district of Epiphania. In addition, Antioch suffered from frequent earthquakes. After such visitations the rebuilding was carried out at imperial expense, as in A.D. 37 when rebuilding was ordered by Caligula. On this occasion the opportunity was taken not merely to replace from public funds what had been destroyed but to improve on it. There was another earthquake of unknown date during the reign of Claudius (A.D. 41–54), in which the great colonnade of the main street fell and three temples were destroyed. The frequency of such disasters played a considerable part in the irregularity of the Olympic games at Antioch.

During the reign of Nero (A.D. 54–68), the peace of Antioch was disturbed by anti-Jewish activity occasioned partly by long-standing gentile resentment at privileges accorded to Jews, such as exemption from military service and from worship of the emperor, and partly by widespread Jewish disaffection and eventually open revolt. Internal dissension among the Jews led to violence in Palestine, with massacres of Jews in Caesarea and Jerusalem. In A.D. 66, Nero appointed Vespasian to govern Judaea, with large forces to enable him to maintain order. The effects of Jewish disorder were felt strongly in Antioch, where there was a large Jewish population, and an outbreak of arson in A.D. 70 endangered the whole city.

Trajan's policy of expansion, towards the end of his reign (A.D. 98–117), brought him to Antioch to plan his oriental campaigns. The city was his headquarters during his occupation of Armenia and Mesopotamia in A.D. 114/5, and it was during his residence in Antioch following these campaigns that the city suffered very severe earthquake shocks which caused great loss of life and destruction of buildings. The shocks were attributed to the anger of the gods against the influence of Christians in the city and gave rise to the outburst of persecution in which the bishop, Ignatius, was sent to his death in Rome and other Christians were executed in Antioch. The rebuilding of the area of the city that had been destroyed enabled improvements to be made in the water supply by means of new aqueducts in Antioch itself and in Daphne, dedicated in the presence of Hadrian in A.D. 129. Further notable additions to the buildings of the city were made later in the second century by Commodus when reinstating the Olympic games after a ban lasting six years. The ban had been imposed by Marcus Aurelius as punishment for Antioch's part in a brief rebellion by the governor of Syria, Avidius Cassius, during which he proclaimed himself emperor, but Commodus' love of sports led him to lift the ban and to extend further at public expense the life of pleasure to which most Antiochenes were devoted. He built a new running track and endowed the old Syrian orgiastic festival of Maiouma, which was held every three years in honour of Dionysus and Aphrodite. Public horse races and wild beast hunts were instituted and public funds were granted to the city to support mimes and dancers. Benefactions of this kind contributed to the popularity of the emperor concerned and to the entertainment of the citizens without making life more stable. The encouragement of public games strengthened the strongly political tendency of rival sporting factions in Antioch and indirectly added fuel to political rivalries which were always ready to burst into flame in a volatile, multi-racial city. On the death of Commodus in A.D. 192 there followed a rapid succession of brief reigns, each ending in bloodshed, and Septimius Severus found it necessary two years later to divide Syria into two administrative sections, Syria Coele and Syria Phoenicia, as well as to punish Antioch for its riotous conduct by depriving it of the title of Metropolis and temporarily transferring the Olympic games to Issus. Antioch did not regain the status of Metropolis until A.D. 212, when Caracalla, planning a Parthian campaign from Antioch, stood in need of popular support.

In A.D. 230 the Sassanid empire supplanted the old kingdom of Parthia, and from this date the new kingdom of Persia contributed a perpetual source of danger to the eastern Roman empire. While this necessarily

added to the importance of Antioch as a military base, it also increased the
fears of its inhabitants in the face of the growing threat from the east. As
a counter-measure to Shahpur I's plans to annex Syria and Asia minor to
his territories, a peace treaty in A.D. 249 did little to restore Antiochene
confidence. There were seditious movements in the city which favoured
Persia rather than Rome. When Shahpur invaded Syria in A.D. 253 and set
fire to Antioch he was accompanied by an Antiochene renegade, Mariades,
who had a following in the city. Prisoners were taken, settled in Persia, and
increased in number after a second invasion in A.D. 260. Antioch was rebuilt by Valerian (253-60), who needed the city as his predecessors had
done as a base from which to organize a campaign against Persia. A new
element in the defence of the city was the fortification of the island in the
Orontes. Valerian's move against Persia was ill-fated, for not only did the
Persians defeat his army in A.D. 260, but they captured Valerian himself
in company with a large number of prisoners. The treatment of prisoners
on this occasion, as in A.D. 253, was generous: they were settled in Persia
and allowed to build their own churches and monasteries. Shahpur was
anxious to make use of the knowledge and skill that he believed would be
found among Antiochene prisoners.

The apparent weakness of Rome in face of Persia led Odeinath, prince
of Palmyra, to assert his independence of Rome. Being given command of
a combined Roman and Palmyrene army for use against Persia, he used it to
secure his own hold over a large part of Syria, and although he was assassin-
ated in A.D. 266/7, his wife Zenobia maintained Palmyrene domination
over the region and became in effect ruler of Antioch. On the accession
of Aurelian (A.D. 270-5), she proclaimed her complete independence of
Rome, and her son Wahballath assumed the title of Augustus in 271, but
in the following year Zenobia's forces were driven from Antioch and
destroyed and she was sent to Rome for public display.

The stability of the eastern empire was restored, and that of Antioch
with it, by the great administrative ability of Diocletian (A.D. 284-305),
under whose direction civil government, finance and defence were reorgan-
ized. A peace treaty with Persia was concluded in A.D. 298. The fortified
Orontes island was rebuilt to include an imperial palace and the city was
equipped with new baths, arms factories and granaries. During the reign of
Diocletian the 'great' persecution of Christians began in 303, lasting until
long after Diocletian's death. The course of the persecution in Antioch is
outlined by Eusebius, as part of his narrative of the events leading up to
the inauguration of the Christian empire under Constantine (A.D. 306-37).
Although it was early in the reign of Constantine that Shahpur II succeeded
to the throne of Persia, an event which marked the beginning of increasing
tension between the two empires as Shahpur planned to win back the territories lost under the treaty of 297, it was not until A.D. 334 that the first

aggressive move was made by the Persians in occupying Armenia. Through-out the intervening years Antioch had been of cardinal importance as the base at which the Roman army was built up and equipped. Antioch was also important ecclesiastically, and Constantine enriched the city with an octagonal Great Church which he did not live to see completed. The mag-nificent building, with its central octagon surrounded by side-aisles and surmounted by a golden dome was built on the Orontes island near the royal palace, for the emergence of the new Christian empire had in no way weakened the religious importance of the emperor. The Christian emperor was not only, as Constantine put it, the bishop responsible for those outside the Church, but assumed responsibilities within the Church as well, as the Christians found in the emperor's attempts to solve the problems created by the Arian controversy. Antioch was drawn into the controversy at an early date. The great council of Nicaea in 325 originated in a council which met at Antioch the previous year, ostensibly to elect a successor to bishop Philogonius but mainly to combat the threat of Arianism. The new bishop, Eustathius, soon gave offence to the empress Helena, and was removed by a council convened at Antioch under the chairmanship of Eusebius. Civil disorder followed his removal and troops were called in to put down the rioting. A further council met at Antioch in A.D. 333 to investigate charges of magical practice made against Athanasius, of which he was cleared in his absence. The determination of the Persian emperor Shahpur to win back Syria, and his policy of persecution of Christians in his realms, disturbed the peace of the east during Constantine's last years. The problems con-cerning the maintenance of a very large army at Antioch, aggravated by a famine in A.D. 333, aroused serious discontent in the city. The emperor's eldest son, Constantius, was sent to the city to raise morale shortly before the Persians moved to occupy Armenia as the first step towards invading Syria. From A.D. 337, when Constantius succeeded his father, the emperor spent much of his time at Antioch, concerned with either military or ecclesi-astical affairs and enriching the city with new buildings. At the dedication in 341 of the Great Church, Constantius emulated his father in presiding over a council at which new creeds were drafted, one of which was probably associated with the name of Lucian the martyr. Despite the disturbances in Antioch arising from the emperor's resistance to Persian expansion and from the acrimony attendant upon his acceptance of the Arian heresy, Antioch flourished during his reign. Its economic prosperity was aided by the opening in A.D. 346 of a new harbour at Seleucia Pieria to receive military supplies. The possibility of economic hardship was not far from Antiochene minds, however, for in 354 it was the fear of famine that drove the inhabitants to petition the tyrannical Caesar Gallus, who was at Antioch during Constantius' absence in Gaul, to alleviate the distress they thought was approaching. Gallus ordered a reduction in wheat prices, which was

opposed by interested parties. Price control was not put into effect and
rioting followed. The anticipated famine began to be felt but Gallus failed
to counteract it, which resulted in renewed civil violence and arson. Gallus
was with difficulty removed from the city on the emperor's orders and
executed. Constantius imposed punishments upon those who had been
associated with Gallus' four years of misrule, and upon the city as a whole.
Attempts to avert open war with Persia were fruitless. Approaches had
been made in A.D. 355, but Shahpur's demands could not be met and the
Persian army occupied Mesopotamia. Constantius directed his Persian campaign from Constantinople, threatened not only from the east but also
from the west, where the Caesar Julian had been proclaimed emperor by
his troops in Gaul and was marching eastwards. Constantius' death in 361
saved the empire from civil war.

Julian's intention to restore the eastern empire to its earlier Hellenism
was soon put into effect. Expecting that the Christian Church would tear
itself to pieces if given scope to do so, he proclaimed freedom of religion
and encouraged the return of the orthodox who had been exiled by Constantius in the interest of state Arianism. Throughout much of Julian's
realm his tolerance had the effect of drawing opposed parties together
rather than separating them further, except in Antioch, where hostility between ecclesiastical parties needed little encouragement from the emperor
to keep it flourishing. Orthodox and Arians had long been bitterly divided
and remained so. The fact that Antioch was an ancient centre of Hellenistic
culture led Julian to concentrate his attention upon the city. He removed
the body of St Babylas from the martyrium at Daphne, where Gallus had
caused it to be reburied, an action which was soon followed by the burning
of the temple of Apollo which stood on the same site. Christians were
blamed for the fire and the Great Church was closed and suffered confiscation of its liturgical vessels. Julian's hopes of a pagan revival in Antioch
came to little. He found the population to be cool towards his policy and
became disillusioned, expressing his contempt for the city in his satirical
Misopogon. The presence of a large Jewish population at Antioch gave
Julian hope that the city would provide a centre from which he could win
widespread support of Jews for his anti-Christian policy, but this again
came to little. It is fruitless to speculate on the length to which Julian's
Hellenizing would have been pressed if he had reigned longer. Antioch was
the base for the Persian campaign which he hoped would re-establish the
prestige of Rome in the east. He carried out sweeping reductions in the
number of palace dignitaries and officers, but the presence of a large army
ensured high prices, and the hardship arising from these was accentuated
in A.D. 360 by famine. Julian remitted taxes and introduced reforms of
the city senate to encourage wider sharing of financial burdens. A drought
in A.D. 361/2 caused a further failure of the wheat crop, and Julian's newly-

appointed senators were more eager to use the economic situation to their own financial advantage than to serve the city, hoarding grain in order to raise prices. Julian reformed the currency and introduced a scheme of publicly-owned land in an attempt to encourage cultivation, but proper cultivation did not take place. Disaffection was felt not only among the citizens but also within the army, and even within the Imperial Guard itself, as a result of Julian's refusal to employ Christians. Julian left Antioch early in A.D. 363 after less than three years of misunderstanding and hostility. His death in battle later in the same year marked the end of organized paganism in the eastern empire, though it continued to flourish strongly in individual areas.

Valens (A.D. 364–78) contributed much to the architectural beauty of Antioch, building the forum of Valens over the Parmenius torrent by channelling the stream through vaulting, above which were erected porticos and finely-decorated ceilings. His ecclesiastical policy was to restore the state Arianism of Constantius' reign, and he subjected the orthodox in Antioch and its surroundings to a rigorous persecution which was alleviated towards the end of his reign on the advice of the pagan Themistius. Arianism was now becoming a spent force in the east, though it continued elsewhere in the empire, and never again was it to form the basis of imperial policy in ecclesiastical affairs. Theodosius I (A.D. 379–95) at once restored orthodoxy, imposing penalties upon heretics and giving back the Great Church at Antioch to the orthodox as their metropolitan church. Economic distress and its attendant disorders were not so readily dealt with. From A.D. 382 to 384 the effects of famine were exacerbated by severe taxation. Senators were impoverished by the demands of public expenditure and public office was something to be avoided if possible. Disloyalty, neglect and oppression on the part of imperial officers caused Libanius to address the emperor on the subject of penal reform. Outbreaks of violence in Antioch in A.D. 387 followed the imposition of yet heavier taxation, leading to an attack upon imperial statues which was tantamount to an attack upon the emperor in person. Fierce punishment followed, in which Antioch was for the third time in its history deprived of its status as Metropolis in favour of Laodicea and stripped of its military supremacy. Its places of entertainment were closed and the distribution of free bread suspended. Senators were imprisoned, and bishop Flavian had to intercede with the emperor to secure the lifting of the penalties. During the reign of Theodosius II (408–50) a visit by the empress Eudocia, while on pilgrimage to Jerusalem in A.D. 438, was the occasion of the extension of the southern wall of the city to take in a further half square mile of new ground, with erection of new buildings, including a basilica and a new gate on the road to Daphne.

The threat to the religious peace of the east was by the fifth century the Monophysite doctrine of the single divine-human nature of Christ. The

Emperor Leo I (A.D. 457-74) supported the orthodox doctrine of the
council of Chalcedon, but in Antioch his policy was threatened when Peter
the Fuller seized the bishopric in the absence of the orthodox bishop
Martyrius. Peter was imprisoned, but shortly afterwards returned to the
bishopric during the brief reign of Basiliscus, to be put to flight again on
the accession of Zeno (A.D. 474-91). Antioch was the scene of perpetual
violence during Zeno's reign. His orthodox bishop, Stephen, was murdered
in A.D. 479. Two years later his army commander, Illus, began gaining
favour in Antioch in preparation for rebellion against the emperor, calling
orthodox Christians and pagan Hellenists to unite under his banner. Avoiding
the appearance of ambition, Illus proclaimed Leontius emperor at Tarsus,
and Leontius installed his court and army in Antioch in A.D. 484. The
usurper was defeated four years later by Zeno, whose closing years were
marked by extreme violence between rival mobs in Antioch. The succeeding
emperor, Anastasius (A.D. 491-518), despite his ability as a reforming
administrator and the harsh discipline he imposed, found it almost impossible to maintain order in the city. Lawless mobs attacked Jews and destroyed their buildings, and an army of Monophysite monks invaded the
city in an attempt to unseat the orthodox bishop Flavian II, to be beaten
off by a combined force of orthodox monks and citizens. Justin I (A.D.
518-27) was as able a ruler as Anastasius and fared little better. Antioch
was out of control of any but rival mob leaders. It is clear that, by the
beginning of the sixth century, the city was set on a course which led
irreversibly to its destruction. Civil disorder obliged Justin to discontinue
the Olympic games in A.D. 520. A succession of terrible fires during 525
was followed by a very severe earthquake in the following year, at a time
when the city was crowded with visitors for the feast of the Ascension.
There was immense loss of life as almost the whole city was destroyed and,
amid the fires which usually followed an earthquake, the citizens looted
and murdered. Rebuilding and rescue work were set in progress by the
emperor, but earthquakes continued until A.D. 528, when the city was
again destroyed. A severe winter following this disaster caused starvation
which imperial gifts of food attempted to alleviate. Once again the rebuilding of Antioch was taken in hand.

From A.D. 528 fighting had broken out on the Persian frontier. Arab
forces in the service of the Persian emperor reached the outskirts of
. Antioch during the following year and were beaten back, taking with them
slaves and loot, after which there were annual campaigns fought against
the invaders by a Roman army depleted by the transfer of troops to Italy.
In 540 the Persians again reached Antioch in the course of an extended
raid designed to collect loot. The emperor Justinian (A.D. 527-65) sent
Germanus to defend the city, whose walls were still only partly repaired
after earthquake damage. There was no time to repair the walls completely

before the Persians reached the city, and the emperor's promise of troops to reinforce the garrison was not fully kept. The Antiochenes offered to buy off the Persians with a ransom, sending the proposal to Khosrau by the hand of Megas, bishop of Beroea, and the Persian emperor accepted the offer. When some Roman troops reached Antioch from the south, there was a feeling in the city that it might be possible to mount a defence against the invaders, and on Megas' return from Khosrau with news of the latter's acceptance of the ransom, he was ordered to go back to report that the ransom would not be paid. The Persians reached the city walls, demanding payment of the ransom that they had been promised, and on receiving a refusal attacked the walls from the river and the mountain slopes. They placed siege engines on the higher slopes overlooking the city. The collapse of the timber framework of a walkway carrying troops along the wall caused a rumour in the city that the walls themselves had been breached. Resistance on the mountain walls gave way and the Roman troops fled down into the centre of the city. The citizens appear to have been allowed to leave Antioch by the gates. There was some opposition to Persian entry by scattered groups, but it was not sufficient to stop the Persian advance through the city. An order was given for the whole city to be burnt excepting the Great Church, which was allowed to stand after being stripped of its valuables. The rest of Antioch suffered systematic destruction.

The rebuilding of Antioch was on a smaller scale than before, for a large area was now left uninhabited and unbuilt. The walls were repaired and in some places straightened, and the river course was altered to help the defence of the walls. The Orontes island may have been abandoned at this time. Labour for the rebuilding was brought in from outside, and the reduced city was provided with churches, hospitals and public buildings. The depleted population was soon further decimated by an outbreak of plague which swept the empire in A.D. 542. The weakened and impoverished condition of Antioch did not hinder the characteristic licentious violence of its civic life, and rendered it more susceptible than before to Persian attack. The refusal of the emperor Justin II (565-78) to pay annual tribute to Persia in A.D. 572 brought a punitive raid into Syria during the following year. Two recent earthquakes had again seriously damaged the walls of Antioch, and the Persian army burned the suburbs of the city before passing westwards to the Mediterranean coast.

In A.D. 602 the eastern empire suffered from a period of brutal rule under Phocas (602-10), who had obtained the throne by murdering his predecessor Maurice. His savagery caused open opposition in Syria and Egypt, and the weakened state of the empire gave an opportunity for Persian troops to reoccupy Syria in A.D. 606/7, perhaps being welcomed as saviours from the hand of Phocas. Rioting in Antioch in 610 was put down harshly. The emperor Heraclius (A.D. 610-41) brought about a

revival of morale and of military strength for a time, but Persian raiding
continued in Syria, capturing Edessa and Apamea and occupying Antioch
for eleven years from A.D. 611. During their occupation of the city the
Persians forced the mainly orthodox citizens to embrace Nestorianism, but
their rule was nonetheless welcomed by many as being preferable to that
of the Romans.

In A.D. 634 the Arabs started expanding northwards, and in 636
defeated the Roman army at the Yarmuk. Heraclius abandoned Antioch
to its fate and retired to Constantinople. By 637 the Arabs were in north
western Syria, meeting little resistance, and in the following year Antioch
surrendered. The city was occupied by a strong Arab garrison, serving as a
military headquarters for attack on Constantinople as it had once, in
Roman hands, served the same purpose against Persia. It remained in Arab
hands for the next three centuries.[3]

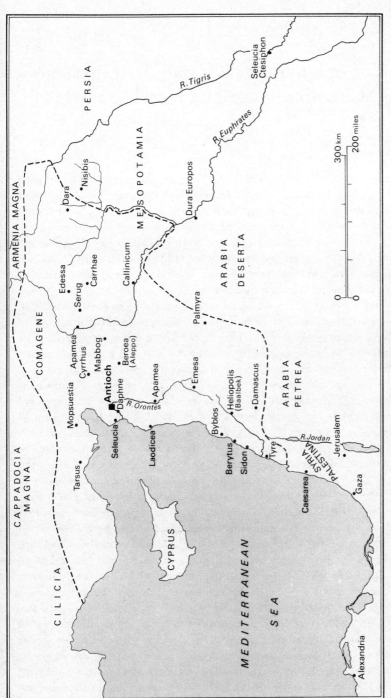

The Patriarchate of Antioch, A.D. 400.
(The eastern border is approximate only)

1

The religious background to Antiochene Christianity: pagan, jewish, gnostic

During the third decade of the first century, the martyrdom of Stephen occasioned the dispersion from Jerusalem of Christians who 'made their way to Phoenicia, Cyprus, and Antioch, bringing the message to Jews only and to no other. But there were some natives of Cyprus and Cyrene among them, and these, when they arrived at Antioch, began to speak to Gentiles as well, telling them the good news of the Lord Jesus' (Acts xi.19 f., N.E.B.). Barnabas was sent from Jerusalem and Paul was brought from Tarsus to serve the growing Christian community in the city, and the germination of this early sowing of the Christian seed produced a vigorous growth with its own strongly-marked characteristics. Antiochene Christianity was to become an expression of the faith immediately distinguishable from its neighbours to north and south, bringing Antioch into prolonged conflict with the great ecclesiastical centres of Constantinople and Alexandria.

In seeking to understand the markedly-individual flavour of Antiochene Christianity, we turn first to the soil in which it germinated, pagan and Jewish, and to the gnostic sects which exercised great influence upon all religious activity in Syria during the early years of the Christian era, for it was converts from these three great religious groups who constituted the primitive Antiochene Church. At the time of the foundation of the Antiochene Church in the mid-first century, each of the three was itself developing. The network of interconnected pagan cults in Syria had grown from the early Semitic conception of *ba'al* into more clearly-defined pantheons of local deities, who in turn had to a considerable extent been overlaid first by the Hellenistic pantheon introduced by Alexander the Great, and then again by the Roman pantheon. Judaism was undergoing a process of re-moulding through the latter half of the first century into a strongly flexible religion more suited to the changed conditions of its existence in the Roman empire. Gnosticism was at this early period in its infancy, but was to produce leaders of great power for centuries to come, whose influence would touch Christianity at many points. It is a complex picture of developing religions, sometimes in conflict with each other, sometimes overlapping, sometimes merging at the edges. The dispersal of Christians northward from Jerusalem after the martyrdom of Stephen carried the Christian gospel into this complex and unstable setting, and in this setting Antiochene Christianity developed its own strongly-marked features.

At the root of the pagan conception of deity in Syria lies the idea of *ba'al*, carrying the primary meaning of ownership or possession.[1] This did not mean the possession of an object or place by a namable deity, for the *ba'al* had no existence apart from its phenomena, but was rather the numen residing in the object, on whose account the object was held in respect.[2] *Ba'al* as owner of a city is identified not by name but often as simply the lord of the place, *ba'al Tarz*, *ba'al Sur*. Every fertile place was the habitation of a *ba'al* whose sanctuary and cult came to be associated with the water and vegetation found there.[3] Inscriptions frequently identify a local *ba'al* by generalized epithets, 'the merciful', 'the compassionate', 'the good and rewarding'.[4]

The absence of individual character in the *ba'alim* other than the character of the places or objects they inhabited made it the easier for them to become identified with alien deities introduced from outside their own regions. They could be taken over and absorbed into a strongly-characterized solar or lunar deity with little power of resistance, having little structure of mythology surrounding them to give them a history and an identity. The venerable figures of El and Elyon, who appear to have enjoyed some kind of supremacy throughout the Phoenician coastal strip west of the Orontes, were early victims, being replaced by the powerful figure of Hadad, who all over Syria came to be called simply *ba'al*, the master, without prejudice to the local standing of other lesser *ba'alim*.[5] El's consort, Asherah or 'Ashtart,[6] was absorbed into the great *dea Syria*, Atargatis, 'our lady Atar',[7] and it is not easy to determine whether Hadad or Atargatis was the dominant partner: Hadad is called 'king of the gods',[8] but a relief at Dura Europos depicts the goddess as being notably bigger and more impressive than the god.[9]

Syrian inscriptions show the ease with which *ba'alim* could become assimilated to Hellenistic figures: at Arsouf, Reshef was absorbed by Apollo;[10] at Tyre, Melqarth by Heracles;[11] at Dura Europos, Be'elshamin by Zeus Kurios;[12] at Edessa, Atha by Venus;[13] at Ba'albek, Nabu by Mercury.[14] Lucian's *De Dea Syria* and Macrobius' *Saturnalia*, while constantly suggesting an indigenous Syrian substratum, reveal a smoothly-Hellenized surface to the cults they describe. At Ba'albek the deity who appears in reliefs, bronzes and statues is Jupiter Optimus Maximus Heliopolitanus, but this great cult centre retained stronger links with its Syrian roots than did, for example, Berytus or Antioch.[15]

Antioch itself shows virtually no traces of its indigenous cult. There are suggestions of the continuance of Syrian culture in the Syriac names of some of its suburbs, in a bilingual inscription,[16] and in references by Chrysostom and Theodoret to Syriac speakers in their congregations,[17] but Hadad and Atargatis were early supplanted by Zeus, Athene and Apollo.

At Daphne, a beautifully-wooded spring to the west of Antioch, which was
held to be the site both of the judgement of Paris and of the metamorphosis of Daphne into a laurel tree, a temple was dedicated to Apollo.[18]
The relative popularity of the various Hellenistic deities fluctuated: under
Antiochus Epiphanes the cult of Olympian Zeus was magnified at the
expense of that of Apollo;[19] under Julius Caesar a statue of the *tyche* of
Rome was erected; during Hadrian's governorship of Syria a temple of
Zeus Soter was built at Daphne; under Trajan temples of Artemis and of
the nymphs were built there; and in A.D. 181, at the restoration of the
Olympic games at Antioch, a temple was dedicated to Olympian Zeus as
patron of the games.[20]

    If the cult of Apollo waned during the second century B.C., it was not a
permanent setback, for steps had later to be taken by Christians to counteract his influence, for example in the translation of the remains of the
martyr Babylas to Daphne by Gallus and the building of a martyrium near
the pagan temple.[21] The middle of the fourth century was not an easy time
for pagan cults in Antioch,[22] and the enthusiastic patronage of Julian on
his arrival at the city in the summer of 362 revealed the fact that there was
little support for them from the inhabitants of the city. Julian visited nine
of the city's greater temples[23] and, in particular, expressed strong disappoint-
ment at the lack of support for the cult of Apollo at Daphne,[24] the renewal
of which was part of his plan for the restoration of paganism. He ordered
the removal of the remains of Babylas[25] in order to purge the spot of
offence to the pagan deity, but his action was soon followed by the destruction of the temple and statue of Apollo by fire.[26] The Great Church
of Antioch was closed and its vessels confiscated.[27] Julian, whose Hellenism
has been called a religion of good citizenship,[28] was by the beginning of 363
executing and exiling members of the army on the ground that Christianity
was treason.[29] The ultimate dominance of paganism or of Christianity had
Julian survived the Persian campaign of 363 must of course remain speculative, but the response of Antioch to the emperor during his residence in
the city suggests that Antioch was by that date predominantly Christian.[30]
Its predominance was strengthened within twenty years of Julian's death
by the action of bands of desert monks who took it upon themselves to
put into effect the anti-pagan legislation of Theodosius I[31] by destroying
pagan temples.[32] Though Antioch itself did not suffer as severely as did the
neighbouring country districts, Libanius' oration *Pro Templis* suggests that
only four of the great temples of the city remained twenty years after
Julian.[33] In the early years of the fifth century Rabbula journeyed in a
white heat of zeal to destroy pagan shrines and suffered for it at the hands
of their priests,[34] for although destruction of temples had been permitted
by law since 399, the temple hierarchies were in no mood to take it lying
down.[35] Not all the emperors following Julian took active steps to suppress

paganism; Jovian, Valens and Gratian were tolerant, and Justinian, who rebuilt and christianized the pagan sites at Daphne and in 529 set in hand a purge of the pagan aristocracy, was stronger against Christian heresy than against paganism.[36] In 468 the arrest and trial of the pagan Isocasius, whose activities came to light through allegations that he had supported the election of Domnus to the see of Antioch in 441, shows the continued life of the old gods,[37] and in 481 the rebellion of Illus against the emperor Zeno, in which he attempted to unite Christian orthodoxy and paganism against Zeno's Monophysite party, indicates the existence of a paganism strong enough to be worth harnessing to political ends. Five pagan priests were prosecuted in Constantinople in 562, two of them from Antioch and two from Ba'albek.[38] The arrest of alleged pagans in 578 in Ba'albek by an imperial commissioner, Theophilus, led to their assertion that they could name associates in every district and city, especially at Antioch, and when their high priest, Rufinus, committed suicide at Edessa to escape torture, further such accusations were made against Anatolius, representative of the praetorian prefect at Antioch, and against the patriarch Gregory, who was said to have witnessed the sacrifice of a boy at Daphne.[39] Gregory's acquittal at Constantinople does not alter the fact that such an accusation against a patriarch was not too absurd to be made. The strange document known as *The Oracle of Ba'albek*, composed in the early fifth century, shows that the Christian monk lived in fear that the old gods could rise again and take vengeance,[40] for the old gods were by no means destroyed, only subjugated, and the failure of the Christian might open the way for their return. At this date Ba'albek was still a strong pagan centre,[41] and a place to be feared. The same was true of Carrhae in the middle of the fifth century. A century and a half after the first edicts of Theodosius against pagan temples, such buildings could be still not merely standing but in working order with priests serving their gods. When we find Syrian writers showing familiarity with pagan deities, Semitic and Hellenistic, we should not assume that they are only indulging their antiquarian interests. Severus in the early sixth century gives an account of the names by which God is known: Elohim among the Hebrews, Aloho among the Syrians and Arabs. God is known by titles such as life-giver, He who cares, the creator, the helper, the strengthener, master, king, all-powerful,[42] the generalized titles accorded to the *ba'alim*. Barhadbešabba recounts the legend of Theodore's arrival at his diocesan town of Mafsoustia (Mopsuestia), a particularly pagan place, he observes, given to the worship of Mopsus. At the bishop's approach, the great man's virtue caused the statue of the god to fall in ruins.[43]

The existence of pagan cult-centres in Christian times does not in itself prove widespread pagan observances among the population; nevertheless the Syrian evidence suggests that during the early years of the Christian era paganism was by no means dead and that, in places, it was a force to be

reckoned with. It was part of the soil in which Christianity was planted
and part of the background against which we must see its growth.

Judaism too was a developing religion, the destruction of Jerusalem in
A.D. 70 having forced upon the newly-constituted Sanhedrin at Jabneh
the task of virtually rebuilding Judaism on the basis of the Torah alone, so
that the Law could be observed in the new conditions of dispersion.[44] The
work of recasting the liturgy and systematizing the Law, begun under
Rabbi Jochanan and carried on into the second century A.D., not only
gave Judaism an ordering of the written and oral Law into a single effective
instrument, but articulated the massive structure of the canon of Scripture
and its exegesis. During the second century, Rabbi Judah the Prince set up
a Sanhedrin in Galilee, and with great foresight set to work to supply a
permanent source of authority for dispersed Jewry, designed to render
Judaism sufficiently flexible and strong to withstand further shocks. A
final definition of the Law was taken in hand, involving an immense task
of codification and explanation, which provided the means for world-wide
Jewry to preserve its identity during centuries of persecution to follow.[45]

In times of persecution it was, of course, an easy step for the persecutors
to force the Jewish population to work on the Sabbath, as in the case of
the renegade Jew, Antiochus, described by Josephus[46] as stirring up the
gentile population of Antioch against his fellow-Jews,

> 'giving them a demonstration of his own conversion to paganism and his
> hatred of Jewish customs by sacrificing after the manner of the Greeks.
> . . . He became a hard task-master over his own people, not permitting
> them to rest on the Sabbath but forcing them to do all that they did on
> other days; and to such a degree of distress he thus reduced them that
> the Sabbath rest was broken not only at Antioch but in other cities also.'

But the Jews succeeded, in spite of such distressing examples of treachery,
in impressing many gentiles by their integrity: their courts, for example,
attracted gentiles because oaths sworn in Jewish courts enjoyed the reputation of being more binding than those sworn elsewhere.[47] Chrysostom
told his congregation of an incident which had taken place only three days
previously. He had seen a decent, honest woman being compelled to enter
a synagogue by a so-called Christian, in order to take an oath concerning
their business. Full of zeal, Chrysostom had rescued her from such abduc-
tion, as he terms it, and had demanded of the man if he called himself a
Christian that he dragged the woman to the haunts of the Jews who had
crucified Christ. The man had replied that an oath sworn there was more
awe-inspiring.[48] Christians also consulted rabbis for healing of sickness, a
practice which Chrysostom describes as resorting to those who confer
healing upon the body and damnation upon the soul.[49] Perhaps it was the

rabbis' reputation for magic, which Chrysostom regarded as satanic, which was the attraction.

The influence of the Jews in Antioch is reflected further in the efforts made by rulers to win their support: not only the Palmyrene Zenobia in A.D. 260, but a century later Julian's policy of wooing the Jews as a powerful ally in his attempt to eradicate Christianity. The Jews were unlikely to be flattered by Julian's condescending comparison of their long-lost sacrificial rites with those of the pagans, but could perhaps conceal their resentment at the comparison if he was to rebuild their temple.[50]

If Christian writers gave expression to their animosity against the Jews, it was doubtless caused in part by their fear of a strong and flexible community which necessarily had many points of contact with the Church, not least in their common use of the Old Testament Scriptures. Christian exegesis had much in common with Jewish;[51] Syriac Christian writings transmit many points of interpretation possibly borrowed from the rabbis.[52] There were elements of similarity between the asceticism practised by Syrian Christians and that of the fringes of Judaism.[53] It is hardly surprising that there should have been some blurring of outlines which went beyond friendly relations at academic level[54] to include a degree of merging that could be seen from the Christian side as a threat to the integrity of the Church. Early in the second century, Ignatius of Antioch warned correspondents against judaizing: 'Do not be deceived by strange doctrines or old fables which are of no value to you, for if we still live by the Jewish Law we acknowledge that we have not received grace'; 'It is absurd to have the name of Christ on your tongue and yet to cherish Judaism in your mind'; 'If anyone teaches you Judaism, do not listen to him'.[55] In the third century, the martyr Lucian of Antioch preached against assimilation to Jewish doctrine.[56] Chrysostom's castigation of members of his congregation at Antioch who failed to distinguish between the two faiths is based upon fear of the attractive power of Judaism. Never ask how many Christians are compromised by judaizing, he advises. If anyone tells you that a great number have done so, silence him. It can only lead to scandal.[57] The excuses made by the judaizers, as Chrysostom quotes them rhetorically, may reflect what was actually being said: 'the synagogue is the repository of the Law and the prophets';[58] 'Jewish fasts have something solemn and great about them';[59] 'Christians used once to observe Jewish fasts';[60] 'the difference between us is negligible. Why not intermingle where intermingling is possible?'[61] From their side, the Jews took part in what might have been considered purely domestic Christian affairs, for example the christological debates of the fifth century, in which they habitually supported the Chalcedonian court party.[62]

The fear occasioned by the tendency of Christianity and Judaism to merge led to frequent outbursts of open hostility which to some extent

were abetted by friction between strict Jews and Hellenizing Jews.[63] The
record of violence in Antioch persists in every century, involving bloodshed and destruction of property. The Church saw the Synagogue simply
in terms of the Old Testament, with no understanding of the development
of Judaism in adapting itself to a world in which there was no longer a
holy city or a temple, and therefore no possibility of the sacrifices which
the Scriptures required. There is no understanding that a Jew could go
beyond the letter of the Law to act with charity in its spirit. Chrysostom
pointed to the legal requirement that, in the observation of Passover, it
was more important for a Jew to observe the feast in the right place, in
Jerusalem, than at the right time. What defence have they, cried Chrysostom
to his congregation, these Jews who nowadays adhere to the right time but
celebrate the feast outside Jerusalem?[64] It is a cruel taunt at those who had
lost their holy place and had painfully rethought the spirit of the Passover
laws. Not only Chrysostom but Christian writers at large applied the term
'Jew' to any Christian who was thought to have denigrated the divine status
of Christ: Paul of Samosata was designated a judaizer,[65] as were Arius,[66]
Sabellius,[67] Nestorius,[68] Macedonius.[69]

It was not easy, in view of their attitude towards the Jews, for Christians
to explain the place held by the Jews in the divine economy. Analogies
culled from the Pauline epistles were fruitful, being used by Irenaeus[70] and
adopted from his work by Eusebius. Judaism was here seen as a temporary
expedient, lying between the non-legal religion of the patriarchs and the
non-legal religion of Christ.[71] The Jews had become accustomed to idolatry
in Egypt and needed re-educating.[72] The theme is picked up by Chrysostom
and Theodoret, and the constantly-repeated polemic may suggest a reason
for the hostility of the Church towards Judaism. Judaism ought to have
disappeared and had not done so. On the contrary, it had refashioned its
cult, reinterpreted its Law, and showed no sign of having run its course.
This refusal to die is hardly accounted for in the Christian explanations of
the matter, and I do not know of any oriental writer who makes sense of it.
The orientals were obliged to attribute the continued vigour of Judaism to
the work of the devil, and leave it at that. A further cause of sensitivity
towards Judaism may be found in the fact that the Antiochene Church
itself was seen by the rest of the Christian Church as lying too close to
Judaism for comfort. It was not a shot in the dark that made Justinian
characterize the christology of Nestorius as 'evil and Jewish doctrine'. The
Antiochenes were perhaps close enough to the Jews for them to feel it
necessary to demonstrate to the world that they were in fact different and,
in doing so, distorted the views of those from whom they wanted to be
dissociated.

Gnosticism was the immense complex of other-worldly religions which affected the whole religious life of the Roman empire and which, being eastern in origin, was of particular concern to the Christians of Antioch and Syria.[73] This complex consisted of elements which could overlap or merge or cross-fertilize each other in a manner that can lead the unwary to see identity where there may be rather a spectrum of finely-graded shades of meaning. Certain elements of gnosticism were of the greatest importance to Antioch, and probably contributed more powerfully than any other single stimulus to the defining of Antiochene theology. Here are reviewed some of the more important figures who played their part in the stimulation of Antiochene thinking to this process of definition.

The serious nature of the threat presented to Christianity by the strongly docetic element in gnosticism as early as the second century is reflected in the passionate warnings of Ignatius against those who deny the true humanity of Christ, though precisely what pagan or Christian communities made this threat is less clear. Simon Magus had gained notoriety further south in Samaria during the first century, though his name seldom seems to be anathematized along with those of Marcion and Mani in later Syrian condemnations of docetic error. The account of the teaching of Simon given by Irenaeus may attribute to Simon gnostic elements which belong to later members of his school,[74] but according to Irenaeus Simon claimed to be an earthly manifestation of God. He was accompanied by a former prostitute, Helen, whom he presented as the first emanation from his own mind, the mother of all, through whom he first conceived in his mind the angels and archangels.[75] In accordance with his will she had descended to the lower regions to generate other heavenly beings, who, in turn, had created the world. They were ignorant of the supreme being and through jealousy confined their mother in a human body and subjected her to insult. Through the ages she passed from one human body to another, through Helen of Troy to her most recent incarnation in Helen the prostitute. The supreme being had come to rescue her, transfigured in the guise of flesh 'so that he might appear among men to be a man, though he was no man', and had previously possessed the body of Jesus. Transmitted through his disciple Menander, who, according to Justin, practised magic at Antioch,[76] Simon's doctrine passed to others. It was renewed by Satornilus (or Saturninus) 'who came from Antioch which is near to Daphne'.[77] In the hands of Satornilus and Basilides, another disciple of Menander who transmitted the teaching to Alexandria, the tradition accumulated mythological accretions and, from Alexandria, appears to have exerted a renewing influence upon the Syrian strain of gnosticism, for the second-century Syrian Bardaisan is described by Eusebius as one who 'formerly belonged to the Valentinian school'.[78] Simon Magus seems to have started a vigorous growth containing within itself the seed of constant renewal as it passed down the succession of his disciples, and it never for long lost contact with its native region,

passing from Samaria to Antioch and then perhaps via Alexandria back to
Syria with Bardaisan. The implication is that docetic teaching concerning
the unreality of Christ's humanity was from the first century rooted in
the east and that in the second century it was strong enough to give rise
to Ignatius' warnings to the Church as he travelled to Rome. It is in this
setting that we may recognize the beginnings of an identifiable Antiochene
christology.

Without doubt the fuel of docetic teaching continued to stoke the fires
of Antiochene doctrine throughout the second century. Marcion of Pontus,
who died about 160, is associated with Rome rather than the east, but his
teaching, which was little concerned with the cosmological fantasies of
mainstream gnosticism and was more concerned with the contrast between
the supreme being of pure benevolence and the legalistic creator-deity, was
of immense influence throughout the east. In Marcion we find strong denigration of the material universe, of the Jewish dispensation as narrated in
the Old Testament, of the Jewish creator-God and of his moral law, and of
the evil of bodily life in flesh and blood. With the two major steps to which
his practical genius gave rise, the creation of his own Church and the editing
of his own bible we are not here concerned, except in so far as the latter
step was designed to excise the entire Jewish Scriptures and anything in
the Christian books which appeared to sanction the material universe, the
life of the human body, and any aspect of Judaism. From the third gospel,
for example, he omitted the birth and infancy narrative as teaching that
Christ was born of a human mother. There is hardly an eastern Christian
writer during the following six centuries who can restrain himself from
anathematizing the memory of Marcion for the damage he did. Among
them we may notice simply Ephrem, who sees the roots of Marcion's dualism not in Paul's contrast of law and grace, but in Greek philosophy[79] and,
to counteract Marcion's influence, celebrates the creatorship of God.[80]
One would not turn to Ephrem's angry denunciation for a dispassionate
estimate of Marcion's teaching, but the fury of his attack shows where a
Syrian of the following century saw the danger to lie, and foremost in this
is the docetic rejection of Christ's human flesh.

The popularity of docetic views of Christ's humanity is further suggested
by the proliferation of apocryphal gospels and other pseudo-canonical
books in Syria during the first two centuries, but the greatest threat to the
Church's understanding of Christ came in the third century. In March, 242,
Mani proclaimed his gospel in Seleucia–Ctesiphon, and launched a religion
which was seen as the greatest external menace yet experienced by the
Church. How far the new teaching was in fact external is debatable, but
many Christians thought it to be so. Ephrem calls it 'the falsehood of India',
by which he means Persia.[81] A rescript of Diocletian calls it Persian, but
may have meant Mesopotamian.[82] Others blamed Egypt for it and remembered stories of Mani's education in Egyptian practices and in the doctrines

of Empedocles and Pythagoras at the hands of an Arab.[83] It is likely to have had its roots in an amalgam of gnosticism and Christianity under strong influence, as Ephrem suggests, of elements from further east.[84] Its *raison d'être* lay in the theological problem of the origin of evil and in the moral problem of how man was to be freed from the hold of evil upon his life, the solution to the problem of evil lying in the division of the whole of existence into two eternally-opposed though unequally-balanced realms, the kingdoms of Light and of Dark, and the solution to the problem of human frailty by the observance of moral and ritual obligations imposed to varying degrees upon the elect and the hearers. The kind of assessment of the religion found in a seventh century Syriac chronicle, which castigates it as being composed of magical practices, human sacrifice, sexual orgy and cannibalism, is absurdly wide of the mark, and its malice could only encourage dreadful cruelty such as the crucifixion of seventy Manichees which the chronicle celebrates.[85] It is not often that one finds in Greek or Syriac any serious attempt to understand what Mani was saying, but Homily 223 by Severus of Antioch is an exception,[86] not in being uncritical but in attempting a point by point refutation.

The complex mythological structure of Manichaeism reflects the dilemma of men and women faced by the opposition of good and evil in their lives. Mani teaches two wholly distinct spheres of existence: Light, representing wisdom, benevolence and order, and Dark, representing malice and anarchy. The invasion of Light by the powers of Dark gives occasion for the Father of greatness to bring into existence the Mother of life, who in turn evokes the primal man armed with light, wind, fire, water and air.[87] These secondary beings are neither eternal nor begotten – they are simply called into existence to counter aggression. The primal man is defeated by the powers of Dark which absorb his light, but a further calling into being of three powers of Light restores him so that he can descend to the abyss and destroy the root of the tree of Dark. The rulers of darkness, the *archons*, are now weakened and become the substance of earth and sky, some of their stolen light becoming sun and moon, some being emitted to form plant life on earth, and some hidden in the first man, Adam. Material substance is thus fashioned out of the substance of the *archons* of darkness, with all the malice and anarchy that they embody, and man alone is a compound of dark matter and an interior spark of light. He belongs to both realms, and the tensions to which he is subjected are derived from his dual origin. To help man in his frustration and torment, Jesus, 'the friend', is sent to protect him from the Dark and to reveal to him his true destiny as a bearer of the Light. The eating of the fruit of the tree of life shows man the truth about his condition, causing him to lament his association with the Dark and to yearn towards the Light. Who is this Jesus, the friend? He is an evocation divinely called into existence for man's salvation, emanating wholly from the Light, and his human appearance is illusory, a disguise adopted for his mission to earth. He is therefore neither really born nor really crucified, nor does he really suffer hunger or weariness or pain, for these are bodily sensations alien to his being. The salvation of man is salvation from matter, the release of the light in man from its association with evil matter, and this salvation is achieved without the saviour's being contaminated by matter. Historical veracity was no concern of Mani, for history is the history of the evil material cosmos and its inhabitants, and Mani was concerned with eternal truths about man's composite nature and ambiguous situation.[88] From the Antiochene viewpoint, the weakness of this analysis of man's condition and solution to his problem lay at its very heart, in that it envisaged a saving power which was in every way insulated from contact with man's material life. This solution was no solution at all and no answer to man's cry for help.

Manichaeism appears to Severus who, although he was bishop of Antioch, was closer to the Alexandrian tradition than to the Antiochene, as being vulnerable in three respects: first, the radical dualism on which it is based is logically self-contradictory; secondly, the myth is nonsense; thirdly, its account of man deprives him of moral freedom.

Mani presents us with two fundamental principles or deities, Light and Dark. A principle must in this context be an ultimate explanation beyond which one cannot go further, an end term on which everything else is dependent for its existence. But if we talk of two ultimates, two end terms, as does Mani, we are in the realm of absurdity, says Severus, for if there are two ultimates there must be some kind of relationship between them, attraction, repulsion or whatever. They exist in a context or framework of some kind, and the context then appears to be more ultimate than the two principles. Or have we now not two principles, Light and Dark, but three, Light, Dark and the principle of repulsion which holds them together but in opposition to each other?[89] This third ultimate is different from Light and Dark, and must be so if it is to hold them apart, so this difference separates it from each of them. But we have already allowed a principle of separation to be itself an ultimate, so the relation of separation between the third principle and that of Light is also a principle, and that between the third principle and Dark is another, so we have now not three principles but five. This progression continues *ad infinitum*. To start with two ultimate principles generates an infinity of principles, but an ultimate is an end, and there cannot be more than one end.[90]

Severus' second point is the illogicality of the Manichaean myth.[91] There is no need to pay detailed attention to this, good debating stuff though it may be, for it suffers from some misunderstanding about the nature of myth. More important is Severus' third indictment of Mani. Mani's ultimate principle of dark matter is by nature evil: everything which is material is by nature bound to sin. But in this case man, who is involved with matter by virtue of his physical body, is deprived of the possibility of good, deprived of freedom of choice, and is no more a responsible moral being than is any material object. Mani's failing here is that he thinks of evil as a substance, whereas it is only the absence of good, just as darkness is only the shutting of one's eyes to exclude the light. Evil is the voluntary deprivation of good, and to do evil is not an inbuilt part of man's being – which would not be moral evil at all – but a culpable act against the good. To deprive man of his freedom to choose good or evil is to degrade him to the level of a piece of wood or stone, in other words to remove him altogether from the moral sphere and from consciousness of moral tension and deprivation, and therefore to render meaningless the concept of salvation. If Mani is right about this, then mankind has no problem to be solved and there is no need of Manichaeism or of Christianity.[92] Severus' reply to Mani in this sermon pays Mani the compliment of treating his doctrine seriously. Severus was closer to the Alexandrian tradition than to the Antiochene, and if we may not put forward his arguments as evidence of properly Antiochene thinking, it is certainly evidence of the strength of Mani's influence in the east in the early years of the sixth century.

Manichaeism was opposed with equal determination by the Mazdaist priesthood in Persia, not on the ground of its dualism, since Persian religion was also dualist, but on the ground of its ascetic and world-renouncing character. The Muslims also took vigorous steps to search out and destroy Manichaeism during the decade following A.D. 775, and with little success, for two hundred years later the author of the Arabic *Fihrist* knew three hundred Manichaeans in Baghdad,[93] although Manichaeism had been the single religious sect excluded from the notable religious tolerance of the court of Baghdad in the eighth century.[94] The ascetic demands which were an offence to Persians and Muslims were precisely the attraction for the Christian monks in Syria. The fearful lengths to which deprivation of physical life could be taken[95] were evidence of real sanctity in Syrian eyes, and the Church could be driven into a defensive position to the extent that in Edessa the term 'Christian' meant Manichaean.[96] Their threat to Christianity was great and lasting.[97]

In this account of gnosticism we must include Bardaisan (A.D. 154-222), not because he was strictly a gnostic,[98] for he exercised too much independence of mind to adhere closely to the earlier gnostic schools,[99] but because he was for centuries to come asssociated in the oriental mind with Marcion and Mani. The three are almost always linked in condemnation. This does not preclude the possibility that Mani learnt from Bardaisan.[100] Apart from his adoption of a complex mythology which bears superficial resemblance to that of other gnostics, his error was seen to lie in his introduction of astrology into his system, but this does not deter Eusebius from quoting extensively from his *De Fato*.[101]

Bardaisan taught that there is one God – a respect in which Ephrem distinguishes his teaching from the dualism of Marcion[102] – and may have envisaged the Trinity as the oriental triad of Father, Mother and Brother.[103] From the one deity derive the five elements, fire, wind, water, light and darkness, and from the opposition of wind and fire the world was created.[104] Thus a principle of opposition is inherent in creation, manifesting itself in the opposition of good (which corresponds to light, right-handedness, mercy, righteousness, justice) and evil (darkness, left-handedness, absence of mercy, righteousness and justice),[105] and in no way may God be thought to be responsible for the existence of evil or of matter.[106] The two roots of good and evil remain in eternal warfare, unreconcilable. The evil touches the free will of man through the influence of the stars, dragging down his intelligence, the highest faculty of his tripartite nature, and depriving him of salvation. The planets are ultimately subject to the will of God, but this does not hinder their partial influence upon man by exercising a derived authority over him. The subjection of the planets to God is their fate,[107] and the freely-willed subjection of man to the planets is his own self-chosen fate. Man thus chooses to act against his true nature and becomes a battle-field in which fate and nature are in conflict for the possession of his soul. If we may take the 'Hymn of the Soul' as evidence of Bardaisan's teaching, the soul in its bodily life is deprived of its celestial robe, its destiny being to ascend from its bodily life to receive again that robe. This separability of man's intelligence from his lower soul and body is attacked by Ephrem: 'Nobody can take away one of the three parts of man any more than he can separate the characteristics of fire. If one takes away one element, one destroys it, for its full perfection lies in its three characteristics, as man is created a threefold unity.'[108] The low status of physical matter in Bardaisan's system leads him to deny a truly human body to Christ, a belief which aroused particular hostility against him. Akhsenaya attacks him for refusing a true body to Christ and for teaching that 'the incarnation did not take place of Mary'.[109] As late as the twelfth century, Bardaisan was still being castigated by Michael the Syrian for the belief that Christ was clothed not with a human body but with the body of an angel.[110] All this is only a step from what we find in most gnostic systems, but it is a step. Docetism was not of necessity gnostic, for Eutyches was no gnostic; the creation doctrine of Bardaisan points more towards monism than to dualism, though the evidence is scanty.[111] The available texts show no evidence of asceticism, which was a characteristic of the gnostic.[112] But the oriental Christians linked Bardaisan with Marcion and Mani and, in his astrological beliefs particularly, saw a threat to their faith which had to be withstood.

The emphasis upon the reality of Christ's humanity, which is the hallmark of Antiochene theology, starts from this point, in its deeply-rooted hostility to the docetism of the gnostics.

2

The interpretation of the biblical record

Išo'dad of Merv, a ninth-century Nestorian bishop, commenting on the creation narrative in Genesis, writes, 'It is necessary to know that first Origen, and after him Basil and others, have claimed that the waters above the firmament are spiritual powers.'[1] What is noteworthy about this comment is that Išo'dad, in tracing the course of a piece of biblical interpretation which he regards as mistaken, should find its source in Origen, six centuries before his own date. Such was the power of Origen that he could still, so long afterwards, be identified as the originator of the type of exegesis that the Antiochenes regarded as being at least dangerous: that is, the use of a biblical text as a springboard from which to leap to higher and more spiritual meanings than might appear on the surface of the text.

Origen had not in fact invented this practice. The Homeric myths had been subjected to this treatment and Philo of Alexandria had habitually treated the Jewish Scriptures in this way, giving the narratives a new lease of life.[2] Philo, however, hardly treated his search for spiritual meaning in Scripture as but one element in a great system, as Origen came to do. In Christian exegesis, Justin, Irenaeus and Clement of Alexandria had paved the way for Origen.[3] He sometimes gives the impression that incidental difficulties in the biblical text oblige him to treat it in a non-literal, non-historical fashion. Thus he finds it necessary to treat contradictions between the gospels as matter for spiritual interpretation,[4] and suggests that the biblical writers could falsify historical fact in order to bring out the spiritual significance of an event or situation.[5] Spiritual truth was often enshrined in what might be called falsehood to the facts, and in such cases the exegete felt at liberty to follow its lead and seek spiritual meanings to the ignoring of historical fact. Indeed such falsifications might be deliberately sown in the biblical text under the guidance of the Holy Spirit in order to lead the exegete to ascend above mere literalism.[6] 'The letter killeth but the Spirit giveth life' was a dictum of St Paul that applied not only to the Jewish Law but to the Christian Scriptures as well.[7] There were in addition many merely factual passages which in their literal sense provided no spiritual nourishment and from which spiritual meaning had to be drawn. So far, Origen's practice might be seen as escaping from difficulties in an *ad hoc* fashion

27

as they occur.[8] But it is very much more integral to Origen's system of theology and philosophy than this, for the exegetical pattern was a pattern that fitted the structure of all existence.[9] Historically speaking, the Old Testament dispensation, the New Testament dispensation and the realm of heaven constitute stages, the shadow of the truth, the image of the truth and the truth itself, reflected in man in his threefold structure of body, soul and spirit.[10] The essence and reality of a thing or of a person are not to be found in mere externals, and one has to rise above externals to the spiritual realms in order to reach the reality. The same is true in the study of natural objects, for each object is and each function is a shadow of a higher spiritual reality.[11] And the difficulties that one finds in applying this principle to nature, says Origen, are analogous to those encountered in the study of Scripture, for here too is an outward and literal sense of the words from which one must ascend to other senses which constitute the real meaning of the words. The bearing of Platonism upon this needs no emphasis.[12] Judaism before Christ shadows the greater degree of reality of the Christian dispensation which, in turn, is an image of the perfect and ultimate reality of heaven. Events took place among the Jews; the Christian can begin to see what those events meant; but not until the end of the ages, the consummation of all things, will the whole truth be known.[13] What matters is not the factual detail of Jewish events but their meaning for the Christian. The children of Israel passed through the Jordan into the promised land without understanding what they had done. That meaning only dawned with the emergence of Christian baptism, by which men pass through water into the promised land of the Church.[14] It was not that the Israelites were too blind to see the meaning: it was rather that there was in fact no meaning at all to their action until Christ invested it with meaning. Similarly there was no meaning to Noah's saving of life by the ark until the saving ark of the Church invested his action with its meaning,[15] nor was there a meaning to any single action or event in the Old Testament. The entire Old Testament was therefore to be read not as an historical record but as a kind of message in cipher to be interpreted by those fit to do so, that is those filled with the Spirit of Christ, for only so could the spirit of the Scriptures be understood. The word of the Old Testament could be understood only in the light of the Word of God made flesh, and the spirit behind the events and the record of them could only be understood in the light of the Holy Spirit of that same Christ. Even so, the exegete must be cautious in finding spiritual meaning in historical narratives, for Scripture contained too many mysteries for certainty. Origen himself was cautious, as his disciples Gregory and Pamphilus described him,[16] and as we find him in his own great Commentaries and Homilies, often propounding alternative interpretations and disclaiming any monopoly of the truth.[17]

How did this work out in practice? De Lubac insists that Origen regarded the literal, historical sense of Scripture as being important, but has to modify his insistence by admitting that it was rather the idea of History that was important to Origen, and that he often passed by individual historical events in order to press on towards the moral and spiritual meanings inherent in them.[18] But how else is History to be understood if not through its particular events? Origen's system demands attention to historical events but his detailed exegesis of passages seldom gives the events the attention demanded by the system. The system provides a ladder by which one passes from the lower to the higher, and Origen is all too anxious to press higher and to leave the lower rungs behind him. Often they are not even touched by his feet in passing. It is, moreover, not the events themselves that concern him on the occasions when he does linger on the lower rungs of the ladder, but the scriptural record of the events. Though the historical has to find a place in Origen's system, he is in no sense an historian: a *Historia Ecclesiastica* such as Eusebius wrote could never have come from his pen. There is no attempt made in his writings to write imaginatively or creatively of the past. His interest begins with the work of the Holy Spirit inspiring the biblical writers to set down their narrative, for it is the narrative which receives meaning in the light of Christ, being written not primarily with a backward reference to the past event but with a forward reference to the reality which it foreshadows. This can be confirmed by reference to almost any page of Origen's Commentaries and Homilies on the Scriptures, where he will be found to dwell on the verbal details of the narrative and only seldom cast further back to the event being narrated. It will be evident that this kind of treatment lays itself open to considerable subjectivity of interpretation unless very closely controlled, and such control was by no means always present even in the work of Origen himself. If Porphyry, that able and forthright critic who had known Origen personally, could castigate such a method of interpretation as 'pretentious obscurity',[19] and could put his finger on subjectivity of interpretation as its failing, much more damaging criticism could be made of the same method as used by lesser men. Such criticism came from the school of Antioch.

It is easy to portray the biblical exegesis of Alexandria and Antioch in sharply contrasted black and white as though spiritual and historical interpretation were divided by an unbridgeable gulf.[20] There was in fact extensive common territory between the extreme positions, and in much of their work the exegetes of both schools trod the same territory, keeping a wary eye on the enemy's position: presented with an anonymous piece of typological interpretation it might be possible to identify it as coming from the pen of John Chrysostom or Theodoret in Antioch or Cyril in Alexandria or Eusebius between the two at Caesarea. But behind Chrysostom would lie the powerful anti-Alexandrian polemic of Eustathius and Theodore of Mopsuestia and their steady concentration upon the historical event, and

behind Cyril would lie the whole range of defences of allegorization and
mystical speculation which Alexandria had built up over centuries. There
were real differences between the two schools, even if they overlapped at
certain points. If the Jewish exegetes had on occasions used allegorical
procedures, as did Philo of Alexandria, it was hardly in the mainstream of
Jewish thought, and we should perhaps see Alexandrian allegorizing as more
closely aligned with that of gnostics such as Heracleon and Basilides and
with Philo than with orthodox Jewish practice.[21] Antioch, however, was
more directly affected by Jewish thinking, and close affinities between
Antiochene and Jewish methods of exegesis have been observed. The tendency of certain haggadic procedures towards allegorism and mysticism
was controlled by Rabbinic rules designed to curb speculation, for instance
Hillel's regulations concerning the use of *a fortiori* arguments, arguments
from the particular to the general and from the general to the particular,
and the proper use of inference.[22] This kind of discipline hardly extended
to the Aramaic Targums, which were virtually exegetical paraphrases of
the Hebrew texts designed to bring them into line with altered situations, a
practice also to be observed in the transmission of Christian Scriptures.
This characteristic can be seen as parallel to the way in which Antiochene
Christians handled their Scriptures.

We may turn first to Lucian. From the late fourth century onwards,
John Chrysostom and Theodoret, writing at Antioch, are found to be consistently quoting a biblical text not precisely identical with any of the
main recensions of the text known hitherto.[23] It is probably of this Antiochene recension that Jerome wrote to Sunnia that apart from Origen's great
Hexaplar version there is 'another version which Origen and Eusebius of
Caesarea and all the Greek commentators call the popular text, and which
by most is now called the Lucianic text'.[24] Jerome was characteristically
scathing about its deficiencies, preferring Origen's text because Origen had
followed proper critical and scholarly procedures. There is truth in Jerome's
criticism, but the absence from the Lucianic text of the critical apparatus
does not mean that Lucian had ignored critical comparison of texts. On the
contrary, he had done precisely as Origen had done, as Theodoret tells us
in his Preface to the Psalter,[25] by comparing the Greek LXX text with the
Hebrew and producing a corrected version, sometimes preferring one
reading to another, sometimes setting two side by side as a doublet. The
Lucianic version became immensely popular, as Jerome's letter suggests,
and became the standard text of the Greek-speaking Church. Part of
Jerome's animosity may have been caused by precisely this popular character of Lucian's work, which sharply distinguishes it from Origen's. His aim
appears to have been to achieve intelligibility and smoothness, regardless of
whatever reading might on purely critical grounds be regarded as 'correct',
replacing pronouns by proper names, introducing words of his own in order

to clarify the sense of a passage, filling gaps in the narrative with his own material.[26] This was, as Jerome saw, unscrupulous by Origen's standards, but Lucian succeeded in his aim of clearing away ambiguities and inconsistencies.

This aim may help our understanding of the difference between Antiochene and Alexandrian treatment of the Scriptures. Lucian started from the position that the important thing was for the scriptural narrative to set out unambiguously what happened on a certain occasion: the written text was a convenient vehicle to convey the details of an historical event to later generations. Origen on the other hand had started from the position that the text itself, originally inspired by the Holy Spirit, contained moral and spiritual lessons to be imparted to later generations, and that the *minutiae* of the text and the establishment of the readings originally inspired were therefore of primary importance. A wrong text would distort the message of the Holy Spirit, since every word, indeed every letter, had its own importance and might affect the interpretation put upon it by later readers.[27]

It is this issue, the primacy of the historical event as against that of the text narrating the event, which is the burden of Eustathius' attack upon Origen's position in his short work *On the Witch of Endor, against Origen*,[28] written in the early fourth century. Origen had written a commentary on the passage in I Samuel 38 which describes Saul's visit to the witch and his vision of Samuel. In accordance with his usual practice he had dwelt little upon the historical situation in which the event took place and had concentrated his attention upon the details of the wording as conveying moral and spiritual teaching relevant to his third-century congregation. The text was a code to be deciphered, a riddle to be solved, for within it lay the words of the Spirit to the third century after Christ. Eustathius works through this passage and Origen's comments upon it in some detail. It is a test case. Origen had regarded every syllable of Scripture as being the vehicle of divine oracles. But how does the matter stand, asks Eustathius, when the text contains the words of evil people, e.g. a mad king and a devil-inspired witch? Are their words divine oracles? Not every word of Scripture, he concludes, can be read as God's words to man, and each passage has to be treated on its merits in the light of the historical circumstances of the event portrayed in the passage. Origen is made to reply, 'Does the Scripture say it or does it not?' For Eustathius, however, words spoken by scriptural characters carry not the authenticity of Scripture but of the person who utters the words. Who would rely upon the words of a witch and a mad king? It is not right to treat Holy Scripture as Origen treats it.[29] Eustathius concludes by turning Origen's own Platonist guns upon himself. Plato says that fables are to be used for educating children. Only suitable fables should be used, after being approved by qualified persons, so that by these fables the children may be taught and their souls strengthened. But of those which they now remember, many ought to be repudiated. Many of the fables of Homer and Hesiod are false and harmful despite the beauty of their language. If then such beautiful pieces of writing should be discarded, how much more should the words of a witch![30] We may well wish that this had been addressed to Origen during his lifetime in order to have the benefit of Origen's reply, for there is much that can be said in answer to Eustathius. But his point remains, that Origen, and the exegetical school of Alexandria with him, lack the specifically historical cast of mind without which an exegete is hardly fully-equipped to handle the Old Testament. Part of what Origen might have answered is implicit in the little Commentary on the same passage written a generation after Eustathius by Gregory of Nyssa.[31] He does not join issue with the precise point that Eustathius has made and there is no evidence that he is specifically answering Eustathius, but the implication of his exegesis is perhaps that although, as Eustathius rightly said, the words of daemons are not to be treated as oracles of God, yet the *record* of the words of daemons may be inspired by God. Too much must not be made of this, for Gregory is chiefly concerned to warn his readers against consorting with purveyors of auguries, divinations and evocations of the dead. What Origen would have made of the viewpoint of the greater Antiochene exegetes and theologians, who did not live until after Origen's death, can only be speculated, and it is perhaps rash to assume that he would have accused them of literalness as he did in his Homily on Genesis: 'He who wishes to take Scripture literally had better join the Jews rather than the Christians. But he who wishes to be a Christian and a follower of Paul must listen to Paul when he says that the Law is spiritual',[32] and in his Homily on Leviticus: 'There are those of our religion who want us to follow the literal meaning and explain what the lawgiver says without any cloud of allegorizing, to use their sarcastic term.'[33] Literalism is a term which could be used of some of the cruder minds of Origen's time, of certain Arabian sects, for example,[34] and of some millenarist groups, but it hardly fits the Antiochenes. There is nothing crudely literal-minded about insisting that an ancient text should be seen primarily in its own terms, a procedure involving an effort at historical understanding and presupposing what may be called a sacramental view of historical events. The Antiochenes themselves used the term 'literal' often enough, contrasting it with spiritual interpretation, but there was no crudity in their understanding of it.

The historical sense is of over-riding importance, and this means the sense which the writer of the text intended. By the faculty of insight (*theoria*), the exegete could determine whether the writer was referring to his own times or to some future event. No Antiochene would have denied the validity of prophecy and if a writer refers to things to come, then that is the historical meaning of his text, and the business of the exegete is to exercise his historical knowledge in deciding to what period of history the prophecy applies.[35] For not all prophecies must be assumed to refer to Christ, nor must it be assumed that because the New Testament applies an Old Testament passage to Christ, that interpretation is the only sense in which the passage may be understood and that the original author meant it to be understood in that way. Against any charge of crude rigidity of mind, we may see here, on the contrary, an elasticity of approach which is in some respects more sympathetic to twentieth-century minds than is the Alexandrian. Apart from verbal prophecy, events also may foreshadow later events. The Antiochenes agree that God works in this way and are prepared to see Old Testament events as 'types' of New Testament events, though in this they are more cautious than were the Alexandrians. For example, Cyril of Alexandria, who was in general much less prone to allegorizing than Origen had been, expounds Hosea ii.23f. ('And I will sow her unto me in the earth, and I will have mercy upon her that had not obtained mercy; and I will say to them which were not my people, Thou art my people, and they shall say, Thou art my God') entirely in New Testament terms, picking up the imagery of sowing – 'the Saviour compares the multitude of believers to corn in a field' – and illustrating it by references to corn in the gospels. Cyril exhibits no interest in the historical setting in which Hosea's words are uttered.[36] Theodoret, however, first places the passage historically and then expounds it typologically: these things happened typically under Zerubbabel, but in reality after the incarnation of Christ the Lord when he betrothed the Church to himself for ever.[37] Theodore of Mopsuestia ignores the hint given in I Peter ii.10 that the passage can have a Christian reference, and treats it in an historical manner, referring to the 'sowing' of the Jews in the district in which the prophet is addressing them.[38] Hosea xiii.14 ('Death, where are thy plagues? Grave, where is thy destruction?') invites treatment in New Testament terms after Paul's quotation of the passage at I Cor. xv, and the Alexandrians cannot do otherwise than accept the invitation: 'God redeems us from the tyranny of death', writes Cyril, 'the instrument of redemption being the death of Christ'.[39] Theodoret characteristically works from a firm historical basis in order to make the typological point: these things happened typically at the return of the Jews to Jerusalem, for hell and death refer to their life as captives in Babylon. But the type is fulfilled in Christ; the things that happened to the Jews were a type of God's care for all men.[40] Theodore will have none of this: 'The passage speaks of the Assyrians', and he will not be persuaded by I Cor. xv to see anything in the passage other than this.[41] Zechariah ix.9 ('Rejoice greatly, O daughter of Zion; shout, O daughter of Jerusalem; behold, thy king cometh unto thee; he is just, and having salvation; lowly, and riding upon an ass, even upon a colt, the foal of an ass') is too

plain in its New Testament reference even for Theodore to ignore it. Cyril
expands it allegorically: the image of a colt, unbroken, uncertain how to
walk, refers to Christ who carries others to spiritual knowledge. It follows
the ass, who represents the synagogue, since the synagogue preceded the
Church in point of time.[42] Theodoret's comment is that the meaning of
the prophet's words is plain, for the king whom the prophet foretold has
come and has destroyed sin by his righteousness, and has destroyed the
pride of the devil by his meekness; and he who rode upon the foal of an
ass had kings to adore him.[43] Theodore begins by anchoring the passage
to history: the king is Zerubbabel. But Theodore then goes on to express
surprise that some commentators understand part of the prophecy to apply
to Zerubbabel and part of it to Christ. There is no distinction in the text
between two figures, for the Law foreshadows Christ, just as in Genesis
xxii.18, 'All nations shall be blessed in thee and thy seed' was spoken
originally of Abraham but was fulfilled in Christ; and Psalm xvi.10, 'Thou
shalt not leave my soul in hell' was spoken by David of the Israelites but
fulfilled in Christ. So Zechariah in the passage under consideration was
speaking of Zerubbabel, who achieved a minor act of salvation through his
actions at Jerusalem, but Christ's great act leads all men to salvation. The
passage does not jump from Zerubbabel to Christ and back again, but
includes both type and its fulfilment at the same time. Theodore notes the
grammatical difficulty that the verse uses the present tense ('thy king
cometh') and says that Scripture varies its use of time and tense throughout the psalms and the prophetic books, and that the reader need not feel
obliged to adhere too closely to a contemporary interpretation just because
the prophet has here spoken in the present tense.[44] Lastly, Micah iv.2 ('And
many nations shall go and say, Come ye, and let us go up to the mountain
of the Lord, and to the house of the God of Jacob; and he will teach us of
his ways and we will walk in his paths; for out of Zion shall go forth the
Law, and the word of the Lord from Jerusalem'). The mountain, writes
Cyril, is the Church gathered from the gentiles, the life of those justified in
Christ and sanctified in the Spirit; or it can be taken as the Christian dispensation rising above the worship of stones and wood by the Greeks.[45]
Theodoret interprets the passage as referring to 'the preaching of the Gospel to the ends of the earth', and rejects an interpretation which links the
prophecy to the return of the Jews from Babylon to Jerusalem because the
Jews did not in fact hasten to the temple on that occasion to embrace their
Laws.[46] Theodore will not agree to this, seeing in the passage only a reference to the return of the Jews from captivity. He expresses astonishment
at those who refer the words to a period long after the return, and who see
in it a type of events which took place in the days of Christ. A type, he
explains, must have a real likeness to the event of which it is a type. John
iv.21 specifies 'neither from this mountain nor from Jerusalem', which

makes it impossible to take Micah's words as prophetic of Christ. The passage, he concludes, means that Israel was restored to its home in Sion in order that the Law and the Jewish cult might run their course.[47]

These passages of comment on the minor prophets point the contrast between Alexandrian use of the text as a jumping-off ground for spiritual exhortation and Antiochene insistence upon the historical foundation of interpretation even if the interpretation goes on to refer to Christ. In Theodore's view, the Old Testament prophet lived in an age which was blind to the more distant future, and could see only a limited distance ahead – as far as the Maccabaean revolt. The river of prophecy runs into the sands and disappears at that point.[48] A few great peaks of Israelite history could be seen as foreshadowing greater peaks in the Christian age to come: the deliverance from Egyptian exile, from Babylonian captivity and from persecution by Antiochus Epiphanes are examples. Outstanding individuals such as David could be allowed such a forward reference to Christ. The Jewish institution of sacrifice could be allowed to prefigure the greater sacrifice of Christ. Events involving water could on occasion point forward to Christian baptism. But Theodore permitted such typological exegesis only on rare occasions, and then only on condition that there was the plainest identity between the external phenomena in both type and fulfilment, e.g. water, sacrifice and so on. This was not allegorizing. It was the practice of *theoria*, insight, which enabled the Christian to see what could not be seen by people living in the old dispensation. It was a recognition that although the age of Law was to be distinguished from the age of Grace, yet both ages were part of the divine strategy, and some degree of continuity was inevitably to be seen running through from beginning to end by those enabled by the Holy Spirit to see it.[49]

Lacking Theodore's five books *Against the Allegorists*, of which Facundus writes,[50] we lack what we may assume to have been Theodore's developed statement of his exegetical position. We are able to turn, in lieu of this lost work, to certain passages in extant works where he repudiates allegorization most forcefully. In his *Commentary on Micah* v.5f.[51] he castigates those who mistakenly allegorize the Scriptures as being 'obliged to compound these absurd fables because they do not understand Scripture's characteristic way of speaking', and in the *Commentary on Nahum* iii.8[52] criticizes 'the empty ostentation of men who want to be able to interpret the names of unidentifiable places'. In his *Commentary on Galatians* there is a more extended attack arising out of Paul's own allegorization of the figures of Sarah and Agar.[53]

'Men who take great pains to falsify the sense of the divine Scriptures and to convert to their own ends all that is written in them actually fabricate foolish fables out of them and propose the name of Allegory to designate their folly, so taking false advantage of the words of the apostle in this passage, as though they were men who think that from him they have gained authority to do away with all interpretations of the divine Scripture, in that they strive to speak allegorically following the apostle's example, not being themselves aware how greatly their own meaning differs from what the apostle says in this passage. For the apostle does not abolish the historical sense of the passage nor does he do away with the events of the distant past, but he narrated those events just as they had taken place and made use of the historical sense according to his own understanding of it when he says, "This represents the Jerusalem of today", and "Just as in those days he who is born according to the flesh persecuted him who was born according to the Spirit". Thus he acknowledges the historical sense of the passage as being prior to all other considerations. For otherwise he would not have said that those things which were "according to Agar" represented "that which is the Jerusalem of today", whose present existence he admitted. He would not have used the term "just as" (*sicut*) of something which he believed not to exist. In using *sicut* he indicated a near comparison, for no comparison could stand if the elements being compared did not really exist. By using *tunc* he deliberately shows that he is uncertain of the exact duration of time. Yet no definition of duration will be necessary if the event never took place. But this is how the apostle does talk. These opponents of mine interpret everything in an opposite sense, wanting the entire historical aspect of divine Scripture to be no more than nocturnal dreams. For they say that Adam is not really Adam when they set about relating the scriptural narrative spiritually – "spiritually" is the word they like to use to designate their absurd interpretation – nor is paradise really paradise, nor is the serpent really a serpent. I was wishing to say this to them, that by distorting historical fact they no longer have any historical fact left to them. But having committed themselves to this kind of scriptural exegesis they have to say what is the basis of their answers to the questions: Who was the first created human being? or how did disobedience come to exist? or how did the sentence of mortality come to be imposed upon the human race? And if they learn these historical facts from Scripture, then necessarily the thing they call "Allegory" is manifest absurdity, superfluous at every turn.'

Theodore goes on to define the meaning of Paul's term 'Allegory': a comparison of actions performed long ago with those which take place at the present time.[54] In short, typology based upon historical fact is permitted, allegory is not. We may wish that Theodore had not chosen the Fall narrative in Genesis as the ground on which to defend historical exegesis, but his point is clear, that typological linking of one event with another must presuppose the historical reality of both events. Historical reality can only be typified by that which is also historical reality, and to depart from this principle is to drift into the realm of 'nocturnal dreams'. The basis of what

Theodore says is his belief that God's action in regard to the human race is one and indivisible. The Scriptures describe one immense act of God in creation and redemption, and Theodore's doctrines of the first state of man in paradise and of the two ages of human history help him to see the whole span of human existence from creation to judgement as constituting one divine act in which chronologically earlier incidents may relate to chronologically later incidents within the same act. This is a theme in Theodore's theology to which we shall return.[55] Here it is enough to suggest that his doctrine that Adam was created subject to mortality enables one to treat human history as being educative from the beginning,[56] with no essential disruption or change of direction occasioned by the fall of Adam.

Events can point forward to events, though it is not often that Theodore allows an Old Testament prophecy to refer to a Christian fulfilment. He begins his commentary on Joel by saying that whereas Hosea spoke of the events of the Assyrian and Babylonian invasions, Joel, contemporary with Hosea, includes also the events following immediately the return from Babylon and those of the Scythian invasion.[57] He proceeds to his verse by verse comment: in Joel i.7, 'the vine' is Israel that has been laid waste; i.9, 'The priests mourn' because of their treatment by the Babylonians; i.17 'the cattle groan' because they suffer from lack of food and break out in search of it; ii.2, 'the day of darkness' has no eschatological significance but refers to the times of Sennacherib; ii.3, 'the land is before them' because it is not yet invaded; ii.10, 'the earth quaketh', not literally, for the prophet is using hyperbole to strike fear into his readers; ii.19, 'the Lord answered' must be taken as future, in accordance with Hebrew idiom; ii.28, 'I will pour out my spirit upon all flesh' does not refer in the first instance to Pentecost, since the prophet could not have known the Holy Spirit in his own person as distinct from other persons of the Trinity. The Old Testament knows nothing of the divine Trinity and must not be made to appear as though it does. The Spirit of God, the Holy Spirit, and similar appellations signify simply the grace and providence of God. Peter could quote that passage at Acts ii.16, however, because the Law foreshadows what is to come, just as David in Psalm xv.10 could speak words whose later reference to Christ's resurrection he could not possibly have known. In this verse of Joel God assures the Jews of his providential care for them, but the prophet spoke metaphorically without knowing it, and the words take on further meaning in the light of Christ. The blood on the earth is that of Christ; the fire and vapour of smoke is the Holy Spirit: the prophet spoke in metaphor but in Christ it becomes literal truth.[58] Only for this one verse in the book of Joel does Theodore allow a New Testament interpretation of the prophet's words. Theodore's refusal at notable points to admit a New Testament interpretation was held by later generations to be scandalous, and the matter was referred to the Council of 553, which declared him heretical. For example, Malachi iii.1 ('the Lord, whom ye seek, shall suddenly come to his temple') refers not to Christ, as other commentators held it to do, but to Maccabaean times;[59] and more scandalous still, the suffering servant passage of Isaiah 53 did not refer to Christ: the prophet used the past tense, and as a past event it must be understood.[60]

Theodore's treatment of the psalms is in keeping with his treatment of the prophets: only three psalms (2, 8 and 44) look forward to Christ. The remainder fall into two groups, those which refer to events in the life of David and those which refer more generally to the providence of God, and it is of importance to Theodore to determine the theme of a psalm before he can treat it in detail.[61] This practice had been observed carefully half a century earlier by Eusebius of Caesarea who, despite his admiration for Origen, was notably Antiochene in much of his exegesis – the effect, perhaps, of his training under Dorotheus of Antioch in the time of Lucian – and it is also to be found in the work of Diodore and of John Chrysostom. Such attention to the overall theme and construction of a psalm is thoroughly Antiochene.

Professor C. Sant[62] has demonstrated an evolution in Eusebius' treatment of scriptural texts, tracing four stages of development: first, the *Prophetic Eclogues*, in which Eusebius does little more than assemble proof-texts to demonstrate that Christ was foretold in the Old Testament; second, the *Demonstratio Evangelica*, where a more literal and historical treatment of the psalms is practised; third, the polemical works against Marcellus, in which Marcellus is criticized for breaking the thought-sequence and structure of passages by ignoring their contexts, and in which allegorical speculation about the meaning of the text is very rarely employed; fourth, the two Commentaries, on Isaiah and the Psalms, in which the weight of the argument is devoted to the historical setting of each passage discussed.[63] Noticeable in these works, composed over a long period of literary activity, is the growth of features which are recognizably Antiochene, until in the *Commentary on the Psalms* Eusebius writes not only in an historical spirit which is foreign to Origen but in one psalm after another differs from Origen's treatment in point of detail. Like Diodore and Theodore he sees in the psalms and the prophetic books references to later events of which the writers could not have been aware, but goes a good deal further than Theodore in admitting Messianic references in the psalms. The references, however, must be plainly present in the text and not read into the text by allegorization. The historical setting of a passage has first to be determined, and then each phrase of the passage must be read in the light of that setting. Failure to proceed in this way distorts the plain intention of the psalmist and leads to a piecemeal treatment in which any phrase can be made to mean whatever the interpreter wants it to mean.[64] Marcellus receives harsh treatment from Eusebius on this ground, and on occasions (e.g. in his treat-

ment of Psalm lxxxii.2) Eusebius rejects curtly 'the other view', which is
presumably that of Origen. Where Messianic references are found, the exegete must closely observe the intentions of the Old Testament writer, as in
the case of Isaiah's references to the coming Messiah, which Eusebius finds
to be systematically grouped to cover the promise of the Messiah, his conception and birth, his prerogatives, titles and offices, in that order. In the
same way the order of the Psalter must be observed, not based, as Origen
had supposed, on mystical numbers, nor on a chronological sequence, but
on a developing sequence of thought. Eusebius insists upon disciplined
study of this kind in order to provide a check upon arbitrary speculation
and individual fantasy, and in this he shows himself to be a child of Antioch.
It is probable that he stands nearer to the moderate historicism of Theodoret than to the extreme hostility to Alexandrian beliefs and methods
shown by Theodore.

We have already noted that in their treatment of the minor prophets
Theodore and Theodoret do not always agree, and that the latter sometimes stands nearer to Cyril than to Theodore. Dr. G. W. Ashby concludes
that by the fifth century Antioch and Alexandria had drawn fairly close in
their exegesis, and that Theodoret shows signs of having accepted the less
narrowly-constricted principles of Diodore and Eustathius rather than those
of Theodore.[65] In other words, Theodore must not be regarded as the most
characteristic Antiochene exegete, even though he is the greatest. Rendel
Harris wrote that Ephrem Syrus and Theodore 'are the men we want to
know, the one for what he said in commenting on the Diatessaron, the
other for what he said on anything, and as being, from a modern point of
view, the greatest of New Testament commentators'.[66] This is splendid
praise and few would dissent from it, but it does not mean that Theodore
was typical of the school which he dominated, nor that all followed him
blindly. Exegesis at Antioch was not monolithic. Theodoret's *concordat*
with Alexandria in 451, however reluctant, may be taken as symptomatic
that by the middle of the fifth century Antioch no longer stood in total
opposition to everything Alexandrian. With the exception of Theodore, it
had perhaps never stood so in respect of exegesis. By the fifth century, the
weight of support for Theodore was already moving from Antioch itself to
centres further east.

The exegetical milieu into which it moved can be seen in the work of
the two fourth-century commentators of east Syria, Afrahat and Ephrem
Syrus. In the work of both men there is a readiness to see prophecies of
Christ throughout the Old Testament, some of which, such as 'the stone
rejected by the builders',[67] had dominical authority for being so treated.
Afrahat allows this verse to attract to it other passages concerning rocks,
e.g. Is. xxviii.16 ('a foundation stone in Zion'), Dan. ii.34 ('a stone was cut
out'), Zech. iv.7 ('a headstone') and iii.9 ('the stone that I have laid'), and

refers them all to Christ – Zechariah, says Afrahat, writes *for us* about the rock.[68] *Homily xvii*, on the divinity of Christ, is not long but contains numerous prophecies of Christ,[69] some of which reveal Afrahat picking up even the least probable suggestion of relevance and forcing it into service, as Zech. xiv.6, 'On this day will be cold and frost', which he sees as a reference to Peter warming himself before the fire in the High Priest's house. Ephrem too is ready to find reference to Christ in the Old Testament, and extends the period of fulfilment beyond the gospels to the Acts of the Apostles, as in his treatment of Joel iii.1ff., 'Your sons and daughters will prophesy . . . blood and fire', which he sees as foretelling not only the crucifixion but also the events of the following Pentecost.[70] His *Commentary on Genesis* and his fragmentary *Commentary on Exodus* however show a remarkable restraint in the use of typology. The seventh-day rest 'was given to them in order that he (e.g. Moses) might show by the temporal sabbath, which God would give to people on earth, the figure of the true sabbath which will be given' in eternity.[71] In Abraham's sacrifice of Isaac, 'the mountain produced a tree and the tree a ram, so that in the ram, which was hanging from the tree and was sacrificed for Abraham's son, might be prefigured the day of him who hung from the wood as though he were a ram, and tasted death for the whole world'.[72] When Jacob poured oil over the pillar at Beth-El (Gen. xxviii.18), 'by the oil which he poured over the stone he showed a symbol of the Christ'; further, 'in the stone was signified the mystery of the Church, through which would come the vows and oblations of all peoples'.[73] At Gen. xxxviii.18 Judah gave his pledges to Tamar, and 'she took from the man his seal with its cord and his staff, and took them as three pledges which might testify of the one of the Trinity who was to be born through her'.[74] Jacob blessing his sons with outstretched arms (Gen. xlviii.13f.) 'clearly depicted the cross'.[75] In the Exodus Commentary the Passover regulations are treated in detail: the lamb is a type of the Lord who was conceived on the tenth day of Nisan, and the fourteenth day of Nisan (on which the Passover lamb was killed) typifies the day of the crucifixion; the unleavened bread is a type of Christ's uniqueness; the bitter herbs a type of his sorrows; the Passover is eaten with loins girt and sandals on their feet, signifying the readiness of the disciples to go out to preach the gospel; the staves in their hands typify the crosses on their shoulders; they eat standing, to signify the bodily position adopted by those who receive the living body of Christ; no foreigner eats the Passover, for nobody other than the baptized receives the body of Christ; the bones of the lamb are unbroken, for though Christ's hands and feet were pierced yet his bones were not broken.[76] At Exodus xxiv.4–7 the sprinkling of the blood prefigures the gospel, by which the death of Christ is given to all peoples.[77] What is remarkable here is not the presence of typology but its rarity, perhaps twenty instances of its use in a hundred and fifty pages of textual comment. In both Commentaries the exegesis is notable for its plain descriptiveness, often no more than a paraphrase of the text, and on occasions failing to indicate a type where most other patristic exegetes would have indicated one; for example, the creator breathing life into Adam's nostrils, Noah's ark, the royal priesthood of Melchizedek. In his treatment of Adam's relationship with the animals in Eden, Ephrem seems almost to invite a comparison with the good shepherd of the fourth gospel in order to avoid it: the animals came to Adam as to a loving shepherd, and each of the herds passed before him fearlessly, the savage and the timid together.[78] At the outset of the Genesis Commentary Ephrem warns his readers, 'Let nobody think that there is an allegorical interpretation of the six days',[79] and indeed he progresses many chapters beyond the creation narrative before he admits any figurative interpretation of the text, and even then it is typology that he employs rather than allegory.

Among Ephrem's rare moments of allegorizing we may note the words, 'Behold, the man has become as one of us', at Gen. iii.22, which to Ephrem 'reveals in hidden form the Trinity',[80] but we also observe that he does not follow Paul in allegorizing the narrative of Sarah and Hagar.[81] Afrahat links the 'rock with seven eyes' at Zech. iii.9 with Is. xi.2, and interprets the seven eyes as the seven gifts of the Spirit – the Spirit of the Lord, of wisdom, of understanding, of counsel, of power, of knowledge and of the fear of the Lord; and he goes further to interpret these as the seven eyes of the Lord which look upon the whole earth.[82] The woman in the parable at Luke xv.8, who loses one of her ten pieces of silver, represents the house of Israel, which has lost the first of the ten commandments on which the remaining nine depend, and so has in effect lost all.[83] In his Diatessaron Commentary Ephrem allegorizes the blind and dumb man at Matt. xii.22 to represent the Jewish people, of whom Isaiah said 'the heart of this people is hard, their ears stopped, their eyes blind'. The healing of the man represents those who came to believe in Christ and received healing of their spiritual blindness.[84] Zacchaeus climbs a big tree as a symbol of his salvation; 'he left the lower depth and ascended to the middle air', and not quite consistently his descent from the tree symbolizes his emergence from spiritual deafness to be made a new man.[85] The fruitless fig tree at Mark xi.12 symbolizes those who were spiritually fruitless under the Law, and in rebuking the tree Christ showed that he was rebuking Jerusalem, because he had sought love in vain in the city. Ephrem rejects too detailed a parallel between the tree and the city, since the tree was not in its season for bearing fruit and Jerusalem was ready to bear spiritual fruit. The incident was in any case not a parable but a sign: 'If it were a parable, [Jesus] would not have found it necessary to say, "If you had faith, etc." but "If you had understanding." It is therefore a sign, not a parable.'[86] Ephrem is, like Afrahat, more concerned with Old Testament types pointing forward to fulfilment in Christ. Christ was crucified in Jerusalem 'in order to reveal the types in Israel', for Deut. xvi.5f. forbids the sacrifice of the Passover anywhere but in the place chosen for it by God, and I Cor. v.7, 'Christ, our passover, is sacrificed', identifies the fulfilling of the sacrificial type with the sacrifice of Christ.[87] It is especially in connection with the passion that Ephrem sees Christ as fulfilling earlier types, in general terms fulfilling the types inherent in the sufferings of Jeremiah, Elijah, Elisha, Samuel and Moses;[88] more specifically as fulfilling the details of David's persecution at the hands of Saul (David was enclosed in a cave, Christ in the depths of humanity; David was unwounded by Saul's spear, Christ undefeated by death; and so on) and Moses' persecution by his people.[89] In this Ephrem was following where Afrahat had led, for Afrahat's Homily xxi, reflecting the persecution of Christians instigated by Shahpur II, pursues relentlessly the typological details of the sufferings of twelve Old Testament figures, Joseph, Moses, Joshua, Jepthah, David, Elijah, Elisha, Hezekiah, Josiah, Daniel, Hananiah and Mordecai,[90] sifting every detail of the biblical record in order to find incidents great or small which could be held to prefigure the passion of Christ. Georg Bert, in the Introduction to his edition of Afrahat's Homilies, sees what he rightly calls Afrahat's 'copious application of typological exegesis' as a link with the exegetical school of Antioch, but it is hard to recall an Antiochene writer in whose work typology runs riot to the extent to which Afrahat allows it. We should indeed not attempt to find any traces of Alexandrian influence in this, for there is nothing of Origen's systematized structure about it, and in Afrahat's work the link between the Testaments is normally one of historical event: certain things happened, and their meaning is made clear by the light of corresponding events in the gospel narrative. Afrahat's use of allegory and typology and his readiness to find prophecies of Christ in the Old Testament suggest a freedom of usage that is not that of Theodore and that reflects the more primitive usage of the Syrian Church. Ephrem is slightly more systematized in his use of figurative and typological interpretations, and is very much more restrained in his use of them, but again there is little sense of systematization as it is found in Theodore – little sense, that is, of working to formulated principles of interpretation, or of Theodore's close integration of exegesis and doctrine. What we find in Ephrem is an attempt at historical common sense: at Matt. xxi. 20, he objects to an interpretation that he has read which makes the words, 'You will say to this mountain, Be removed', apply not to a mountain but to a daemon, for there was no daemon present when Jesus spoke the words, whereas the mountain present was obvious – he was standing on the Mount of Olives.[91] We also find interpretations linked closely to the setting in which they were spoken: at the transfiguration Peter asked to be allowed to build three tabernacles because in the quiet of the mountain he was rejoicing at their escape from Caiaphas and

Herod, and Christ's first announcement of his passion was fresh in his mind.[92] Again, Christ's angry outburst to the twelve, 'O perverse generation', is made to precede the choosing and sending out of the seventy-two, a juxtaposing of the narratives of Matthew and Luke which doubtless reflects the Diatessaron text, but which gains a sharper point in Ephrem's commentary in its suggestion of cause and effect in Christ's relations with his disciples.[93] This kind of writing is far removed from the allegorical speculations of Alexandria, and may be seen as characteristic of the indigenous habit of mind which was temporarily submerged by the immense domination exercised by Theodore in the fourth century, and to which Syrian exegetes returned when that domination was challenged by Henana in the sixth century. Indeed, the exegesis of Gregentius of Zafār in the sixth century may suggest that Theodore's influence had never penetrated to regions remote from the great Syrian centres of learning such as Edessa and Nisibis.

Is it possible to trace this indigenous Syrian exegesis further back in time to an earlier date than that of Afrahat and Ephrem? It may be that something of the sort can be found in the work of Theophilus of Antioch, *ad Autolycum*, written in about 182. Theophilus was a Syrian by birth, coming from a region near the rivers Tigris and Euphrates, which 'border on our own region'.[94] More important than this is the influence of Theophilus in the fifth century upon Narsai at Edessa and Nisibis, and upon James Bar'adai at Edessa.[95] P. Gignoux examines the use made of Theophilus by Narsai,[96] identifying ideas common to both and showing that Theophilus represents 'the tradition of the School', which was transmitted to Narsai through the work of Afrahat and to a lesser extent through that of Ephrem.[97] R. M. Grant sees strong Jewish characteristics in Theophilus' *ad Autolycum*,[98] but it may be that for an explanation of Theophilus' idiosyncratic and eclectic theology we should look rather to the tradition of the eastern Syrian Church. His exegesis has much in common with that of the moderate literalism that we have observed in the work of Afrahat and Ephrem.

That Theophilus' treatment of the biblical text is not to be easily categorized is plain from the disagreement of scholars in their estimation of it: R. M. Grant sees it as the first example of characteristically Antiochene literalism;[99] to F. L. Cross it is nearer to the allegorical manner of Alexandria;[100] both views can be supported by reference to Theophilus' text. Theophilus sets out what is said in the creation narrative of Genesis, quoting it at considerable length, but in allegorical manner he sees the relationship between the heavenly bodies as representing that between God and man. The heavenly bodies 'contain the pattern and type of a great mystery, for the sun is a type of God and the moon of man'.[101] The sun is unchanging in its power and radiance, whereas the moon wanes and is reborn as does

man when he passes through death to resurrection. The fixed stars typify
the settled piety of the good man, the wandering planets the instability of
the man who abandons God's law and commandments. The creation of
waters leads Theophilus into an analogy between safe anchorages and the
Church, and between threatening rocks and the heresies which bring ship-
wreck to man's salvation.[102] Wild beasts are the unrepentant among men.
Birds fly upwards like the righteous, but birds which have wings and do
not use them are the earthbound among men.[103] Creatures proceeding from
the waters are blessed by the Creator, a sign that man in rising from the
water of regeneration at baptism will also receive blessing.[104] Much of this
sounds as though it were written by an Alexandrian rather than by an Antiochene, and it may be that we see here the influence of Philo of Alexandria.
Comparison of Theophilus' account of creation with Philo's *de Opificio
Mundi* and *Legum Allegoria* suggests that Theophilus knew at least the first
of them. The darkness which covered the face of the earth is to Theophilus
caused by the heavens, which covered earth and water like a lid:[105] to Philo,
air is by nature dark 'when left to itself', and this unillumined air 'spread
over and completely filled the immensity and desolation of the void'.[106] To
Theophilus the Spirit moving on the face of the waters suggests a mingling
of two elements, air and water, the two together penetrating the earth at
every point to nourish growing things:[107] to Philo the water seeped into
every part of the earth 'as though the earth were a sponge saturated with
moisture'.[108] To Theophilus, the sun, moon and stars were created later in
time than things growing on the earth so that philosophers could not attribute earthly growth to the activity of the sun and moon:[109] to Philo, God
knew in advance that man would look for the plausible explanation rather
than the true one, and 'would suppose that the regular movements of the
heavenly bodies are the causes of all things that year by year come forth',
and therefore created the growing things before the heavenly bodies.[110]
To Theophilus, birds and fish are of one nature:[111] to Philo, birds are sisters
to aquatic creatures, 'both being creatures that float'.[112] Parallel passages
of this kind suggest that Theophilus may have drawn upon Philo's work,
but if this is so, more striking is the fundamental dissimilarity of the two
writers, for the massive allegorical structure which Philo builds on the
Genesis narrative is entirely ignored by Theophilus. In *Legum Allegoria*
Philo develops a detailed examination of the dawn of human psychological
development, built upon the creation of Eve from Adam's rib.[113] The only
possible point which could suggest that Theophilus had assimilated this is
his idea that Adam and Eve were morally neutral before the Fall, which
has something in common with Philo's conclusion that mind and sense perception are neutral or inactive until awakened to their proper activities.[114]
But a reading of the two texts leaves a strong impression of the imaginative
versatility of Philo and of the down-to-earth plainness of Theophilus. If

there are parallels between their respective works, they are slight. There are abundant instances of Theophilus taking a factual and literal view where Philo allegorizes: for example, the four rivers flowing from Paradise are to Philo four virtues, prudence, self-mastery, courage and justice,[115] while to Theophilus they are four rivers and no more, two of which 'border on our regions'.[116] This is the unmistakable voice of Antiochene exegesis which we shall hear again in the work of Diodore, Eustathius, Theodoret and the Syrian fathers. It is the rejection of cosmological myth and the restrained use of biblical allegorization, the fixing of attention upon things known and understood as means of apprehending the unknown, that is characteristically Antiochene and Syrian, seen here as early as the end of the second century. This was 'the tradition of the Church' inherited by Afrahat and Ephrem and handed down by them to Narsai.

The indigenous Syrian tradition received an infusion of new Antiochene blood early in the fifth century. The first step towards the re-creation of Syrian theology by Theodore was the translation of Theodore's work into Syriac, almost the entire labour of translation being completed before the death of Theodore himself in 428.[117] The process began after the death of Ephrem in 372 or 373 at Edessa, when the scholarly Qiiōrē began to replace the older curriculum of the school by the work of Theodore, and we first encounter references to 'the Interpreter', namely Theodore. Ephrem, great as he was in many ways, represented a more primitive Syrian culture which was now to be superseded by a new order. This change established Theodore as the great doctor of the Syrian Church until the first signs of reform or reaction appeared a hundred and fifty years later. In the work of translation Qiiōrē was assisted by Hībā, or Ibas, whose far-sighted statesmanship on behalf of the teaching of Theodore brought him into trouble with his Monophysite opponents. 'The holy Theodore interpreted the scriptures in Greek and Mar Hībā, bishop of Edessa, translated [them] from the Greek into Syriac, together with other men trained in the divine scriptures'.[118] His assistants were Kūmī, Dani'el, the archdeacon Prōbā and Ma'nā of Shiraz. To this group of devoted scholars Edessa owed not only Syriac texts of Theodore but also of the Clementine *Recognitions*, Titus of Bostra, Eusebius of Caesarea and Diodore of Tarsus, in addition to a great deal of Greek philosophical work. The condemnation of Nestorius at Ephesus in 431 carried with it an inevitable attack upon Theodore, who was held to be Nestorius' master, and the proper understanding of Theodore's exegetical principles was an essential weapon in the hands of his supporters at Edessa. The defection in 432 to the Monophysite party of Rabbula, bishop of Edessa,[119] and his consequent setting in motion of a counter-movement of notable Monophysite translations made it the more necessary for Theodore's work to be widely available and properly understood. Hībā himself, bishop of Edessa for a brief period and under continual attack, was deposed

and imprisoned at Antioch until 450,[120] and not even the declaration of
his orthodoxy at Chalcedon in the following year could regain him his
episcopal see. Nevertheless his championship of Antiochene theology and
exegesis continued to be a powerful influence until his death in 457. The
school of Edessa never regained its earlier leadership as an Antiochene
centre and was closed in 489 by imperial decree.

At some point between the death of Hībā and the closing of the school,
a second and greater Antiochene centre came to the forefront still further
eastward, in Nisibis. The first great head of the school of Nisibis, Narsai,[121]
was only indirectly concerned with exegetical matters, turning rather to
homiletic and moral instruction – in spirit perhaps a Chrysostom rather
than a Theodore – but his championship of Theodore against attack[122]
shows where his sympathies lay, and the list of works attributed to him
by Ebedjesu includes commentaries on the Pentateuch, Joshua, Judges,
Ecclesiastes and the prophets.[123] Under his rule the study of Theodore,
'the doctor of doctors',[124] gave coherence to the entire curriculum of the
school, liturgical, literary, lexical, grammatical and theological. The adoption of Theodore as the doctor to teach the eastern Syrian Church did not
call for total abandonment of all that had been taught in Edessa before
this time: Narsai stood on the shoulders of Afrahat and Ephrem in order
to extend his reach.[125] The exegetical tradition established by Narsai was
thus to some extent already formed. His work lay in the redirection of
that tradition and not in original exegetical work of his own, which may
account for the disappearance of his commentaries and the silence of his
successors about his personal contribution to the tradition.[126] Nevertheless
we have enough of his work to enable us to recognize the extreme literalism
of his treatment of the text. His homilies on the Creation follow closely
the path trodden by Theodore. At Gen. i.2 the spirit moving on the face
of the waters is for Narsai, as for Ephrem, Theodore and Theodoret, the
wind, not the Spirit of God.[127] The creation of sea-creatures from the
waters means literally that they were engendered by the water: 'The waters
brought forth innumerable species of animals, reptiles, birds, marine mon-
sters and deadly creatures. O Power, for whom difficulties are made easy
according to his will, who formed numberless species from the water! He
made the birds out of water . . .'[128] In over eighty pages of the Syriac text
of these homilies, the nearest approach to typology is perhaps Narsai's
treatment of the tree of life in Eden:

'By the tree of life [God] announced to us the creation of the world to
come, and in his good will he planted it in the place of punishment. The
desire for the fruit bore hard upon the young Adam. When he would
have eaten it, the fruit of life would renew him. By the narrative of the
two trees [God] showed us the two worlds, and as though to children
he wished to reveal his (nature) concealed in a symbol. By the tree of

knowledge he led [Adam] towards earthly riches, and by the tree of life he announced to him heavenly riches.'[129]

Of allegorization or spiritualizing of the text there is no sign whatever, and this not in formal commentaries but in homilies, where we might expect some moral or spiritual lessons to be drawn from the words. Narsai, in the strictest Antiochene manner, refrains from any such extravagance. The exegetical basis for scriptural study at Nisibis was to be the unspeculative historical method of Theodore.

Narsai was followed during the first decade of the sixth century, by a notable exegete, Elisha bar Quzbaie, who completed the work of translating Theodore into Syriac - Theodore's *Commentary on Samuel* - and undertook original work of his own in commentaries on Joshua, Judges, Job and possibly the Pauline epistles,[130] all of which is lost to us. His reputation was such that three centuries later his work was quoted by Išo'dad of Merv, the indefatigable collector and compiler of the work of the greater Nestorians. Also lost and known to us through Išo'dad are the commentaries of Abraham de-bet Rabban on Joshua, Judges, Kings, Canticles, Bar Sirach and the Prophets,[131] and those of Mar Aba on Genesis, the psalms, Proverbs, Wisdom, Ecclesiasticus, Isaiah, some Pauline epistles and possibly the gospels. Mar Aba carried further the work of translation by producing a Syriac version of the liturgical work of Theodore and a Syriac translation of the Greek Old Testament. A further step in the development of Antiochene exegesis at Nisibis is found in the lectures delivered in the middle of the sixth century by Paulos, in which he set out to elucidate and categorize Theodore's principles by cross-fertilizing them with Aristotle's *Organon* (translated into Syriac by Paulos himself) and *de Hermeneutica*.[132] Paulos treats systematically the questions that the exegete must ask himself when he has a text before him: what kind of work is this - historical, prophetic, proverbial, didactic? What authority does it carry? - the authorship of individual books of Scripture must be examined and their relative authority estimated. What is the quality of the text within its *genre*? Paulos applies this scheme to the Scriptures, discussing the familiar topics of typology, prediction of future events and their fulfilment.[133] This was lecture-room work which gives an interesting glimpse of the systematic way in which study of the Scriptures was conducted at Nisibis. The questions to be asked reveal clearly the kind of critical and historical approach inherited from Theodore.

The first sign of dissension within the ranks of Theodore's disciples may perhaps be seen in the defence of Theodore enshrined in the canons of the synod of Seleucia-Ctesiphon in 585.[134] Why, after so long a period of dominance, should Theodore need defending? Henana of Hadiab, who had been teaching at Nisibis since before 571,[135] was reputed to be a dissident element in the Nestorian fold. He was a man of great learning and of immense influence upon his pupils. Among his known exegetical work, most of which is lost, were commentaries on Genesis, the Prophets, the Psalms, Proverbs, the Wisdom literature, Mark and the Pauline epistles.[136] In general he was to lead the practice of biblical exegesis away from the long-established tradition of Theodore towards something less rigidly historical – less narrowly constricted, as it would have seemed to him – and more in accord with the more relaxed principles of Theodoret and Chrysostom or of the primitive tradition of east Syria as exemplified by the work of Afrahat and Ephrem. To his opponents it seemed as though he were leading straight back to the allegorism of Origen, 'the pagan of pagans'.[137] A test case was his treatment of the book of Job, which Theodore had rejected as a late Hellenistic composition. The second canon of the Nestorian synod of 585/6 under Išo'yabh I accused Henana of 'venturing to say that the man of God, Moses, had written the book of the blessed Job', and of having used the commentary of Chrysostom.[138] Samples of his exegesis preserved by Išo'dad reveal his allegorizing cast of mind: Matt. xx.7, 'No man has hired us' refers to the teachings of the gospel not yet fully revealed, and Matt. xxii.4, 'my oxen and my fatlings are killed', predicts the martyrdom of the saints[139] – comments that Theodore would not have permitted. In his *Treatise on the Friday after Pentecost*,[140] Henana expounds the principle on which the Old Testament can be interpreted prophetically. The Law, he says, is both heard and seen, spoken and performed. Thus the advent of Christ was predicted for us in two ways,

> 'by prophetic words and by symbolic actions. The prophetic words are the following: [Gen. xxii.3] "In thee shall all the nations be blessed"; [Gen. xlix.10] "Until he shall come to whom it belongs, and for whom the nations wait"; [Deut. xviii.15] "The Lord will raise you up a great prophet from among your brothers"; [Num. xxiv.17] "A star shall proceed from Jacob"; [Ps. ii.7] "the Lord said to me, thou art my son"; [Ps. viii.1] "Eternal, our Lord, may thy name be magnified by the whole earth"; [Ps. xlv.7] "That is why, O God, thy God has anointed thee with an oil of gladness above thy fellows"; [Ps. cx.1] "The Lord said to my Lord, sit at my right side"; [Ps. lxxxix.36] "Thy throne shall be like the sun in my presence". The actions are: the sacrifice of Isaac, the slaughter of the lamb, the raising up of the serpent, the sojourn of Jonah in the sea and in the belly of the fish, in addition to other actions which there is no need to mention here.'

Henana's willingness to abandon Theodore's exegesis along with Theodore's theology sowed seeds of discord from which the School of Nisibis never recovered. His exegetical innovations were perpetuated in the work of pupils such as Isha'ia of Tahal,[141] but his anathematization was a serious blow to him. The catholicos Sabrišo reaffirmed the anathema upon 'all who reject the expositions, traditions and teachings of the tested doctor, the blessed Theodore, the Interpreter',[142] and on the suggestion that Henana might succeed to the bishopric of Nisibis in 608/9, the anathema was again renewed. From having had many hundred students, the School was left, after the death of Henana in about the year 612, with only twenty,[143] the majority having transferred to other schools already in existence or having founded their own communities elsewhere.

The long-term effects of Henana's reform can be observed two hundred years later, when in the middle of the ninth century Išo'dad, while remaining true to the memory of Theodore,[144] was also prepared to abandon Theodore in favour of other interpretations of the biblical text, often allegorical. Ephrem, Cyril of Alexandria, Gregory of Nyssa and Chrysostom appear shoulder to shoulder with Theodore.[145] His exegetical principles appear to be unexceptionably Antiochene: 'It is necessary that with every word of Scripture we should observe these four things – the occasion, the place, the time, the persons who are involved in it',[146] which brings to mind the systematization of Paulos' lecturing at Nisibis. In his preface to the Psalms Išo'dad expresses his opposition to allegorical treatment 'which suppresses the reality in order to put something else in its place'. Historical interpretation 'explains things as they are', whereas allegorical interpretation he claims to have been invented by Origen and to be conducive to 'impiety, blasphemy and lies'.[147] Išo'dad explicitly rejects allegorical interpretation of Matt. xii.43, 'when the unclean spirit is gone out of a man', of which 'allegorists and others say that the unclean spirit is the error received from Satan to be within man, but came out of a man, out of the people of the Jews, in which it had dwelt . . . but, the Interpreter refers it to an individual man's spiritual state.'[148] Origen's interpretation of the parable of the sower, in which 'sixty fold' refers to the virtue of widowhood, is mistaken: Matthew refers here to married people, not to widows.[149] In his comment on Genesis i.7, he tells the reader that

> 'it is necessary to know that first Origen and after him Basil and others have claimed that the waters above the firmament are spiritual powers. Origen giving the scriptures an allegorical interpretation understands [this passage] in such a manner. Having once decided that men are represented by the water, he thought stupidly that the waters above the heavens are therefore spiritual powers.'[150]

The fragments of Išo'dad's commentaries on the minor prophets and psalms[151] show such constancy to Theodore that the work is not far removed from being a *catena* of Theodore's remarks on the passages in question. Throughout his commentaries he constantly discusses etymological derivations of names, supporting his conclusions with Greek and Syriac evidence; he discusses the relative chronological reliability of John and the synoptic gospels, always in favour of the former – Matthew's gospel was written 'not in the order in which it was spoken and done by our Lord, but according to another plan which he thought would be in agreement with his doctrine';[152] John, on the contrary, was careful about chronological detail;[153] scribal errors in the text are noted and corrected,[154] including what Išo'dad holds to be the mistaken insertion of a marginal gloss into the text of John xxi.25: 'The Interpreter says that these words are not in the text of scripture, but were put above on the margin . . . and afterwards were introduced into the text.'[155] All this is purely Antiochene, yet at other times Išo'dad is prepared to allegorize on his own account as though he had never learnt from Theodore how to comment on a text. At Luke i.51 'the mighty' are the demons, the pagans and the Jews;[156] at Luke iv.18 'the captives' are those who suffer violence from the tyranny of demons;[157] at Luke v.2 'two boats' signifies circumcision and uncircumcision.[158] In the birth narrative of John the Baptist, the tying of his father's tongue signifies 'the tying of the nation and the gentiles by error; but in the loosening of his tongue, their loosening from error . . . and the renewal they receive from Christ. But his translation to the wilderness typifies our translation from earth to heaven.'[159] At Matt. viii.20 'the allegorists interpret the foxes as covetous thoughts', but no censure of the allegorization is expressed.[160] At the entry into Jerusalem, 'Jesus went on foot from Jericho to Bethphage to typify the labours and vexations of human nature. The beasts ridden from Bethphage typify the abrogation of fatigue and its liberation from tribulations to the repose that is in heaven. It further typifies riding on the clouds of heaven'.[161] There is room to doubt whether Theodore would have countenanced this as an example of typology. It sounds Alexandrian, and van de Eynde concludes that the allegorical sense of Scripture figures largely in the exegetical work of Išo'dad, sometimes being employed in a quite arbitrary fashion.[162] The eclectic usage of Išo'dad is part of the inheritance of Henana, whose continuing influence is clear from the canons of the synod held by catholicos Yohannan bar Abhgar a century after Išo'dad.[163]

The animosity shown towards Henana by those who claimed to remain loyal to the tradition of Theodore, and the accusations of Alexandrian treachery levelled at him, may lead us to see the matter of biblical exegesis as being more central than perhaps it was. That it was important to Antiochenes there can be no doubt, not because it was the central point at issue, but because it was an essential avenue of approach to that point. Antiochenes and Alexandrians did not anathematize each other primarily because of their opposed standpoints on the matter of exegetical method but on matters of Christian doctrine directly concerned with the salvation of man, and if Christians were to get the latter point right (from whichever standpoint) then they had to understand the Scriptures aright as a preliminary. But it was, I believe, a preliminary and not the last ditch. We may look in this light upon the variability of the attitudes of Antiochenes towards exegesis. We have noticed briefly in this chapter the extreme instance of Theodore himself; the less rigid historicism of the majority of Antiochenes and of Syrians both before and after Theodore; the possibility of an individual mind moving, perhaps under pressure of doctrinal controversy, towards a more pronounced historical emphasis in exegesis, as in the instance of Eusebius; or in the opposite direction, as in the instances of Rabbula and Henana; or adopting a moderate position without appearing to see the need to argue the matter at all, as with John Chrysostom; and these variable standpoints co-existing at various points round a circumference whose centre was the salvation of man's soul. If that was the centre where the real battle was fought, the Scriptures provided a map of the battlefield, a history of the battle up to the time of Christ, and a vision of the cosmic scale of the conflict to its ultimate and inevitable outcome. The general who misread his map was thought to have little hope of leading his army victoriously to participate in the final triumph.

3

Historiography in the Eastern Church

While all religions are in a sense historical religions, the claim of Christianity to be a historical religion takes its stand upon doctrinal ground rather different from that of any other of the major religions, in that it claims that the historical person of Christ is of cosmic significance. Christ is seen as central to the proper understanding of the world in which he is incarnate and, although the articulation of this central significance of Christ varies as Christian doctrine changes its emphasis over centuries, and even within the patristic era itself, the claim for Christ's centrality remains, whether his significance is seen in relation to the objects and processes of the natural world or to the events of human history. Patristic historiography must be seen in the wider context of the religious and philosophical standpoint of its writers. It does not fall within the scope of this chapter to examine the Alexandrian view of human history, but such an undertaking would need to set the matter in the framework of the Platonist spirituality of Philo and Origen.[1] Eusebius lies nearer to our purpose, for all Antiochene and Syrian historical writing is to some degree beholden to him, and we must pay attention to his vision of human history as having achieved its goal in the Christian empire. We shall also need to note the philosophical and doctrinal basis of Theodore's view of man and his development. These great writers and their different views of the historical process were of seminal importance, even though their Greek and Syrian successors could readily abandon the underlying presuppositions and could appropriate to their use only the formal characteristics of their masters' work. Eusebius could teach Syria how to write history though the Syrians did not so easily accept from him what they should be writing about, in part perhaps a consequence of the circumstance that not all of his great output of work found its way into Syriac, and in part because they were embarrassed by the association of his name with the founding fathers of Arianism. Theodore, on the other hand, could show them why to think historically, though from his pen they received no formal historical work analogous to the *Chronicle* or *Ecclesiastical History* of Eusebius to give them a pattern to follow.

Eusebius, standing at Caesarea midway between Antioch and Alexandria, tempered his admiration of Origen with a reverence for the observed fact which is wholly Antiochene, and nowhere is this more apparent than in his historical writing. This is not to say that he was simply an annalist recording events with detached objectivity. He saw human history as exhibiting a pattern in which the patriarchal age of faith was recapitulated in the Christian age of grace, the two ages being separated by the intervening Mosaic age of Law. The age of the last things had begun with Christ and had achieved its consummation in the conversion to Christianity of the empire under Constantine, a theme which had occupied Eusebius' attention long before his final exultant statements of it in his Constantinian writings and *Theophany*.[2] The articulation of this theme demanded nothing less than a full-scale exposition of the history of man from the beginning to the end, demonstrating the various civilizations, empires and dynasties that had succeeded each other throughout the known world. Only so vast a canvas could show how these disparate elements had been drawn together under the hand of God with the majestic inevitability of the physical chaos drawing together into creation at the beginning of time in obedience to the power of the creative Word of God. 'By the express appointment of the same God, two roots of blessing, the Roman empire and the doctrine of Christian piety, sprang up together for the benefit of men. For before that time the various nations of the world such as Syria, Asia, Macedonia, Egypt and Arabia had been each subject to different rulers. The Jewish people too had established their dominion in the land of Palestine. And these nations, in every village, city and district, driven by some spirit of madness, were engaged in perpetual and murderous war and conflict. But two mighty powers, the Roman empire, henceforth ruled by a single sovereign, and the Christian religion, subdued and reconciled these contending elements.'[3] It is a noble conception and it is nobly executed, and we shall not be misled by the dry tabular presentation of the theme in the Canons of the *Chronicle* into thinking of it as an academic exercise in chronological computing. The vision was that of a young man, and the composition of the *Chronicle* was achieved, we may assume after many years of work, before Eusebius was forty years of age. The further elucidation of this theme of the cosmic significance of Christ occupied the second half of Eusebius' life, and was examined from many angles, historical, doctrinal, philosophical and exegetical.

Eusebius was not the first to have attempted a presentation of comparative chronology in which events in one nation were aligned with events elsewhere. Sextus Julius Africanus had done something of the same kind in his *Chronographia* in 221, and Hippolytus in his *Chronica* in 234, and the fragments of the great pagan Porphyry show that he had drawn up a comparative chronology of Greek and Roman events from the fall of Troy.[4] Eusebius made use of his predecessors' work, particularly that of Africanus, altering its dating with remarkable freedom in the interests of chronological principles characterized by A. Momigliano as 'something between an exact science and an instrument of propaganda'.[5] Faced by conflicting sources, Eusebius could be forced into a juggling with dates that seems on occasions to have reduced the exact science to guesswork, as in his attempt to date the crucifixion by aligning the fifteenth year of Tiberius, A.D. 29 (from St Luke), the spring of A.D. 31 (from Africanus) and the eclipse of the sun recorded by Phlegon in the Olympiad 202/4. It was habitual with Eusebius to make divergent sources fit each other wherever possible rather than to assume that one was right and others wrong, and it is plain that he did this on grounds of principle rather than as a convenience, for he could be severe on inaccuracy where he detected it: he castigated errors of dating by Greek, Egyptian, Chaldaean, Roman and Hebrew chronographers.[6] Accurate dating was far from being a matter of indifference, and to categorize the *Chronicle* as propaganda in no way implies dishonest manipulation of material to make it support a thesis. There was indeed a thesis to be propagated, the demonstration of the slow progress of mankind from barbarity and diversity to civilization and unity in Christ, and the steps of that progress needed mapping as accurately as the wide assortment of sources permitted. Eusebius taught the Church to be concerned 'with the pattern of history rather than with the detail',[7] but if the details are wrong the pattern is distorted. The historian's task was to set accurately-dated detail in its overall pattern, so that the reader might see his place in the whole sweep of human affairs from the creation of the world.

The lesson in accurate dating was not lost upon Eusebius' successors, and we may hope that he would have accepted with good grace their strictures upon his own lapses. The composite sixth-century *Ecclesiastical History* of Zacharias Rhetor claims to carry on the narrative begun by Eusebius, Socrates and Theodoret,[8] and gives the impression of being a continuation of Eusebius's *Ecclesiastical History* rather than his *Chronicle*, but there are passages early in the work which indicate familiarity with the latter. Zacharias starts his work in Eusebian fashion with a discussion of the accurate computation of dates, showing that the current Syrian computation of the years from Adam to Abraham falls short by 1374 years, and demonstrating the superiority of Greek chronology over Syrian in comparative tables to the year A.D. 570.

The anonymous *Expositio Officiorum Ecclesiae*,[9] after an introductory chapter describing Eusebius' chronological computations deriving from a request at Nicaea that he should undertake this work, gives an extended treatment of the chronology of Eusebius and of the patriarch Išoʻyabh. Since creation took place in April, why does Eusebius date the beginning of the year from October? The author answers by saying that creation took place in Spring, a season of the year in which growing things could begin their growth, leading to the first harvest in the following September and the beginning of the first full year in October.[10] He goes on to Eusebius' treatment of solar, lunar and hebdomadal chronology,[11] bringing his work nearer to the subject matter of its title with a chapter devoted to the instruction by Išo'yabh that the divine offices should start in December, not at the beginning of the secular year in October.[12] In all this there is no suggestion of criticism or correction of Eusebius' dating: Eusebius is in fact called 'the blessed Eusebius', and is accorded the highest recognition as an authoritative source for this kind of enquiry.

The seventh-century *Chronicon* of Jacob of Edessa[13] is an unambiguous continuation to the year 692 of Eusebius' *Chronicle*, with additional later material. After a laudatory introduction concerning Eusebius' *Chronicle*, a lengthy discussion of the details of the dating shows that Eusebius errs in counting three years too many.[14] Jacob's own *Canons* consist of three columns, one presenting Persian dates, one Roman, and one showing a running total of 385 years starting with the twenty-first year of Constantine. The three columns are enclosed on left and right by flanking columns of commentary, following the layout of the Armenian version of the Eusebian *Canons*. Jacob pays Eusebius the compliment of adopting his format, but it may be doubted whether a seventh-century Syrian Monophysite would see the empire and its ruler in the favourable light that illuminated them in Eusebius' eyes. The latter's vision of the peaceful unity of all nations under Christ could hardly have stood up to the facts of subsequent political and military history on the eastern frontier of the empire. Nor does Jacob in all respects accept Eusebius' dating. His strictures upon Eusebius' chronography are taken up by succeeding historians, for example the eleventh-century Elias of Nisibis' *Opus Chronologicum*.[15] Elias claims that his dating is based upon the Eusebian *Canons*,[16] being content often to note discrepancies between Greek, Hebrew and Syriac dating of events without attempting to elucidate the difficulty, and he can follow Eusebius against the corrections of Jacob of Edessa. Jacob had criticized Eusebius for saying that Levi begot Qehath at the age of forty-six when he must have been less than forty-one, but Elias reverts to Eusebius' computation of forty-six.[17] For Elias the establishing of events two thousand years before his own time is not an antiquarian exercise, but the tracing back to its head waters of a stream running through to the age of the Arab invasions, and the Hebrew patriarchs have as great relevance to his own story as have Roman emperors and Muslim caliphs.

An anonymous Syriac Chronicle, possibly from the eighth century,[18] begins with creation, and after following Eusebius into the Christian era at A.D. 303 indicates a change in his main source: 'At this point the Chronicle which we have taken from Eusebius comes to an end. Hereafter we have drawn upon the writing of Socrates' , and he relies upon Socrates until he changes again to local Mesopotamian sources which he enumerates. This degree of precision about sources is refreshing, and its root is to be found in Eusebius' method in the *Ecclesiastical History*.[19] It was Eusebius' achievement to have set the writing of ecclesiastical history upon a proper formal basis that could serve as a framework for future work. The Eusebian *Chronicle* is a work of primary importance in the formation of the Church's understanding of its own origins and rôle, and Monophysites and Nestorians alike accepted gratefully the gift of a chronological framework and method which enabled them to make sense of the past and which could be extended indefinitely into the future as the divine purpose was further revealed.

But within this framework, what was the content of the revealed purpose? For Eusebius it was the universal rule of the one God reflected in the universal rule of the one emperor. God foretold to Abraham 'that he shall be a father of many nations, and says expressly that in him shall all the nations of the earth be blessed, directly prophesying the things which are now being accomplished in our time',[20] that is in the world-wide dominion of Rome. 'To whatever quarter I direct my view, whether to the east or to the west or over the whole world, or toward heaven itself, everywhere and always I see the blessed one yet administering the self-same empire.'[21] The monarchical rule of the emperor reflects directly that of the divine ruler, as can be seen in Eusebius' construction of his *Oration in praise of Constantine*, where he begins by setting out the theological basis of imperial rule. 'One divinely favoured emperor, receiving as it were a transcript of the divine sovereignty, directs in imitation of God himself the administration of the world's affairs.'[22] In primitive times polytheism was correspondingly reflected in the political fragmentation of tribes and peoples,[23] but Eusebius felt that a much more serious problem was posed by disunity within the Roman empire itself, exemplified by the warfare between rival emperors and by persecution of the Church. Internal strife within a structure that was 'a transcript of the divine sovereignty' was self-contradictory, and its existence demanded explanation. The construction of the *Ecclesiastical History* in three phases suggests that the problem grew no easier as the 'great' persecution of 303 merged into civil war.[24] Disunity within the Church seems to have disturbed Eusebius less than disunity within the empire. The *Ecclesiastical History* indeed records outbreaks of heresy and of schism, but not with very much consistency and with an absence of attention to the doctrinal points at issue that has been frequently noted. The author's mind was not really engaged with the seriousness of the matter. Heresy is presented as a question of aberrant individuals or small groups whose disaffection could be easily contained when it had been properly refuted. With tenacity Eusebius adhered to his theme, the unity of the empire as a 'transcript' of the rule of God.

Eusebius' enthusiastic championship of this theme found little acceptance in the east, for although it found hearers in Byzantium who were ready to put it to their own political uses, I know of no evidence to suggest that during the christological conflict that convulsed the following centuries, the king's party (the Melkites) made use of Eusebius' conception of Roman *imperium* to justify their loyalty. Eusebius had shown them how to write history, and what they wanted to write about was not necessarily what their master had written about: they accepted his historiographical framework and filled it with their own material. In the first place, doctrinal dispute was now too major a concern to be shuffled into the background; in the second place, the unity of the world under God was now hardly even a legal fiction. Syrian historians were aware of the pressure of tribes from the north,[25] and some of them showed more concern with the Latin empire in the west than Eusebius had shown,[26] but relations between Byzantium and Persia were in themselves enough to sour any eulogy of universal peace.

The narratives of Ammianus Marcellinus, Zosimus, Procopius of Caesarea, Agathius and to some extent Socrates, Theodoret and Sozomen, show that during the three centuries preceding the Muslim invasions the periods of peace on the eastern frontier were few and precarious. The removal of the centre of gravity of the empire to the east during the early part of the fourth century reflects something of the gravity of the threat from the Sassanian kingdom. From that time onwards Persia was a continual menace to Roman stability in the east, and it was against a background of political instability against which Christian lives had to be lived, churches maintained, doctrinal innovations thought through and assessed, conciliar decisions reached, books written.

The striking characteristic of Syriac Histories and Chronicles of this period is not simply the paucity of reference to the constant military and political disturbance but the attitude towards it which the writers appear to adopt. It is remarkable that the Syrian historians do not recognize the fall of Antioch in 540 to have been worth more than a passing mention. For a detailed account of the political and military causes of the disaster, the course of Khosrau's approach to the city early in the year, the part played by the Christian bishops in bargaining for the safety of cities attacked on the way westwards, the bargaining for Antioch itself carried on by Megas, bishop of Beroea, the failure of the defences of the city through neglect of a strong point outside the walls occupied by the Persians, the flight of the defenders and the subsequent slaughter, the quantity of treasure looted from the ruined city – for all this we have to turn not to the Syrian historians whose theological roots lay in Antioch but to the *Belli*, book ii, of Procopius of Caesarea,[27] written in Constantinople soon after the events described. The explanation of the lack of interest shown by the Syrians is not that they had lost contact with their Antiochene roots: the theological battles in which Antioch had figured so largely during the preceding centuries constitute the main subject matter of their Histories and Chronicles; the praises of their heroes are sung and resung. The explanation of their neglect of the fall of Antioch must lie elsewhere, and their attitude towards it is in general terms characteristic of their treatment of all secular events, however catastrophic.

In the twelve books of Zacharias Rhetor's *Ecclesiastical History* no interest is shown in secular affairs until book vii, from which point the work is from the hand of a later interpolator, and the circumstantial account of incidents occurring in and soon after 502 seems to reflect an interest of the interpolator which was not shared by Zacharias himself. It is a curiously eclectic narrative, and appears to know nothing of Khosrau's destruction of Antioch in 540, though the fragmentary state of the text of the later books may be to blame for this. The sixth-century *Edessene Chronicle*, composed of very diverse elements, shows no concern with military engagements between Byzantines and Persians but records an invasion of Byzantine territory by the Huns.[28] Barhadbešabba's *History* is devoted entirely to ecclesiastical matters and exhibits no interest in their political context.[29] In general the copious Acts of the Martyrs concentrate attention upon their immediate subjects too closely to be concerned with wider issues, but there are exceptions to this, as in the seventh-century *History of Bar-'Idta*. Here we are told of the rising of 'Bahram the tyrant' against Khosrau II in 591, Khosrau's flight for protection to Maurice and the army of the 'Romayē' sent by Maurice in response. The relevance of this to the life of the saint is Bar-'Idta's prophecy of the overthrow of Bahram.[30] There is also noted the murder of Maurice at the hand of Phocas in 602 and Khosrau's consequent attack upon Dara, Edessa, Jerusalem and Alexandria: 'then came the Greeks who smote and plundered and destroyed', but Bar-'Idta's monastery was spared and even protected by a guard.[31] Khosrau's simulated toleration of Christianity under the influence of his debt to Maurice is reflected in a seventh-century Syriac Chronicle by an anonymous writer: 'Although Khosrau appeared to show favour to the Christians on account of Maurice, nevertheless he persecuted our people with hatred', but he favoured Yazdin of Karkha as Pharaoh favoured Joseph, suggesting perhaps the precarious hold of Yazdin upon the favour of the king.[32] Another Chronicle records an attack by Khosrau I on Antioch in 560, a date which we may assume to be twenty years too late.[33] Another document places the attack upon Antioch in 532, and specifies that a ransom of two centenaria of gold was paid before the invader retraced his steps by way of Edessa,[34] which reads like a conflation of the abortive plan to attack Antioch in 531 and the destruction of the city in 540 when the ransom was ten centenaria. Rather more notice is taken of the Arab invasions. The *Chronicle* of Jacob of Edessa says that Mohammad was active in Palestine, Phoenicia and Tyre in the eighth year of Heraclius (618) for purposes of trade.[35] This dating is quite possible, since Mohammad's first real success was with the pilgrims from Yathrib/ Medina in 620, and he had certainly travelled north before that. The *History of Marouta*, composed by Marouta's successor Denba during the seventh century, says in passing that 'the emperor Heraclius and the Romans invaded and laid waste the country of the Persians. Our blessed father [Marouta] was not troubled by this ill fortune, but remained with courage and dignity at the head of the faithful',[36] and in more detail that a letter was sent from 'Mohammad ben Abdullah, prophet of God, to Khosrau son of Hormizd, king of Persia', which Khosrau tore up because Moham- mad's name preceded his own, causing Mohammad to declare that God would so tear up the Persian kingdom.[37] The seventh-century *Maronite Chronicle* records accurately that Mo'awiya was proclaimed caliph in Jeru- salem in 660, and adds that the amirs and Arabs offered him their right hands but that he would accept no peace with the Romans.[38] There is little sign that the Arab invasions were seen to constitute a specifically religious threat earlier than the eleventh-century *Chronology* of Elias of Nisibis. Elias devotes considerable space to his account of the Arab invasions from A.D. 622 and notes that in 638 a mosque for the first time replaced the Jewish temple in Jerusalem.[39] From his viewpoint in the eleventh century, Elias could have made much of this as being prophetic of the religious per- secution that was still far away in 638, but he does not do so. The Arab invasions are treated in the same way as the Persian invasions of the pre- vious century, as incursions by an alien people rather than by an alien religion that could pose a threat to Christianity.

What does this evidence of secular and political awareness on the part of the Syriac historians amount to? Little, perhaps, both in its extent and in the importance that is attached to secular matters.[40] There is no suggestion that they were in any way alert to Eusebius' conception of great tides of human affairs sweeping inwards to the shore under the hand of God, nor even (as they might well have been excused for thinking) that the great tide of the age of grace was ebbing before the successive onslaughts of Per- sian Magianism and Arabian Islam. They appear to have discerned no such tides, only individual waves breaking perhaps uncomfortably, but leaving the sufferers able to carry on their Christian vocations. They do not even dispute the truth of Eusebius' vision: it is plain to them that the kingdom of God is not of this world, and that the ebb and flow of nations is not what the Christian gospel is concerned with. Their eyes are fixed elsewhere. Political and military events appear in their narratives as a background to the main action, throwing into relief the action of saints such as Bar-'Idta or Marouta, but more often as a piece of detached information whose omission would hardly effect their narrative. To turn from this body of historical writing to the mass of exegetical and homiletic work produced during these centuries is to confirm the impression received from the historians, that the ecclesiastical writers of Syria and Mesopotamia show a remarkable detachment from worldly circumstances whose violence can seldom have been conducive to sustained scholarly pursuits. The problems which they found pressing were those posed by disunity within the Church itself rather than those posed by the struggles of mankind on a wider canvas.[41]

Detachment from the world combined with some restriction of the field of vision is found in the fifth century in the *Ecclesiastical History* of Theodoret of Cyrrhus. Theodoret sees himself as the continuator of Eusebius' *Ecclesiastical History* ('Eusebius the Palestinian has written an *Ecclesiastical History* from the time of the apostles to the reign of Constantine, the prince beloved of God. I shall begin my history from the period at which his finishes'),[42] although it is not easy to see how a continuation of Eusebius' narrative is possible in the terms in which Eusebius had conceived it. The end to which creation had been moving was not for Eusebius the end of the world but the rule of Christ uniting mankind in brotherhood under God's anointed emperor.[43] If this end had been achieved under Constantine, what continuation was possible other than a song of praise for the achievement of God's purpose? This is the note upon which Eusebius ends. By the first half of the fifth century, when Theodoret wrote, the sky has darkened again and the song of praise is more restrained, for already in his second chapter Theodoret is looking back to the days of Eusebius' own lifetime when 'Arius, who had been enrolled in the list of the presbyters and entrusted with the exposition of the holy scriptures, fell a prey to the assaults of jealousy'.[44] Eusebius' jubilation was, in fact, premature, and the harsh story of conflict had still to be told, with emphasis now upon what Theodoret calls 'opportunities for dispute and contention' within the Church itself. His *Ecclesiastical History* is virtually a history of the progress of Arianism, with occasional interludes covering for example the renewal of paganism under Julian from 361. In formal terms, Theodoret follows Eusebius closely, and in this sense, as well as in his beginning at the chronological point where Eusebius ends, his work is a continuation of that of Eusebius. It is the purpose that is different, the synoptic view of what is happening. To observe the growth of Eusebius' conception of cosmic history we have to pay attention not only to his specifically historical writings but to his entire *corpus*, and to observe the divergence of Theodoret from this conception we have in the same way to look not only at his *Ecclesiastical History*. Eusebius' massive *Praeparatio* and *Demonstratio Evangelica* move parallel to the *Chronicle* and the *History* in tracing the self-destructive elements inherent in paganism even at its finest, leading to the emergence of Christianity and the dawn that breaks upon all mankind with the birth of the Church. Theodoret's *Graecarum Affectionum Curatio* is superficially similar to the *Praeparatio* and *Demonstratio* of Eusebius in its erudition, and to some extent in its subject matter, but we do not detect in it the note of the inevitability of mankind's march out of darkness into the present light. Its characteristic tone of voice, as its title suggests, is that of a physician arguing reasonably with a patient who has only to put his mind to the matter to recognize the course of treatment which must lead to restoration of his health. The patient is still sick: paganism is by no means a thing of the past. The diagnosis is clear, the treatment is prescribed, but the patient has still to accept it. Paganism, Arianism and Monophysitism are the three sicknesses of the soul afflicting man, and Theodoret's literary output is concerned with their cure. There is no suggestion of a golden age upon earth when the threefold cure will be universally achieved, nor any suggestion that this could be achieved in political terms as envisaged by Eusebius. On the contrary, a condition of the dawn of the Kingdom of God was the total rejection of this world and its values to an extent that was regarded even by Egyptian ascetics as ostentatious.[45]

This is the theme of Theodoret's *Historia Religiosa*,[46] which gives an account of Syrian hermits, some already dead by the time in which Theodoret wrote the work, and some known personally to him and still living, mostly near Cyrrhus. Their holiness is seen in their rejection of the world, their complete neglect of matters of dress, their savage mortification of the flesh, their totally-enclosed lives which prevented any communication with their fellow men, their indifference to what befell them. Afrahat alone abandoned the life of withdrawal for a time in order to descend upon Antioch to confront the Arian Valens in defence of orthodoxy.[47] It is Theodoret's proud boast that he had once set eyes on Afrahat, 'and I have enjoyed the blessing of his holy hand when I was a young boy and accompanied my mother on a visit she made'.[48] In these hermits we see the fierceness of a primitive desert culture almost in the environs of Antioch itself, and may wonder whether the radical dualism of soul and body implied by this rejection of the world was part of the indigenous Syrian culture, or rather an importation of an element from further east.[49] That it was strongly rooted by the fifth century is evident from Theodoret's veneration for its practitioners and from John Chrysostom, both in his troubled championship of asceticism in his early work *On the Priesthood*[50] and in his frequent exhortations to his flock at Constantinople to forsake the world.

The other-worldly conception of man and his destiny receives its most coherent formulation at the hands of Theodore of Mopsuestia, whom we may see as giving new expression to an idea which, whatever its origins, was strongly rooted in Syrian Christianity. Theodore sees man's predicament primarily in historical terms, extended along a temporal axis, rather than in ontological terms in a philosophical manner, even though Platonic implications remain embedded in his thought.[51] Along this temporal axis he developed his idea of the two ages or *catastases* of man: 'We first experience our present condition and then, through the resurrection of the dead, are changed to the likeness of Christ.'[52] The change is from an imperfect state of mortality, mutability and corruptibility to a perfect state of immortality and immutability, from disobedience to obedience. Baptism presents the believer, if we may so express it, with an undated cheque to be cashed at a time unknown to ourselves but known to God.[53] The fundamental characteristic of the first age of man is the mortality which is the result of disobedience to the will of God. R. A. Norris finds no evidence that Theodore believed that Adam was created neither mortal nor immortal,[54] though such a conception would consort well with his view of the divine education of mankind and was to some degree part of the Syrian tradition.[55] Man's faculty of choice between good and evil requires a true moral freedom which in combination with human mutability leads inevitably to the exercise of free will, and thence to sinful disobedience.[56] In emphasizing freedom of will Theodore was following the voluntarist emphasis of Afrahat and Ephrem.[57] Sin is here seen not as a failure of God's purpose, since it is an inevitable consequence of divinely-given human freedom, which is itself essential to man's moral education.[58] Man is educated in the knowledge of right and wrong by the Law, and in learning obedience is led towards the promise of blessedness inherent in baptism. In the second age of man this promise is fulfilled in man's living the heavenly life of likeness to Christ, no longer needing educative Law and no longer subject to mutability and death, but in perfect obedience to the divine will.[59] Such a conception of the destiny of the human race is radically different from that of Eusebius, and in its other-worldliness is more firmly rooted in the Syrian tradition than is Eusebius. Theodore shares with Theodoret and his fellow Syrians an implied pessimism concerning mankind which was more in keeping with the facts of late fourth-century life in Syria than was the optimistic heralding of the consummation of the purpose of God for man which is found in Eusebius' work. Whatever the pattern of human history might be, it appeared that Eusebius had misread it even while he was teaching posterity so splendidly how to read it.

What then was the task of the Syrian historian? He had learned not to see patterns in earthly events too readily, and his adoption of a more modest aim was itself an achievement, analogous to Theodore's refusal to see prophecies and types scattered at large through the Scriptures. The historian could restrict the scope of his vision to the history of that institution for which the Syriac-speaking Church was renowned, its great schools, and the work of this kind listed by Assemani indicates the popularity of the *genre* in Syria. Up to the middle of the seventh century we find histories of the schools written by Elisha bar Quzbaie, the successor of Narsai, Abraham de-bet Rabban, Elias of Merv and Michael Gramqaya,[60] but we may turn our attention more closely to the *Cause of the foundation of the schools* by the seventh-century Barhadbešabba of 'Arbaya, who became bishop of Halwan.[61] This remarkable document is of no great length – of the order of 9000 words of Syriac – and its object is to give an account of how the School of Nisibis came into being, but in the pursuit of this aim it presents astonishingly varied material, including Old Testament history, anthropology, philosophy, psychology, the history of education, the narratives of the gospels and Acts, and some account of the theologians of Antioch, before at last reaching the Syrian Church and its schools.[62] All this is held together by the theme of God's education of man to fit him for heaven – a series of widely-ranging variations on a theme derived from Theodore. The concept of the two ages of man and the need for education to equip him for the second age is stated at the beginning. Man has been given a twofold life, the first mortal, the second perfect and immortal. 'As God has created us, so will he give us new life by his grace and by his wisdom he will translate us from here to heaven, and that power which nothing could withstand during the first phase of our education will encounter no obstacle in the second.' Although we are ungrateful sinners, 'he has supported us with life-giving laws, which from century to century are established for our benefit', above all the Law of Moses. After this stage of our education we receive the glorious gift of Christ.[63] This general statement of the theme, derived unmistakably from Theodore, is then worked out in detail, starting from first principles with the eternal and ingenerate nature of God, and progressing to an analysis of the created order. Man occupies a central position, linked to the spiritual and to the material order,[64] and Barhadbešabba again follows Theodore in rejecting any suggestion of the divinization of man,[65] for man remains firmly among the creatures. There follows an extended discussion of man's faculty of intelligence and of his misuse of freedom.[66] Angels and men alike were from the beginning subject to education, the former during the first six days of creation, the latter in Eden when Adam was shown all living creatures in alphabetical order and was taught the earliest laws.[67] Adam refused the discipline of the school, threw away his writing tablets and erased from them the letters of the Law, and so was expelled from school to work the soil. Various schools succeeded that of Adam, those of Abel and Cain, of Noah and Abraham, until the 'school of perfect philosophy' was founded when Moses taught the Law afresh to unwilling pupils who had set up a new and inanimate schoolmaster of their own on the rostrum.[68] Solomon too founded a school to which men came from the ends of the earth to learn, and was followed by the schools of the prophets. Barhadbešabba proceeds to a briefly eclectic and not wholly accurate résumé of the Greek schools of Plato, Aristotle, Epicurus, Democritus, the physicists and Pythagoras, with some mention of the schools of Babylon, India and Persia,[69] before reaching the school of

Christ in which the fulfilling of the Mosaic Law began on a mountain analogous to Sinai, and in which the head prefect was Peter.[70] Thus Barhadbešabba reaches the point at which he can contrast the apostolic school of
Antioch with the Jewish-Hellenistic school of Philo at Alexandria, where
scripture 'was explained allegorically to the detriment of history'.[71] After
Nicaea, Eustathius opened a school at Antioch, James at Nisibis with
Ephrem as commentator on the scriptures, and Alexander at Alexandria
with Athanasius as his commentator. We must presumably understand
these schools in a non-institutional sense. Diodore, whose pupils included
Basil, John Chrysostom, Evagrius and Theodore, 'achieved more than any
other in the science of philosophy and in exegesis',[72] and on his consecration to Tarsus left Theodore, 'who like a good physician reunited into
one body the traditions and *pušaqa*[73] which were scattered, in such a manner that he articulated them with great skill and learning'. Like a sculptor,
he laid out and fitted together the separate limbs of knowledge.[74] A direct
line of descent is traced from Theodore through Nestorius to Theodulos,
Narsai and Barsauma almost as though it were the manual transmission of
the apostolic succession, Narsai and Barsauma receiving a blessing from the
hands of Theodulos, as the author has learnt from Akhsenaya (a source
quoted reluctantly since Akhsenaya was 'a bad worker').[75] We have thus
by a circuitous route reached Edessa almost at the end of the story, but it
is at this point that Barhadbešabba can tell us most. He writes of Rabbula's
defection from the Nestorian camp, attributing it to animosity arising from
Theodore's public rebuke of Rabbula on a point of exegesis and of Rabbula's destruction of the manuscripts of Theodore's work then existing at
Edessa, with the exception of the Commentaries on John and Ecclesiastes,
which had not yet been translated into Syriac.[76] The school of Edessa
flourished under Quiiōrē, who used the traditions of the Syrian Church
derived from Addai and transmitted by word of mouth until incorporated
in his own work by Ephrem. Qiiore caused the work of Theodore to be
translated into Syriac as a basis for study at Edessa.[77] Narsai's direction
of the school was brought to a close by the wiles of Satan, and Narsai
moved to Nisibis, where he was encouraged by Barsauma to open a school
in that city, thus filling the Persian empire with the knowledge of the fear
of God.[78] When Barhadbešabba reaches the succession of Henana to the
directorship in 572, his own equivocal position becomes apparent. He
had studied under Henana and appears to have written this work during
Henana's lifetime, in full knowledge of the reformation carried out by the
latter and the replacement of Theodore's system by a theology more con-
ciliatory to Alexandria. Barhadbešabba devotes some pains to showing his
respect for the Nestorian doctors, Diodore and Theodore, although he
does not say very much about Nestorius himself, and he had during the
troubles at Nisibis concerning Henana deserted his master Henana and

supported the Nestorian party. Yet he concludes the present work by a eulogy of Henana's industry and scholarship, his authority as a speaker, his richness of spirit, his ability to write as effectively as he spoke, and his literary output. 'He is sweet, merciful, patient and does not seek his own glory', and Barhadbešabba prays for God's protection of him.[79] A sixth-century Syriac work which praises both Theodore and Henana can only give rise to confusion about the standpoint of its author,[80] and leave a suspicion that Barhadbešabba suffered from the bad conscience of the renegade whose deserted master still lives to reproach him for his apostasy.

Barhadbešabba's *Cause of the foundation of the schools* works a narrowly-circumscribed vein but works it deeply, probing the 'cause' to the beginning of human history and beyond. It is also open-ended, bringing the enquiry to the author's own times without suggesting that the story can go no further. In these two respects the form of his work reveals its difference from that of Eusebius, whose columns of nations spread across the page in their simultaneous advance towards their ordained end in the fourth century. It differs also from some Syrian historiography which is transmitted to us as *Ecclesiastical History* but which attempts hardly at all to take a synoptic view of Christian affairs in the Eusebian manner, and consists rather of collections of essays, each devoted to a particular topic or person. Barhadbešabba's own early *Ecclesiastical History* gives us accounts of a number of noteworthy Christians, orthodox and heretical, barely grouped in chronological order, and preceded by a brief summary of fourteen heresies. The piecemeal arrangement of the work is emphasized at the conclusion of the last two studies, those of Narsai and Mar Abraham, each of which ends with the ascription, 'To Christ, his Father and the Holy Spirit be glory and honour for ever and ever. Amen.'[81] Continuity is precluded where each section is self-contained. In formal terms it resembles the manner of the collections of lives of the saints, of Eusebius' *Martyrs of Palestine*, Theodoret's *Religious History* and of the copious accounts of Syrian and Persian martyrs, in which the *acta* of individuals are treated in isolation from those of their fellows. The sectarian histories, on the other hand, devoted specifically to the advancement of Nicene or Nestorian or Monophysite doctrine, flow more easily in chronological sequence, on the occasions when the state of preservation of the manuscripts permits a judgement about their form. Zacharias Rhetor, for example, as far as the point at which his *History* disintegrates into fragments, is successful in forming a continuous narrative in the Monophysite interest in the manner of Theodoret's orthodox Antiochene anti-Arian narrative.[82] The sectarian history is written in the belief that a doctrinal point can be demonstrated by historical exposition: the facts have only to be stated for the truth of the doctrinal issue to be manifest to the reader. The record speaks for itself. Barhadbešabba is explicit about it:

'It is by comparisons . . . that one distinguishes truth from falsehood, as
one does sweet from bitter, light from darkness, short from long, tasty
from tasteless; so too the good and the wise stand out from the evil
and the wicked. It is for that reason that we recount the histories of
heretics and their evil ways, in order to highlight the real love of the
fathers and their consistency in the orthodox faith'

– that is in the Nestorian faith.[83] The author of the *Pseudo-Dionysian
Chronicle* asks rhetorically[84] what is the use of reading such things as a historical narrative if admonition is not included in the narrative. The events
are enough by themselves, and if the events did not teach us a lesson, the
events were a waste of time. And indeed the author does not point any
moral but leaves the events to teach their lesson. The effectiveness of the
method can be overestimated, but it is characteristic of the Antiochene
and Syrian presentation of their case and it is analogous to their understanding of the scriptural record.

4

The doctrine of the nature of God

The sixth-century historian Barhadbešabba of 'Arbaya[1] opens the third chapter of his History with an identification of two main groups of heretic: first, those who 'offended against the economy of our Saviour in saying that he did not take flesh, but that he appeared by an illusion, such as Simon, Menander, Cerinthus, Valentinus, Cerdo, Basilides, Mani, Marcion'; and secondly those who 'committed a great error concerning the divine nature'. He names Theodotion, Artemon, Paul of Samosata, Photinus, Arius, Eunomius, Aetius, Macedonius, who say 'that the Word is a creature and a work (of the Father), who by grace became God, and who do not confess that he is of an (eternal) essence, but teach foolishly that he was created before all'.[2] It may be thought curious that a Nestorian should identify the threat to 'the economy of our Saviour' as residing in the gnostics rather than in Monophysites of more recent date,[3] but in his identification of two great matters of doctrinal definition, the nature of Jesus Christ and the nature of the Godhead, as the main issues to concern a sixth-century historian, he brings to the forefront the two matters of dispute which had exercised the best minds of the Church from early centuries. These two doctrines affected Syrian Christianity in different ways. The doctrine of the nature of God, which Barhadbešabba places second, was the first to become a matter of concern, and it is to that doctrine that we turn first.

We are given a glimpse of trinitarian doctrine in its early formative stage in the work of Theophilus, who wrote in Antioch at the end of the second century but probably represented the tradition of the Syrian Church east of Antioch. To him falls the distinction of being the first Christian writer to use the word 'Trinity' (*trias*) of God, when he writes of the Genesis creation narrative, 'The three days which were before [the creation of] the heavenly bodies are types of the Trinity of God and his Word and his Wisdom.'[4] The Old Testament antecedents of the terms 'Word' and 'Wisdom' are clear: the Word is that spoken by God at creation, carrying with it the power to bring things into existence, this conception becoming refined philosophically by the mind of Hellenistic Judaism; Wisdom is the personified female figure who appears in the Old Testament literature of the third century B.C., described as eternal and as proceeding out of the mouth of God, identified with divine power immanent in the universe.[5] To Philo the light of the first day of creation was 'intelligible light', which is the image of the divine Word. To another Jew, Aristobulus, Wisdom has the character of pre-cosmic light. That Theophilus should associate Word and Wisdom with the days before the creation of the luminaries of heaven is perhaps to be expected in view of his dependence upon Jewish sources.[6] His Old Testament and Hellenistic sources helped Theophilus to associate Word and Wisdom with God as immanent in his creation; but he takes the matter further.

The function of the Wisdom of God is to 'found the earth', which may mean to set in order the unformed matter, the chaos, created by the Word. Wisdom is the agent of God in his providential care for the universe, ordering seasons and natural processes in addition to inspiring the prophets.[7] So far Theophilus is hardly breaking new ground. In his treatment of the Word, however, he goes further afield to draw on Stoic sources which may again have reached him through Philo. In Stoic thought the Word is Reason expressed in voice or word, and in Theophilus we find a distinction between the Word of God residing in the Deity and the Word of God uttered or expressed in divine activity. The few lines in which he makes this distinction were to have far-reaching effects upon Antiochene thinking. 'God, having his own Word internal within his own bowels, begat him, emitting him along with his Wisdom before all things. He had this Word as a helper in the things that were created by him, and by him he made all things.'[8] 'But when God wished to make all that he determined on, he begat his Word, uttered the firstborn of all creation.'[9] The Word residing within God is characterized by the term *endiathetos*; the Word uttered or emitted as the agent of creation, by the term *prophorikos*. In what sense can the internal Word be called personal other than that of the vaguely personified Wisdom of later Judaism? The Word internal to God before utterance is no more than an attribute of God: 'If I call him Word, I name but his sovereignty', as 'if I call him Judge I speak of him as being just . . . if I call him Fire I but mention his anger'.[10] This attribute or function of God was then begotten or uttered as 'the firstborn of all creation' in order to act as the creative agent of God. Theophilus quotes John i.1 to demonstrate that 'at first God was alone, and the Word in him', but when God walks in the garden to talk with Adam and Eve the Word assumes the person, that is the rôle or character of God, for the occasion.[11] The Word, in short, only becomes personal in any recognizable sense after his begetting or utterance. Theophilus calls this Godhead a Trinity, but by fourth-century Nicene standards the term may only be attributed to his conception in a most inexact sense, for there is no kind of equality of persons such as characterizes the Trinity of the Nicene definition. Theophilus speaks of God, the totality of the Godhead, uttering his Word and his Wisdom: he does not speak of the Godhead being eternally threefold in structure, Father, Word and Spirit. Despite his distinction of being the first Christian writer known to use the term Trinity, it is hard to regard Theophilus as a trinitarian at all. His God is rather a Unity with ill-defined offshoots or personified qualities. After three quarters of a century we find similar ideas occurring and gathering new force in the theology of Paul of Samosata.

If we regret that Theophilus is only represented by one extant work, we must regret still more that Paul of Samosata is represented by not even one, and that our knowledge of his doctrine reaches us through the bitterly unsympathetic notices of Councils which condemned him and individuals who repudiated his views.[12] Paul's episcopacy at Antioch covers the period during which Antioch came under the domination of Palmyra, the capital of Commagene, some two hundred miles south east of Antioch near the Persian border and a meeting place of important trunk roads. In 259/260 the Palmyran prince Odeinath defeated Shahpur I of Persia and brought Palmyra to a degree of power which threatened Roman control of the east.[13] His successor Wahballath ruled under the regency of Queen Zenobia, taking the titles of *rex* and *imperator*, and in 271 of *Augustus*.[14] The Syrian element of the population of Antioch found Palmyran rule more congenial than that of Rome, and for eleven years the city was under the control of Zenobia. The same eleven years mark the episcopate of Paul. Nothing is known of Paul's origins or education. He appears first in the partly Jewish milieu of Palmyra,[15] where monotheistic cults of all kinds tended to merge and cross-fertilize each other. Paul's appointment to Antioch is held by G. Bardy to have been partly political: Bardy describes him as a kind of Palmyran viceroy in Antioch.[16] but this is disputed by Fergus Millar,[17] who shows that his title *ducenarius* was no more than an affectation arising from his vanity. Paul was a self-styled *procurator* and set himself up on a procuratorial throne. The records concentrate upon theological issues and not political. Making all allowance for their hostile bias, the documents describing Paul's life and conduct show him to have been theatrical, egocentric, vain, financially dishonest and sexually unchaste. His women's choir, his throne, his guard of honour, his lawsuits and his ecclesiastical pomp gave rise to fierce criticism.[18] He was, however, a man of undoubted ability and of sufficient personal power to attract and hold widespread support including that of a number of bishops, especially in the less Hellenized areas,[19] but the national and cultural aspect of his influence must not be over-emphasized.

A council was convened at Antioch, perhaps by Helenus of Tarsus, in 264, attended by bishops of neighbouring dioceses most nearly concerned with events at Antioch. 'Dionysius of Alexandria was invited to attend the council', writes Eusebius, 'but, pleading as his excuse both old age and bodily weakness, he postponed his coming, and furnished by letter the opinion that he held on the subject in question',[20] the subject being Paul's doctrine. Paul 'espoused low and mean views of Christ', Eusebius tells us, 'contrary to the Church's teaching, namely that he was in his nature an ordinary man'.[21] As an account of Paul's doctrine this leaves much unsaid, but it shows how the next generation regarded him. Bardy gives his opinion that Dionysius was invited on grounds of personal distinction rather than that of Alexandrian involvement in Antiochene affairs, though Dionysius was deeply concerned over the doctrinal standpoint of Paul.[22] There could be no compromise between Paul and the Origenist tradition of Alexandria. The Council met, and after many sessions convicted Paul of inventing new doctrines and obtained from him a promise of amendment. 'On his promising to change, Firmilian adjourned the proceedings, hoping and believing that the matter would be fittingly concluded.'[23] The hope and belief of the Council, thus expressed in the synodal letter that it circulated before adjourning, were ill-founded. Paul changed neither his life nor his teaching and ignored personal appeals made by neighbouring bishops. The Council met again in 268 without its former chairman, Firmilian, and without the great weight of Dionysius: both were dead. Not content this time with normal procedure, the bishops put forward as their advocate a priest of Origenist views, Malchion, 'a learned man', says Eusebius, 'who also was head of a school of rhetoric, one of the Greek establishments at Antioch'.[24] Stenographers were present to record the proceedings. Malchion was well chosen: he was the intellectual equal of his bishop and was a professional disputant. The course of his argument with Paul left the assembled bishops in no doubt about Paul's heresy, and they deposed him from his bishopric and excommunicated him, appointing a successor who would be more acceptable to Rome. Eusebius describes Paul as refusing to accept the Council's decision and refusing to vacate the 'house of the Church'.[25] 'The emperor Aurelian, on being petitioned, gave an extremely just decision regarding the matter, ordering the assignment of the building to those with whom the bishops of the Christian religion in Italy and Rome should communicate in writing.'[26] Until Palmyran rule in Antioch ended with the defeat of Zenobia, the two parties each maintained their separate bishops in opposition, but the defeat of Zenobia by Aurelian in 272 carried with it the disappearance of her bishop.

Paul is heard of no more except as a name constantly anathematized by later theologians of widely differing views who often appear to have treated Paul as a convenient whipping-boy to take the blame for doctrinal aberrations with which he had little connection, and whose knowledge of Paul's teaching was expressed in the formula, 'Christ was only a man', to be transmitted from generation to generation for centuries after Paul's death. Eastern writers obtained most of their information about him from the brief remarks of Eusebius, from Theodoret and from epitomized Syriac chronicles. As soon after Paul's time as the fourth century, Ephrem has virtually nothing to say about him. We should not expect much analysis of the views of an opponent in sermons addressed to the faithful, and in his *Sermones de Fide* Ephrem simply includes in a list of heretics 'the Paulianists'[27] (the name by which Paul's adherents are designated in the nineteenth Canon of Nicaea), but even in his *Contra Haereses* Ephrem gives no more information than that the Paulianists were rejected 'because of their perversity'.[28] The reduction of Paul's doctrine to a formula is already at work in Theodoret. His *History* shows that he possessed a good deal of detailed knowledge, but in *Eranistes* he found it more convenient to dramatize the matter succinctly: 'The judge is enthroned. Paul is brought before him. "You said I was a man; you have no life with me. You did not know me; I do not know you." '[29] In his letters the convenient formula is disseminated more widely: to Flavian of Constantinople, 'There is another gang of heretics . . . Photinus, Marcellus and Paul of Samosata assert that our Lord was only human',[30] and in a letter to the monks Paul's teaching is reduced to the sentence, 'A mere man was born to the Virgin.'[31] Severus of Antioch, in his great compilation entitled *Philalethes* quotes Nestorius: 'we put before their eyes the term "Mother of God" and the term "Mother of man", so that it is inescapable that we do not fall into Manichaeism nor into [the error] of Paul';[32] and 'Paul said that the Word inhabits a man – I quote his own words, from the impious Paul of Samosata in the dialogue with Malchion.'[33] Despite Nestorius' rejection of Paul, the early sixth-century Monophysite Philoxenus of Mabboug, writing his *Twelve Chapters against those who maintain two natures in Christ*, in the course of an anathema pronounced against Nestorius and Diodore associates Paul with their views: Diodore, having embraced the true faith and having come into the orthodox Church, 'fell into the heresy of Paul', which is later defined, 'Paul said that Christ is a man like a prophet.'[34] A seventh-century Maronite chronicle draws more directly upon the details given by Eusebius and Theodoret: Paul desired to please Zenobia because she had a leaning towards Judaism, and was led away to the sect of Artemon. Paul himself was not far removed from fornication, for beautiful women adhered to him and sang in his name. There follows an account of his excommunication, his refusal to leave the 'house of the Church', the appeal to Aurelian and the emperor's judgement against Paul.[35] Paul's association with the heresy of Artemon appears again in a Syriac chronicle to the year 724: 'Paul adulterated true doctrine and renewed the heresy of Artemon.'[36] An undated Nestorian document drawing upon Theodoret and Syriac *epitomes* picks up the point made earlier by Severus when it says of Nestorius, 'The patriarch said, we do not say that [Mary] bore a man, in the manner that Paul of Samosata confessed that Christ was simply a man; nor that she bore God, as Apollinarius confessed, but we say that she bore Christ, God and man.'[37]

Barhadbešabba of 'Arbaia lists Paul among heretics who held that the Son is a creature,[38] and claims that Narsai had been attacked in Edessa 'because he adhered to the thought of Theodore and Nestorius, disciples of Paul'.[39] Paul is still the father of heresies seven hundred years after his brief episcopate at Antioch. His name is associated with others who specifically rejected his teaching. His views are pressed into service not only in trinitarian dispute ('the Son was a creature') but in christological dispute ('Christ was a mere man'). To what extent can these later judgements upon him be justified in the light of the documents relevant to his trial?

The doctrinal point which brought Paul into conflict with his fellow bishops was the divinity of Christ. Malchion, in his confrontation with Paul, was not content merely to bandy scriptural texts, but sought the philosophical root of the matter, and the extant fragments of the dispute, assembled by Bardy and de Riedmatten from later documents, indicate the level at which the dispute was conducted. The question at issue was that of unity and multiplicity; if two units interpenetrate, what kind of unity is possible which maintains the individual identity of the components? Does not a human being show a real union of apparently incompatible elements, spiritual and bodily? May there not then be a real union of divine spirit and human flesh in Christ without any lowering of the former? Is there not a distinction between divine inspiration in the prophet and divine indwelling in Christ? But the root of the matter lay in defining not the relationship of the divine Word to the man Jesus of Nazareth but that of the divine Word to the Godhead whose Word he is. Paul was facing the weight of the Origenist tradition of Alexandria,[40] which with slight variations of terminology still remained the theology established by Origen himself.

Origen had seen the divine Wisdom (or Son, or Word – the terms are interchangeable) as existing not as an impersonal attribute of the Godhead in the manner of Theophilus, but personally, and by definition from eternity, since God can never have been without his Wisdom. The independence of the two divine persons and the subordination of the second person is expressed forcibly by Origen: 'The Son is not greater than the Father but inferior to him'; 'the Saviour and the Holy Spirit are . . . far superior to created things, but the Father is even higher above them than they are above the highest created thing'.[41] Origen's conception of the Son is at root a late-platonic idea of an intermediary figure designed to link the perfection of God to the imperfection of created matter, which is not unconnected with the gnostic hierarchies of heavenly beings fulfilling this function of bridging the gap between perfection and imperfection.[42] Origen was postulating a necessary mediator between God and man. At almost any cost, the transcendent holiness of God had to be safeguarded from contaminating contact with the material world. The difficulty of maintaining any kind of divine status for the 'second God' Origen met by saying that the Son proceeds from the Father like an act of will proceeding from a mind.[43] Wisdom, since it proceeds from God, is generated out of the divine substance itself . . . of one substance with that body of which it is the outflow or exhalation.[44] From Origen's position nevertheless it does not require many steps of argument to separate the Son from the Father to such an extent that it is impossible to attribute to him any real divinity of nature at all, but in the theology of Dionysius of Alexandria and of the priest Malchion at least an attempt was made to regard the Son as being of one substance with the Father, however distinct in person. Paul of Samosata, faced at his trial with what looked like a radical separation of Son from Father, allowed no terminology of distinct persons within the Godhead.[45] God is a single substance and a single person, whose Word is within himself until it is uttered. Paul does not appear to use Theophilus' distinction between the indwelling Word and the uttered Word, but the similarity of their positions is unmistakable, for both see the Word attaining recognizable personality only when it is uttered. Before utterance the Word 'existed in God like reason in the heart of a man', wrote Epiphanius,[46] expressing what he held to be Paul's teaching, and from the emphasis that Paul's opponents laid upon the status of the Word as the creative agent of God it may be inferred that Paul held a view in some way opposed to this, namely that the Word was no more than an impersonal force. Paul's use of the word 'begat' to describe the mode of utterance of the Word by the Father may suggest that the Word must be more than an impersonal agent, but whatever personal subsistence is implied by this term amounts to little in view of the charge against Paul that he depersonalized the Word. It is difficult to pin down his meaning, and to see in it anything more than that God possesses an immanent power or quality which emerges before creation into some kind of manifestation of divinity and that this manifestation was in some way effective in the act of creation which followed and later in Jesus Christ.

Consideration of the relationship between the uttered Word and Jesus of Nazareth brings us back to Malchion's question whether there may not be a real, substantial union of the spiritual with the earthly. To this Paul's answer was emphatically that there can not be: the Word of God and the man were substantially separate.

'The man Jesus is anointed, the Word is not. The Nazarene is anointed, our Lord . . . Mary did not give birth to the Word since she is not before all ages. Mary received the Word and is not older than the Word; but she gave birth to a man like ourselves, though better in all respects since the grace which is in him is of the Holy Spirit.'[47]

The distinction is expressed by Severus, voicing what he held to be Paul's

view, that the Word dwelt in Christ without consubstantial unity with the
humanity, just as the clothing which covers a man's body is different from
him and not part of him.[48] Leontius expresses the point briefly: 'The Word
is greater than Christ, for Christ became great through wisdom.'[49] The Word
took possession of the man Jesus at his birth without substantially altering
the manhood of Jesus – another seminal idea destined to bear fruit during
the following century. Man and Word simply 'come together'. Their mode
of union is 'participation', 'communion' and no more, for a truly substantial union would compromise the dignity of the Word. The bishops at the
council denied that the status of the Word would be so compromised.[50]
The Syriac *Florilegia* records a fragment of the debate:

> *Paul.*   The Word cannot be composite without forfeiting his status.
> *Malchion.* The Word and his body are not composite?
> *Paul.*   On no account may they be composite or mixed.
> *Malchion.* If you do not wish to admit the composite nature, it is in
>   order to avoid saying that the Son of God was united sub-
>   stantially with his body.[51]

The bishops put forward the analogy of the unity of body and soul in man.
To Paul 'this is a different kind of constitution',[52] but the bishops see it as
different only in degree, not in kind.[53]

Paul's theology was able to stand up to the attacks levelled at it perhaps more strongly than it appeared to his contemporaries to do. On both
counts – on the one hand his view of the relationship of the Word to the
Father within the Godhead, and on the other his view of the relationship
of the Word to the man in Christ – there is more to be said in his defence
than his opponents allowed, and the defence was later to be developed by
Theodore of Mopsuestia. The weakness of the forces arrayed against Paul
lay in its Origenist basis in starting its thinking about God from multiplicity
rather than from unity. It started from the conception of three divine persons (or even of two) since it required from the outset a shield or buffer
between the perfection of God and the imperfection of matter. Antiochene
theology began from the unity of the substance and sought to draw out
the persons of the Trinity from the single Godhead without destroying the
unity. In historical fact the Antiochene conception of unity proved to be
stronger than the Alexandrian conception of multiplicity, and the definition
of Nicaea in 325 leant more heavily upon the Antiochene tradition than
upon the Alexandrian. To Alexandrian minds Paul of Samosata appeared
to be a unitarian. To Antiochene minds Origen appeared to be a tritheist.
Both views were mistaken, but the independent theological opinions of
Rome and Asia Minor came nearer to Paul than to Origen. Paul's own
articulation of the various elements of his theology may have left much to
be desired: the fragmentary evidence makes it hard to judge. But much of

the evidence reaches us through men who were unable to see anything but danger and falsehood in the views of the vain ecclesiastic of Antioch. Further, Paul's view of the relation of the Word to the man Jesus has this characteristically Antiochene merit, that it places emphasis upon the true humanity of Jesus. We have had occasion above to observe the emphasis placed by Antiochene biblical exegesis upon the facts of human history divorced from fanciful explanations or allegorizations, and the same emphasis is to be observed in Antiochene doctrinal thinking. The human experiences of temptation, hunger and pain, were real human experiences or they were meaningless. It is something of this sort that Paul is saying in his insistence that it is not the Word who is anointed but the man Jesus. Paul's theology was far from being a lost cause when it was condemned by the bishops at Antioch in 268. Its further developments were yet to carry it far, fed on its way by tributaries of thought from other traditions but never entirely losing its own identity.

One of the tributaries derived from the teaching of Sabellius, who had been excommunicated by Callistus of Rome at some point between 217 and 222, and who was associated in later tradition with Egypt. Those who refer to him – and few later writers could keep their hands off him – are more united in their repudiation of his views than lucid in their exposition of them. But his main point is plain in outline, that God is a single divine substance who manifests himself in three ways, when creating, redeeming and sanctifying. Dionysius of Rome says that Sabellius taught that the Son is the Father and the Father the Son;[54] Eusebius says that he held God to be one person known by two names, Father and Son.[55] Whether or not Sabellius himself used the analogy, it became common to describe the Sabellian God as an actor who plays three different parts, holding up a different mask (*prosopon, persona*) before his face for each part.[56] This is not identical with the teaching of Paul of Samosata, who had distinguished identifiable qualities or energies within the Godhead and had described these qualities as assuming some kind of personal identity when the divine economy demanded it.[57] With Sabellius there seems to have been no question of separate personal identities of any kind within the Trinity. One God acted in a certain way to create and we call him Father; the same God acted in a different way to redeem and we call him Son; in a different way again to sanctify and we call him Holy Spirit. There is here no Trinity of persons, only a Trinity of names. It was the reputation of unitarianism which adhered to Sabellius' memory. An eighth-century Syriac chronicle characterizes his teaching, 'He said that the Trinity was one person, and that the body and blood which we receive at the altar is that of the Trinity.'[58] The teaching of Sabellius was at any rate a potent idea which seems to have reinforced the doctrine of Paul of Samosata and given it fresh life in the mid-fourth century in the mind of Marcellus of Ancyra, who must be

considered at this point not because he was an Antiochene but because his
teaching lay in direct descent from that of Paul.[59]

Eusebius, in two works composed to refute Marcellus, denounces him
as Sabellian. If Marcellus believed that Christ 'was the Word united with
God, eternal and unbegotten, one and the same with God, known by the
two names "Father" and "Son", of identical substance and one in person,
then he put on the mantle of Sabellius'.[60] Marcellus pretends to oppose
Sabellius, 'yet falls into the same error'.[61] They join 'like faithless Jews'
in claiming to know God.[62] Marcellus is one in faith with Sabellius, and
Sabellius was excommunicated.[63] There is much more of the same kind.
The fact is that Marcellus' teaching was by no means identical with what
we know of Sabellian teaching, and that 'Sabellian' was a general label
ready to hand in the fourth century for Origenists to attach to any teaching
that did not meet their requirements in distinguishing between the persons
of the Trinity: any suspicion of merging the three persons was dubbed
Sabellian.

The doctrinal views of Marcellus exhibit the features familiar already in
those of Paul of Samosata, but he adds his own contribution. His doctrine
is supported constantly by biblical quotation,[64] but there is substance in
the accusation by Eusebius that he does not know his bible well enough.[65]
Nor was he a philosopher, and repudiates those who are 'led astray by philosophy'.[66] It has been suggested that he was pagan before he was Christian,
hence his lack of ease in wielding the polemical weapons required by doctrinal controversy. Yet his views were acceptable to many contemporaries
of unquestioned orthodoxy until his Sabellian tendencies obtruded themselves to such an extent that his associates severed their connection with
him. Virtually indistinguishable from his Antiochene predecessors is his
doctrine that the Godhead is indivisible, the Monad, possessing within
himself the impersonal Word as an energy or function of God.[67] The Word
could not be called 'Son' until born of the Virgin, and therefore God could
not be 'Father' until this moment. Eusebius makes much of this: if what
Marcellus says is true, that the Word is to be identified with the Father,
then 'it is clear that the Father was no Father, since there never existed his
Son; similarly, since there was no Son, there never existed a Father'.[68] The
omission of the words 'the Father' may be noted in the creed which Marcellus submitted to Rome: 'I believe in God almighty'.[69] The Word became
operative at a certain moment in time and became possessed of individual
personality as the Son for the purpose of the redemption of man,[70] and
from the incarnate Son came the Holy Spirit, breathed upon the apostles
as recorded in the fourth gospel. The peculiar contribution added by Marcellus to this teaching was his belief that in accordance with I Cor. xv.24ff.,
the reign of the Son will end when he 'delivers up the Kingdom to God the
Father', and that then the Son will return to the Father to be 'what he was

before', that is the impersonal Word.[71] The Monad, in other words, expands into a Dyad at the moment of incarnation, into a Triad at the gift of the Holy Spirit, and back to the Monad at the last judgement when Christ's rule is ended: an expansion and contraction akin to the movement of the human heart. The Trinity is thus an episode in the divine life, a rhythmic heartbeat in the life of God.

Marcellus dissociated himself from Sabellianism, Eusebius tells us, and indeed what Marcellus has to say about the Trinity carries the matter well beyond what Sabellius is reported to have said. It is linked constantly though perhaps crudely to the fourth gospel, but this did not save it from condemnation.[72]

Contemporary with Marcellus, and equally indebted to Paul of Samosata as far as one can judge the fragments of his doctrinal writing that are extant,[73] is Eustathius, who was translated from the bishopric of Beroea to that of Antioch in 324.[74] Like Marcellus he was an advocate of the term *homoousios* at Nicaea in 325, for like the rest of this school of theologians he seems to have held the Word of God to have been from eternity a function of God, and rejected any theology which regarded the eternal Word as personally distinct from the Father. The Word, as incarnate Son, inhabited the body of Jesus in the manner of deity inhabiting a shrine; the body was his 'temple', 'house', 'human instrument', and the suffering experienced by the human body was independent of the indwelling Son. His deposition from his bishopric in 326[75] was achieved by his enemies as a result not of his doctrine but on charges concerning his personal conduct and his alleged insults to the empress Helena.[76] Outbursts of rioting calling for military intervention in Antioch followed his condemnation and on the appointment of a new bishop a large party of Antiochene Christians refused to recognize the newcomer and separated themselves. The Eustathian Church remained in this separated state for eighty years, long after Eustathius himself had died in exile.

Marcellus also suffered condemnation and exile, but in his case he faced not trumped-up personal accusations but charges arising out of the doctrinal point concerning the personal independence of the members of the Trinity. Marcellus never wavered in his belief that the unity of God is the vital point to be held against any tendency to separation of the divine persons, although he was capable, at a crucial moment, of some duplicity in suppressing the more original and striking aspects of his doctrine. At Nicaea he had defended the term *homoousios*, and was to refer in later years to his championship of orthodoxy on this occasion. It was to stand him in good stead. Ten years after Nicaea, in 335, he was stung by the dominance of the Origenists, led by Eusebius of Nicomedia but inspired doctrinally by Asterius the Sophist, to publish an attack[77] not only on this extreme wing of the party but also on the more moderate Origenists such as Eusebius of

Caesarea, who himself replied with a fierce counter-accusation of Sabellianism. It is this work, *Against Marcellus*, and its sequel *On the Theology of
the Church*, that remain our chief sources of information about Marcellus'
teaching, for Eusebius frequently quotes the words of his opponent.[78] A
synod of Eusebians was called at Constantinople in 336, Marcellus' book
was condemned and he was exiled. In the following year he suffered banish-
ment a second time, having on Constantine's death been reinstated to
Ancyra, where he possibly had some contact with Athanasius and aroused
the fears of the Eusebians that Athanasius was mustering support for himself. In 340 we find Marcellus defending himself before Julius of Rome,
pleading his orthodoxy at Nicaea and presenting as proof a creed for
Rome's approval.[79] He can hardly have been disingenuous in presenting a
statement of belief which was to all intents the creed of Rome itself, and
in omitting any mention of his idea of the Trinity as an expansion and
contraction of the Godhead. Julius accepted his defence and took him
into communion with the Roman church. In 341 the dedication of Constantine's 'Great Church' at Antioch was the occasion of a council of nearly
a hundred eastern bishops of varying degrees of Origenism, who took the
opportunity to reiterate their excommunication of Marcellus[80] and their
belief in God as three individual persons held in relation to each other by
a common will. 'If anyone teaches or holds in his heart anything other than
this faith, let him be anathema . . . Marcellus of Ancyra or Sabellius or Paul
of Samosata.'[81] The joint emperors, Constantine's sons, wanted a settlement
of the dispute,[82] and in 342 or 343 a fresh synod was convened at Serdica,
the modern Sofia, attended by three hundred western bishops and seventy
eastern bishops.[83] The demand by the latter for the exclusion from the
synod of Marcellus and Athanasius having been rejected by the western
delegation, they left in anger, leaving the westerners to reaffirm their approval of the two disputed brethren. They reaffirmed their belief in God
as 'one divine substance' as against 'three distinct persons' of the Origenists,
but they did so without actually using the terminology of Marcellus[84] –
perhaps the first sign that they were wearying of a dispute which divided
Christendom over the terminology of one man. The eastern bishops met at
Sirmium in 351 to deal with Photinus, a disciple of Marcellus.[85] All the
familiar points were passed in review and condemned – that the Son did
not exist before the incarnation; that the persons of the Trinity comprise
one divine substance; that the essence of God expands and contracts
according to the divine purpose. The emperor Constantius II had already
exiled Marcellus in 347, and even Athanasius had withdrawn his championship of his old supporter at Nicaea.[86] The west wanted peace and agreed to
the deposition of Photinus from his bishopric, implying thereby the withdrawal of their support from his master. Little more is heard of Marcellus,
who lived out his exile for another twenty-three years and died in 374.

There is evidence that shortly before his death he approached his old ally Athanasius through an intermediary, the deacon Eugenius, and that Athanasius was not unsympathetic to the approach.[87] For the venerable Athanasius to reveal himself to this stage as still not unsympathetic to Marcellus and the Sabellianism with which his name was associated could have been a severe blow to hopes of unity, but no lasting damage seems to have been done: within a year of Marcellus' death a large number of his followers produced a document asserting the eternal sonship of the Word, repudiating specifically Marcellus' doctrine of the Word being reabsorbed into an impersonal status within the Godhead and thus losing his sonship.[88] It was a direct overture to the Nicene party, and despite the misgivings of Basil about the danger of receiving crypto-Sabellians into communion[89] their approach was welcomed.

The attractive force of the doctrine with which Marcellus is associated is indicated by the continued life of the separated Eustathian Church in Antioch until it was reunited with the Nicene Church in 414. It continued at first, on the death of Eustathius, under the leadership of a priest, Paulinus, who was consecrated bishop in 362, and remained under continual pressure to reunite with the Nicene Church at Antioch. But the Nicene faith included belief not only in the single substance of God but also in the three distinct persons of the Trinity, and the Eustathians dared not risk association with others who, as it appeared to them, had one foot in the Origenist camp. Paulinus' fears that his party might defect after his death led him to consecrate Evagrius in 388, and resistance to pressure was maintained.[90] On the death of Evagrius the Eustathian Church seems to have carried on without a bishop until 414, when it capitulated to the persuasion of Alexander, the Nicene bishop. 'By soft persuasion of words', writes Theodoret, 'and alluring them by repeated exhortation, he united the Eustathians to the body of the Church.'[91]

The Origenist tradition was rooted in Alexandria, but one of its strongest branches was associated with Antioch. Its other branches, notably in Asia Minor and Palestine, where Origen lived during the latter part of his life, we shall touch only incidentally. The sweep and self-consistency of Origen's system of theology, apart from its deep-laid philosophical foundations, were sufficient to ensure its widespread influence long after the death of Origen himself.

The aspect of Origen's thought which concerns us here, and which demands rather clearer definition than we have so far given it, is his conception of the Word in relation to the Father. God's nature is 'uncompounded intelligence', perfect unity, complete in its immutability and untouched by any form of existence which is subject to change or multiplicity.[92] And yet his nature is perfect love, which demands an object to be loved, a creation. A relationship can be postulated between the transcendentally perfect God

and a creation which is finite, material and therefore subject to corruption
and change, by envisaging an intermediary being who in some sense shares
the attributes of the Godhead and in some sense those of the creation. 'We
seek a being intermediate between all creation and God, in other words a
mediator.'[93] In such a manner Origen approaches his doctrine of the Word.

> 'We are lost in reverent wonder at Jesus, who has recalled our minds
> from all sensible things which are not only corruptible but are destined
> to corruption, and has raised them to honour the God who is above all
> with prayers and a righteous life, which we offer to him as being inter-
> mediate between the nature of the uncreated and that of all created
> things.'[94]

There will be seen here the difference between Paul of Samosata's conception of the Word as an adjectival quality of the Godhead, and Origen's conception of an intermediary being. Origen is emphatic in rejecting the former:
'Let nobody imagine that we mean anything impersonal when we call him
the Wisdom of God . . . the Son of God is his Wisdom, hypostatically (personally) existing.'[95] To Origen, the Word is classed generically with a host
of other subsidiary divine beings, however far he may transcend them in
rank, in knowledge, in power and in sharing the divine will. Whatever per-
fections are attributed to the Word as understood by Origen, not even
Origen's warmest supporters can entirely bridge the gap which exists
between the Word and the Father in this system. 'Although we may call
him a second God', writes Origen against Celsus, 'let men know that by the
term "second God" we mean nothing else than a virtue capable of including
all other virtues, and a reason capable of containing all other reason what-
soever which exists in all things.'[96] Yet the term 'second God' stands. In
his Commentary on John, Origen makes clear that the Word is above all
created beings, and yet that the relation of created beings to the Word is
analogous to that existing between the Word and the Father; and therefore,
says Origen, we find Jesus in St Mark's gospel rejecting the adjective 'good'
as applied to himself, since the adjective applies only to the Father, and in
St John we find Jesus saying, 'My Father is greater than I'.[97] He is the image
of God's goodness,[98] eternally generated by an extra-temporal process
which was not to be defined as any kind of act in time,[99] generated to be
a distinct, individual existence, a second person, to whom Origen added a
third person to complete the Trinity not by reason of philosophical necessity but because he was part of the biblical data: 'Of the existence of the
Holy Spirit no one indeed could embrace any suspicion, save those who
were familiar with the law and the prophets, or those who possess a belief
in Christ.'[100] It is not hard to see how such teaching would appear to Christians of the cast of mind of Paul of Samosata and Marcellus as being tritheist, and yet we find this teaching strongly established in Antioch itself

before the end of the third century by men contemporary with Paul. The centre of Origenism at Antioch was the school of Lucian.

We should perhaps seek for an explanation of the attractiveness of Origenism in the all-embracing completeness of Origen's system, of which the preceding brief sketch of his doctrine of the Trinity is but one element. His system is an articulated theology, with all the attraction that a developed system possesses. It is possible that Lucian's contact with Origenism may have arisen from his work on the text of the bible,[101] for it is improbable that Lucian's scholarly and critical achievement could have been carried out in complete isolation from the immense work of Origen in this field, and it has been suggested that he obtained codices from Alexandria to assist his work.[102] If this is so, Lucian may have imbibed Origenist doctrine without at the same time adopting his method of scriptural interpretation: Origen's flights of allegorical interpretation are far removed from the literalism of Lucian's pupils, who presumably learnt their literalism from their master. Close-knit though Origen's system was, it was possible to abstract certain elements from it, and if Lucian in fact adopted Origen's theology without adopting also his exegetical method, he was doing no more than was done later by Eusebius in Palestine and the Cappadocian fathers in Asia Minor.

Apart from his textual work Lucian wrote little (some small books and some short letters), says Jerome,[103] but his name is associated, probably rightly, with one of the creeds that emerged from the Council of Antioch in 341, and possibly with the earlier creed of the Council of Nicaea. The acceptance of the Nicene creed by some of the Origenists present at Nicaea may have been due to its having Lucianic associations of some kind. His connection with the creed of Antioch in 341 is better attested.

Of the four creeds issuing from this Council[104] the second and longest was the formal doctrinal declaration of the assembled bishops.[105] Of the others, the first was a refutation of the charge that they were Arians, with an added shaft directed against Marcellus; the third was a personal defence offered by an accused bishop, Theophronius of Tyana, to which the Council added a further anti-Marcellan anathema; the fourth was apparently an afterthought dispatched hastily to the west for the approval of the emperor Constans, though its purpose is by no means clear. The second creed extends to over four hundred words of Greek, including quotations of the first and fourth gospels, and makes quite clear its Origenist view of the relationship between the persons of the Trinity, 'the names . . . denoting accurately the peculiar subsistence, rank and glory of each that is named, so that they are three in subsistence, and in agreement one'.[106] It is certainly not an Arian creed, since its second clause defines the Son as 'begotten before the ages from the Father, God from God'. It does not say that the Son is 'of one substance with the Father', *homoousios*, but that the Son is the 'exact image of the Godhead, substance, will, power and glory of the Father'. He was in the beginning with God as John i.1 attests. He is 'unalterable and unchangeable'. At its conclusion it specifically rejects certain tenets of Arius, namely that there was a time before the generation of the Son, and that the Son was a creature, a work of God. Sozomen says that Lucian's disciples claimed that they had found a copy of this creed written by Lucian's own hand.[107] If this tradition of Lucian's authorship, or at the least his doctrinal approbation, is correct, it shows him to have maintained belief in a Trinity of individual persons standing in a relationship of superiority and inferiority to each other.[108] The creed adopts the Origenist position on the matter, and quite consistently rejects the Arian exaggeration of Origenism at the same time as it rejects the Marcellan extreme in the opposite direction. The son is here a true image or likeness of the Father, but the dangerous word *homoousios*, 'of the same substance', is avoided. The wording of this creed has points in common with that of the creed put forward in self-justification by Eusebius at Nicaea, sixteen years earlier,[109] as though Lucian's party was reasserting its old allegiance to its master. That the Lucianists should do so suggests that his name carried real weight, not only as a martyr (he had been put to death by Maximin Daia in 312) but as a theologian, and renders it questionable whether the Lucian described by Alexander of Alexandria[110] as having been excommunicated in 268 for heresy along with Paul of Samosata is the Lucian with whom we are dealing. The excommunicated Lucian remained out of communion during three episcopates at Antioch. A strong statement of the identification was made by C. E. Raven.[111] Raven sets out the conflicting and mutually contradictory fourth-century estimates of Lucian: according to Alexander he followed Paul of Samosata; according to the apology alleged by Rufinus to have been presented by Lucian at his martyr's trial, he repudiated Paul's theology;[112] Epiphanius agrees with this, and claims that he was on the contrary the fountain head of Arianism;[113] the Lucianic creed of 341 specifically excludes Arianism. On the ground of Lucian's great reputation for scholarship and sanctity, Raven concludes that whatever Lucian was, he was not 'an Arian, and a muddle-headed Arian at that', and traces a hypothetical development for Lucian from a Paulian position to an Origenist position, suggesting that he was forced to develop his views in order to fit the demands of a consistent spiritual and intellectual life. As a Paulian he would have held that the Word was no more than a quality or faculty of the Father, from which he moved to a position which allowed a greater distinction between Father and Word and a personalizing of the latter; from this he moved to a realization that the Word incarnate in Christ must be personal, and therefore that Christ could not possess both the personal Word of God and a normal human soul. The final position is represented by the Confession at his trial and the creed of 341, both of unimpeachable Origenist orthodoxy. Raven puts too much weight on the Confession, whose authenticity is probably more questionable than he allows, but the removal of this piece of evidence does not destroy his case. It may be asked whether a man who had once been excommunicated for adherence to Paul of Samosata would have ever regained sufficient ground to be held in veneration by the opposite party and would have been resuscitated in 341 to give weight to that party's creed. It is not imperative to sweep aside Alexander's evidence of excommunication as referring to somebody else, since the process of excommunication, recantation and rehabilitation as an Origenist could well account for the conflicting contemporary evidence.[114] It has been suggested, to give credence to the excommunication story, that Lucian was excommunicated by Paul of Samosata himself on account of the divergence of their theologies,[115] but there is no mention of such an event in the accounts of Paul's episcopate, and Lucian's fame as a scholar would hardly permit his excommunication to be passed over in silence by Paul's biographers. The question remains unsettled.

This is not to say that Lucian is to be blamed for the theological excesses of some of his pupils. In the heated pagan atmosphere of Alexandria, Origenism could turn into Arianism, and heretical bodies of various descriptions (e.g. Meletians) could range themselves under the banner of Arius. Thus the Collucianists, as they were proud to call themselves, attracted theologically heterogeneous elements which brought the name and the master himself into disrepute. Arius himself is not included in the list of Lucian's pupils by Philostorgius,[116] who was in a position to know, though Arius styles himself 'Collucianist' in one letter,[117] and even the better-accredited of Lucian's pupils tended to push their master's doctrine further than he would have approved. The fact is that Lucian had sent out from Antioch an able and well-trained group, many of whom received bishoprics, united in devotion to Lucian himself and in common hatred of all that was represented by Paul of Samosata, Sabellius, Eustathius and eventually Marcellus. Arius struck the first blow which reunited the group in 318,[118] but Asterius was the theorist of the party and Eusebius of Nicomedia its organizer. Sympathetic, but holding some reservations, Eusebius of Caesarea added the weight of his scholarship to the group, though as a possible pupil of Dorotheus of Antioch[119] he could not claim to be strictly a Collucianist. Later centuries have tended to think of the group as Arians, but they did not think of themselves in this way: they called themselves Lucianists and their opponents called them Eusebians. The *Life of Lucian*[120] describes them loyally surrounding Lucian in prison, but at Nicaea only three, Theognis, Maris and Eusebius of Nicomedia, supported Arius strongly enough to refuse at first to sign the creed. And in Antioch in 341 they dissociated themselves vigorously from Arius, prefacing their creed with the words, 'We have neither become followers of Arius – for how should we who are bishops follow a presbyter? – nor have we embraced any other faith than that which was set forth from the beginning. But being constituted examiners and judges of his faith, we admitted him to communion rather than followed him.'[121] The party may have had a stronger bond of fellowship than Arius had ever provided, namely their loyalty to Lucian, as was recognized by Arius himself when he first canvassed their help in 318. Epiphanius' ·distinction between Lucianists and Arians is probably justified.[122] The hard core of Lucianists seems to have been composed of nine or ten men, Eusebius of Nicomedia, Theognis of Nicaea, Maris of Chalcedon, Menophantius of Ephesus, Athanasius of Anazarbis, Antony of Tarsus, Leontius of Antioch, the sophist laymen Alexander and Asterius, and possibly Arius himself, who had charge of the Church at Baucalis in Alexandria, to whom may be added some half a dozen active sympathizers such as Eusebius of Caesarea. The widespread support commanded by Arius outside the limits of this group has little to do with loyalty to the memory of Lucian or with Antioch, and with Arianism as such we are not here primarily concerned. Some account must however be given of Arius' doctrine in its relation to that of Antioch.[123]

It is unsafe to attempt a reconstruction of Arius' theology from much of what his opponents wrote about his thought. G. C. Stead has shown that the reliability of Athanasius as a source is dangerously variable, and that the most reliable of his accounts of Arianism, namely that contained in *De Synodis* 15, shows Arius to have been a more careful and less extravagant thinker than he is often made to appear. Despite T. E. Pollard's strong advocacy of the Lucianic tradition of Antioch as the main influence upon him, recent studies place Arius within the Origenist tradition of Alexandria, though his Origenism is strongly leavened by the Platonism of his day and by elements drawn from other sources, perhaps Peter of Alexandria, Methodius and Dionysius of Alexandria.

Arius appears to have taken to an extreme length Origen's insistence upon the absolute supremacy of the Father, that whatever can be said about the Son – that he is the power of God, wisdom, truth, image, logos – the Father is greater than these. These titles apply primarily and in reality to the Father, secondarily and derivatively to the Son, 'in a manner of speaking'. But Arius takes this further to draw his line of demarcation not between Father and Son within the Trinity, as Origen had done, but between God and every other being, classing the Son with the other beings. God is himself logos, truth, wisdom, and he reveals a delegated or generated logos, truth and wisdom in the Son. The term 'logos' thus appears on both sides of the line dividing God from other beings, laying Arius' fragmentary literary remains open to the misunderstandings from which they have suffered ever since. Arius probably preferred to use the term 'Son' rather than 'logos', and 'beget' rather than 'create', when writing of the generated second person, though the verb 'create' may well have occurred during the course of the controversy, and the memory of the term have been carried over by Athanasius into his summary of what Arius wrote.[124] Arius' opponents saw his teaching as placing the Son unambiguously among the creatures and as denying the eternal fatherhood of God. But Arius' qualification that the Son, though generated like other creatures, is 'not as one of the creatures' suggests that he was at least cautious in his thinking. Arius' caution may have led him to adopt the method of Dionysius of Alexandria, a method not unknown elsewhere in patristic writings, of weighing apparently contradictory terms against each other in order to achieve an overall balance of statement. Any one term may be insufficient or misleading if used alone, but in conjunction with others contributes to a balance of mutual qualification which sets in a wider context the crudity of each individual statement. A kind of *via media* between extremes can be established by such a method.

Arius' belief that the Son was to be placed in the realm of other beings was qualified to some extent by his insistence that the Son was unique among such beings. He could moreover call the Son 'God', though not 'true God'. The glories and dignities the Son received from the Father were not mere titles, but were real: he was in reality glorious, and enjoyed a dignity unknown to other generated beings, their 'beginning' and their 'chief'. Moreover, the dignity of the Son was such that we cannot speak of his having originated within the time sequence which was the proper setting for the creation or generation of all other beings. Origen had seen the difficulties here, and had overcome them by speaking of the generation of the Son as an eternal process rather than a specific act. Arius, having committed himself to placing the Son among 'all other beings', however great the Son's dignity and priority, is obliged to speak of his generating as an act rather than a process. But how does one speak of an act that is performed outside the sequence of time? The book of Genesis speaks of creative acts of God before the creation of sun and moon, which mark the passage of time, and perhaps it is thus that Arius feels able to avoid the word 'time' altogether. He does not say 'there was a time when the Son was not', but simply 'there was when the Son was not', a phrase which his opponents regarded as being simply evasion, a verbal trick to avoid a difficulty.[125]

The picture of Arius as an almost cynical spinner of words, which is the picture of him that we receive from his enemies, as one who taught that the Son is 'merely' a creature, is probably an injustice, though the fact remains that to whatever high degree the Son is said to be superior to other beings, he is on their side of the line which separates them from everything that is meant by the term 'true God'. This was in itself sufficient to secure his condemnation at Nicaea, as it was also enough to deny him any kind of support in Alexandria itself. Arius' affinity with some aspects of Antiochene thinking is close enough for the question of his sources to be still open. Whatever he meant by his claim to be a 'fellow-Lucianist' of Eusebius of Nicomedia – and the term need not mean that he had studied under Lucian personally – much of his support came from Antiochenes who had personally sat at Lucian's feet. Yet few pupils of Lucian appear to have been able to accept his teaching in full, or for long.

Eusebius of Nicomedia accepted it and wrote to a fellow bishop to enlist support, giving his own teaching that the Father alone is ingenerate, the Son created by the Father and not participating in any way in the substance of the Father, nor deriving his existence from the substance of the Father, but different by nature. And this, he says, is not merely our opinion but is scriptural.[126] Nevertheless Eusebius subscribed the Nicene Creed, along with its conclusion, 'Those who say "there was when he was not" and "before his generation he was not" and "he came to be from nothing", or those who pretend that the Son of God is "of other *hypostasis* or substance" or "created" or "alterable" or "mutable", these the Catholic and Apostolic church anathematizes.' Subscription failed to save Eusebius from three years' exile. His change of front at Nicaea can perhaps be accounted for if, as has been suggested, the creed of the Council had had some connection in the past with Lucian, but it is also likely that a politician such as Eusebius would have seen the direction in which the emperor's mind was working, and would not sacrifice his political ambition out of loyalty to an Alexandrian presbyter.

Another disciple of Lucian who was able to accept Arius' teaching was Asterius, the sophist from Cappadocia, not ordained to the priesthood because of his apostasy during the great persecution, during which he sacrificed to idols.[127] Athanasius' remark concerning a piece of Arian teaching, 'This is what Asterius the sacrificer has written, and Arius has copied it and handed it on to his friends',[128] suggests that Asterius exercised no little influence upon the formulation of Arian doctrine at an early date. Asterius had written, says Athanasius, that the Son, being a creature of God, could be compared with other creatures such as a cricket or a caterpillar.[129] And yet, in a letter written in defence of Eusebius of Nicomedia shortly after Nicaea,[130] Asterius could write of the three persons of the Trinity, and at Nicaea could, like Eusebius, subscribe the creed and in effect abandon Arius. The explanation may be, once again, that his loyalty to the memory of Lucian was greater than his loyalty to Arius. During the following decade, when Eusebius of Caesarea and Marcellus were engaged in combat, one of Marcellus' targets was the doctrine of Asterius, in particular certain statements and formulae which have clear connection with the creed of Lucian presented by the Lucianist party at Antioch in 341. Whatever rash opinions Asterius was uttering during the early 320s, his settled belief seems to have been the creed of Lucian, and the points of agreement between that hallowed document and the creed of Nicaea may account for Asterius' abandoning Arius at Nicaea in order to subscribe a creed which was associated with his master. This is in outline the reconstruction presented by G. Bardy in his *Recherches sur Saint Lucien et son école*. It is a picture of a group of men who were briefly (for perhaps the seven years between 318 and 325) pulled out of their natural orbit by the attraction of a foreign body passing close to them. The Arian attraction was however not sufficiently powerful to hold them, and for their various reasons they reverted to their courses as Lucianists and left it to others to pursue the comet which had come so near to destroying them.

Lucian does not appear to be associated by later Syrian writers with Arianism. The Syrians liked to probe the historical roots of doctrines, establishing a succession of teaching, orthodox or heretical, which set a contemporary situation in historical perspective. They had long memories to preserve the names of the founding fathers of truth and error: we have already noted their reluctance to allow the memory of Paul of Samosata to lapse and they constantly trace their Nestorian faith back through Theodore and Diodore of Tarsus. It is hard to think that if Lucian had been the spiritual father of the leading Arians of the first generation they would have allowed the point to pass unnoticed. On the contrary, the few specific references to him in subsequent Syrian writers seem to be laudatory. His biblical recension is of course frequently in use by writers as widely separated chronologically as Theodoret in the fifth century and Išoʻdad in the ninth, who deplored Arianism. So strong an opponent of Arianism as Severus of Antioch writes of him as 'Lucian the martyr, the blessed friend to labour', and cites his authority as equal to that of 'our blessed Syrian doctors, Mar Ephrem and Mar Jacob and Mar Isaac and Mar Akhsenaya', that is, Philoxenus.[131] An eighth-century chronicle records that 'Constantine established Drepanum in honour of the martyr Lucian, who was buried there.'[132] It is possible that the paucity of reference to Lucian stems from embarrassment – how does one write of a heresiarch who was also a blessed martyr? But nothing of this kind of embarrassment inhibits Syrian treatment of Eusebius of Caesarea, whose renown as a scholar occasioned the translation of a number of his works into Syriac in the fifth century, and yet whose Arian affiliations they did not shrink from describing. The eighth-century chronicle which records Lucian's shrine at Drepanum records also that 'Eusebius Pamphilou, bishop of Caesarea, was known as a writer, many of whose books are preserved', that is, in Syriac.[133] The eighth-century Maronite chronicle tells that Eusebius assumed the name of Pamphilus, his teacher at Caesarea.[134] The seventh-century Jacob of Edessa begins his *Chronicle* by a careful statement of how it picks up the historical narrative where Eusebius' *Chronicle* ends.[135] A ninth-century Monophysite

Chronicle records the Council of Nicaea, with the excommunication of 'Arius and his companions, Eusebius of Nicomedia, Theognis and Maris . . . Among those bishops already mentioned were famous men, Jacob of Nisibis, Alexander of Alexandria, Patrophilus of Constantinople, Eustathius of Antioch, Eusebius of Caesarea . . .'; Eusebius is classed here among the 'famous men' and we may note in passing that the three excommunicated bishops are remembered as Arians, not as Lucianists.[136] The *Nestorian History*, writing of Nicaea, places Eusebius among the Arians while recognizing his respectability in other respects: 'Alexander reunited twenty bishops and excommunicated Arius with those who held his doctrine. Among the bishops was Eusebius of Caesarea, who composed the *Chronicle*.' After the excommunication, 'Eusebius of Caesarea, Eusebius of Emesa and Ourighanis, met again and demanded that Athanasius free Arius.'[137] Barhadbešabba, writing with knowledge of later Arian intimidation of their opponents in Syria, says that at Nicaea only eleven bishops were unwounded 'by reason of the affliction of the heretics', and names them, all east Syrians excepting Eusebius of Caesarea and Eusebius of Nicomedia.[138] The writer's knowledge of Nicaea is often confused, but he contributes to the evidence of how later Syrian writers could see Eusebius as both eminent as a scholar and at the same time an Arian. A bifocal historical vision of this kind could well have been applied to Lucian if he had presented them with a similar problem of focus. But there is nothing in what the Syrians say of Lucian that suggests that they regarded his doctrinal teaching as being in any way suspect, and the 'Eusebians' are unambiguously grouped under Arius and not under Lucian in Syrian memory. If Bardy's reconstruction is right, one would expect it to be reflected east of Antioch in subsequent writings a good deal more strongly than it appears to be.

Nor was it the case that east of Antioch Lucian escapes censure because there was widespread ignorance of Arianism. Syria was undoubtedly well represented at Nicaea in 325. We must probably discount later stories concerning Ephrem's presence at the council. Gregory of Nyssa's *Vita* says nothing of it, although Ephrem's opposition to Arianism is mentioned in the context of a general statement of his attitude to heresy: 'He hated equally the false confusion of Sabellius and the insane division of Arius . . . He detested the most absurd opinions of Apollinarius.'[139] A mention of Nicaea might be expected here if Ephrem had been present. Barhadbešabba relates how Simon bar Sabba'e, bishop of Seleucia-Ctesiphon and catholicos of Persia, was summoned to attend, and that because there was at that time trouble on the Roman frontier, Mar Simon was afraid to make the journey and sent an apology for his absence by John, bishop of Arbela, and Šahdost, a presbyter. His letter is quoted, 'If it were not for the pagans who have a desire for our blood, I would be willing to attend', and he pledges support for 'the fathers who are persecuted for the true faith'.[140] Barhadbešabba

was writing towards the end of the sixth century,[141] and his remarks about
Arian persecution of the orthodox as early as 325 suggests a reading back
of fifth-century Arian troubles in Syria to an earlier date. We have noted
Barhadbešabba's record of nine east Syrian bishops present at Nicaea who
were, with the two Eusebii, the only bishops present unwounded by the
heretics,[142] which again shows Barhadbešabba's distorted view of the power
wielded by the Arians before the council, and raises some doubt about the
accuracy of his computation of nine east Syrian bishops at Nicaea, despite
the fact that he names them.[143] Syria was very well represented at Nicaea,
and therefore possesed first-hand knowledge of the points under consideration. Afrahat, however, in the middle of the fourth century, appears to be
quite unaware of Arianism. His Homily 14, an 'Admonition against the
quarrelsomeness in our own times' addressed to the Christians at Seleucia-
Ctesiphon,[144] is an extraordinary compilation of biblical examples of the
sins of pride and greed and the virtue of meekness, but there is not a word
about Arianism as a source of dispute, and one can only speculate upon
what the delegates of Simon bar Sabba'e at Nicaea had reported back to
their catholicos about the importance of the proceedings. It may well be
that they had not understood very much of the debate. Afrahat's Homily
17 on the divinity of Christ[145] could hardly avoid reference to Arius if
Afrahat had been aware of the weight Arius carried, but again no mention
of him appears. It is particularly surprising in view of Afrahat's personal
contact with Arianism when he descended upon Antioch and confronted
Valens in defence of orthodoxy.[146] But Theodoret's narrative of this incident, like that of Afrahat's healing of the emperor's favourite horse,[147]
suggests that Antiochene legends concerning its heroes were not all based
upon fact.[148] Afrahat's silence in his Homilies concerning Arianism suggests
the possibility that the philosophical terms in which the Arian dispute was
conducted rendered it strange to those who had been trained in the unphilosophical tradition of the desert and prevented them from fully appreciating
what was at stake. Certainly Afrahat reveals no such appreciation.

The fact that the orthodox Church in Syria received severe treatment
from the Arianizing emperors is not in doubt. The degree of severity reflected partly imperial policy and partly the presence of the emperor himself, for those in sympathy with current policy would naturally feel their
hand strengthened by the emperor's presence in their district and would
feel themselves to be in an advantageous position to make public, even
violent, demonstration of their convictions. It is thus no accident that in
the *Chronicle of Edessa* we should read that 'in the year that Ephrem died
the people separated themselves from the Church of Edessa because of the
attack by the Arians',[149] for Valens seems to have spent the late summer of
373 in the region of Hierapolis.[150] Theodoret's account embellishes this
bald statement: 'Valens, after depriving the flock of their shepherd, had

set over them in his place a wolf. The whole population had abandoned the city and were assembled in front of the town when he arrived.' The prefect was ordered to disperse the crowd, but when this failed and Valens himself had been consulted, an attempt was made to coerce the clergy to communicate with the Arian bishop or suffer exile, and eighty people were exiled to Thrace. Their bishop Barsai was already in exile on an island off the Phoenician coast.[151] Theodoret makes no attempt here to distinguish between the true Arians and the compromise party of the Homoeans, who during the reign of Valens were in the ascendant, although he was well aware of the difference, as his treatment of the ecclesiastical policy of Constantius II makes clear. He accounts for the Arian Leontius of Antioch lowering his voice during the doxology by saying that Leontius feared 'the terrible threats which Constantius had uttered against anyone rash enough to say that the Son was unlike the Father'.[152] He writes of 'the anger shown by Constantius against the party who asserted that the only-begotten Son of God was a creature'.[153] He describes Constantius calling together the bishops at Antioch in order to secure a denial of the formulae 'of one substance' and 'of different substance'.[154] And after all his criticism of Constantius, he allows at the end that 'even if Constantius, led astray by those who influenced him, did not admit the term *homoousios*, at least he sincerely accepted the meaning underlying it, since he called the divine Word the true Son begotten of the Father before all ages, and those who dared to call him a created being he openly repudiated'.[155] In short, Theodoret describes Constantius as steering a middle course between Nicenes and Arians, with a leaning towards the former. Valens, on the other hand, is treated by Theodoret as a thoroughgoing Arian from the moment of his baptism by the extreme Arian Eudoxius of Constantinople in 367, and implies that his actions were influenced by the combined force of his Arian wife Dominica and of the court.[156] The rescript of Spring 365, ordering the expulsion from cities of bishops previously exiled by Constantius and recalled by Julian, was an attempt to restore some kind of order to a situation deliberately disordered by Julian,[157] and since the recalled bishops had been largely Nicene, their renewed expulsion by Valens was seen as a blow struck for the Arians. Theodoret makes much of Valens' persecution of orthodox bishops and clergy in the east, though in fact such action was interrupted more than once, by the rebellion of Procopius at Constantinople for six months from October 365, and for three years by Gothic wars on the Danube from 367. There was virtually no repressive legislation from the hand of Valens,[158] but the eastern Church undoubtedly suffered individual *ad hoc* acts of repression directed at orthodox bishops. If Valens' policy was intended to be a continuation of the toleration of Milan,[159] it did not look like that to Theodoret from April 372, when Valens began to devote his attention seriously to eastern affairs. Eusebius of Samosata was deposed in 374 and replaced by an Arian.[160] Edessa was deprived of its bishop and eighty of the laity were exiled with him.[161] Flavian, Diodore and Afrahat led open opposition to Arianism in Antioch[162] and the monk Zeumatius made his protest on the Euphrates.[163] Theodoret characterizes the reigns of Constantius and Valens as encouraging Arianism, the one by indifference, the other by malignity.[164] From the accession of the strongly orthodox Theodosius I in 379, Arianism in the east was doomed to extinction, and a succession of legislation within his first two years brought about its rapid end.[165] Arianism found its home among the Romanized Goths. The mind of the eastern Church was in any case now increasingly occupied with the problems of christology.

There may be a danger that in thinking of the Arian opposition to orthodoxy we should envisage the latter as a uniform theological structure founded on the definition of Nicaea. It is unlikely to have been the case. The further east, the less susceptible would theological thinking have been to Hellenizing influence, and it is probable that primitive Syrian thinking spread as far west as the Syrian-speaking environs of Antioch itself: as far, that is, as the monks described by Theodoret in his *Religious History*. We catch glimpses of ancient Syrian observance which was the soil in which apostolic Christianity was planted. Theodoret describes Simeon Stylites occupying his column between the years 422 and 429, surrounded by crowds of pilgrims kept at a distance by his disciples, who alone had access to him.[166] Theodoret was as a young man an eye-witness of what he describes. His explanation of the effect of the saint's action upon the pilgrims is that God on occasions commands his prophets to perform outrageous acts in order to emphasize their teaching, and cites Jeremiah, Hosea and Ezekiel as examples. It was the astonishing novelty of Simeon's action which, in Theodoret's view, caught the imagination of the pilgrims. But pillars were a common feature of semitic religions,[167] and there is evidence of the practice of climbing them for religious purposes. The Ugaritic texts from Ras Shamra tell of a king mounting a tower to offer sacrifice.[168] Lucian of Samosata describes the two great pillars at Hierapolis,[169] and says that there was a custom whereby 'a man goes up one of these *phalli* twice a year and remains on the top for seven days', receiving the names of worshippers called up to him from below and offering prayers on their behalf.[170] It is hard to think that there is no cultural connection between Lucian's pagan stylite and the Christian stylites of Antioch, and it is possible that Theodoret's educated sensibility could blind him to the more primitive intuitions held by the unlettered pilgrims, and that we should recognize here an outcrop of primitive observance that could seem strange to a scholar educated in the Hellenic tradition as was Theodoret. It is *a priori* improbable that in the realm of Christian doctrine we should expect to find doctrinal categories and norms identical with those found in Greek-speaking

regions further west. The evidence we possess of Afrahat's teaching from
the early fourth century is that here again are signs of a primitive outcrop
of belief and that the orthodoxy of Antioch or of Alexandria was not
identical with that of Edessa. Afrahat's Homilies do not express Christian
doctrine in philosophical terms but mainly in moral terms derived from
the bible: thus he can profess his faith in Father, Son and Holy Spirit
invoked at baptism.[171] But Spirit, the semitic *rûh*, is feminine, and in
Homily 18 the Holy Spirit represents the feminine element in the deity as
the Father represents the masculine element. The Gospel according to the
Hebrews, as quoted by Origen in his *Commentary on John* (ii.12), contains
the words, 'The Saviour himself saith, Even now did my mother the Holy
Spirit take me by one of my hairs and carry me away.'[172] The feminine
element in the Godhead is reflected in Muslim criticism of the Trinity, and
we find the ninth to tenth-century Christian Al Kindi having to defend the
concept of Trinity against the idea that Christians thought the Trinity to be
composed of Father, Son and Mother.[173] Doubtless this feminine element
is later reflected during the Nestorian dispute in the importance attached
to the Virgin *theotokos*, the queen of heaven, but its roots go far back into
primitive semitic culture to the great female deities 'Astart of Phoenicia,
Allath of Arabia and Atargatis, *Dea Syria* herself, at Hierapolis, and it is
reflected in the constant emphasis upon the rôle of women in semitic
cultus from early pre-Christian times to the fifth century A.D.[174] We should
probably be right in assuming that the eighty people exiled by Valens with
their bishop from Edessa held a doctrine of God containing some such
trinitarian elements as these rather than the carefully articulated doctrine
of Athanasius.[175]

The decline of Arianism in the east during the last quarter of the fourth
century does not mean that the question of the triune nature of the Godhead could from that time be shelved, nor that the problems raised by the
doctrine of the Trinity were solved. In the first place, renewed preoccupation with the problems concerning the nature of Christ (a matter which,
as we have seen, had already come to the front in the controversy surrounding Paul of Samosata) required that a close watch should continue to be
kept upon the prior question of the nature of God, for whatever conclusions might be reached about the relationship of the divine to the
human in Jesus Christ, both elements in that relationship demanded as
clear definition as they could be given. In the second place, the question
of the triune nature of God was reopened in the sixth century in a form
which, though quite distinct from Arianism, was inevitably called Arian,
and old animosities were for a time renewed in the east.

The christological dispute, involving great Antiochene theologians such
as Diodore, Theodore, Nestorius, Theodoret, Apollinarius and Severus,
and extending not only west but far eastward into the Syrian desert, Meso-

potamia and Persia, brought to the forefront violent conflicts of theological principle and occasioned a succession of synods and imperial publications which vainly sought to bring peace to the divided Church. Our only concern at this point is to indicate the constant renewal of the doctrine of the nature of God articulated at Nicaea in 325 and confirmed by the councils of Constantinople in 381 and Ephesus in 431. Thus the council of Chalcedon in the autumn of 451, while being primarily concerned with christology, found it necessary to reaffirm the Nicene definition and to press the point in a postscript to the creed: 'Those who say, There was when the Son of God was not, and Before he was begotten he was not, and that he came into being from nothing, or that he is of a different substance, or that he is mutable – those the catholic and apostolic Church anathematizes.'[176] In 482 the emperor Zeno vainly attempted to unite the east by the publication of his *Henotikon*, which again explicitly reaffirmed Nicaea,[177] and successive synods which reaffirmed the *Henotikon* by implication reaffirmed Nicaea, as at Antioch in 513 and at Tyre in 514. The emperor Justinian's address to Constantinople in March 533 states his belief in the consubstantial Trinity as the only possible basis for ecclesiastical unity,[178] and his legislation confirms the same basis.[179] Justin II attempted a new *Henotikon* in 571,[180] built upon the same Nicene foundation. This definition was seen as the essential first step to any forward move out of the christological problems which engulfed them, and it was accepted as authoritative by Nestorians and Monophysites alike. Nobody in the east from the fifth century onwards would have returned to Arianism as a live option, but the point needed to be made clear each time a step forward was attempted.

There remains, however, the curious theological disturbance which centred on the figure of John Philoponus, 'the grammarian', whose philosophical studies in Alexandria led him and a few disciples to propound a doctrine of God which denied the Trinity altogether. In book 5 of his *Categories*, Aristotle considers the term 'substance', subdividing it into primary substance, which is particular and individual, and secondary substance, which is universal or generic. An example of primary substance is thus a particular individual man, whereas 'mankind', as the species to which the individual belongs, is secondary. Secondary substances can in loose speech be treated as though they are individual units: for example, the species 'man' or the genus 'animal' can be spoken of as being particular units. But says Aristotle,[181] 'this is not true to fact, for what is meant [by secondary substance] is a quality. A secondary substance is not an individual unit.' He guards against secondary substance being seen merely as an accidental quality such as the colour white, which may or may not apply to the individual man, by showing that species and genus *must* apply to the individual, but secondary substance is nonetheless a quality defining what sort of individual is under consideration. What happens when this is applied to the trinitarian conception of God? Here the term 'God' becomes generic, and therefore a secondary substance, 'a quality, not an individual unit'. Attention is focussed upon the substantial reality of the three individual units, Father, Son and Spirit, who share the generic description, 'God'. The term 'God' denotes substance, even if secondary, and is therefore not merely adjectival as are the terms 'holy' or 'eternal'. But it is near enough to mere adjectival status for Aristotle to have seen the need to warn his hearers that secondary substances are not accidental in the adjectival manner of 'white'. It is characteristic of Aristotle to turn our attention towards the individual particulars at the expense of the more general conception. With 'God' relegated to the status of secondary substance, we are left with three individual *hypostases* whose definition is that they share a common nature, a *phusis* or *ousia*, called God. It was precisely against such division of the Godhead into three that the Nicene fathers had drawn up their creed two centuries earlier. Arius had seen Son and Spirit as created beings; John the grammarian saw Father, Son and Spirit as being virtually three equal, individual heavenly persons who share the generic quality 'God'. It is not Arianism, but it is clear why the sixth-century theologians who still adhered to the Nicene definition should be able to brand as Arians the grammarian and his followers such as Conon and Eugenius. John may simply have been speculating, following an interesting train of thought as philosophers do to see where it would lead, but it was dangerous to speculate in public on such explosive matters at a time when the Church was trying to keep its foothold on the rock of Nicaea in order to keep its head above the troubled waters of christological dispute. Nicephorus Kallistus outlines John's progress through the logical analysis of Aristotle, the distinction between particular and universal terms, 'from which he concludes that when we profess the nature of Father, Son and Holy Spirit, we say that they are three separate units and persons'.[182] A joint statement was issued from Alexandria and Constantinople against those who dared to think or teach that there are three separate gods, three separate substances, three separate natures, or a plurality of substances or natures.[183] An anathema was composed denouncing John's doctrine as 'full of unbelief and contrary to the document on the sacred Trinity composed by our father Theodosius [of Alexandria] and to the doctrine of the fathers who truly taught the word of truth':[184] that is, above all, the fathers of Nicaea. Theodosius writes in this connection of 'the polytheism of Arius',[185] but he knows well where the philosophical root of the matter lies: the tritheists have picked up a word used by John Chrysostom, who had written of the 'particular substance' of the incarnate Word, and have interpreted its meaning as a separate, particular substance or *ousia*. 'That term "particular" is one that they have cooked up in philosophical circles, following the lead of Aristotle on that subject', and Theodosius goes on to the distinction between a particular man and the generic term 'mankind'. 'God forbid', he concludes, 'that this should be accepted by Christians. They are the progeny of Arius and of the polytheism of the pagans.'[186] But the grammarian was no Arius, nor was the time ripe for such teaching to take hold. The dispute was nevertheless not confined to Alexandria and Constantinople, and Severus of Antioch considered the heresy to be of sufficient importance to warrant a full-scale refutation. His *Liber contra impium grammaticum*, composed in about the year 520,[187] is in the massively repetitive style which he favoured, relying upon copious quotation of the fathers approved by him, mainly Cyril of Alexandria, Athanasius, John Chrysostom and the Cappadocians. Long sections of the work are virtually a *catena* of the words of other theologians. Severus goes back to definitions of terms, for that is the level at which Philoponus must be answered. The term substance signifies something that exists. God exists and possesses his own peculiar substance. The fact that God is triune in structure does not affect the point that He is one and therefore possesses his substance as does every existing entity.[188] Severus has already implied that the error of Philoponus is fundamentally one of method. The latter had started in Aristotelian manner from the observed phenomena of three persons, Father, Son and Spirit, and had treated their common deity as a quality shared by them. Severus starts from the unity, the genus or substance, as the primary term, and proceeds from this premiss, that the divine substance is one and indivisible. *Hypostasis*, he continues, signifies the existence of a single entity or person.[189] Thus the term 'man' is a generic, substantive term, embracing the whole human race made in the image of God, whereas individual men are *hypostases*, standing as it were in the second rank of the logical structure, mere participants in the generic substance and each distinct from all other *hypostases*.[190] Thus the generic term God is shared by the three persons of the Trinity, while each person of the Trinity is a distinct *hypostasis*: their 'being' is common, but the manner in which each enjoys that common being differs in each case, the Father ingenerate, the Son begotten from eternity, the Spirit proceeding from the Son eternally. Scripture reveals this knowledge, but the manner in which the Son is begotten and the Spirit proceeds is closed to us.[191] From this point Severus begins to move towards the particular application of the principle which was most pressing in the sixth century, the relation of the particular human and divine *hypostases* to the single entity, Christ, and having embarked upon this matter Severus devotes the remainder of his work to it, and we will not follow him thither at this point. Philoponus and his followers caused enough stir to draw the fire of Severus and for the documents to be translated into Syriac, but the mind of the Church was now no longer primarily focussed upon the trinitarian question.[192]

5

The use of Greek philosophy by the Eastern Church

It is only in a general sense that the Christian writers of Antioch can be called Aristotelian. The sense in which the term is admissible is that which credits them with an Aristotelian frame of mind or outlook, and this is probably true of many of them even when they had little knowledge of Aristotle's work and joined the chorus of patristic condemnation of many of his philosophical tenets. Aristotle's concentration of mind upon observable facts finds some analogy in the Antiochene emphasis upon historical events and upon the humanity of Christ, but this much hardly allows us to see Aristotle as a direct influence upon their thinking. In so far as they refer to him, it is usually to demonstrate his errors, and like all Christians of a philosophical turn of mind during the first four centuries after Christ, they find Plato more congenial. It was the Syriac-speaking Church to the east of Antioch which, in the centuries after Antioch itself had ceased to be important as an intellectual centre, adopted Aristotelian logical method wholeheartedly for reasons which are not in all respects clear and which are certainly complex, and then elevated a serviceable logical tool into a closed system such as Aristotle himself might well have repudiated. It was the Syrian Church that transmitted the entire Aristotelian corpus to the Arab world,[1] and so played an important rôle in saving Aristotle for the west.[2] But in this Antioch itself played no part. Indeed it can be said that Alexandria, that nursery of Platonists, contributed demonstrably more to the study of Aristotle than was ever true of Antioch.[3]

Although Antiochene Christianity was biblical and historical rather than philosophical, it did not exist in a philosophical vacuum. Syria and Palestine, though inferior to Athens and Alexandria as centres of philosophy, had made a contribution that was far from negligible and whose continuity over several centuries suggests vitality in its philosophical tradition. We may pass in brief review the names of Antiochus of Ascalon, who died in the first century B.C.; Nicolaus of Damascus, historian as well as philosopher, whose adaptations of Aristotle excited the Syrians four hundred years later to make a Syriac translation of his work;[4] Nichomachus of Gerasa in the second century A.D., concerned in his *Theological Arithmetic* with Pythagorean number mysticism;[5] Numenius of Apamea, an important and

96

influential second-century figure in the development of Platonism;[6] the formidable figure of Porphyry, born about 232 at Tyre, through whose eyes
later centuries read his master Plotinus, and whose *Isagoge* to Aristotle's
Categories was to become the almost obligatory approach for Syrian study
of Aristotelian logic;[7] Iamblichus, from Chalcis in Syria, who died about
336, an important systematizer of the work of his predecessors;[8] and four
of the seven philosophers who went from Athens to Persia when Justinian
closed the school of Athens in 529, namely one Syrian, two Phoenicians
and one from Gaza.[9] This succession of notable philosophers over several
centuries does not suggest that the study of philosophy was uncongenial to
thinking minds east of the Mediterranean, nor that the study of theology
in Antioch during that period could have been pursued in isolation from
the currents of philosophical thought. From the first century Christian
thinking had been under the greatest debt to Philo Judaeus for his integration of Platonic concepts into the structure of Judaeo-Christian thought.
It may be doubted how far he was an original thinker, but the influence of
his Platonized Judaism was of seminal importance.[10] The Platonism of the
Middle and Neo-Platonists was derived not only from Plato himself, but
from an eclectic blend of the more mystical elements of Plato's thought
with Aristotelian logic and theology and to some extent with Stoicism,[11]
but the Aristotelian and Stoic elements were introductions into what was
in essence a metaphysical structure derived from Plato.

In a cultural *milieu* that was predominantly Platonist, a Christian could
of course be open to Platonist influence without being aware of it, and it
could find a place in his unexpressed assumptions particularly in respect of
elements in Platonist thought which were not altogether inconsistent with
a Christian standpoint. The doctrine of transcendent Ideas, fundamental to
any kind of Platonism, may be taken as an example. The concept of Ideas is
developed through the Platonic dialogues to demonstrate the class of transcendent entities or universals distinct from sensible things, 'patterns, as
it were, fixed in the nature of things. The other things are made in their
image.'[12] The Ideas are alone completely objective, separate from particular existing things, changeless, eternal.[13] The craftsman mending a broken
shuttle is making a copy of 'the Idea according to which he made the
other shuttle', and the Idea of a shuttle is 'precisely what a shuttle is'.[14] So
too every beautiful thing shares in the absolute beauty of the Idea of the
beautiful;[15] a bed and table share in the Ideas of bed and of table.[16] These
universals are 'given' elements in our knowledge, their influence spreading
downwards into the fragmented, dissolving world of physical things. In the
attempt to apprehend the Ideas, the human mind has to ascend: thus in the
Republic[17] Socrates plots geometrical points along a straight line to illustrate
the ascent of reason from the lowest realm of unrelated images to the higher
realm of physical perception of related objects, thence to mathematical

entities of which the physical objects are images, thence to the realm of
Ideas, of which the mathematical entities are themselves a kind of mythi-
cal presentation. This is the process of dialectic.[18] In the *Phaedrus*[19] the
dialectical method is defined as the uniting under one Idea of separated
particulars by means of synthesis. Dialecticians thus rise from the particular to the universal by practice of the logic which is 'the keystone of the
whole structure of knowledge'.[20] Man is born into this world with a soul
reincarnated from a previous life in which there has already been some
degree of apprehension of the Ideas.[21] The soul is reborn with recollection
of the Ideas. The dialectical process is a ladder of ascent only for those
who have undergone the rigorous intellectual training that fits the few to
be philosophers, but every man is born with innate knowledge upon which
he acts constantly and blindly in everyday acts of recognition of objects.
Dialectic is a method of achieving fuller apprehension of what is already
known to be there. The Ideas are the end term of a journey of rediscovery.
The difficulties inherent in Plato's doctrine of Ideas are recognized with
remarkable objectivity in the *Parmenides*, anticipating many of the objections to be raised by Aristotle.[22] Prominent among these difficulties is the
precise definition of the relation of particular to universal, which is not
sufficiently covered by terms such as 'shadow' or 'imitation'. It was to
fill this gap that Plato's philosophical descendents filled the cosmos with
hierarchies of semi-divine beings, developing the original conception away
from strict dialectic in the direction of the mystical and spiritual realm. The
mystical element had been increasingly present in Plato's own thought,[23]
but by the Christian era had gone far beyond anything envisaged by Plato.
This was the cultural atmosphere breathed by educated Christians, and it
did not demand too great a side-step for them to express scriptural data in
terms of late Platonism. Christian adoption of Platonism could take the
form of conscious use of Platonist categories to enable Christian doctrine
to be presented to the pagan world, or it could be an unconscious assumption of common factors. In the work of eastern Christian theologians we
may look for such unstated assumptions at points of stress, where we are
made aware of the presence of an extraneous or distorting element present
in an argument.

We may notice, as an example of residual Platonism in a setting of Christian doctrine, the twofold nature of Theodore of Mopsuestia's account of
the sinfulness of Adam.[24] The first of the two strands of doctrine follows
the traditional interpretation of the Genesis narrative: Adam was created
sinless, and through spiritual pride and ambition rebelled against the divine
will and fell into a state of arrogant self-will, that is the state of sin. The
result of this fall was the sentence of mortality passed upon him.[25] The
sentence of mortality was inherited by his offspring but not his guilt, for
to Theodore the responsibility of human will for its own actions and its

own guilt must be maintained. Mortality can be inherited but not guilt. Side by side with this in Theodore's teaching there lies a different strand which shows Adam as created mortal in readiness for the educative process which was to follow, but mortality carries with it the necessity of moral weakness, and Adam was helpless when tempted by Satan. Sin is here not the result of free choice of evil but rather of weakness consequent upon possession of a mortal body. Adam's descendants inherit his mortality, by virtue of which they too fall into sin.[26] In the first of these two strands of teaching, sin is the cause of mortality; in the second, mortality is the cause of sin. R. A. Norris traces Theodore's attempt to reconcile these two strands by maintaining that although Adam sinned voluntarily, God knew in advance that he would do so and passed sentence of mortality upon him from the beginning in anticipation of his sin.[27] What is the origin of the idea of mortality carrying with it the inevitability of sin? It is certainly not part of Christian tradition that matter is essentially evil, and the roots of the idea should be sought somewhere in the Platonist tradition. In the Socratic dialogues there is a consistent dualism of soul and body, though it varies in its intensity: perhaps the *Phaedo* puts the matter most strongly, with its emphasis upon the grossness of the material body, its obtrusive presence and its untrustworthiness. The aim of human activity must be to achieve total detachment from the body.[28] Among the Middle Platonists, Numenius expresses most powerfully the idea that matter is wholly separate from God and is the physical manifestation of evil.[29] His successors in the Platonist tradition considerably modified this strain of oriental dualism. To Plotinus the individual soul is a remote stage of the outflow of energy from the One, and in its turn the irrational level of the soul transmits to the body something of its life,[30] and the body unites with the soul in experience of bodily passions. Evil originates in the body and communicates its weakness to the irrational soul.[31] This is less radical than Numenius' teaching in its separation of soul and body. Porphyry associates the soul more closely with Intelligence than Plotinus had done, and the body remains a distraction and hindrance to man's highest function of contemplation, and returns at the end to the physical sphere from which it originated.[32] It is not possible to identify among the later Platonists a precise source for Theodore's view of the evil inherent in material existence, and probably we can go no further than to recognize it as simply an element of generally Platonist provenance which remains as an extraneous element in its biblical setting.

The diffusion of Platonism in eastern Christianity during the first few centuries may be seen in its permeation of the thought not only of Theodore but also of those in radical opposition to his christological teaching. The fragments that remain of the proceedings at the trial of Paul of Samosata in 268 are sufficient to show that his Antiochene judges maintained a generally Platonist view of the relation of soul to body. The ontological

separation of soul and body is expressed in fragment 16,[33] in which man
is described as being composed of flesh and of 'somebody' within – the
'interior man' of fragment 30. The soul-complex is the real person encased
in a fleshly covering. At the date of the council which condemned Paul,
the Middle Platonist schools were teaching the essential oneness of all souls,
a sharing of the outpoured energy of the One, by diminishing degrees but
still a real sharing down to the lowest level of soul, permitting transmigration
of the human soul to the bodies of animals and birds.[34] The human soul
contains all the higher stages of the world of spirit, the divine hypostases.[35]
The *Acta* of 268 are too fragmentary to enable us to trace any direct connection between the bishops at Antioch and the pagan Platonists, and
direct connection is in any event improbable, but the idea of some degree
of 'interpermeability' within the spiritual realm was at any rate a possibility
at that date. It would not have been thought absurd in philosophical circles
to hold that divine spirit could reside in a human soul. The bishops were
not of course saying precisely this: they described this kind of permeation
of the human by the divine as God being 'con-natured' with the man,[36]
and there was no idea in their minds of a loss of transcendent energy in
the divine descent.[37] But their teaching has a Platonist ring to it.

Something of the same sort is true of the teaching of Apollinarius at
Antioch in the following century. In his defence of Monophysite christology he employs a number of concepts which are associated with the Neo-
Platonism of his time. His use of the idea of a tripartite division of the
soul[38] goes back to Plato himself and was current in later Platonism. Plotinus, though not consistent in the matter, writes of the tripartite soul,
rational, sensory and vegetative,[39] in which the rational element is man's
link with Intelligence. Albinus takes up the hint given by Plato in the
Phaedrus[40] and distinguishes three faculties in the soul.[41] As a Christian,
and specifically as a Monophysite, Apollinarius is committed to a view of
the intermingling of soul and body which forbids denigration of the body,
but there remains a substratum of dualism in his thinking which is a common factor in all late Platonist writing. Plato's image of the charioteer
driving a rebellious team is echoed in Apollinarius' conception of the
rational soul controlling the body. The nature of the rational soul is to
tend towards its source in God and to conform itself to God's will; nevertheless it is linked to its lower soul and to its body, and even without the
attention it has to bestow upon the latter in its capacity of controller, it is
subject to mutability and weakness and can itself be mastered by the body.
The grace of God is thus not an arbitrary force compelling man to act
against his own will, but an attractive force seeking to draw man in the
direction which it is his true destiny to follow.[42] This has striking parallels
in Plotinus. He writes of the body not as a prison but as an unstable element
demanding intervention and control by the rational soul,[43] and in the atten-

tion it bestows upon the body the soul may lose its proper orientation towards the realm of Intelligence and become so preoccupied with the body that it becomes subject to rebirth. For the rational soul is derived from the outflow from the One, and as the expression of its Intelligible archetype it is subject to some degree of determination[44] which takes the form of an innate tendency towards the good. In so far as such language can be used of the One, the motivation of its process of emanation is good will.[45] The emanation, as it recedes or falls, experiences the urge to return, since every being seeks to return to its cause,[46] and the true freedom of the being lies in its conformity with the will of the One. The fragmented soul yearns upward, and its freedom consists in its following that yearning rather than the downward attraction forced upon it by the body to which it is attached. *Mutatis mutandis* this account of human freedom and of grace is not far from the way in which Apollinarius treats the matter. The connection of Apollinarius with Platonism should be seen in terms of parallels rather than precise influences.

It is in keeping with these indirect Platonist parallels that when Antiochene writers made specific references to Plato they should generally express approval. Theodoret's *Graecorum Affectionum Curatio* singles out Plato for praise. It is Plato, 'the prince of philosophers', who is quoted to demonstrate the irrelevance of stylistic grace when the truth is at issue[47] – he whom Theodoret had already praised for his own mastery of style.[48] The mutual contradictions of philosophers are admitted by Plato, 'the first of the philosophers',[49] as are the errors of the Greeks in paying homage to man-made gods.[50] On the subject of creation Plato is right in saying that its purpose is that the creatures should be like their creator;[51] that the cosmos was created not of necessity nor to furnish the creator with praise from his creatures,[52] but out of the good will of the creator; that the cosmos derives not only its outward form but its essence from its creator.[53] Theodoret quotes the *Timaeus* on creation in time,[54] and acclaims this as a 'marvellous passage'. Plato presents us with the Word of God as the agent of creation,[55] and after stepping aside to quote Euripides, Theodoret returns gratefully to Plato, 'for I approve when he uses terms similar to our own concerning the fate of the cosmos'.[56] Plato writes correctly of the providence of God controlling the cosmos;[57] he pays heed to Moses on the subject of punishment;[58] he writes of the rejoicing of the blessed.[59]

Theodoret quotes or makes an identifiable reference to over a hundred and fifty passages of Plato. He refers unambiguously to only three passages of Aristotle: *Topica* v.3, concerning which Theodoret repeats what he has read in Clement of Alexandria about Aristotle calling faith 'the criterion of knowledge;[60] *de Anima* ii.2, concerning Aristotle's refusal to include plants in the category of animals;[61] and *Nicomachean Ethics* i.8, in which Aristotle includes worldly property and health among his requirements for goodness,[62] a matter on which he is compared unfavourably with Plato. Among the Peripatetics, Aristoxenus is quoted for his view of the character of Socrates,[63] and Aristocles is credited with two biographical trivialities concerning Aristotle.[64] Later Platonists receive more generous notice. Porphyry is quoted as evidence for the failure of philosophy to attain absolute truth,[65] and a catena of quotations from his work supports Theodoret's case against the gods,[66] against sacrifices[67] and against oracles.[68] In the same way he makes use of Plotinus[69] and Numenius.[70]

Theodoret's sympathetic use of Platonist sources does not blind him to the fact that they can also be cited as hostile to Christianity. Porphyry's hostility[71] is turned to good account, for it strengthens Theodoret's own case to be able to draw support even from his opponents.[72] Nor does Plato himself escape censure: he is accused of vacillating in the matter of the use of legend,[73] of mingling truth and error,[74] of permitting worship of the gods,[75] of teaching the creative power of the Word without reference to the Father.[76] Nor should it be over-looked that Theodoret's generally favourable estimate of Platonism reflects to a great extent the bias of those from whom he derived his knowledge of Platonist texts, namely Eusebius and Clement of Alexandria. Of the passages to which we have drawn attention, almost all are derived from Eusebius' *Praeparatio Evangelica*, usually much abbreviated, and there is little evidence that Theodoret had read any Platonist texts at first hand other than Plotinus' *Enneads* book iii, Porphyry's *History of Philosophy*, and *Life of Pythagoras*, and possibly Plato's *Symposium*.[77] Theodoret is not a philosopher at all, and there is no attempt in his work, any more than in that of Eusebius, to grapple with the major issues argued by the philosophers. He presents issues that are central to his own position and uses suitable passages from philosophical texts when they support his own case. The Platonists are more useful in support than are the Aristotelians, and consequently receive far more sympathetic notice in the *Curatio*. His use of their work suggests that the Christianity preached in Antioch during the fifth century was in general more closely aligned with Platonism than with Aristotelianism. It may be argued that his *Eranistes* is evidence to the contrary, since it concludes with a series of demonstrations, loosely syllogistic in form, of Theodoret's arguments against Dioscuros of Alexandria.[78] Since the time of Porphyry, Aristotelian logic had become closely woven into the fabric of Neo-Platonism, and it is probable that Theodoret would have been hard-pressed to disentangle Aristotelian elements from Platonist, and that argumentation of this kind was part of an educated Christian's armoury without specific attribution to its origin. Antiochene Christianity was in its essence unphilosophical,[79] and its innocence of serious philosophical thinking is paradoxically the measure of its reputed debt to Aristotle. The Antiochene characteristically thought in terms of history and Scripture, and it is in relation to these that we have observed the close attention to *phenomena* and to detailed examination of the facts of each matter under consideration, which is held to be Aristotelian in spirit. But we may look in vain for an attempt to base their historical or scriptural standpoint upon a logical or metaphysical foundation derived from Aristotle. The Antiochenes appear to have been unaware of the possibility of such support or uninterested in making use of it.

The eastern Church has little to show of the influence of Stoic thought,[80] but apart from traces of its presence in the later transformations of Platonism and Aristotelianism, there are signs of its presence in the work of Theophilus in the second century and of Nemesius in the fourth. R. M. Grant identifies Stoic elements in Theophilus' *Ad Autolycum* i.4, on the attributes of God, and i.5, on God's presence making itself felt through his works.[81] In the latter passage the presence of soul is inferred from the visible manifestation of its working in a human body, from that of a steersman inferred from the passage of a ship, from that of the sun from the glare in the sky, from that of seeds within a pomegranate from the evidence of the visible rind, from that of a king from the evidence of the existence of his laws: so too the divine Spirit, the principle of cohesion in the cosmos, is to be inferred from the structure and behaviour of the material creation around us. Stoic elements are also present in Theophilus' distinction of the Word internal within God (*logos endiathetos*)[82] and the Word expressed by God (*logos prophorikos*). To Theophilus the Word is impersonal, an attribute of the Father analogous to his wisdom, strength and power,[83] and only attains limited independence when it is emitted with his wisdom for the purpose of creation. Whether Theophilus was aware of his debt to Stoicism may be doubted,[84] for he seems unaware of the moral nobility inculcated by Stoicism and can only castigate Stoics for sexual licence.[85] A closer contact with a Stoic source has been argued in the case of Nemesius of Emesa's dependence upon Posidonius, though here again the element may have reached Nemesius through an intermediary, in this case perhaps Origen or Galen.[86] Throughout *De Natura Hominis* Galen's influence is felt, on occasions rising to the surface in direct quotation.[87] Ideas common to Nemesius and Posidonius appear in *De Natura Hominis* i.2, where Nemesius places man on the boundary between the intelligible and the phenomenal orders, giving a unity to the whole of creation which he sees as arguing a single creator. So too in all animate creatures there is a unity between insentient elements such as hair and sentient tissues, flesh and bodily organs. The wholeness and unity of man is constantly being pressed upon us by Nemesius; thus he rejects the Neo-Platonist conception of some measure of separation of man's higher intellectual faculties from his lower vegetative faculties of soul in favour of a more unified Stoic psychology. At i.5 there can be felt the influence of Posidonius in the discussion of the greater power possessed by plants in the earliest days of creation; again at i.6, where Nemesius emphasizes the balance of Nature in man's having to make for himself clothes and shelter, and in having to seek the help of medicine to correct the balance of his constitution; again at xlii.60, where he puts forward as evidence of a creator the perfect balance of the cosmos as seen in the regularity of its patterns and functions, the regular recurrence of the rise and fall of stars, seasons, day and night. Nemesius rejects strongly any conception of fate, and argues that Providence on the contrary leaves room for human free will. He cannot follow Stoic doctrine to its ethical ideal of freedom from moral struggle: the full and free functioning of human will is essential to Nemesius' conception of human morality and is at an opposite moral pole from Stoic *ataraxia*.[88] Nemesius' over-riding aim, to demonstrate the unity of man's being, is set in a mosaic texture of references to earlier philosophical and scientific thought, sometimes explicit, sometimes indirectly suggested, and probably seldom derived from first-hand knowledge of the works in question. Thus there are suggestions of Plato's *Timaeus*,[89] and rather more definite traces of Aristotle's *Historia Animalium*,[90] *De Generatione et Corruptione*,[91] *De Partibus Animalium*,[92] *De Anima*[93] and *Ethica Nichomachea*.[94] However indirect the route by which Nemesius received knowledge of Plato, Aristotle, Posidonius and Galen, his work reveals a mind that is more genuinely interested in matters of psychology, biology and cosmology than any that we have noticed in preceding pages. He is perhaps not a philosopher, but is able to appreciate philosophical work when he reads it.

The philosophical tone of voice becomes still more marked when we turn south to the work of the Christian philosophers of Gaza in the generation following Theodoret, for here we find topics followed through at some length in a real attempt to meet opposing arguments on their own philosophical ground. Aeneas (d. 518) and Zacharias Rhetor (d. after 536) adopt Plato's dialogue form to argue the immortality of the soul, the resurrection of the body[95] and the doctrine of creation,[96] and pass in review a good deal of current Neo-Platonist thinking on these topics in addition to that of earlier philosophers. Aeneas' interlocutor, Theophrastus, an Athenian, maintains a Platonist view of the pre-existence and immortality of the soul as the Form of the body, ending with the death of the body. Axitheus, the Christian disputant, agrees with Theophrastus that there is much to commend in the teaching of Heracleitus, Pythagoras and Plato, and thinks it best to 'pass by Aristotle in silence',[97] but criticizes various Platonist doctrines of reincarnation – that human souls are reborn into animals appropriate to their character, kites, wolves or asses; or that souls are reborn into beings of their own kind, a wolf becoming again a wolf, an ass becoming an ass, and so on, as is argued by Plotinus, Porphyry, Iamblichus and others. It is no punishment for a lustful man to become an ass, but merely an opportunity for further lust: it is like a thief being introduced into a temple and invited to help himself to its contents. The teaching is reduced to absurdity: on this principle Odysseus should be reborn as an ant since he is prudent and industrious.[98] If we are reborn, why do we remember nothing of our previous life? Axitheus brings the dialogue to its main theme, that death is no evil but a translation of the whole person to a higher state, the true evil being the sinful will of man that can reverse this beneficent destiny. Human freedom is essential to an argument in favour of a beneficent Providence.[99] Human desire and emotion are necessary effects of man's possession of a body, and need direction by the higher faculty of the soul if they are not to take charge like frightened horses in the absence of a driver. Discipline, education, law, reason, study of the good, human intercourse and knowledge all help to direct the body to its proper functions.[100] The good man does not fear death, for since his life is ordered and controlled he does not change into something else at death but rises to 'the first principle'.[101] This enables us to find moral justification in the apparent injustices of human life. The conditions of each man's life are ordained by the foresight of Providence.[102] The doctrine of immortality may seem to imply that all individual souls are part of a single universal soul. All things are indeed one, and each fills the whole, as Plotinus says, but only in the manner in which each separate shoot of a tree contains the whole tree in itself. From a single seed spring many, yet all are one without any one being identical with its original.[103] Every single entity has its own beginning: only God exists in eternity before creation, as Porphyry, Plotinus and Plato teach.[104] But argues Theophrastus, do not commentators on Plato interpret his teaching on creation in terms of natural causation, as a body can be said to create its own shadow? Logically, replies Axitheus, a creator must precede his creation.[105] God's willing of the cosmos to ultimate dissolution does not imply negligence or failure, for dissolution is the inevitable end of a composite body: the individual elements of matter are mutually hostile and fall apart.[106] A human person is composed of matter and Form, and the matter suffers dissolution just as grain falling into soil appears to die, but it dies in order to live again, for the human soul calls it from its sleep.[107] The tone of this dialogue differs from that of Theodoret or Eusebius in that it shows a philosophically-inclined mind pursuing Christian subject matter, rather than a biblically-inclined mind introducing quotations from philosophers on occasions when they can be made to fit. The same is true of Zacharias' *Disputatio*, which is largely dependent upon Aeneas for its contents. Both writers give us a restatement of Christian doctrine in Platonist terms, pursuing a course dictated not by scriptural *data* but rather by what can be inferred from the nature of substances, from causation, temporality, necessity and so on. Logic forbids Zacharias to draw certain conclusions;[108] a certain argument is based upon a false premiss;[109] syllogistic reasoning must be observed (contemporaneity can only be predicated of material objects; matter cannot be predicated of God; therefore God is not contemporaneous with creation).[110] The pagan physician puts forward a geometrical demonstration of the eternity of the cosmos: the sphere is the perfect figure, having neither beginning nor end; the cosmos is spherical, therefore it has neither beginning nor end. The Christian attacks the major premiss: a geometrical figure has its beginning in a geometrical definition, in this case definition of a centre and a radius.[111] These are the terms of reference, and we are far indeed from Theodoret's scorn of logical spiders' webs. It is such philosophical terms that we frequently encounter in religious disputation when we look further eastward from the Mediterranean coast.

It can hardly be accidental that the growth of western philosophical thinking in eastern Syria and Mesopotamia coincided with their adoption of Theodore of Mopsuestia as 'the Interpreter' of theology to the east, and that Theodoret attempted to clarify his diphysite christology in *Eranistes* by syllogistic reasoning. The Monophysite controversy demanded that disputants should argue in philosophical terms. In about 520 Severus of Antioch begins his *Contra Impium Grammaticum*, levelled at John Philoponus, in the manner of an elementary commentary on Aristotle's *Organon*, spelling out the ABC of universals and particulars with a care that almost suggests that Philoponus needs teaching his business. He was, however, challenging a formidable philosopher on his own ground.[112] The argument turns on the distinction between universals and particulars and on the terminology by which they may be expressed. The term *ousia* is a universal term signifying 'genus' or 'kind'; *hypostasis* is a limiting term signifying a single entity or person.[113] Thus 'God' is a generic term common to Father, Son and Spirit, each of whom has his own distinct hypostasis, having their 'being' in common but differing in the manner in which each enjoys that being – ingenerate, begotten or proceeding. The complexity of a man's soul-body nature does not preclude him from being a single hypostasis; so too is the incarnate Christ a single hypostasis, though a complex of divine and human natures.[114] The grammarian's error lies in thinking that the divine element in Christ consists of the whole *ousia* of Godhead, whereas in fact it consists of the individual hypostasis of sonship.[115] The union is between two particulars, the divine Word and the child of the virgin Mary, not between Godhead and Manhood, as though the whole genus 'Man' were composite with the divine element in Christ. If the grammarian really means that the generic substances are united, he is saying that the whole of the Trinity is incarnate in the whole of the human race.[116] He will argue against us that each hypostasis partakes of the whole, that the divinity of God is not divided up into three parts, but each partakes of the whole without diminution of it; that each hypostasis of the Trinity is perfect God.[117] But Peter, Paul and John can share in one genus and substance of manhood without each individually constituting all mankind. In other words, what is true of the universal is not necessarily true of each particular. To say that the flesh of Paul is consubstantial with the substance of all human kind is not to say that he participates in the lives of Peter and John.[118] The grammarian's error lies in a confusion of hypostases under cover of a single *ousia*, the error of Sabellius and of Marcellus.[119] It was all too easy to apply the closure to a dispute by throwing at one's opponent the names of notorious heretics, but the Monophysite issue was not at bottom a matter of mud-slinging but of careful definition of terms, and it has many times been observed that if the definitions had been more careful there would have been less acrimony. Severus is here pressing careful definition upon a widely-acclaimed Aristotelian commentator who has perhaps been guilty of allowing a brilliant hypothesis suited to seminar discussion to overflow into public debate. The great patriarch dispatches the wayward philosopher with ponderous lucidity, and though he cannot refrain from shouting 'Sabellian!' after him, he has shown how keenly aware he is that Monophysite doctrine is a philosophical matter to be defended in philosophical terms. But Antioch was by now within a quarter of a century of destruction at Persian hands, and the reign of philosophy within its walls was to be short-lived. The immediate future of Greek philosophy was to lie further east.

That Syria early recognized the philosophical nature of the Monophysite question is suggested by its demand for the logical work of Aristotle which deals particularly with the points at issue. During the second quarter of the fifth century Aristotelian philosophy was being taught at Edessa.[120] The British Library codex dated 411 containing a Syriac version of Eusebius' *Theophany* contains also a Syriac commentary on Aristotle's *Categories* of Alexandrian provenance.[121] The work of Hībā in making Theodore available to the Syriac world was accompanied by an upsurge of interest in Peripatetic thought, and Hībā's pupils Kumi and Proba were instrumental in securing its naturalization within the sphere of eastern theology. Proba translated Aristotle's *De Hermeneutica* and *Analytica Priora*, and fragments remain of his commentaries on Porphyry's *Eisagoge*[122] and on the two works of Aristotle that he had translated. It will be noted that the association of Aristotle's logic with Porphyry's interpretation of it is already present in the fifth century: the two became virtually synonymous in the Syrian mind, and when they write of Aristotle as 'the philosopher' they habitually mean Aristotle as filtered through Neo-Platonist understanding of his thought. The decline of the school of Edessa and the rise of Nisibis served only to shift the centre of Aristotelian studies further east.

Paulos, known to the west as Paul the Persian, who studied in Nisibis in the early sixth century before his election to the bishopric of the same city, shows marked Aristotelian characteristics in what remains of his work.

His lectures on the interpretation of the Scriptures were transmitted to the west by Junilius *De Partibus Divinae Legis*.[123] In the manner of the Aristotelian Categories, Paulos subdivides the Scriptures into four main types, history, prophecy, proverbs and didactic writing (i.3–6), and goes on to analyse their authority, authorship, quality, arrangement and subject matter (i.7–11). The subject matter falls into three divisions, God, the present age and the future age,[124] each division being subdivided; for example his treatment of Providence in the present age subdivides it into the two categories, general and special, and the special category is itself subdivided under five heads: Providence revealed by divine law, by divine works, by divine words, by angelic intervention and by human rule (ii.3–10), each division and subdivision illustrated by scriptural citation. It is the work of an analytical mind attempting to impose order upon the heterogeneous contents of scripture.[125] In the first half of the sixth century Sargis of Riš'aina, who was trained as a Monophysite and defected to the Chalcedonian party,[126] wrote extensively on Aristotelian logic,[127] including work on the *Categories*, on the relation of the *Analytica Priora* to the rest of Aristotle's work, on the *schema* in the *Analytics* and on *De Hermeneutica* iii; he translated into Syriac the pseudo-Aristotle *De Mundo*, a *De Anima* no longer extant in Greek, Porphyry's *Eisagoge* with the Aristotelian *Categories*, a philosophical work on parts of speech and a treatise on agreement and disagreement and on the concept of Being. A. Vööbus tells us that Sargis was the first to translate from Greek into Arabic.[128] The Nestorian Aba of Karkar, who was influential in the court of Khosrau II between 590 and 628, made use of his knowledge of Greek by writing a commentary on the complete logical work of Aristotle.[129] Barhadbešabba's *Cause of the Foundation of the Schools*[130] contains an extended treatment of the doctrines of God and creation couched in the unmistakable analytical tone of Aristotle. Just as for a created being the term 'was' is anterior to 'is', so for a non-created being 'eternal being' is anterior to 'is', and is the cause of any being of which 'is' alone can be used, since if it 'is' and has not 'eternal being' it had a beginning. God himself is Being; the creature possesses Being only derivatively. Creatures may be divided into the following classes: material, animate, living, reasonable, spiritual – in which Barhadbešabba appears to divide the human soul unscripturally into vegetative and rational. These gradations differ not in respect of their generic Being, but in respect of their particular modes of Being: the bull is superior to the stone in its life and sensory faculties; the angel is superior to man in his natural immortality; God is superior to all in his essence and eternity. Man is linked to God by his faculty of reason, which functions through three faculties, mind, sense and thought. Desire, anger and will are under the direction of Intelligence, purifying the animal forces of the soul and leading man to wisdom.[131] The tone is Aristotelian, the subject-matter sometimes Neo-Platonist, as we would expect. The same Aristotelian tone is present in Ahoudemmeh's treatise *On Man*.[132] The soul possesses two faculties, rational and vital, from the second of which derive anger and desire. Desire lies between the two poles of moderation and extremity,[133] anger between the poles of fear and bravery.[134] The rational soul possesses faculties of knowledge, reason, intelligence and thought. Ahoudemmeh places each of these faculties between its own poles,[135] in relation to the others and in relation to will as servants of a master.[136] He analyses the interaction of soul and body and the springs of human behaviour and action: 'Everything lies between opposites.'[137] He moves on to the sensory experience of man, which supplies information about the world to man's body 'from below' just as the rational soul influences its movements 'from above'. The senses are each linked to a bodily organ, and Ahoudemmeh goes into some anatomical detail to place each organ correctly in relation to the others.[138] Thus he can demonstrate that by its situation in the body the stomach (desire) can inflame the kidneys (concupiscence) or the liver (anger).[139] He gives examples of good and bad actions in which the various faculties of soul, senses and body all dovetail in playing their respective parts.[140] 'A person is thus fused into a unity by the action of soul and body',[141] the whole being analysed as lying under the hegemony of reason and in accordance with the Aristotelian doctrine of the Mean.

The *Liber de Unione* of Babai in the seventh century shows an Aristotelian cast of mind in its structure and contents. The first book of the twelve is concerned with the logical and metaphysical foundations of the enquiry into the christological question which is Babai's main concern. God is beyond man's apprehension since he is beyond space and time, and therefore he cannot be spoken of in terms signifying relation to other beings. Only beings within space and time are susceptible of relational terms, and if God came within the scope of such terminology he would not be God.[142] Then what kind of language is appropriate? Descriptive language is permissible on the condition that it is understood to refer not to God's being but only to his observed activity. Terms such as 'light', 'life', 'spirit' are to be used not as describing accidental qualities possessed by him, but as descriptions of his creatorship, for these are blessings given to us and are to be understood in relation to his activity, not his being. God is being; God is life; God is spirit: these may be inferred from his revealed activity, but he remains incomprehensible to beings who have not the vocabulary to define one who is beyond space and time.[143] But even analogical language is to be used with caution, for an analogy is not identical in all respects with its subject. We may talk meaningfully about the nature of Adam, even though he is beyond our observation, for we can observe human nature in men around us, but to use the term 'Word' of the second person of the Trinity is not the same use of language. 'A mind is not without a word, nor a word without a mind.'[144] This inference from human minds to the divine mind may seem to be using language in the same way as when we make the transition from observed human nature to Adam's nature, but the use of the term 'mind' of God is itself analogical and cannot be a direct description of what he is. Babai exercises the same care in the use of language about God consistently through this long book, and constantly warns his reader to be on his guard against the careless language of his opponents, Cyril, Henana, the gnostics, the Theopaschites, the emperor Justinian. To whatever extent this kind of discussion of logical and metaphysical preliminaries is derived in detail from Aristotle's *Organon* and *Metaphysics*, its attitude of mind is Aristotelian. Philosophy had by the time at which Babai was writing become closely integrated into Syrian theology.[145]

In the judgement of A. Vööbus, the School of Nisibis lost its intellectual vigour early in the seventh century,[146] and as other schools such as those at Seleucia-Ctesiphon and Baghdad rose in public esteem, so the literary output of Nisibis diminished. The work of translating and commenting continued elsewhere. Severus Sebokht (d. 666/7) translated into Persian a commentary on *De Hermeneutica*, and was probably the editor of the Syriac text on which was based the Persian *Compendium of Logic*. He produced original work on Aristotle's *Rhetoric* and *Analytica Priora*.[147] Athanasius of Baladh (d. 686) translated Porphyry's *Eisagoge* into Syriac. Henanišo (d. 699/700) wrote a commentary on Aristotle's *Analytics*.[148] Išoʻbokht of Rewardašir, who was ordained before the end of the seventh century, wrote on Aristotle's *Categories* and on the concept of possibility.[149] Jacob of Edessa (640–708), described by Maurice Brière as a polygraph who left his mark on many aspects of Syriac literature,[150] translated the *Categories*. Silvanus of Qardu in the first half of the century wrote on the *Eisagoge*, the *Categories*, *De Hermeneutica* and Neo-Platonist philosophy.[151]

From the eighth century we have commentaries on Aristotelian logic by Mar Aba II (d. 751) and Dawid bar Paulos, and translations by the Maronite Theophilus of Edessa (d. 785),[152] and the *Dialectica* of John of Damascus, who was ordained before 735.[153] This work constitutes the first part of *Fons Scientiae*, and is neither a translation of the *Categories* nor a commentary, but rather a free paraphrase in which he picks out key passages from the original, omits the accompanying discussion and on occasions adds a little of his own. He reads Aristotle's text in a curious order, reaching nearly the end of *Cat.* v, for example, and then retracing his steps to the end of *Cat.* iv and the opening of *Cat.* v. He is to some extent dependent upon Porphyry.[154]

We have followed in outline the course of philosophical work in the east as far as the ninth century and may leave it at a point of great importance in the history of philosophy, the work of Hunain ibn Ishaq and his son

Ishaq ibn Hunain at Baghdad, who between them spanned almost the complete century. They completed a massive programme of translation from Greek into Syriac and thence into Arabic, including not only a great part of Aristotle's work but also Plato, John Philoponus, Alexander of Aphrodisias, Themistios, Olympiodorus, Simplicius, Iamblichus, Porphyry, Proclus and perhaps Theophrastus.[155] The Arab world was not generally conversant with Greek and depended upon Syriac intermediaries,[156] and it was of importance for the future understanding of Plato that Hunain collected and transmitted interpretations of Plato's thought untouched by the Neo-Platonist tradition.[157] Hunain and Ishaq were neither the first translators of Greek philosophy into Arabic nor the only ones, but their work was of major importance in the process of transmission. From this point onwards Aristotle belonged to the Arab world.[158]

The eastern Church needed Aristotle for his logic: it is the *Organon*, or parts of it, which occurs repeatedly in Syriac translations and commentaries from the fifth century onwards, filtered through Porphyry to the extent that in the Syrian mind the two were virtually inseparable. Nestorians, Monophysites, Maronites and Chalcedonians were alike obliged to fight their doctrinal battles with the weapons forged by the Neo-Platonist Aristotle.[159] But the *Organon* is not the only work of Aristotle which appears in the Syriac lists, nor was the Monophysite controversy the only matter of concern in which the help of Aristotle was valued. Second in importance to the logic, but more important than any other work of Aristotle, was the *Meteorology*. Astronomy had been taught at Edessa in the early fifth century,[160] and from the seventh century we hear of original astronomical work such as that of Aba of Karkar;[161] Silvanos of Qardu's work combatting astrology;[162] Severus Sebokht's work on the darkness and phases of the moon, on the astrolabe,[163] on the constellations, and an astronomically-based cosmography in eighteen chapters, to which he added eight further chapters of answers to questions on astronomy, mathematics and chronology.[164] From the late eighth century Timotheos' work on the stars is recorded by Assemani.[165] Hunain ibn Ishaq in the ninth century wrote a great compilation of medical and astrological knowledge;[166] his son Ishaq translated Aristotle's *Meteorologica* and Alexander of Aphrodisias' commentary upon it, and Theophrastus' *Meteorologica*. Baumstark lists a number of anonymous astrological manuscripts in Syriac; 'Signs of the Sun, Moon and Stars according to the Chaldaeans'; 'the Book of the Victor and the Vanquished', attributed to Aristotle; manuscripts containing interpretations of Daniel and of prophesies attributed to Ezra.[167] We may associate this concern with astronomy and astrology with the fluctuating relations between the Church and the Magian establishment of Persia throughout these centuries. The *Acta* of the martyrs, Syrian and Persian,[168] reveal the demands of the Magians that Christians should worship Ahura Mazda, the sun,[169] under threat of deprivation of rights, financial penalties, destruction of churches or martyrdom.[170] To the Magian the existence of nations, as of individuals, was dependent upon the heavenly bodies, supreme among whom was Ahura Mazda, and since it was demonstrable that the stars followed a determinate course, the life of man was wholly determined by their influence.[171] The Church reacted vigorously to Magian pressure and to its associated astrological beliefs and determinism. A great deal of Christian apologetic, not only in the east, was directed against fatalism, and especially regrettable is the loss of Diodore's work mentioned by Photius.[172] Magical practices, also dependent upon belief in a cosmic sympathy between material and spiritual realms which bound the daemonic sphere as rigidly as the human, were employed to ensure freedom from the grip of fate, and these too were fought by the Church throughout the empire.[173] The continuing hold that astrology and magic exercised upon men's minds is shown in the event at Berytus in the fifth century when the murder of a slave for magical purposes revealed widespread addiction to such practices.[174] In the east Theodore of Mopsuestia wrote against the Magians,[175] and in Syriac we have the work of Elisha bar Quzbaie in early sixth-century Nisibis,[176] and of Johannan de-bet Rabban.[177] The impact of Magian astrology was felt throughout the empire and even took root in Islam: its impact upon the Church was immense. Faced by a religious cult which was closely linked to astronomy and which could to some degree be presented in scientific terms, and which could appeal to Stoic conceptions of an ordered and unified cosmos,[178] the eastern Church perhaps saw a weapon ready to its hand in Aristotle's *De Meteorologica*. If it did not enjoy the immensely wide use that was accorded to the *Organon*, it was used a good deal more widely than the ethical, biological and political work of Aristotle. The Cambridge codex of Nicolaus *On the Philosophy of Aristotle* provides a Syriac compendium of Aristotle's work to supplement the already-translated *Organon*.[179] Versions of *De Caelo* and *De Meteorologica* appear early in its list of Aristotle's works. The tenth-century *Syriac Lexicon* of Abu-l-Hasan bar Bahlul lists seven works of Aristotle, six pertaining to different parts of the *Organon* and the seventh to *De Meteorologica*.[180]

We may perhaps also see an Aristotelian element of intellectual toughness and rationality infused into the perpetual struggle of the eastern Church against the astrological excesses of gnosticism in its various forms, and against the influence of thinkers such as Bardaisan and Mani who to varying degrees were aligned with Christian thought. Here we return to the indefinite region of 'habits of thought' rather than the adoption of specific Aristotelian tenets. Christians were not alone in standing opposed to the irrationality of much gnostic thought, for much of their anti-gnostic polemic can be matched, point by point, in the attack launched upon gnosticism by Plotinus.[181] They join in opposing the gnostic refusal to allow the creation of the cosmos to have been the work of God and hence to allow respect for the material creation as a work of God;[182] they oppose the neglect of moral discipline that derives from the gnostic conception of election to salvation;[183] they oppose the mythological presentation of gnostic doctrine and the refusal to argue rationally.[184] Whether or not Mani is to be classed as a gnostic, Severus attacks him on precisely these points in his Homily cxxiii.[185]

Severus begins characteristically with the fundamental question, what does Mani mean by the term 'principle' when he contrasts his two principles of light and darkness? These principles are held by Mani to be uncreated, eternal, infinite, the cause and root of all. But, says Severus, you cannot maintain two supreme principles of equal status. 'Which of the two shall we say is the cause of the other, in order to attribute to it the name "principle"? Since neither is the root of the other, neither is truly a principle at all.'[186] In any case it is absurd to maintain that darkness is an infinite principle, since Mani's darkness is equated with matter, and matter is finite. The concept of a 'material principle' is a contradiction in terms. But the very concept of 'two principles' is itself contradictory, since that which is separated from something else, as these principles are separate from each other, 'occupies its own place' and not that of its opponent, and is therefore finite, and finite entities are material. How then can these 'finite principles' be uncreated?[187] Further, if these two principles are separate, what holds them apart? We have to introduce a third principle, also uncreated and eternal, which must in its nature be different from the other two principles, and still more principles to separate the third from the first and the second, and so *ad infinitum*. Where does the root of the error lie in this impossible belief? Severus identifies it as lying in Mani's attribution of evil substance to darkness, whereas he should have treated darkness as merely the absence of light, and therefore without substance.[188] Darkness, *heššokha*, is a strongly positive concept to Mani, occupying a geographical region to the south. Mani is thus not thinking rationally at all, but in mythological terms.[189] He must not, then, support his views by reference to the *Timaeus*. Plato was mistaken in attributing eternity to matter, but never made the mistake of attributing evil to matter as Mani does.[190] Darkness being the deprivation of light, we may not blame God if somebody chooses to shut his eyes and exclude the light, nor may we turn darkness into a deity.[191] Similar ideas underlie the mystical aphorisms of Evagrius, which set out somewhat repetitively the content of the Christian *gnosis*.[192] Against dualism of any kind the Unity-in-Trinity of the Godhead is expounded from different angles of approach. Thus at the outset of book i: nothing is opposed to the first good (no eternal second principle), because opposition resides in qualities and qualities in bodies. Opposition can only exist in the realm of creatures, not in that of principles; therefore there

cannot be two opposed principles.[193] Towards the close of book vi Evagrius rejects the introduction of numerical concepts into the Trinity: 'The
blessed Triad is not like a tetrad or a pentad, for these are numerical concepts, whereas the blessed Triad is a simple essence.' 'The numerical triad
is obtained by the sum of units, but the blessed Triad does not exist by
numerical addition, but being a numerical triad.'[194] Since the concept of
number is foreign to the Godhead, the opposition of two eternal and infinite principles is absurd. There is also found in these aphorisms a refusal to
accept the widely-held view of matter as evil. 'By the contemplation of
true knowledge you will find [Him] in everything, because our saviour has
created all things with wisdom.'[195] Intellect contemplates incorporeal and
corporeal beings alike, but how can it do the latter if it has no sensory
organs with which to do it, and how can one then despise the human body
which carries the senses?[196] We find here also the refusal of substantial
existence to darkness, evil and ignorance: death is a secondary consequence of life; sickness a secondary consequence of health; evil of good.
Evil is the sickness and death of the soul.[197] Light and darkness are acci-
dents pertaining to the air; good and evil, knowledge and ignorance, are
accidental to the soul. Good and knowledge are primary, evil and ignorance
secondary.[198] 'Spiritual riches consist in spiritual knowledge, and spiritual
poverty in ignorance, but if poverty is the deprivation of knowledge it is
evident that riches are anterior to poverty, health to sickness.'[199] The Christian mystic admired by the Syrian monks had his doctrine founded upon
philosophical principles clearly opposed to the dualism of gnostic thought,
and he showed them that it is possible to follow the way of enlightenment
into the vision of God without embracing the anti-intellectualism of Valentinus or Bardaisan or Mani. The Origenism of Evagrius may have been too
strong for Syrian taste, but he stood with them against the onslaught of
gnosticism and taught them a spirituality built upon philosophical foundations, and he attempted to argue his position rationally.

There is a further point to be made in relation to the Syrian adoption
of Aristotle. The *Metaphysics* is not a work that ranks high in the Syriac
lists of Aristotle's writings. Nevertheless it was translated and known, and
its contents are too relevant to Nestorian beliefs for it to be credible that
its relevance passed unnoticed. Of the points on which Aristotle disagreed
with Plato, the most important concerns the fundamental Platonic doctrine
of the substantial reality of the universal Ideas and the affinity of particular
objects to the Ideas. Particulars participate in the reality of the Ideas at
far remove, deriving from them their form and their being and whatever
shadowy degree of reality they may possess. This fundamental Platonic
concept was explicitly denied by Aristotle, and the denial constitutes a
major theme of the *Metaphysics*. For Aristotle a universal is not a substantial reality but is simply a philosophical term, a way of denoting a class of

objects. The universal has no separate existence apart from particulars and would not continue to exist if the particulars disappeared, and the notion of particulars participating in the greater reality of the Ideas fails to stand up to examination. What, he asks, are the Platonic Ideas supposed to contribute to the particulars? As regards our knowledge of objects the Ideas are no help, as even Plato himself had suspected,[200] for the Ideas are not actually present in the objects to be understood. Nor do the Ideas contribute to the existence of the objects, since as universals they cannot be present in the objects which participate in them. Further, 'objects are not in any accepted sense derived from the Ideas. To say that the Ideas are patterns, and that objects participate in them, is to use empty phrases and metaphors fit for poetry.' Nor is the relation of a particular object to its Idea a matter of likeness: 'a man may be like Socrates whether Socrates is alive or not'; and a single object may possess attributes which participate in more than one Idea at the same time, as for example a man participating in the Idea 'animal' and the Idea 'two-footed'.[201] Aristotle concludes a lengthy exposition with the statement that 'the Ideas have no bearing whatever' upon our understanding of the causation of particular objects.[202] The universal does not partake of the particular, for since the particulars of one class are not all identical a single universal cannot be attributed to them.[203] There is no justification for the belief in the independent existence of the Ideas in a realm that is 'more real', the reality of particulars depending upon and participating in them.[204] On the contrary, reality is an attribute of each particular thing,[205] for 'each particular thing is one and the same with its essence . . . To have knowledge of the particular is to have knowledge of its essence.'[206] Is it possible to conceive of a house apart from its bricks?[207] 'There is no need to set up an Idea as a pattern . . . The completed whole, such-and-such a form induced in this flesh and these bones, is Callias or Socrates.'[208] The completed whole is the substance and essence of a thing, and we do not need to look outside the thing for the ground of its reality, not even to look for universals, for we know of no universals apart from particular things in which they are manifest, no houses apart from their bricks, no Callias or Socrates apart from their flesh and bones. Aristotle's world is a world of real individual things separated from all other individual things, each one in the process of achieving its full actuality of substance.[209] In actuality the object is at any given moment what it is and nothing else, and potentially is what it might become,[210] and cannot be a composite of more than one substance: it is itself and not something else. If particular things cannot be of composite substance, and if in particular they cannot be composite with the infinite,[211] the bearing of this metaphysical doctrine upon the possibility of a composite Christ, a mingling of the divine and the human, is plain.[212] The residual Platonism found in the early Nestorian texts, e.g. Theodore of Mopsuestia, was an element that could only with difficulty be reconciled to a theology which denied the possibility of hypostatic participation between the divine and the human. They could be reconciled only if the Platonic doctrine of participation were wholly ignored. *Mutatis mutandis*, this is precisely what the Monophysites were obliged to do with Aristotle, for their insistence upon divine-human participation in Christ required them to turn a blind eye to Aristotle's denial of the possibility of such participation, although they could use Aristotle's logic and astronomy. The bearing of this upon Monophysitism is not our concern here. The Nestorians cannot have been unaware of this aspect of Aristotle's philosophy, central to his thought as it is, and it is a matter of surprise that it does not appear more explicitly in their philosophical defence of their position.

Perhaps the greatest contribution that Greek thought made to the Syrian Nestorians was to stiffen their polemic by teaching them to define, to distinguish, to categorize. They may not have seen very clearly what were the pre-Christian Athenian roots from which their Syriac logic books were derived, and they certainly saw Aristotle through late-Platonist eyes and differentiated but little between Pythagorean, Stoic and Platonist elements in what was transmitted to them. They absorbed what Greece had to give because they needed it, and it became integrated into the older structure of their religion, adding a weapon to their intellectual armoury without which the forces of Magianism and gnostic speculation might have overwhelmed them.

6

The human experience of Christ and the salvation of man

The golden age of Antiochene theology lies in the century between the birth of Diodore of Tarsus in about 330 and the death of Theodoret in about 458, the period in which it attained its most complete articulation and during which in particular it developed its christology. During this period we find Diodore, widely held to be the father of Antiochene christology; Theodore, its most systematic and most extreme exponent; Nestorius, its most notorious and its most hated advocate; Chrysostom, its most moderate adherent and the one whose work was best known in the west; Theodoret, its historian; Hībā (Ibas), instrumental in facilitating its dissemination in the east; a formidable company of witnesses. Diodore's claim to paternity needs to be qualified in the important respect that the Antiochene tradition was already in existence in embryo well before his birth. The fourth century received the Antiochene formulation of the doctrine of Christ's nature rough-hewn from its predecessors and shaped it with greater precision.

Before the full formulation of the tradition we find Ignatius of Antioch in the early second century already expressing with great force his opposition to gnostic docetism concerning the reality of Christ's human nature and of his human experience. The letters of Ignatius are not documents in which one would expect to find carefully-articulated statements of doctrine, since they are the work of a man being led to his death, written in haste in a mood of exultation at his imminent martyrdom. Their passionate outbursts of jubilation are combined with admonition concerning the ecclesiastical problems that Ignatius is leaving behind him. Whether or not B. H. Streeter was right in seeing Ignatius' continual harping upon the themes of unity and obedience as a reflection of a troubled episcopacy at Antioch,[1] and a fear on the part of the bishop that his removal might encourage his flock to revert to their characteristic disorder, there can be little doubt that it reflects the danger presented to the oriental Church by those who denied the authority of God in the incarnate Christ and that of Christ in his bishops. The emphasis here is upon the authority of God objectively manifested in the episcopate, upon the will of God objectively manifested in the person of Christ, and upon the call of Christ to the Christian to follow him to martyrdom, a following which is possible only if

Christ's death – and *ipso facto* his human life – was a fact of history. The relationship between the reality of Christ's human experience of death and the call to the imitation of Christ was important in Antiochene and Syrian spirituality, a point to which we shall return. Here we simply note the emphasis upon the objective, historical element in early Antiochene thought exemplified in the letters of Ignatius, before passing on to the great age of Antiochene theology in the fourth century. Gnostic docetism had been the enemy in the early second century as it was in the fourth, and the defence of the human experience of Christ was the perennial pre-occupation of Antiochene theologians.

By the fourth century the questions concerning Christ's nature had become more complex and the formulation of answers rendered more difficult by the emergence of a new factor which claimed the immediate attention of theologians without fundamentally altering what had in any case to be said in a world threatened by Mani's docetic teaching. References to Eustathius in Theodoret's *Eranistes* give several brief catenae of quotations from his work, and what Eustathius has to say about Christ could well have been the substance of a reply to Mani. 'If anyone considers the generation of [Christ's] body, he will find clearly that after being born at Bethlehem he was wrapped in swaddling clothes and was brought up for some time in Egypt because of the evil counsel of the cruel Herod, and grew to man's estate at Nazareth.'[2] 'The Word built a temple and carried the manhood, keeping company in a body with men.'[3] Again, 'He took from the virgin the limbs of a man.'[4] But it becomes plain that Eustathius is fighting a different adversary when he asks, 'Why do they, in the inventions of their earth-born deceits, make much of demonstrating that Christ assumed a body without a soul?'[5] The new opponent is not saying, as Mani had said, that Christ did not possess a truly human body, but that he did not possess a truly human soul. In either case it was the true humanity of Christ that was under attack and which had to be defended. The new adversary was Arius, and though the denial of a human soul in the incarnate Christ was an aspect of Arianism that received no emphasis at the Council of Nicaea, within a short time Eudoxius could give unambiguous expression to it: 'The Son of God was incarnate but not made man. Instead of the [human] soul there was God in the flesh.'[6] Later expressions of this version of an emasculated Christ at the hands of Eutyches and Apollinarius were to meet universal condemnation, but in the mid-fourth century it was the Antiochenes who stood most strongly for the full humanity, body and soul, of Christ. That Eustathius was fighting on two fronts may be suggested by juxtaposing two of Theodoret's quotations of his work, the first of which is directed towards those who, like Arius, denied the human soul of Christ: his soul is rational, Eustathius asserts, 'and of the same substance as the souls of men, just as the flesh is of the same substance as the flesh of men, coming from Mary';[7] the second towards those who, like Mani, denied the human body of Christ: 'If he is incorporeal and not subject to touch, nor can be apprehended by eyes, he suffers no wound, nor is nailed, nor has part in death, nor is buried in the ground, nor shut in a grave, nor rises from a tomb.'[8] Eustathius' stand against the Arians cost him dear, for a year after Nicaea he was deposed from his bishopric by the Arian-dominated synod of Antioch and four years later, in 330, was driven into exile in Trajanopolis.

It was at about this time that Diodore was born. His name constantly recurs long after his death as the master who taught Theodore and John Chrysostom, as the spiritual master of Theodoret (he could hardly have been more, since Theodoret was born at about the time of Diodore's death), as the man who was most nearly responsible for giving shape to the Nestorian heresy and who, despite his work against paganism and heresy and his championing of the creed of Nicaea, was himself attacked by Apollinarius and Cyril of Alexandria in 438 and condemned in retrospect at Constantinople in 499. In consequence of his condemnation, his immense output of literary work has virtually disappeared, and we have only fragments left to us that can with tolerable certainty be attributed to him. His writings treated cosmology and natural science, Christian doctrine, apologetics and exegetical work on biblical texts in the historical manner characteristic of Antioch. Diodore was Antiochene by birth and training[9] and may have received training also at Athens, if we may interpret in this way the reproaches of the emperor Julian in 363, who complained that he turned his Athenian wisdom against the celestial gods and had been afflicted with sickness in retribution.[10] He lived an ascetic monastic life near Antioch,[11] devoted to the teaching of young Christian men, until exiled by the emperor Valens in 372. He was consecrated bishop of Tarsus to the north west of Antioch six years later, and was declared by Theodosius to be one whose teaching was a standard by which the orthodoxy of others could be assessed,[12] an opinion fiercely disputed by orthodox theologians of the following century. Diodore did not in all respects agree with the doctrinal views of Paul of Samosata, but in the extant fragments of his work we find the separation of the divine from the human in Christ, the two elements co-existing in harmony; we find the moral progress of Christ through his early years, 'progressing in dignity towards a better state', leading to the ratification of his moral perfection at his baptism.[13]

Diodore would permit no confusion between the divine Word and the human Jesus.

'I hear them say that he who was received by Mary and born of her is creator of all . . . Thus is the creator of all a man . . . If he who is born of Mary is truly man, how did he exist before heaven and earth? If he is prior to these, he is then no man . . . If he is on the earth, how is he prior to the earth? . . . How is the son of David the creator of David and maker of all?'[14]

'Do not name the divine Word with bodily names, for you ought not to call the divine Word a body since he is without limitation.'[15]

'The divine Word is born of the Father before eternity, the one from the One, but the form of a servant is a child of the blessed mother in later times, a man from the holy Spirit.'[16]

'Who was he who was circumcised? Who was he who was brought up in the Jewish manner? Indeed, the man born of Mary. Is he not to be distinguished from the divine Word?'[17]

'The power of God overshadowed Mary so that she fashioned the temple in such a way that the Word was not mingled with the body.'[18]

'When we hear that the Son of Man came down from Heaven, we understand that it was not he who is the seed of David but he who is from the Father before all time.'[19]

'We do not understand that there were two sons of the Father, but the divine Word was the one Son of God by nature and the man born of Mary as the descendant of David.'[20]

'Is the man from David's seed from the substance of God? Is not the divine Word of the substance of the Father, the man of David's seed from the substance of David?'[21]

'The question, *Where have you laid Lazarus?* was spoken out of our human condition, but he that called, *Lazarus, come forth*, and him four days dead, goes beyond human power.'[22]

If Diodore in this way teaches an ontological distinction between divine and human in Christ, he also insists that the distinction did not lead in practice to any kind of twofold activity, for the Scriptures know only one person, Jesus Christ. The Scriptures do not say, this element is from above and that from below, this from God and that from David, for both elements are both God's and David's, just as in man soul and body join, the invisible with the visible, the immortal with the mortal.[23] On this point, where one wants further elucidation, the fragments give us no more. It is far from clear that Diodore observed his own exhortation to treat Christ as one, for there are passages in which he distinguishes sharply between the impassible Word and the suffering human Jesus of Nazareth.

'Who is he who on the cross said that the thief would [that day] be with him in Paradise? For he who dies was buried and did not rise the same day . . . It is improbable that he would both be buried and be alive to lead the thief to Paradise.'[24]

'At that time the earth trembled and the sun changed its course for him born of Mary, the temple of the divine Word through whom the saving of man was effected . . . For the cry, *My God, why hast thou forsaken me?* belongs not to the divine Word. It is in respect of his bodily life that he cried out because he was forsaken.'[25]

'It is clear that the little child who was conceived by Mary and was born of her was the seed of Abraham and of David . . . This one born of Mary went about as a man, was weary, dressed as a man, hungered and thirsted, was crucified, his side was wounded and blood and water flowed from it, and his crucifiers shared his clothing. He died and was buried, and when he rose he showed his disciples that he had flesh and bones, who no more would undergo suffering and death. Forty days he ate and drank with his disciples, and ascended from his disciples on a cloud in their sight. And that he will come again as he ascended we have already said and have demonstrated from the divine scriptures. We have also demonstrated that the divine Word, who was born of the Father from eternity, is not susceptible of change and suffering, did not walk about in bodily form, was not crucified, nor died, neither ate nor drank nor was weary, but remained bodiless and unlimited, since he never departed from the divine form.'[26]

In Diodore's view the human Jesus was nonetheless different from the rest of mankind by virtue of the indwelling of the divine Word. 'When the Lord was in the womb of the virgin and part of her substance, he had not the honour of sonship. When he was fully formed and was the temple of the divine Word, receiving the only begotten, then he received the honour of the name.'[27] Cyril of Alexandria quotes Diodore as saying, 'The man from Mary was clothed with the rank of Lord, but he who at first was in no way superior to us was hardly worthy of the name and honour due to the Son and to God immediately after he issued from the womb.'[28] So, concludes Cyril, according to Diodore there are two Sons, and Christ is a new God who came into being at a point in time when the Word entered the human Jesus. This is hardly just to Diodore, who would certainly have repudiated any such idea. The divine Word, as he constantly repeats, took possession of the human body and operated through it. Human occupation of a house, to use Diodore's own analogy, does not render the house human, and divine occupation of a temple does not render the temple divine. It may well be said, despite Diodore's assertion to the contrary, that he offers us two persons, one divine and one human, but hardly two Gods, one eternal and one temporal. The fragments of Diodore's work which escaped the destruction consequent upon condemnation on grounds of heresy give us little basis for understanding his mind and little idea of the power that he undoubtedly possessed.

What we cannot tell from the fragments of Diodore's work is the extent to which he gave theology a fully-rounded statement as an articulated system of thought. The elements of such a system had long been present in Antioch and awaited only the integrating force of a constructive theological mind. This was supplied by Theodore at the end of the fourth century. More of his work would have survived for our use were it not that his name grew to be associated indissolubly with that of his most celebrated pupil, Nestorius, but we possess enough of it to form a clearer impression of his teaching than we can of Diodore's, and we can recognize in it the signs of a remarkably constructive mind worthy of his great opponent, Apollinarius. At the root of his thinking lies the characteristically Antiochene insistence on human freedom. Whatever the term 'salvation' may mean, it must never be interpreted in such a way as to deprive the Saviour of the full and free humanity which is an essential element in the restoration of man to his proper destiny.

Constantly and with great care Theodore states his view of the way in which the divine and the human elements in Christ should be understood. At the very least, the two elements were never confused. R. V. Sellers, who goes to great pains to demonstrate the essential identity of Antiochene doctrine with Alexandrian, concedes that

> 'as it is seen from certain angles, the teaching of the Antiochene theologians would seem to be that of "two Sons": their constant use of the term "conjunction" when speaking of the union, their description of the action of the Logos in taking man's nature as an "indwelling", and their determination to "separate" the natures of Godhead and manhood in Christ, each of which, they assert, has its *prosopon* – all these features of their doctrine might seem to indicate that for them Jesus Christ is not one *prosopon* but two'.[29]

Of course Theodore does not teach that Jesus Christ was 'two Sons', and specifically rejects such an idea: 'We do not speak of two Sons. We confess, rightly, one Son, since the dividing of the natures ought of necessity to be upheld, and the indivisibility of the unity of the *prosopon* to be preserved.'[30] It is hard to think that the violence of the condemnation of Theodore and the Nestorians as heretical was occasioned simply by the fact that 'some of their expressions were unsatisfactory', as Sellers puts it. *Prima facie*, those with whom Theodore disputed were in a better position to judge his meaning than anybody else could be, and more recent work on Theodore's christology has in general supported their estimate of his thought.[31] In their estimation Theodore defended the inviolability of the human nature of Christ to a length which denied the possibility of real union with the divine Word. Support for their view of his teaching lies in his separation of biblical passages concerning Christ and spoken by Christ, into those which appertain to his divinity and those which appertain to his humanity: for example, the words 'I cannot do anything of myself' (John v.30) 'are hardly appropriate if they refer to the divine nature, since they imply weakness . . . but they make the best sense if they are understood of the human nature.'[32] When we read in the Scriptures that Christ was honoured or glorified, or that he was given domination, we must not understand it as referring to his divinity but to his humanity,[33] for nothing can be given to the divine Word. When Paul writes 'God sent forth his Son, born of a woman' (Gal. iv.4), 'the apostle is referring to the man, to him who was made of a woman.'[34] Theodore always distinguishes the divine from the human. The two elements consitute two separate centres of will, so that Christ himself speaks of the Word in the third person singular, 'I have done everything according to his will and good pleasure . . . The divine Word, who has assumed me and joined me to himself, faithfully gives me the victory.'[35] The Word urged the human Jesus towards perfection and assisted him,[36] the initiative always residing in the Word and the willing, voluntary response to the initiative coming from the man. The two elements are never described as co-operating as equals but always being in a relationship of initiative and response. The human characteristic is voluntary obedience, involving moral struggle, 'training the soul to defeat its passions and to bridle the lusts of the body'. If this struggle is taken to be anything other than a true struggle against true temptation, then it becomes 'no more than the gratification of a love of display'.[37] The initiation of moral effort resides in the Word and the human will responds.

It is impossible to reconcile this teaching with the crude view that 'God the Word was changed into a human being',[38] for such language Theodore held to describe a being who is not human at all. God 'assumed' humanity, God 'inhabited' a man, and the humanity is real. The divine Word 'assumed a complete man, consisting of a body and an immortal and rational soul'.[39] There can be no question of the divine element inhabiting the human in such a way that the human provides the body and the divine the soul, thus constituting one person, for humanity consists not simply of a human body but of body and soul together. If the human side is bodily only, then it is not fully human. 'We marvel at those heretics who are unwilling to concede that our Lord asssumed a soul.' 'It is evident that a soul is part of a man.'[40] 'He did not take a body only, but the whole man, composed of a body and of an immortal and rational soul.'[41] Jesus 'grew in wisdom', which cannot refer to the divine Word nor to his body, but to his human soul. 'It was not the death of the body which it was important to abolish, but that of the soul, which is sin.'[42] It is man's sin that has to be overcome, and sin is a condition of arrogant disobedience within the human will. The only salvation from that condition is a reversal of disobedience, a voluntary willing to return to a relation of obedience to the divine will. This reversal must, to be worth anything at all, take place in a man, though the initiative and assistance in doing so comes from the Word.

To define the relationship of the Word to the man, Theodore uses the term 'inhabitation', repudiating any kind of mixture of the two elements to produce a *tertium quid* which is neither purely divine nor purely human. The divine 'inhabits' the human as God inhabits a temple,[43] but the outward expression of this inhabitation as observed by others, the *prosopon* of the union, is one person, Jesus Christ, and Theodore adduces as an illustration of this kind of language in ordinary human life the hardly satisfactory instance of the oneness of husband and wife, who are one while remaining two centres of consciousness, and body and soul, which combine to form a single person while remaining distinct entities.[44] 'The essence of the divine Word is his own and that of the man is his own, for the natures are distinguished but the *prosopon* is perfected as one by the union . . . Both natures constitute one *prosopon*.'[45] Because of this outward appearance of oneness we are able to speak, by a kind of legal fiction called the *communicatio idiomatum*, in terms which transfer the properties of the human element to the divine and vice versa. By virtue of 'the marvel and sublimity of the union, what is due to the one is due also to the other'.[46] 'Whenever the scripture wishes to speak of things that happened to the human nature, it rightly refers them to the divine nature because they are superior to our own nature.'[47] Thus adoration accorded to the man Jesus is admissible because of the indwelling Word, not because of any specifically human quality. There is a sense in which God may be said to inhabit every existing thing in consequence of its dependence upon its creator not simply for its creation but for its continued existence, and this kind of inhabitation by God is universal. But this is not what Theodore wishes us to understand of the inhabitation of the man Jesus by the divine Word, which takes place as an act of divine will according to God's good pleasure. 'Since he is unlimited and uncircumscribed by nature, he is present to all. But by good pleasure he is far from some and near to others',[48] choosing those who are worthy of his presence. The moral development of Christ, growing in wisdom, was not the cause of God's choice of him but the result of the choice, for the inhabitation began at the moment of conception,[49] enabling the growing boy to take advantage of the assistance of his divine inhabitant without at any point being obliged to do so as he would if in some way the divine and human natures had been merged into a composite being. Thus Theodore does not find it easy to answer the thorny question whether the divine Word was born of the virgin Mary and whether she is to be termed *theotokos*. The Word plainly did not have his origin in Mary's womb, for he was begotten before all ages,[50] but since the Word was already inhabiting the infant who was born, the term *theotokos* is not inappropriate. 'When they ask whether Mary was the mother of man or the mother of God, let us answer that she was both: the first by the nature of the fact, the second [by the relationship of the Word to the humanity which he had assumed].'[51]

If she was mother of God, she was also mother of man. A similar answer could be given to the question whether anything that happened to the man happened to the Word. In a sense it did, but by the nature of the case in a different sense, 'by nature, or by virtue of the relationship'.[52] Through their close association within a single *prosopon* of Christ the two elements could be said to share each other's properties, as we have seen, and the human experience of birth can be transferred to the divine inhabitant.

Theodore starts from the belief that man's salvation can only be achieved in a manner that is morally acceptable by the deliberate and willed action of man. The fact that, as Theodore describes it, man is given divine assistance in this, and that he is called to it by divine invitation, does not detract from the all-important human achievement of responding to the divine call and willing to effect the reversal of the fall of Adam. There is nothing defensive about Theodore's repeated distinction of the human from the divine in Christ, as though he were trying to frame a formula which would produce a perfect hypostatic union but failing to do so. It is, on the contrary, as though starting from the full humanity of Christ he felt his way towards a definition of the minimum divine influence that was reconcilable with the scriptural data and which would give a satisfactory account of the man's action in overcoming his inborn disobedience. He framed his thought in biblical categories rather than philosophical, unlike most of those who followed him, and this was partly what led his opponents into finding difficulties in his christology. They linked him with Nestorius in one direction and with Paul of Samosata in the other direction, despite his own rejection of Paul as 'an angel of Satan' in company with Arius and Asterius. But Theodore's detractors were in one respect not wholly wide of the mark, for though his doctrine of the nature of the divine Word in relation to the Father within the Godhead was certainly not that of Paul, he shared with Paul, as with the Antiochene school in general, the determination to start his thinking from the manward end and to work from that point towards a christology, whereas his opponents started from the godward end and worked towards their christology from that point. The two schools, Antiochene and Alexandrian, in starting from opposite ends could hardly be expected to understand the virtues of each other's position.

Sometimes, indeed, little attempt seems to have been made either to understand their opponents' case or to present their own in a manner that might have met opponents half way. This is probably true of Nestorius, whose single-minded concentration upon a narrowly-circumscribed area, presented with what sometimes appears to be a wilful disregard for intelligibility, was the cause of his tragic downfall. The narrow area was that which it was the mission of Antioch to defend, the reality of Christ's human nature and experience. Nestorius probably added nothing to the common stock of Antiochene thought that was not already present in the work of his immediate predecessors, and indeed covers a much narrower field than did Theodore. This may be due to our ignorance of most of what he wrote, for his work was destroyed when he himself was deposed from his bishopric, and only the devotion of those who remained loyal to him and fled to more congenial Syriac-speaking surroundings east of Antioch preserved a copy of his immense and repetitive *Book of Heracleides*,[53] which was discovered at the end of the nineteenth century. This work, whose English translation covers nearly four hundred pages,[54] contains teaching which could be contained in a very few pages. Such was the narrowness of the front on which Nestorius chose to fight Cyril.

Nestorius was Persian by birth, and came from Germanicia in Syria Euphrates to be educated in Antioch under Theodore. Ordained to the priesthood, he became well known for his preaching.[55] Theodosius II, faced by great difficulties in filling the vacant see of Constantinople in 428, secured his consecration, and Nestorius at once showed himself to be headstrong and passionate. Rivalry for domination of the eastern Church may have contributed to the opposition of Cyril of Alexandria. Nestorius soon aroused in addition the disapproval of Rome by questioning the rightness of a papal judgement against a group of Pelagians who had migrated to the east in exile.[56] Within four years the powerful combination of Alexandria and Rome had destroyed him, and from 431 he spent the rest of his life, perhaps twenty years, exiled first in Antioch and then in Egypt, his followers being denied the right to call themselves Christians.[57] The issue which brought to an end his brief and tumultuous tenure of his bishopric was his difficulty in countenancing the term *theotokos*.[58] Nestorius found it hard to come to terms with the title although it had been widely used and although Theodore himself had not explicitly rejected it. It was the language of devotion, possibly associated in popular use with the primitive cult of the virgin mother. For whatever reason, Nestorius defended his nervousness about the term to Celestine of Rome:

'We find here no little corruption of orthodox doctrine . . . It is no petty complaint, but one similar to the festering disease of Apollinarius and of Arius. For the union of the Lord with man in the incarnation they make a mixture which results in a blending and confusion of both elements. There are even some of our own clergy . . . who openly blaspheme the divine Word who is consubstantial with the Father, representing him as having received his first origin from the virgin mother of Christ . . . So they make the origin of the Godhead of the only-begotten the same as the origin of the flesh which was conjoined with it, and they make it die with the flesh; and in speaking of the deification of the flesh and its transition to Godhead they rob both flesh and Godhead of their real nature. But that is not all. They dare to treat the virgin mother of Christ as in some way divine, like God. I mean, they do not shrink from calling her *theotokos* . . . This title is not suitable, for a real mother must be of the same substance as that which is born of her.'[59]

It is to him a dangerous term, but he did not entirely forbid its use: 'I have said often that if any simple soul among you or anywhere else takes delight in the title, I do not object to it, but do not let him make a goddess of the virgin.'[60] By *communicatio idiomatum*, the term *theotokos* can be used of the virgin if we transfer the honour due to the Word to the bodily temple he inhabits.[61] Let the virgin be called *Christotokos*,[62] or the offending term be qualified by *anthropotokos*.[63] Nestorius claims that he did not himself seek dissension but was asked to adjudicate between those who disagreed over the use of the term, and that he had himself suggested the use of *Christotokos* in order to bring the dissentient parties to agreement.[64] It is not impossible that Cyril had stirred up the dispute in order to force Nestorius into a position in which he had to make a public pronouncement on that question, for Cyril's conduct at Ephesus in 431 suggests that he was determined to secure Nestorius' deposition.

The charge against Nestorius was that he separated the divine and the human elements in Christ to such an extent that they constituted two separate personal entities with no proper union between them. Even the clergy of Constantinople turned against their bishop by submitting a document showing that his teaching was in agreement with the heresy of Paul of Samosata. Nestorius objected that his hesitation over accepting *theotokos* had never received a fair hearing. His words, 'I could not give the name of God to one who was two or three months old',[65] were picked up by Theodotus, as Nestorius himself records.[66] He complains that when Theodotus reported these words, Cyril never enquired whether the words had meant that the two-month-old Christ was not God, or whether that it was not as God that Christ was born and not as God that he was two or three months old. For the latter is doubtless what Nestorius meant, that God could not, in his eternal and immutable being, undergo human birth. While we may have little sympathy with the failure of Cyril, as judge at the trial, to find out what the accused meant, we may have some sympathy for those who in place of argument were subjected to epigrammatic fragments of this sort. It was the kind of insouciant treatment of weighty matters which first alienated Celestine of Rome and which Socrates called his 'levity of mind'.[67] Nestorius was making the point which he elsewhere expresses soberly enough, the fundamental Antiochene doctrine that there must be no confusion between Godhead and manhood in Christ. 'You do not confess that [Christ] is God in his substance', he writes, addressing Cyril, 'in that you have changed him into the substance of flesh, and he is no more a man naturally in that you have made him the substance of God, and so he is neither God truly and by nature, nor man truly and by nature.'[68] There is no change of substance from divinity into manhood; there is equally no mixture or confusion of substances in Christ.[69] If you propose a hypostatic union of divine and human in Christ, then 'as the body endures the suffering of death . . . so also God the Word, who was united for the completion of the natural union, must endure naturally all the sufferings of death.'[70] It is intolerable to Nestorius that Cyril's hypostatic union of divine and human should attribute the human sufferings of Christ to the eternal and impassible Word, 'the human fear and the betrayal, the interrogation, the answer, the smiting on the cheeks, the sentence of the cross, the way thereto, the setting of the cross upon his shoulder . . .', and so on through the passion narrative. And all this 'they shamelessly attribute to the divine nature through the union of the natural *hypostasis*: God suffering the sufferings of the body because he is naturally united in nature, thirsting, hungering, in poverty, in anxiety . . . and the properties of God the Word they set at nought and make them human.'[71] It is an insult to the Godhead to make him human: it is depriving man of his dignity to make him divine. It is, moreover, destructive of man's salvation, for just as man's willing participation is essential to his salvation, so is the initiative of God, and no christology is admissible which detracts from the fully transcendent majesty of the Word. It was a matter sufficiently important for Nestorius not only to preach on the question[72] but to make it the subject of a treatise addressed to Cyril.[73] God had been operative in the formation of the first Adam, and the restoration of man equally demanded his assistance, for it was beyond man's power to achieve his salvation unaided.[74] Thus no theology is valid which permits a mingling of the divine with the human in a hypostatic union which destroys the divinity with the humanity and deprives man of his salvation.

The association of the two natures was a matter of divine initiative and the willing response of a free human soul. It was the Arians, in Nestorius' view, who wrongly deprived Christ of a human soul, an error which resulted in their having to say that Christ suffered and died of necessity, having no human will to choose or to reject suffering.[75] Nestorius insists on the voluntary nature of the association between the divine and the human in Christ, in order to preserve the freedom of will required by real humanity. 'The union of God the Word with [the attributes of a man] is neither hypostatic nor natural but voluntary, consisting of a property of the will.'[76] What kind of union does Nestorius propose? He does not take us far beyond the repeated assertion that the divine and the human each has its own *prosopon*, and that Christ has a single *prosopon* in which the two, human and divine, coexist without merging. As seen by others, Christ is one and indivisible, but the two *prosopa* meeting in him retain their individuality. 'The only begotten Son of God and the son of man each have their own *prosopon*, and in Christ it is one *prosopon* of Christ.'[77] 'In the flesh the Word was revealed and therein he taught, and therein and by means thereof he acts',[78] just as in the eucharist he takes bread to be the *prosopon* through which he acts.[79]

These points are repeated with variations of detail throughout the great length of the *Book of Heracleides*, supported by copious scriptural reference and by frequent reference to the Council of Nicaea as supporting his own position against that of Cyril: 'I have kept without blemish the faith of the three hundred and eighteen who were assembled at Nicaea',[80] and indicating his agreement with his patristic predecessors: 'What have you found in my letter that is contrary to the deposit of the fathers?'[81] Cyril, on the contrary, is declared to be self-contradictory and heretical, and resorts to bribery and intimidation in order to gain his ends.

It need hardly be said that Cyril makes precisely the same claims as does Nestorius for the biblical support for his teaching and for its conformity with the tradition of the fathers. The fact that to many of his contemporaries and to others in later times he appears as one of the most unattractive figures in the annals of the Christian Church must not blind us to the merits of his thinking, as it seems to have blinded Nestorius and Theodoret. The latter, who in the interests of peace had paid lip-service to the domination of Cyril after the downfall of Nestorius, greeted the news of Cyril's death in 444 with jubilation at the demise of one 'who was born and bred to ruin the churches'.[82] Was Cyril in fact saying something fundamentally different from what Nestorius was saying, or were they only emphasizing different aspects of the same theology and defending that same theology from the danger of exaggeration at different points? R. V. Sellers believed that this was the case.[83] They themselves were in no doubt about the differences, though it does not appear that either paid much attention to what the other was saying. There is of course much common ground between them: neither would allow that the divine nature is to be identified with the human nature in Christ; neither would allow a merging of human and divine to produce a third type of nature which was neither man nor God, though Nestorius constantly accused Cyril of this; both insist on real divinity and real humanity. Against Nestorius' teaching that the immutable and impassible Word cannot have suffered physically and that Christ's sufferings appertained to his humanity alone, Cyril insists that the Word experienced all that the flesh endured: 'He made his own a body which was capable of suffering, in order that he might be said to suffer in that which had a passible nature, although he himself remained impassible in his own nature.'[84] The humanity, body and soul, was used by the Word as a vehicle of human experience, created by him for the purpose. In this humanity God experienced everything that the man experienced. At no moment did God cease to be the immutable and transcendent ruler of the universe but at that geographical location and for that duration of time he also limited and contracted his divine experience to human scale in order to know, see and feel as a human being does. He retained his divine consciousness throughout the thirty years during which he experienced humanity. Thus Cyril can claim that his account of it allows for the fully human experience which Nestorius demands, and also allows for the fully divine experience of manhood and death which Nestorius does not provide in his own account. But Nestorius asks repeatedly, is the experience that Cyril describes as human experience really human at all? For Nestorius, as for his Antiochene predecessors, real humanity implies moral autonomy. R. A. Norris has shown[85] that Theodore departs from the Platonic conception of the contemplative function of the human soul by giving it a primarily moral function, man's rationality residing in his moral autonomy.[86] Nestorius constantly asserts the voluntary nature of the union of Word and man in Christ, and the erroneous doctrine of his opponents in this respect. 'We shun those who describe the incarnation [as residing in] an *hypostasis* of nature and not in a voluntary *prosopon*.'[87] This does not mean that the union is only one of identity of will, but that human freedom of will is the main characteristic of the human soul and that therefore full freedom of choice was available to the man Jesus of Nazareth. His moral growth was real and his temptations were real. Had he therefore the freedom to break his association with the Word and live simply as a good carpenter? Was he therefore free to choose disobedience and sin if he had willed to do so? The Antiochenes would have been forced by the logic of their position to answer in the affirmative. Cyril's position on the other hand did not demand such an answer, for the Alexandrian-Platonist tradition held the human soul to be the rational, contemplative element in man which linked him to the timeless and intelligible realm of God, the point at which man participates to some degree in the divine substance out of which the soul is formed. For the Platonist there is none of the earthward-orientated moral quality in the rational soul of man that is described by Theodore and implied by Nestorius. In the matter of the moral autonomy of man the Antiochenes saw Cyril as least convincing, and this is the main point at which Nestorius attacks him. Cyril had not paid sufficient attention to the one question which every Antiochene theologian regarded as primary, 'What is a real human being like?' Cyril's position implied that the primary question was rather, 'What was this single and indivisible person like whom we call Christ?' The emphasis of Antioch was moral, that of Alexandria metaphysical. Looking back at John Chrysostom it is possible to see in him the Antiochene emphasis at its most characteristic, in his lack of interest in metaphysical subtleties in order to expound the moral demands of the faith. To John Chrysostom we shall return in the last chapter.

The metaphysical nature of Cyril's thought may have been conditioned by an interest as fundamental to him as was the moral interest to the Antio-chenes. H. Chadwick demonstrated twenty-five years ago that Cyril's vigorous support of a virtually Monophysite theology was not primarily a desire for political domination of the east but was eucharistic.[88] In the eucharist we receive 'the body of Christ', a belief which for Cyril demanded a fundamental union between the spiritual and the physical in the conse-crated element of bread. It was this that Cyril designated 'hypostatic union', and if it applied to the eucharistic elements, as Cyril had applied it for seven years before the Nestorian controversy arose, it had to be applied to the person of Christ as well. Nestorius said that this forced Cyril to say that the divine element was capable of suffering. Cyril replied that the divine could 'suffer impassibly', which Nestorius rejected as word-spinning non-sense despite its use by Stoic philosophers, and demanded that the dis-pute should be conducted at an intelligible level in terms of human moral responsibility rather than in terms of 'impassible passibility'.[89]

The fifth session of the Council of Chalcedon in October 451 proclaimed its definition: 'Following the holy fathers, we all teach with one accord one and the same Son, our Lord Jesus Christ, . . . who for us men and for our salvation, according to the manhood, was born of the virgin Mary, *theo-tokos*, one and the same Christ, Son, Lord – only-begotten, confessed in two natures, without confusion, without change, without division or separ-ation. The difference of the natures is in no way denied by reason of the union; on the other hand the peculiarity of each nature is preserved, and both concur in one *prosopon* and one *hypostasis*.'[90] Both parties, Antio-chene and Alexandrian, claimed that the definition gave them the victory.

'When I was silent, [wrote Nestorius of his exile] and the authority to say these things had been taken away from me and I was not believed, God raised up those men, who were believed when they said these same things as I, which were the truth, without there being any suspicion therein of their having said these things out of friendship or out of love for me. And God brought not these things about on my account. For who is Nestorius? Or what is his life? Or what is his death to the world?'[91]

This was nobly said, and we may hope that Cyril would have expressed himself so, had he not been seven years dead. In fact, Leo had at Chalce-don with statesmanlike caution given expression to the two unassailable propositions that Christ is one person and that humanity is not identical with divinity. The definition sets limits to further discussion of the matter, condemning as heretical the doctrines of Nestorius at one extremity and of Eutyches and Apollinarius at the other.[92] If there was a victor, it was the combination of Rome in the person of Leo and the imperial capital, Con-stantinople, in the person of the emperor Marcian. But sooner or later

Nestorian christology would have to face Monophysite christology on the latter's own, that is philosophical, ground.

The authoritative definition of Chalcedon, which Nestorius hailed as what he had always taught, was not Nestorianism as the world came later to understand the term. Moreover later Nestorianism was hardly even what Nestorius himself had taught, for its root and branch separation of the two natures in Christ barely conformed to his own insistence that Christ was a single *prosopon*. Even if the Antiochene fathers guarded themselves against the accusation of positing a divided nature in Christ, the fact that their doctrine could be pushed to that extreme, and that its extreme form could be regarded as stemming directly from their work, suggests that this was at least a vulnerable point in their christology. Antiochene insistence that since man had sinned, man had to reverse the effects of the Fall, and their vigorous opposition to anything that detracted from the full humanity of the Saviour, may have hindered them in recognizing the strength of the Alexandrian conviction that if man had sinned, only God could achieve man's salvation. A drowning man cannot save himself, and a purely man-made salvation is no salvation at all. How can man be saved by man when man's mind 'is a prey to filthy thoughts'?[93]

One of the acutest minds associated with Antioch, Apollinarius – an Antiochene by adoption though of Alexandrian parentage – saw this as something more than a mere weakness in Antiochene theology. Insofar as he overlaps chronologically with the Antiochenes whose work we have noticed in this chapter, he was a slightly older contemporary of Diodore of Tarsus,[94] and came into conflict with him in about 350. He was bishop of Laodicea, a seaport some fifty miles south of Antioch on the Syrian coast, a man of great literary output and of great reputation for his learning. As late as 373-4 Jerome attended his lectures and seems to have suspected no heresy in them,[95] although it was at about this time that Apollinarius' characteristic christology was beginning to find expression in his work, and at this time that he went into schism, consecrating Vitalis as bishop of Antioch to minister to his own followers. The attempts of Basil to bring Apollinarius back to the fold were unavailing, and he was condemned as heretical by a synod in Antioch in 379.[96] His influence was widespread even after his death, but his sect disintegrated and was largely reabsorbed into the orthodox Church.[97]

An Alexandrian Platonist at heart, his target was the Antiochene Christian humanism which he saw as a dangerous dividing of Christ's nature into its two elements resulting simply in a divinely-energized man, a prophet but not a saviour. If merely 'receiving' God makes a man divine, then anyone can be divine.[98] Apollinarius was not blind to what the Antiochenes were really saying: he understood that they were rejecting the Platonist conception of the rational soul and were associating the soul much more strongly with will to act, and he opposed them on precisely this ground. A mind of this description could not co-exist in perfect unity with the divine mind of the Word in Christ.[99] If the human mind is such as the Antiochenes said that it is, then it partakes of sin, an inference from which they would doubtless not have shrunk but which to Apollinarius was unthinkable,[100] for it implies that Christ was 'simply the old humanity once again, a living soul but not a life-giving spirit'.[101] Any kind of union in Christ which combined the divine Word with a human soul would lead to the submerging of the human in the divine and to a consequent loss of human freedom. It was, strangely, in the interest of human freedom that Apollinarius opposed the apostles of human freedom at Antioch. Human will, he argued, is free but weak. It suffers from instability, inability to determine to follow the good and to adhere to its determination. Such a will in conjunction with the divine immutability of the will-to-good present in the Word of God could not avoid being dominated, and would become merely obedient to its divine partner. Men and angels had in the beginning been made free, and God would not revoke this blessing.[102] The mode of union proposed by Apollinarius derives from his Platonist view of the constitution of man's soul as comprising soul itself (the principle of life which distinguishes animate from inanimate) and spirit (the element which links man to God).[103] Soul is a faculty shared by all sentient beings, animals and birds as well as man, and there is nothing distinctively human in the possession of soul. Spirit, on the other hand, is the faculty by which man apprehends the intelligible realm and which is the distinguishing mark of man.[104] Since spirit is of divine origin and gives man natural affinity with divine Spirit, that divine Spirit can take the place of human spirit in a man without disrupting the essential structure of the man. By the substitution of one spirit for another, man is relieved of his crippling mutability without being deprived of his humanity. Apollinarius' argument could be put in syllogistic form: spirit inhabiting flesh is a man; but Christ is spirit inhabiting flesh; therefore Christ is a man. By this means human flesh, which comprises both body and animal soul, can be led to its salvation by spirit, for there is no question of spirit achieving salvation through escape from the flesh, as an orthodox Platonist would argue. Apollinarius was a Christian, and the doctrine of the resurrection of the body was part of his creed. It is thus possible for Apollinarius to speak of Christ as possessing a single centre of will, as being one person,[105] without jeopardizing his divinity or his humanity. Like his Nestorian opponents (excepting Babai in the seventh century) Apollinarius presses into service the analogy of soul and body in a single human being, so that just as one can speak of 'a man', transferring the attributes of his body to his soul and *vice versa* by virtue of his essential oneness, so can one speak of 'one Christ', transferring divine and human elements. The divine Word takes the place of the human spirit in Christ by

a process of self-limitation or contraction (*kenosis*) without thereby affecting his cosmic function as divine Spirit. 'The conjunction with the body
does not involve the limitation of the Word so as to leave him nothing but
bodily existence.'[106]

Apart from his schismatic act in setting up his own sect, Apollinarius'
fault was perhaps that he was too original, for theological originality was
not much favoured in the twin centres of establishment at Rome and Constantinople. The Alexandrians borrowed largely from him either in ignorance or in pretence of ignorance.[107] Cyril of Alexandria was fairly close to
his ideas, using his *Profession of Faith* addressed to the emperor Jovian
under the mistaken impression that it was by Athanasius. The Cappadocians, Basil and the two Gregories, were embarrassed but sympathetic,
taking what they could from the great Antiochene and often weakening
it in the process.[108] To Theodore the christological theory proposed by
Apollinarius failed to do the one thing that was of primary importance: it
failed to save man. Theodore saw no virtue in a scheme of salvation in
which God alone conquers sin. Sin is a human condition springing from
man's arrogant will, and it is not a morally acceptable solution of the problem for God to take man's place in the struggle. The only victory worthy
of the name would be a victory gained by a person who was subject to the
dictates of that arrogant human will and who had overcome them.[109] Christ
must be seen as human in this full sense, or the salvation wrought by him
becomes simply a *fiat* imposed on man from without. Theodore was not
as boldly speculative as Apollinarius, and perhaps never achieved a fully-
articulated theory of the union of the divine and the human in Christ. He
made clear what the conditions of that union had to be, full divinity inhabiting full humanity, and beyond that confined himself to similes. Apollinarius used the Platonist psychology of his day to attempt a real explanation, which nevertheless failed to fulfil the human condition required by
Theodore. On this ground the Antiochenes showed no mercy to one of
their city's boldest thinkers: every Nestorian writer for centuries to come
was to anathematize his name along with that of Arius.[110] To Theodore the
very terms of the problem are questionable in the form in which Apollinarius sees them: the Fall from innocence, inherited guilt, universal punishment;[111] and the solution of the problem turns the world into a stage
on which God works out his wrath and his mercy, in defiance of man's
responsibility.[112] God would not do as much for man as Apollinarius
claims, for it is contrary to divine love to over-rule human freedom.[113]
Apollinarius proves too much to be true to life. If Theodore's attack upon
this christology is trenchant, perhaps the most consistently carried-through
attack is that of Theodoret, whose work did not suffer the fate of so much
Antiochene writing, relieving us of the need to piece together his views

from fragments preserved from destruction. The main focus of his polemic was Cyril of Alexandria, but he traces Cyril's teaching back to Apollinarius and then follows the roots back until he is satisfied that he has disclosed the roots of their errors in the gnosticism of the first and second centuries. In the course of his exposition he has much to say about Paul of Samosata, Sabellius, Marcellus, the Lucianists and the Nestorians, so that he affords us a useful backward glance over a wide sweep of theological thought.

Apollinarius had taught that in Christ the human spirit, distinct from soul, was replaced by the indwelling Spirit of the Word. Theodoret will have none of this. 'Apollinarius describes the Master's body as endued with a soul, but deriving I know not whence the idea of a distinction between soul and intelligence [e.g. spirit], deprives intelligence of its share in the salvation achieved.'[114] The phrase 'I know not whence' is less a profession of ignorance than of derision, for Theodoret knows well enough the Platonist origin of the idea: 'Apollinarius did indeed assert that Christ assumed a soul with the body, not the reasonable soul [spirit] but the soul which is called animal, *phutikos* . . . He had learnt the distinction between soul and mind [spirit] from the foreign philosophers.'[115] Apollinarius' psychology is defined by Theodoret also in the *Ecclesiastical History*, where he says that Apollinarius 'affirmed that the reasonable soul, which is entrusted with the guidance of the body, was deprived of the salvation effected. For according to his argument, God the Word did not assume this soul, and so neither granted it his healing gift nor gave it a portion of his dignity.'[116] Theodoret's ground for rejecting this view is here made plain, that if the 'reasonable soul' or 'mind' or 'spirit' is as it were removed and its place taken by the divine Spirit of the Word, then whatever benefits accrue to the assumed human body are not enjoyed by the reasonable soul which is displaced. But if this displaced faculty is a real part of a human being, then it is not an entire human being who benefits from the incarnation of the Word, and salvation is only partial. Theodoret puts it another way: if the reasonable soul is displaced in the act of incarnation, then the reasonable soul is not saved, so it appears 'that the incarnation of God the Word had taken place not for the sake of reasonable beings but of unreasonable beings'.[117] If Christ is to be seen as saving man, then Christ must be seen as a whole man or the act of salvation is mere play-acting, 'pantomime . . . farce . . . tragedy', as Theodoret wrote of Cyril.[118] Theodoret rejects the psychology on which Apollinarius' doctrine is built, that is the distinction between spirit and soul. 'Holy scripture on the contrary knows only one, not two souls, and this is plainly taught us by the formation of the first man. For it is written that God took dust from the earth and formed man, and breathed into his nostrils the breath of life, and man became a living soul.' And at Matthew x.28 our Lord warns us to fear him who is able to destroy both soul and body in hell.[119] This is the appeal from philosophy to the bible which is characteristic of Antioch, the appeal from what Theodoret regarded as baseless speculation to the certainty of the historical record.

If Apollinarius was the master who had disseminated this teaching, Cyril was his apt pupil, and the main issue taken up by Theodoret against Cyril was whether (as Theodoret maintained) the divine Word assumed humanity or whether (as Cyril maintained) he became human. Cyril saw the Antiochene view as postulating two separate beings pretending to be one; Theodoret saw Cyril's view as postulating a mixed being who was neither recognizably divine nor human. The formula to which Theodoret returns constantly is: one divine Word inhabiting one human being, constituting one Christ. He disclaims originality in this, as when he quotes I Corinthians to Eusebius of Ancyra, ' "we know in part", says the apostle, and again, "If any man think he knows anything, he knows nothing yet as he ought to know." So I hope that I may hear the truth from your holiness . . .' This passage follows a statement of his doctrinal position:

> 'I have been taught to believe in one only-begotten, our Lord Jesus Christ, God the Word made man. But I know the difference between flesh and Godhead and I regard as impious all who divide our one Lord Jesus Christ into two sons, as well as those who, travelling in an opposite direction, call the Godhead and manhood of the master Christ one nature.'[120]

To the monks of Constantinople he writes,

> 'They affirm that I preach two sons because I confess the two natures of our master Christ,[121] and they refuse to perceive that every human being has both an immortal soul and a mortal body, yet nobody has yet been found to call Paul two Pauls because he has both soul and body . . . Precisely in the same way, when calling our Lord Jesus Christ both Son of God and Son of Man, as we have been taught by divine scripture, we do not assert two Sons, but we do confess the peculiar properties of the Godhead and the manhood.'[122]

Theodoret is making the point that Nestorius had made concerning the humanity of Christ, but perhaps with greater care than Nestorius had shown to safeguard himself against the charge of dualism.

During the years 430 and 431 Cyril wrote copiously against Nestorius, beginning with *Adversus Nestorii blasphemias*, then three short addresses to the emperor Theodosius II and his sisters under the title *De recta fide*, and a summary of his points of attack in the *Twelve anathemas against Nestorius*. The last-named work called for further elucidation in three Apologies and brought Theodoret to the defence of Nestorius.[123] Theodoret was not alone in thinking Cyril's *Twelve anathemas* to be Apollinarian:

'The blessed John [of Antioch] had written to the very godly bishops Eutherius of Tyana, Firmus of Caesarea and Theodotus of Ancyra, denouncing these Chapters as Apollinarian, and at Ephesus the exposition of these Chapters was the cause of our deposition of the Alexandrian.'[124] In the same letter Theodoret writes of 'the poison of the twelve Chapters'. Elsewhere he describes them as 'sprouted without doubt from the sour root of Apollinarius',[125] and declares that 'we can never communicate with anyone who has not previously repudiated the heretical Chapters'.[126] Theodoret's own reply to Cyril, *Reprehensio duodecim capitum*[127] takes the points one by one. Cyril had anathematized anyone who refused to acknowledge the virgin Mary as *theotokos*, 'for she gave birth in natural manner to the Word of God made flesh'. Theodoret is ready to use the term *theotokos* 'not because she gave birth in a natural manner to God, but to man united to the God who had fashioned him', for 'God the Word was not changed into flesh, but the form of God took the form of a servant'. Cyril had further anathematized those who refused to confess that the Word was in Christ united personally, in *hypostasis*, with the body of the man. 'If the author of these statements means by the hypostatic union that there was a mixture of flesh and Godhead', writes Theodoret, 'we shall oppose his statement with all our might and shall refute his blasphemy, for mixture is of necessity followed by confusion, and the admission of confusion destroys the individuality of each nature. Things that undergo mixture do not remain as they were.' Cyril had emphatically denied such a belief. Some people, he complains, are saying that he holds 'a mixture or confusion or blending of the divine Word with the flesh . . . but I am so far from holding anything of the sort that I look upon it as insane'.[128] But Theodoret's fears were grounded on terminology such as we find in Cyril's next letter: 'We say that two natures are united.'[129] Theodoret stood with his fellow Antiochenes in denying the possibility of the uniting of natures, *hypostases*, and this was what he meant by mixture and confusion. Cyril had described the union of natures as 'natural union'. Theodoret replies that what is natural is involuntary, like hunger, breathing, sleeping. Natural union leaves no freedom of voluntary action to the man Jesus. The basis of man's salvation is a relationship with God not of compulsion or necessity but 'because he put into operation his loving kindness'. Jesus lived in godly fear; he offered supplication to the Father with tears; he could not save himself and appealed to the Father to release him from death: this was the action of a real man, 'mortal, susceptible of suffering, afraid of death'. But if Cyril says that Christ was in truth divine, then Christ could not have suffered, since the divine is by definition impassible, so 'how could there be a passion?'[130] If Cyril says that the divine Word did in fact suffer, then why was incarnation necessary? God could have suffered on our behalf without incarnation.[131] Cyril, in short, is accused of not only making nonsense of the incarnation

and of Christ's passion but of making them irrelevant. These points Cyril
did not meet to Theodoret's satisfaction, but resorted to bullying: a letter
from Theodoret to Andrew of Samosata in the year following Cyril's
Twelve anathemas likens him to that other Egyptian, Pharaoh, who persecuted Israel.[132]

In view of an exchange of this kind, and of Theodoret's repeated asser-
tions that he could never be reconciled to Cyril or to any who thought like
him, it is not easy to see on what grounds he did eventually come to terms
with Cyril's doctrine. Cyril appears to have met Theodoret as near half way
as he could. His letter of reconciliation[133] avoids using the offending term
'one nature' in describing Christ, and affirms that Christ possessed two
natures 'consubstantial with the Father in respect of his divinity and with
us in respect of his humanity'. Theodoret was able to accept this, but we
can detect a measure of embarrassed defensiveness in the terms in which
he reported his change of front to the exiled Nestorius.

> 'Your holiness is, I think, well aware that I take no pleasure in culti-
> vated society nor in the interests of this life nor in reputation, nor am
> I attracted to other sees. Had I learnt this lesson from no other source,
> solicitude for the city over which I am called to preside would suffice
> to teach me this wisdom . . . Let nobody therefore persuade your holi-
> ness that I have accepted the Egyptian writings as orthodox with my
> eyes shut, because I covet any episcopal see. In truth, after constant
> reading and careful examination of them, I have found that they are
> free from all taint of heresy, and I have hesitated to put any stress upon
> them though I have certainly no love for their author, who was the
> originator of the disturbances which have agitated the world. For this
> I hope to escape punishment in the day of judgement, since the just
> judge examines motives.'[134]

Theodoret hastens to add that his reconciliation with Alexandrian theology
in no way reconciles him to the treatment that Nestorius has received at
Alexandrian hands: time does not change him like the centipedes and
chameleons who imitate the colour of their surroundings. The price of
peace with Cyril was that the Antiochenes should disown and anathematize Nestorius, and Theodoret drew some comfort from the terms in which
John of Antioch had done this, 'in that it is laid down not in wide general
terms but with some qualification. For he has not said "We anathematize
his doctrine" but "What he has either said or believed other than is war-
ranted by the doctrine of the apostles".'[135] Peace with Cyril did not restrain
the joy with which Theodoret celebrated the news of Cyril's death in 444.
'At last and with difficulty the villain has gone', he wrote jubilantly to
Domnus. 'Knowing that the fellow's malice has been daily growing and
doing harm to the body of the Church, the Lord has lopped him off like a
plague and has taken away the reproach from Israel.' The mixture of meta-

phors may perhaps be excused in view of the fact that Cyril had towards the end been contemplating breaking the peace and reopening the controversy, this time with Theodore of Mopsuestia as the object of his anathema. Bury him deep, pleaded Theodoret, with a heavy stone on top 'lest he should come back and show his changeable mind once more'.[136]

There is just a hint of seriousness behind this talk of Cyril's return, for Theodoret knew well that ideas have long ancestry and the present manifestation of an idea is only the visible tip of an iceberg. He was therefore concerned not only with the present manifestations of heresy but with the shapes it had taken in the past, which to some extent condition its present shape. The historical dimension in Theodoret's work was thus not only the result of academic desire for knowledge but was part of the attempt to understand the present and to shape its course in the day-to-day task of ruling a diocese of eight hundred churches. Theodoret's three dogmatic dialogues entitled *Eranistes*, the beggar or collector of scraps, derive their title in part from the diverse, and to Theodoret disreputable, antecedents of Cyril's doctrine. Describing Cyril's 'patchwork' at the opening of *Eranistes*, he writes,

> 'To call our Lord Christ simply by the appellation "God" is the way of Simon, Cerdo, Marcion and others who share this abominable opinion. The acknowledgement of his birth from a virgin, coupled with the assertion that this birth was merely a process of transition and that the divine Word took nothing of the virgin's nature, is stolen from Valentinus and Bardaisan and the followers of their fables. To call the Godhead and manhood of the Lord Christ "one nature" is the error stolen from the follies of Apollinarius. Again, the attribution of capacity for suffering to the divinity of Christ is stolen from the blasphemy of Arius and Eunomius. Thus the main principle of their teaching is like beggar's rags.'[137]

It is not entirely absurd to trace in this way a family resemblance between Arius and Cyril, horrified though the latter would have been at the suggestion, for Cyril's early writings are Athanasian in doctrine, and Athanasius and Arius were contemporary offshoots, albeit in different directions, of the mighty tap-root of Origen. These elements, along with the gnostics of two centuries earlier than Origen, Theodoret sees as the distant source of the stream which now, centuries later, flows dangerously at his door. The threatening flood is a long way from its source, but the water is the same.[138] Theodoret's fears for the future were not ill-founded. The extreme form of Alexandrian Monophysitism, as taught by Cyril's successor Dioscorus, reduced the human element in Christ dangerously near to total deprivation of humanity, as was recognized with alarm by wiser heads in his own party.[139]

Just as Nestorius had been deposed by the Council of Ephesus in 431 under the domination of Cyril, so Theodoret and Hībā (Ibas) of Edessa were deposed at Ephesus in 449 under the domination of Dioscorus.[140] Antiochene theology was on the retreat. Under the combined attack from the emperor's Chalcedonian policy of enforced compromise and from Alexandrian Monophysitism, the Antiochenes found a more congenial setting further east in Edessa, where the leadership of Quiiōrē, who died perhaps in 436/7,[141] and then of Narsai, had established in the School the work of Theodore in Syriac as the foundation of Edessene teaching. While the School was allowed to remain in existence its work of translation and commentary enabled Antiochene theology to secure a firm foothold in the east, but under Monophysite pressure the School was closed in 489, and again the centre of Antiochene teaching moved eastwards into Mesopotamia.[142] Narsai was by this date already in Nisibis, where he was building up a previously-existing School with the help of the bishop, Barsauma. Not all the scholars from Edessa joined him in Nisibis, and the dispersion after 489 did much to disseminate Nestorian teaching in the east.[143] At Nisibis, as at Edessa, the Nestorians came under strong attack from Monophysites. Under the directorship of the great Abraham de-bet Rabban from about 510, attempts by the emperor Justinian to bring about a reconciliation between the two factions by instituting a discussion of their theological differences at Constantinople came to nothing,[144] and coincided with a formidable upsurge of Monophysite activity in eastern Syria instituted by John of Tella. The account by the Nestorian monk Bar 'Idta of his training at Nisibis under Abraham gives no hint of the critical situation in which the Nestorians lived. He paints a charming picture of Abraham walking among the cells of his novices in the evening to encourage them. He made the young Bar 'Idta recite to him the work of Theodore of Mopsuestia, Abba Isaiah, Evagrius, Gregory of Anzeyanzo (Nazianzum), the 'Book of Histories', the Sayings of the Fathers, the works of Basil of Caesarea and the book of Mar Nestorius called *Heracleides*, 'which in my days had but recently gone forth from Greek into Syriac'.[145] Scholarly work proceded calmly at Nisibis in face of a massive programme of ordinations to the Monophysite priesthood and continual attempts to remove Abraham from his directorship. The School was closed for two years in 540,[146] its closure coinciding with a change in the policy of toleration hitherto pursued by Khosrau I. The policy of Monophysite expansion was carried on throughout the second half of the sixth century by James Bar'adai as bishop of Edessa[147] and Ahoudemmeh as Metropolitan, who between them carried their teaching far into Persia. The School of Nisibis reopened on a small scale, having lost most of its scholars to Seleucia on the Euphrates, and carried on a constantly threatened existence until the end of the century, when the efforts of Henana to reform its theology and to oust the influence of Theodore threatened its Nestorian principles from within and virtually

destroyed it.[148] The position of the Nestorian Church may have been eased
by their being given a status in Persia superior to that of the Monophysites,
the latter being given superiority in Syria, but Khosrau's toleration in 612
was suspect: he was too much under the influence of his Monophysite
queen Širin to be trusted.[149]

The eastward migration of Antiochene theology from its place of origin
is thrown into relief by the aims of Monophysite polemic in Antioch at the
end of the fifth century and the beginning of the sixth. The Monophysite
Church owed not a little of its success in attracting to itself men whose
theological ability was matched by their capacity for administration. Cyril
was one such, and in the sixth century James Bar'adai; and between the
two, Severus of Antioch, the brevity of whose two periods in occupation
of the patriarchal see of Antioch (512–18, 531/2–36) is counterbalanced by
the quantity of his written work and the vigour with which he expounded
Monophysite doctrine and harassed his opponents. But his opponents are
found to be the imperial Church of Constantinople as much as, or even
more than, the Nestorians.[150] Much of the force of Severus' writing lies in
his avoidance of wearisome repetition of formulae and his eagerness to
argue his case from first principles. The matter did indeed call for careful
definition, and Severus does not shirk the necessary task of investigating
the meaning and relationship of such terms as being, substance, *hypostasis*,
prosopon and mixture. The Nestorians had claimed that the two distinct
hypostases in Christ were united in one *prosopon*, but Severus sees this
as meaning only a rather loose association of partnership or brotherhood
like the union of Peter and Paul in their apostleship, or of God and his
prophets.[151] Severus demands a union in Christ that is closer than this, in
which the constituent elements can no longer be numbered as two nor
described as retaining their individual existence after the union.[152] The
accusation that the Monophysites teach a doctrine of 'mixture' arises from
thinking in material terms, from the use of analogies drawn from physical
conjunctions of solids and liquids to form mixtures that may or may not
be separable into their original constituents.[153] But entities of different
kinds cannot be mixed, separably or otherwise,[154] and this principle applies
not only to a putative mixture of spiritual and physical but also to that of
the divine will and human will in Christ: the two wills are of different
orders of being, and no such mixture of God and man is possible even at
the level of will.[155] This sounds as though the Monophysite Severus is con-
ceding his opponents' case but in spite of his denial of the possibility of a
'mixed' Christ he asserts the over-riding importance of the unity of a person,
and therefore in the instance of Christ the impossibility of the human will
functioning separately from the divine will and the impossibility of its being
free to reject God's calling.[156] An individual person has a single centre or
source of his being, to which different bodily and mental operations owe

their inception;[157] the different operations performed by Christ cannot be attributed to his divine element or to his human element separately, for he cannot be divided in this way any more than can an ordinary man. The Aristotelian analogy of burning wood is used by Severus to show the phenomenon of wood becoming, 'as one thinks', entirely fire, but nevertheless it remains wood; the burning ember 'performs the operation of the fire'.[158] Thus does the humanity of Christ remain human while performing the operation of the Word. Are then the constituent elements of Christ in reality one or two? In reality one, as every person is one, and the duality exists in the realm of thought (*theoria* or *epinoia*), which is nevertheless a realm of reality and not a realm of mere abstraction from the realm of physical existence.[159] Despite the accusations levelled against the Monophysites that they were one with Apollinarius, Severus rejects strongly the idea that in Christ the divine Word took the place of the highest human faculty. He quotes with approval the words of Cyril, 'I do not say that the body was deprived of a soul, but that it was endowed with an intelligent spirit.'[160] It is possible to unite in one person the distinct entities of divinity and humanity without having to take away some human element to make room for the divine, in the Apollinarian fashion, or to reduce the union to mere 'inhabiting' of the human by the divine in the Nestorian fashion. The human soul does not inhabit the human body; it is united with it. Nor is the humanity in Christ swallowed up by the divinity, as a drop of water would be swallowed and lose its identity if poured into the sea.[161] It may be doubted whether this was humanity as Theodore and Theodoret had understood the term, for hypostatic union of human and divine would, as Severus says, prevent Christ from suffering ignorance.[162] Nor would Severus' distinction between a man's will and the man who performs the act of willing have satisfied them when the distinction came to be applied to Christ, for in its application it distinguished between Christ's human will, as the agent of volition, and the composite man-Word who was the ultimate source of the volition.[163] It was precisely the composite figure at the source of the acts of volition who was in question, and to the Nestorian fathers any kind of composition was as fatal to the divinity of Christ as it was to his humanity.[164] Even the moderate Monophysitism of Severus would have failed their fundamental requirement of attributing to Christ unadulterated humanity.

Yet in the first decade of the sixth century who was there to maintain the Antiochene tradition against Severus? Theodoret and Hībā had been dead for half a century, and Severus' conflict was with extremists in his own camp and with the compromising of Chalcedon and the *Tome* issued in 449 by Leo of Rome.[165] In so far as the dispute was with Nestorians, it was with the increasingly remote figure of Theodore, whom Cyril had always regarded as a more formidable opponent than Nestorius himself.[166]

Shortly before Severus' death in 538, five Monophysite bishops argued their case before Justinian. 'It is necessary', they said, 'first of all to suppress the documents of the Romans to which the bishops of the episcopal sees have subscribed', and secondly to reaffirm the anathema imposed on Diodore, Theodore, Theodoret, Hībā, Nestorius and Eutyches.[167] There was apparently no opponent of more recent date worth the trouble of an anathema. Nestorianism nevertheless exhibited a tenacity in adhering to its faith and a resilience which in the course of time could transform its eastward migration into missionary ventures to the far east. Its dearth of constructive theological thought after the death of Theodoret was expressed in a forthright generalization by F. C. Burkitt when he said that the Syrians revealed mediocrity in all that they touched: they could only assimilate and reproduce.[168] This is largely borne out by the evidence of their theological work during the centuries following their exodus from Antioch. Much, of course, has disappeared or at least is not available to us.[169] We read of theological work by Johannan and Išoʻyabh and Henana in the sixth century and Surin in the seventh, which might change our opinion if we had more of it at our disposal.

Some indeed we have. The writings of the desert monks suggest that if Nestorian thought did not exhibit strong powers of growth and if it lacked the stark black and white outlines of Monophysite christology, it had yet some comfort to offer to the solitary, for Christ's humanity brought him within reach of their own harsh experience of desert life. In this respect the epistle to the Hebrews spoke powerfully to their condition. We may notice, for example, the *Explanations of the Liturgical Feasts* by the sixth-century Cyrus of Edessa.[170] Leaning heavily upon the theology of Theodore, though practising greater freedom in interpreting the Old Testament typologically,[171] Cyrus demonstrates the distinction between the human and the divine *hypostases* in Christ: the Word 'assumed from us a perfect man, showed him to be an exact observer of the divine commandments, made him live beyond all sin and perfected him in all righteousness'.[172] It was in pursuance of exact observation of the commandments that Christ fasted, and his fast was to be distinguished from the fasts of Mani, Marcion and Bardaisan in that whereas they based their practices on their false doctrine of the evil of matter,[173] Christ's fast began the voluntary process of rectifying Adam's disobedience,[174] to be continued voluntarily by his Church,[175] and initiating the Church into the life of heaven in which man is freed from indigence and becomes immortal and immutable.[176] Through Christ's real humanity he is united to man, and has thus renewed human life, indeed all material creation, just as he has renewed the spiritual realm through the union of that realm with his spiritual reality.[177] A blacksmith uses a pair of iron pincers to forge a new pair of pincers: God uses a rational man, Jesus of Nazareth, to bring to perfection other rational men in his likeness.[178] The sharp outlines of the doctrine which gave strength to the Monophysite in his solitary struggle may seem softened here in the concept of the humanity of Christ leading his fallen brothers in their willingly-embraced schooling for heaven, but this teaching was not without its own power of attraction, for Cyrus (as all Nestorian writers) constantly turns to the theme of Hebrews iv.15, 'He was like us in everything except sin.' It was the companionship of Christ that gave the Nestorian monk his strength.

This theme finds expression again in the seventh century in the *Liber Perfectionis* of Sahdona.[179] The solitary has to overcome the pain of separation from his friends and compatriots in order to become brother to the divine Son who is from eternity but who is not ashamed to call us his brothers in return.[180] But Sahdona has come under the reforming influence of Henana,[181] and this influence seems to have contributed little but confusion to his christological thinking. Henana's reformation took the form of a relaxation of the extreme Antiochene position advocated by Theodore, perhaps seeking to reinstate the milder form of the Antiochene tradition. It was seen by Theodore's orthodox disciples as an unambiguous defection to the Alexandrian school and it is in such terms that it is castigated by Babai in the seventh century. Cyril and Henana are alike guilty, in Babai's view, of uniting the Word and the humanity in Christ so indissolubly that they either compromise the divinity of the Word or imply a separation of the Word from the divine Trinity of which he is by nature a member.[182] If they were correct in holding Christ to be a composite being, then the Word is removed from the infinity natural to him, and is subjected to finitude and measure.[183] We have not the materials at our disposal to form a just estimate of Henana, but Babai at least was very clear that Henana had gone over to the enemy. Sahdona appears not so much to have adopted Cyrillian doctrines as to vacillate unhappily between Cyril and Theodore. He can on the one hand write of the union of the divine Word and the humanity in Christ as constituting a single, unique *hypostasis*,[184] a position refuted specifically and in detail by Babai,[185] who distinguishes between the terms *hypostasis* and person with precision. For Sahdona the single person of Christ is a natural hypostatic *parsupa* (*prosopon*), not just a pretence of union in which his humanity can be separated from its divine possessor as a portrait can be removed spatially from its subject or an ambassador from the king he embodies.[186] 'Their *parsupa* is natural and not imaginary thanks to the indissoluble union of the two natures.'[187] What does Sahdona mean by 'natural'? In the context of patristic christology the term usually connotes the complete hypostatic union of the two elements in Christ, as opposed to the Antiochene conception of voluntary indwelling or inhabitation or assumption of the humanity by the Word. Sahdona's opposing of 'natural' not to 'voluntary' but to 'imaginary' leaves the contrast less clear than one could wish, but seems to align him with Cyril rather than with

Theodore. On the other hand he can also write in Antiochene fashion that John i.14, 'the Word was made flesh', means that the Word 'inhabited' the flesh,[188] and that the real humanity of Christ's soul and body was the 'temple' of the Word, and that the 'assumed' body is raised to the honour of him who assumed it just as the purple takes to itself the honour of the king who wears it.[189] He refers to the human soul and body combining to constitute a single person, but also employs this over-used analogy to demonstrate not only the unity of the single person but also the distinctness of the two constituent *hypostases*.[190] Sahdona's chapter on the obedience of Christ reversing the disobedience of Adam, and on the voluntary nature of this obedience, is derived unmistakably from Theodore's soteriology,[191] and the Pelagian ring of his treatment of grace calls to mind accusations of Pelagianism made against Theodore and Nestorius: 'We receive the blessing', he writes, 'as a kind of just reward for our conduct, and in which we rejoice as arising out of our own effort, and which we enjoy as the labours of our hands, without the shame and confusion which would be ours if we had received it by grace and without labour.'[192] We may well doubt whether a theology which vacillated between the terminologies of Cyril and of Theodore could offer a way forward, and indeed whether it reflects adequately what Henana himself had meant. The vitality of seventh-century Nestorianism is to be seen more clearly in the uncompromising ferocity of Babai than in Sahdona, though we should see Babai rather as a systematizer of four centuries of Nestorian thinking than as an original thinker in his own right. He writes with clarity and power in compiling a detailed exposition of the common stock of Nestorian theology, but there is not much that is his own.

We have in an earlier chapter drawn attention to Babai's *caveat* concerning the use of analogical language in religious discourse and his insistence upon careful scrutiny of terms to determine their relation to the matter under consideration.[193] The rational mind of man can distinguish between elements in a complex experience and hold them apart for inspection, though in the experience itself the elements operate simultaneously as a unified whole. The analogy of the light and the warmth of the sun, illustrating the divine and human elements in Christ, is allowed to be useful so long as the user remembers that it is 'the rational mind' which separates the light and the heat.[194] This may seem to argue for the hypostatic unity of Christ, in so far as the separation of the two elements of his nature appears here to be an abstraction constructed by the mind of the theologian, but light and heat are in truth different. Babai does not defend the reality of the intellectual realm in Platonist terms as does Severus.[195] Light is found without heat in certain luminous stones and in the eyes of wild animals, he explains, and heat is found in mustard which burns the tongue without giving light. Both elements, moreover, take possession of the atmosphere at sunrise and leave it at sunset without affecting the constitution of the atmosphere, for their conjunction with the atmosphere is not in any way a mixing of constituents. Light, heat and atmosphere interpenetrate mutually but remain distinct, and the distinction is real not in the realm of intellectual necessity but in observed fact. Again Babai (in what reads like a specific reply to Severus) demands caution: some conjunctions of constituents can produce inseparable mixtures, as the mixture of liquids or of flour, dust and ash; but solid mixtures of grains, though occupying a bigger volume than each of the constituents by itself, can be separated. In short, not every conjunction of elements can be used as an analogy of the nature of Christ. But the sun's light and heat in the atmosphere can be so used, as can the conjunction of evaporated moisture with the atmosphere. In each of these instances there is conjunction without mixture or alteration of the constituent components. This Babai will allow as an analogy of the mode of union of the divine Word with 'his man', in which the reception of the human component does not in any way mix with or alter the constitution of the Word or of the Trinity.[196] By definition the humanity could not in any case add to the Trinity, since the Trinity, being perfect, can receive no further addition of perfection even by conjunction with a perfect man. Three perfect lights cannot have more light added to them by the introduction of an additional burning substance, nor can lose light by the withdrawal of one of the three: in that which is infinite the part equals the whole. The incarnation of the Word affects the Trinity neither by addition nor subtraction.[197] The union of human soul and body Babai rejects altogether as an analogy in the context of his strong attack upon Severus. Soul and body interact upon each other, he argues, and both suffer together, which when applied to the incarnation of the Word leads to the Theopaschite heresy of which he holds Severus to have been guilty. The real failure of Severus' body and soul analogy lies in the fact that the relation of soul to body in a man is not a true parallel to the relation of divine and human in Christ. The function of the soul is to give animate life to the body, but this was not the function of the Word in Christ, who possessed his own human soul. The function of the Word was to fulfil the purpose of God in leading mankind to salvation. If this was the function of the human soul, then every human possessor of a soul would be saved simply by virtue of possessing a soul. The analogy is too faulty to bear the weight that Severus puts upon it.[198] We may think that Babai has missed Severus' point, which was that whatever the function of the soul may be, soul is different from body and yet does combine with body to constitute one person. It is not a question of what the soul does to the body but of the soul's sacrificing its separate identity to help constitute a person. Severus' analogy is concerned with structure, not function.

In his refutation of Apollinarius, Babai puts forward the argument (despite Severus' denial that Monophysites believe any such thing) that Mono-physites see Christ as a mixture of divine and human elements. Babai's examination of the term 'mixture' leads to his defining it as the indissol-uble conjunction of properties: in a mixture of wine and water it is the properties of wine (colour, degree of liquidity, temperature) that are mixed with the corresponding properties of water. Apollinarius would have us understand that certain properties of the Godhead are in Christ mixed with certain properties of the man. But Babai has already argued that in the Godhead there can be no separation of properties from essence. We do not attribute light and life to God as properties or attributes: we do not say, 'God *has* life' but 'God *is* life'. Even being itself is not an attribute of divinity: 'God *is* being', not 'God *has* being'.[199] On this ground Babai will have nothing to do with any doctrine of mixture of properties. The divine nature is one with its properties and is indivisible.[200] Further – here Babai turns his attention to Cyril and Henana – if a composite divine and human being combines the infinity of the one constituent with the finitude of the other, the resulting composition can be neither fully infinite nor fully finite. To what *genus* then did Christ belong? This is not simply a wrangle about classification: it is a question of possibility and impossibility, for a being cannot be neither finite nor infinite. What kind of *tertium quid* is intended by Cyril and Henana?[201]

Babai accepts the challenge of Cyril's objection that the Nestorian pos-ition destroys proper understanding of the elements of the eucharist.[202] It had already been suggested by Nestorians, e.g. by Cyrus of Edessa, that there could be something less than a complete hypostatic merging of spiritual and material in the consecrated elements.[203] Babai is character-istically forthright on the matter, using it to illustrate his contention that Christ is one person by assumption and by participation, not by nature; he is one Christ in two natures, 'just as that body on the altar is one body mystically with the body which is in heaven [that of the ascended and glorified Christ] through virtue and sanctification and in name', though separate from the ascended body of Christ by distance.[204] Again, he writes of the action of the Holy Spirit at the annunciation:

'Just as with the priestly invocation in the prayer over the mystery of our salvation, when the priest says, "May the grace of the Holy Spirit come and descend upon this bread and this cup, and may he make it the body and blood of our Lord Christ", at the same moment as the words of the priest, in a flash, we believe that the sacrament is made and the grace of the Holy Spirit descends and makes perfect the mys-tery of our salvation, that they may become the body and blood of Christ . . ., one body, not two bodies, although the bread is one thing by its nature and the body by its nature something different, and although the natures are here separate from each other, yet through the virtue and the operation of the consecration there is one body, one bread.'[205]

Again, the Trinity receives no addition 'from that body which is daily broken upon the altar'. The material and the spiritual are embraced in a single *parsupa* of sanctified bread and of Christ.[206] Christ is *the bread of life*: the bread broken upon the altar, 'through the prayer of the priest and the descent of the Holy Spirit, receives virtue and becomes the body of our Lord . . . through union, not by nature. The bread, preserved in its nature, is the body by virtue of the union, and the body, remaining in its own nature, is the bread by the union.'[207] Babai can write of 'his body mystically sacrificed daily in the Church for the remission of our sins',[208] without feeling himself obliged to agree to a doctrine of fusion of the spiritual and material in the eucharistic elements of a kind which he denies to be true of the body of Christ himself. If Babai is accused of denying the real presence in the consecrated elements,[209] he would perhaps say in reply that if 'real' means what the Monophysites meant by 'natural' or 'hypostatic' union of two constituents to form a single new *hypostasis*, then it is only a repetition of the impossible position they had adopted concerning the incarnation of the Word. Whatever alleged actions of the Word he had rejected as rationally unacceptable in the one was no less unacceptable in the other. The Monophysites failed to distinguish properly between clothing and 'being clothed', between arms and 'being armed', between the body and 'being embodied'.[210]

It is in keeping with his attempts at clear definition that towards the close of his *Liber de Unione* Babai attains the climax of his exposition not by way of an outburst of impassioned rhetoric but by a final book of definitions of the titles used of Christ, first those pertaining to his divine status, then those pertaining to his incarnate state, concluding with the all-important terms assumption, habitation, temple, vestment, adhesion, union. This section of his work constitutes a survey of much that Antiochene theology had represented during the previous centuries. The term 'Word' is thus especially appropriate not only as denoting the expression of the Father's mind ('a mind is not without a word, nor a word without a mind')[211] but as a warning against thinking this divine mode of expression to be simply 'a virtue and operation' without subsistence, as Sabellius and Paul of Samosata had taught.[212] The terms relating to the incarnation must be used with precision, for each of them (habitation, temple, vestment, adhesion, union) says something of its own about Christ. A man puts on a garment and does not 'inhabit' it; fishes inhabit water and do not 'put it on'. Equally, the terms 'habitation' and 'temple' are not synonymous since not every habitation is a temple. Fishes adhere to the water they inhabit and a garment adheres to the body of its wearer, but the term 'unity' does not apply in these instances. Christians are united in their faith but it is not a unity of adhesion, for this requires physical propinquity. The union in Christ of the divine Word and the man contain all these different modes of coming together.[213] In no sense may we apply to Christ a concept of adhesion in which one constituent limits itself in order to fit the other, nor a concept of union that pertains to particular purpose of limited duration, as the union of man and woman for procreation.[214] 'That which is infinite cannot be compounded [with anything else] and cannot be involved in natural and hypostatic union, only in a union that is voluntary and personal.'[215] We may not use the analogy of human soul and body, nor that of Caesar and his distant ambassador, nor that of the love which unites separated lovers:[216] the first analogy expresses propinquity, which is appropriate, but also involves hypostatic union; the second analogy lacks the element of propinquity; the third expresses concord of mind and will but again lacks propinquity.[217] Analogies are at best partial, and a full statement of the mode of union in the incarnation of the Word requires all the analogies together to express the propinquity and the unity of will while excluding the concept of a hypostatic compounding or mixing. We may see Babai's book as the most exhaustive statement of Nestorianism after Theodore, different from Theodore's work, however, both in point of originality of mind and of being an expression of a developed Nestorianism which had absorbed the habit of philosophical analysis into its system. The Nestorians remembered its author as 'Babai the Great', even though we may doubt whether the Antiochene tradition received new impetus in his exposition of it. The voice is the voice of Babai, but the mind is still that of the three revered doctors, Diodore, Theodore and Nestorius.

It was a turn of events hardly to be expected that a theological tradition founded not only upon much that seems to have been indigenous to Syrian thought but also carrying the authority of the great triad of Antiochene doctors should have been beaten from its stronghold and reduced to a struggling minority in the east. That it should fare roughly at the hands of imperial policy exemplified by Chalcedonian theology is less surprising than its being driven out of Syria by a theology built upon Alexandrian foundations. The emperor's authority was not in question, and disputes with Constantinople were theological not political.[218] Zacharias Rhetor's account of the imperial envoy, Juvenal, trying to persuade the monks of Neapolis to embrace the Chalcedonian faith and meeting their objections with the formula, 'It is the will of the king', gives a hint of formidable political power wedded to ecclesiastical persuasion. The monks were in this instance put to death singing psalm 78, *They lay waste Jerusalem.*[219] But the Antiochene faith was driven out of Syria not so much by the Chalcedonian Church as by the Monophysite. W. H. C. Frend has suggested the linguistic separation in Syria between town and countryside, the strong

Jewish community in Antioch which supported imperial policy against
dissident Nestorians, the absence of Antiochene influence over communities of individualistic and extremist monks in outlying regions, and the
ascetic practices of Marcion and Mani, whose docetic teaching was nearer
to Monophysitism than to Nestorianism.[220] These elements may have combined to expel Nestorianism. We may also refer to an observation made
above, that from the fifth century the Monophysites produced a succession
of remarkable men such as Cyril, Severus, John of Tella, James Bar'adai,
whose power of leadership could not be matched by the Nestorians. In
addition, the Syrian monks were faced by the gods of the pagans,[221] whose
terrors were by no means to be faced with equanimity, and the more uncompromising forms of Monophysite teaching gave assurance of a divine
Christ smiting the powers of hell, and thus provided comfort and confidence that could appear to be undermined by Nestorian insistence upon
the primacy of the human Jesus of Nazareth. Confronted by the power of
Atargatis, 'Ashtart and Adonis, Iarhibol and 'Aglibol and Ba'al in his many
forms, an unambiguous God in human form, endued perhaps with a divine
body brought from heaven and impervious to human weaknesses, as Eutyches would have had them believe, may well have given them the assurance they craved for. The claim of Theodore, that man's perfidy must be
reversed by man if man is to be saved, may have seemed cold comfort in
their harsh desert warfare with the supernatural powers of evil.

   And yet this is not quite the last word on the matter, for in point of
fact the Antiochene tradition lived on. There were still those who found
comfort in their harsh warfare in the belief that the Saviour was 'like us in
all things apart from sin', as they read in the Epistle to the Hebrews. There
was strength to be derived from the Man of Sorrows. To this aspect of the
matter we turn in the last chapter.

7

Antiochene theology and the religious life

It was to the Letter to the Hebrews that the Antiochenes turned especially for assurance of God's presence with them in the tribulations of this present age, and for assurance of salvation in the age to come. The Monophysite monk found strength in the divinity of Christ: the Nestorian found it in his humanity. 'The Son did not shrink from calling men his brothers when he says, "I will proclaim thy name to my brothers . . . The children of a family share the same flesh and blood, and so he too shared ours" ' (Heb. ii.12, 14). Christ and his human brothers are 'all of one stock'. This does not lower Christ, says John Chrysostom, so much as it raises man and confers honour upon him by bringing man, 'the creature made from nothing', into association with 'the true Son of the divine substance'. 'Do you see wherein the likeness lies? In the flesh and blood . . . It is the heretics who shrink, hiding themselves in shame because they say that he only seemed to come in flesh and did not do so in fact . . . He showed his brotherhood with us in fact, not in imagination and pretence.'[1] There was of course nothing in Chrysostom's exposition of this passage from Hebrews which Monophysites would dispute. Cyril's successor at Alexandria, Dioscorus, was condemned and exiled at Chalcedon for refusing to subscribe to the doctrine of Leo and for his alleged partiality for that of Eutyches, that the flesh of Christ was no human flesh but a heaven-sent likeness of human flesh, and from his exile in Gangra he wrote to Domnus of Antioch protesting that he believed no such thing as this. If there was any difference between Christ's flesh and ours, he wrote, then it makes Paul (that is, the Letter to the Hebrews) a liar. 'There is no difference in nerves, hair, bones, veins, stomach, heart, kidneys, liver, lungs and everything else', along with a rational human soul and mind, but 'without seminal fluid and lust. Otherwise how could he be called our brother? He is like us, not in pretence as the Manichaean heresy holds, but in truth.'[2] It is doubtful whether the Nestorians would have admitted Dioscorus' reservation concerning seminal fluid, for the primary consideration in their view was the act of will in obedience to the Father rather than physical structure in rendering Christ sinless. But the Alexandrian patriarch could assert the reality of Christ's human body as could the Nestorians, differing from them in his view of the relationship of that body to the divine Word, which is not the point at issue here. It was, however, precisely the relationship as defined by the Monophysites which destroyed the real bodily identity of Christ with 'his brothers'. Dioscorus appeared to Theodoret and Hībā to be paying only lip-service to Hebrews ii.12. The importance of the bodily identity to the Nestorian monk is expressed by the seventh-century Sahdona, writing on the solitary life. Separation from normal human intercourse with friends and compatriots is anguish at first, he writes, but then he finds fellowship with Christ in the pain of separation, and though he does not lose his sadness, the sadness is joyful. The solitary is bound in love to the Father whose fatherhood exists from eternity, and he becomes brother to the divine Son who is from eternity and who 'does not shrink from calling us his brothers', and he wins the love of the holy Spirit who places us in motherly fashion under the protection of his holiness.[3] It is the bodily identity of man with Christ which brings man within the sphere of the divine family, and herein lies the spiritual confidence of the Nestorian monk.

The qualifying clause in Dioscorus' statement of Christ's humanity quoted above derives from Hebrews iv.15, in which passage Christ, 'because of his likeness to us, has been tested in every way, only without sin'. The wording of this passage has been thought to be ambiguous, in that 'without' may suggest either that Christ was tempted and did not succumb to sin, or that he was tempted in every way apart from the temptation to sin. The latter interpretation, if it means anything at all, removes Christ from the one human experience which would confirm most strongly his oneness with other men, and makes a pretence of real incarnation. Dioscorus shows himself unable to accept this fulness of incarnation in denying sexuality to Christ. The Nestorians, without overtly referring to sexuality, nevertheless emphasize the completeness of Christ's humanity. Cyrus of Edessa in the sixth century expresses this in the simile of a blacksmith who forges a new pair of iron pincers and uses an old pair of iron pincers to do the job: so God forges a new manhood by using the old manhood as his instrument.[4] There is here no implied exception of sexuality or of anything else from Christ's human experience. Cyrus puts emphasis upon the renewal of all things in Christ, spiritual things through their affinity to his spiritual nature, material things through their affinity to his bodily nature.[5] Nothing is excepted. Babai sees Christ as having to win immortality by the exercise of obedience to the Father's will (a major theme in all Nestorian writing) and associates this with his growth in wisdom and stature (Luke ii.40). Baptism at the hands of John did not confer remission of sin but adopted sonship, just as sinless infants have committed no sin to require remission but receive sonship at their baptism. Christ's temptations immediately following upon his baptism were real, just as his agony at Gethsemane was real. 'It was fitting that God should make the leader perfect through suffering' (Hebrews ii.10). By his suffering Christ learnt obedience and was made perfect. The crucifixion was the final phase of all the suffering endured by Christ, beginning with the temptations and including the whole range of human deprivation.[6] There is again no suggestion here of excepting Christ from the trials imposed by human sexuality any more than of excepting him from any other form of temptation to disobedience. Sahdona more specifically associates the imitation of Christ with the rejection of the satanic pride 'whose filthy streams have flowed in us all through all kinds of channels', leading us to hold those bodily channels in horror, namely our bodies' craving for feeding and for lusts.[7] It is Christ's humility in putting on the form of a servant which enables him to unite with man in man's sinful pride and through his obedience to lead man upwards. In a later passage Sahdona's exposition merges into prayer: 'Thou knowest, O high priest of the religion we profess, the sufferings of our race, you who have been susceptible to sufferings like ourselves apart from sin, who hast experienced the flesh and its weakness. Cleanse us of its passions by thy grace, Lord, so that its weakness may be assisted by thee, the high priest who purifies us.'[8] Whatever temptations assail Sahdona in the desert, Christ has experienced them before Sahdona, and this oneness with Christ is the ground of his hope.

Imitation of Christ is then no empty form of words, for if Christ was affected by temptation and persecution the disciple can expect no less. 'Above everything else', writes Barhadbešabba, 'it is our Lord Jesus Christ who has been the cause of troubles throughout the world: "I came not to bring peace but a sword".' He and his followers endured suffering and still do endure it.[9] The writer is primarily concerned in this passage with the merciless hounding to death of the Nestorian Sisinnius by Cyril, and passes on to the similar treatment suffered by Nestorius himself. But, he says, this is nothing new: it is characteristic of all who follow Christ. This is a recurring theme in the homilies of John Chrysostom. In order to 'enter his rest' (Heb. ii.18) one must first have endured Christ's suffering. He knew suffering not as God knows it but as man knows it, for God is impassible but the flesh of Christ suffered affliction and temptation no less than our own.[10] It is therefore not the Christian's part to seek a life of ease, for all who live in Christ suffer persecution. 'This age is an age of warfare, of suffering wounds and shedding blood and mourning'; our prayer is not for peace but for deliverance from the time of trial; our joy lies in following Christ to the cross, renouncing everything earthly as soldiers of Christ engaged upon spiritual warfare.[11] The strongest emphasis is laid upon this in the twenty-eighth homily on the sufferings of the faithful, in which Hebrews xii.2 is central: 'looking to Jesus on whom faith depends'. 'If he who had least occasion to be crucified was crucified for us, how much more is it fitting that we should bear all things bravely?'[12] 'If you are a disciple, Paul says, copy the master, for this is the work of a disciple.'[13] The theme is picked up again in the next homily. Christ shed his blood for us: you have not yet shed yours. 'If God chastises every son whom he receives, those who are not chastised are perhaps not his sons.'[14] The vehemence of the great preacher is evident even in the printed word. 'Our offering to God is praise (Heb. xiii.15), and the imitation of Christ in everything so far as is possible.'[15] Always Chrysostom returns to that theme. Even if the Christian be spared persecution, following Christ demands constant struggle against proud self will. 'It is right', says Akhsenaya, 'that every man who desires to follow God should emulate the following of the apostles, and that he should despise and reject everything which is visible and deny the whole world.' The bondage which the world imposes is not a quality inherent in the nature of the world but in the corrupted desire of man, a sickness in man which leads him to desire what is not beneficial, as a fevered man desires water.[16] Akhsenaya identifies three stages in the pursuit of perfection: law, righteousness, and the rule of Christ, the third stage being characterized by the injunction, 'Take up your cross and follow me' and inaugurated by rebirth from the bodily life to the spiritual. 'Participation in the sufferings of Christ does not consist in a man's giving alms and in showing kindness to the needy, but in his dying wholly to this world.' There are no rewards in the spiritual life, for the life is itself the reward.[17] The following of Christ's bodily endurance is the constant theme of the *Liber Perfectionis*.

> 'Christ fasted forty days for you, lacked sleep for you, prayed for you; a pilgrim and poor, he had nowhere to lay his head; wearied by the burdens of the way, he endured fatigue, he who had strengthened the paralytics with a word to make them leap up; giving the banqueters wine which he had made from water, he himself was affected by the heat and asked humbly for water to drink.'[18]

'Everybody knows what fatigue and vexations the Lord of the universe suffered in the body which he had put on for us, in which he endured tribulations and poverty with his disciples' in order to teach us patience in our own tribulations in the ascetic life.[19] The disciple follows the example of Christ in the hunger and thirst and fatigue of the way, obeying his injunction, 'Take nothing for the journey' (Luke ix.3).[20] 'Let us rid ourselves of the earthly burden of the body, and let us run lightly in the footsteps of our saviour.'[21] Much is made of those forerunners of Christ who forsook the world, Abraham, Jacob, Moses, Elijah and John the Baptist, and like them 'Christ himself, coming for the redemption of the world to live in the midst of it and lead it to safety, always hastened to the desert'.[22] The desert dwellers 'raise their eyes to Christ to contemplate the sight of him and to stretch out their hands to him, conversing with him face to face as between friends'.[23] In book 12 Sahdona devotes much space to the sufferings of Christ imitated by the faithful, not only those since his passion but those before it whose lives were types of his suffering, 'for they saw him afar off' (Heb. xi.14), and as they imitated him, let us imitate them in our turn.[24] Withstand evil, therefore, 'and you will be the companion of the saints of old, and even more you will be companions of Christ'.[25] The 'contemplation of the sight of Christ' of which Sahdona speaks is what Theodoret terms the angelic life of perpetual communion,[26] but the account of the Syrian monks given by Theodoret, and still more by Jerome,[27] suggests turmoil of spirit induced by a crushing sense of unworthiness in following Christ. The struggle to fix their attention upon their master took the form of a violent subjection of bodily needs, even essential needs such as sleep and food. The body had if possible to be reduced to nothing at all in order to deprive it of any power to interrupt contemplative prayer.[28] John Chrysostom's idyllic portrayal of the peace of the monastic life on the mountains round Antioch may well be an idealization of that life as seen from the tumult of the city, for he often contrasts the angelic calm of the monks with the ferment of city life, the self-indulgences, the torments of love for a dancing girl seen in the theatre, the inflammatory effect of prostitutes.[29] Chrysostom had been a monk himself and knew what it was to follow Christ into the desert, but he was an orator, almost a poet, and we may be forgiven for preferring the more sober account given by Theodoret, who tells us not of angels descending upon the ecstatic monks, but of the monks' agony and struggle and sense of dereliction and constant interruption by admiring crowds from the city. 'One has to drive oneself to every good work', says Abba Isaias, 'even when one does not desire to do it', and he repeats the phrase over and over again.[30]

We may pause to glance briefly at a particular manifestation of the desire to follow Christ, the deliberate attraction of martyrdom by provocative action. This had been one of the characteristics of the Palestinian martyrs during the 'great' persecution of 303, as recorded by Eusebius,[31] but even at a time when the Church was not suffering persecution something of the sort could be done. The desire to follow as literally as possible the footsteps of Christ led Rabbula of Edessa westwards to the banks of the Jordan[32] and probably to other sacred sites associated with the life of Christ.[33] Baptism in the Jordan was followed by a literal adoption of Christ's command to give up all to follow him, and Rabbula embraced total poverty. Not long afterwards, in company with a companion he went to Ba'albek to attack the pagan sanctuary,[34] an action which the author of the *Vita* interprets as an attempt at self-induced martyrdom. The two Christian fanatics were attacked by the temple priests and left for dead, with wounds on their bodies similar to Christ's wounds.[35] Rabbula was still a follower of Nestorius at this stage of his life,[36] and the literal identification of himself with the human suffering of Christ was a powerful motive in this action and during the whole of his episcopate.

Hebrews iv.15, 'Because of his likeness to us, he has been tested in every way, apart from sin', was not only an inspiration to the imitation of Christ's earthly sufferings which supported the desert monk. The verse carries a further implication which the author of the Letter to the Hebrews develops and which was of importance to Syrian Christianity. If Christ is one with the human race, then he can stand as the champion of the human race in pleading man's case before God, or in the terminology of Hebrews, he can act eternally as man's high priest. One of the main functions of the Levitical high priesthood was the offering of the liturgy within the Holy of Holies on the day of Atonement, when the high priest acted as man's representative before God.[37] This theme is taken up at Heb. iv.14ff.:

> 'Since therefore we have a great high priest who has passed through the heavens, Jesus the Son of God, let us hold fast to the religion we profess. For ours is not a high priest unable to sympathise with our weakness, but one who because of his likeness to us has been tested every way, only without sin. Let us therefore approach the throne of our gracious God, where we may receive mercy and in his grace find timely help' (N.E.B.).

The Letter goes on to demonstrate the superiority of Christ to the Levitical high priest, who shared the sinfulness of his fellow men and had therefore to 'make sin-offerings for himself no less than for the people' (Heb. v.3). Christ made the offering of his prayers, and 'because of his humble submission his prayer was heard . . . He learned obedience in the school of suffering' (Heb. v.7f.) and achieved perfection unattained by the Levitical high priests. He is thus superior to the high priests as was Melchizedek to Abraham (Heb. vii.1–10; Gen. xiv.18ff.) and is 'high priest for ever in the succession of Melchizedek' (Heb. vi.20, vii.23). Our great high priest has no need to offer daily sacrifices for his own sin and that of his people, for he offered that sacrifice once for all on the cross, and now 'lives always to plead on their behalf' (Heb. vii.25).[38] The reason why this epistle should have taken so strong a hold upon Antiochene minds is not difficult to discern. Its strong emphasis upon the reality of Christ's humanity and his brotherhood with the rest of mankind and his learning of obedience to the divine will were well suited to the humanist tendency of Antiochene Christianity and to its passionate rejection of gnostic doceticism. It was much that one man should have learned perfection through suffering and thus should have given his disciples a figure to imitate; it was much more that this man, risen and exalted to the heavens, should stand eternally before the judgement seat pleading the efficacy of the offering of his own obedience which he had once made. The Christian's confidence in the efficacy of this plea was based upon the complete manhood of him who made the plea. For the Antiochene, the manhood of Christ was far from being merely a pawn to use in the christological war of words: it was the lifeblood of his ability to live bravely in this world and of his hope of heaven. It was vital not only to his theology but to his religion.

In the surviving fragments of the *Commentary on Hebrews* by Cyril of Alexandria we find expression of the characteristically close fusion of the divine and human elements in Christ into an inseparable unity that the Antiochenes regarded as nullifying the doctrine that was central to their belief. On occasions his language can be unexceptionable from the Antiochene viewpoint:

> 'He was like his brothers in all respects, inasmuch as he stooped to take the form of a servant, for he was made Son of Man, brother of those who are of the seed of Abraham, that is our flesh and blood . . . He was made high priest by virtue of his humanity. Although as God he receives sacrifices from all, yet as flesh he is victim.'[39]

> 'Taking an animate mind and body from the blessed Mary *theotokos*, he was like his brothers in all respects, that is like ourselves. Therefore he became our merciful and faithful high priest.'[40]

An element of doubt concerning the humanity of the sacrificial victim may be felt when we reach the words, 'The Son offered himself as an innocent victim to the Father', the Son here presumably being the composite Christ, divine and human,[41] and the doubt may be increased by Cyril's exposition of the words, 'Having then a great high priest': 'The Word, being made like ourselves and having suffered for us in the flesh, then became our high priest, not offering another victim but himself acting as the lamb.'[42] In the Antiochene view this salvation would appear as no salvation at all, since it is not an offering of true man but of a composite being.

For John Chrysostom we can 'approach boldly' (Heb. iv.16) only because of the complete humanity of Christ: he did not merely take the likeness of flesh; he took flesh itself.[43] He fulfilled every requirement laid down for high priesthood – chosen from among men, their representative before God, offering sacrifices for others, bearing patiently with the ignorant and sinful.[44] But he is no earthly high priest in the Levitical mould, for though he ministers 'in the real sanctuary' (Heb. viii.2) he sits to do so at the right hand of God, and earthly ministrants stand to their ministering. This is the 'real sanctuary' of which the Jewish Holy of Holies was a shadow, just as Jewish offerings were a shadow of his offering,[45] and were designed simply as a ritual and ceremonial cleansing of outward defilement, not as cleansing the soul of sin (Heb. ix.10). Our need is not for a cleansing of that which fills the atmosphere and thence infects the body, as do plagues, but of that which directly deforms the soul, as does avarice. It is for the cleansing of our sin, not of our ritual uncleanness, that Christ pleads.[46] He offered his sacrifice once and goes on pleading just as we go on making our frequent memorial of his one sacrifice in the eucharist.[47] Babai Magnus, who we may regard as reflecting in the seventh century a great deal of Syrian thought before him, is clear that the high priesthood of Christ pertained to his humanity, not to his divinity. The divine Word entered the flesh at Christ's conception and his rational human soul was added forty days later.[48] The soul and body grew in wisdom and stature, not the Word, just as in our own lives we progress but our sonship received at baptism is not affected by our growth. 'Christ learnt obedience in the school of suffering, and once perfected, became the source of eternal salvation for all who obey him, named by God high priest in the succession of Melchizedek' (Heb. v.8f.).[49] The wise know, says Babai, that this refers to his humanity, not his divinity. It was not the Word who offered sacrifices to the Father, for 'all that the Father has are mine', and 'I and the Father are one' (John xvi.15; x.30). But of his humanity it is written, 'He offered himself without blemish to God' (Heb. ix.14), where Paul shows that the high priesthood pertains to the Lord's man, to the form of a servant, not to the form of God.[50] Babai returns to the same point later in *Liber de Unione*, when considering the various titles by which Christ is known. His title 'high priest' is fitting 'because we have come to the knowledge of the truth through him, and because he has brought us out of the power of darkness and has led us to the truth, and he bore sin and fixed it to his cross and gave us propitiation and redemption in his blood'. These matters pertain to his humanity since the divine Word has no blood to shed, nor is recently received into heaven, being one with God by nature. Therefore it pertains to his humanity.[51] Babai is concerned with the theology of the high priesthood; Sahdona with its practical efficacy. Hope, he says, lifts the soul behind the veil of the firmament into the heavens and places it near the high priest who washes our sin and intercedes for us and shows the soul its future bliss.[52] This high priesthood of Christ is a practical means of securing God's forgiveness, and so in writing to a brother who had forsaken his profession Sahdona's advice is that he should leave his sin and persevere in confessing the great high priest, who may purify the backslider from his sin. 'Let us therefore approach boldly the throne . . .'[53] The high priest has suffered for us and now it is for us to use boldly the great gift that he has given us, to bring ourselves within the sphere of his intercession.

This is not to say that the monks' concentration upon the imitation of Christ was the prerogative of the Nestorian, rather that for the Nestorian the bodily experience of Christ provided a particular focus of attention and a source of inspiration and strength which derived from his theology. Similar emphasis is found elsewhere than among the Nestorians, for example in the *Asceticon* of Abba Isaias.[54] The ascetic aim is to achieve humility, the elimination of 'seeking honour and glory from men, as the gospel tells us, but having only the Lord before our eyes and his commandments, to desire to please him alone';[55] 'keeping constantly before our eyes the humility of the Lord, his conduct and his bearing . . . Thus when the heart labours [the man] grows accustomed to good, remembering the Lord at all times and waiting for him with great love.'[56] When the Lord sees the effort of will expended by the disciple, 'he gives himself to him entirely', bringing forth in him the christlike qualities for which he has wrestled.[57] 'I am as though seated upon the Mount of Olives with the Lord and his apostles . . . I will be constantly with them, imitating their fervour and their conduct.'[58] Isaias has a long analogy of a city occupied by a usurper who destroys the images and laws of the rightful king and enslaves the citizens, who plead with the king to drive out the usurper. 'It is impossible therefore for the soul to enter into the rest of the Son of God when it has not in itself the image of the king . . ., the soul which has not in itself the likeness of the king Jesus.'[59] The image of Christ is formed in the disciple by the gracious gift of God in response to the disciple's determination 'to walk in the foot-steps of our Lord Jesus'. 'Believing in him consists of walking in his foot-steps.'[60] Just as in the animal world like mates with like, so in the spiritual world the imitation of Christ leads by grace to likeness of him and partici-pation in his body, his will being that man should be like him in all things.[61] In time of spiritual struggle to achieve this likeness, the disciple's prayer does not seek to tell God what is necessary: the prayer is, 'Our Lord Jesus, you are my help. I am in your hands. You know what besets me. Help me. Do not leave me to sin against you, I who am outcast.'[62] The Lord knows what besets us because, as Isaias has reminded us more than once,[63] he was 'like us in all things, apart from sin'. This is the work of a Monophysite ascetic, whose fervour of mystical union with the divine Son was strongly rooted in contemplation of the earthly life of Christ and in the struggle towards conformity with that life. His prayer is directed towards 'our Lord Jesus'.

The historical foundation of the spiritual life underlies the anonymous *Expositio Officiorum Ecclesiae*, which sees in every detail of the daily offices a repetition and imitation in word and movement of the narrative of Christ's life, death and resurrection.[64] We have in an earlier chapter observed the author's presentation of the offices as a kind of liturgical drama. He uses the term 'mystery' (*'raza*) to denote this drama, defining 'mystery' to mean a representation of something that is not present: a portrait of a king is a mystery, he says, or a house built as a copy of another house. Ecclesiastical mysteries represent in the present the events of the past or the future; or places unseen by us, such as heaven, Jerusalem, paradise, the whole world; or persons not visibly present to us, such as Christ and the angels.[65] On the feast days in particular the Church presents not doctrine but historical events, the nativity, epiphany, passion and ascension of Christ, Pentecost, and the finding of the cross. These events are not prophecies or types or beginnings; they are accomplished ends, completed actions.[66] The author's interpretation of the Church's re-enactment of these events is not a systematic commentary on the offices but takes the form of answers to questions posed by others or by himself concerning the intentions of Išoʻyabh in ordering the offices. Nevertheless we can see from his answers something of the way in which the life of Christ was represented in the daily worship of the Church, bearing in mind the author's warning that no 'mystery' can depict the reality completely.[67]

The element of dramatic representation is present also in the *Homilies* of Theodore on the eastern liturgies of baptism and the eucharist. 'Every sacrament consists of the representation of unseen and unspeakable things through signs and symbols', and Theodore distinguishes between the degrees of representation achieved by images, which are a closer likeness to their originals, and shadows, which are a less close likeness.[68] But in a sacramental action the question is not simply a difference of external likeness to an original, that the actions in the Christian symbolism look more like their original than did ancient Jewish ceremonies. It is not that the Christian liturgy is a 'better performance' than the Jewish, for the difference to Theodore lies in the fact that while both in their different ways enact the things of Christ, the Christian enactment possesses a spiritual content and a grace imparted to the participant in a way that was not true of the Jewish ceremonial. There is no play-acting about baptism: 'When at my baptism I plunge my head I receive the death of Christ our Lord . . . and when I rise from the water I believe that I have symbolically risen.'[69] 'We receive from [baptism] participation in this second life without question or doubt.'[70] So too in the consecration of the elements in the eucharist, the bread and wine are signed with the cross to show that they are in truth Christ's body and blood and are not merely described figuratively as being so: 'He did not say, "This is the figure (*tupos*) of my body" but "This is my body"; and in the same way with the cup, not "This is the *tupos* of my blood" but "This is my blood", to show that since [the bread and wine] have received the grace and coming of the holy Spirit, we should not look at their outward nature but should receive them as being the body and blood of our Lord.'[71] But while these liturgical actions go beyond being simply imitations and reminders in that they confer grace, we receive this grace while we are still in the body – in Theodore's terms of the two ages of history, in the first *katastasis* – and have yet to enjoy its full fruition. We are still living in the age of hope of good things to come. Paul, says Theodore, 'taught that we are baptized so that we might imitate in ourselves the death and resurrection of our Lord, and that we might receive from our memory of the happenings that took place the confirmation of things to come'.[72] 'We sacramentally perform the events that took place in connection with Christ our Lord, in order that, as it has been shown to us through them, our oneness with him may strengthen our hope.'[73] The liturgical action has a backward reference in its imitative aspect and a forward reference in the grace of future immortality and immutability which it confers. 'Great is the sacrament which is performed, and awe-inspiring and worthy of credence is the virtue of the symbols, which will without doubt grant us to participate in the future benefits.'[74] The assurance of heaven confessed by baptism needs to be maintained during the remainder of the recipient's earthly life by the eucharist, which also does not confer immediate bliss but strengthens the disciple's hold on heaven. It gives not the life itself but the promise of it:

> 'He has given us the hope to be associated with him in these good things to come.'[75]

> 'All these things will happen to you in reality at the time appointed for your birth at the resurrection; for the time being you have for them the word of Christ our Lord, and in the expectation of this taking place you rightly receive their symbols and their signs through this awe-inspiring sacrament, so that you may not question your participation in future things.'[76]

Participation lies in the future: but what of the present? The spiritual warfare of this life is of course training for the life to come, and Theodore's doctrine of the educative value of the exercise of human will is repeated by others: it appears for example in John Chrysostom's account of suffering as education;[77] in Cyrus of Edessa;[78] in Barhadbešabba's long preparation for his narrative of the great Syrian schools by describing the process of education to which man has been subjected ever since the garden of Eden.[79] The 'angelic life' of the ascetic, described by Afrahat, John Chrysostom, Theodoret and other Syrian fathers is not devoid of its harshness and its frustrations, as we have noted above. Nor would the Syrian fathers wish to understate its harshness, since the endurance of hardship is itself the sign of following Christ's footsteps. If the religious life as Chrysostom describes it could bring the consolation of visions of angels, it could bring also the realization of the appalling severity of warfare against the devil.[80] The Christian may be helped in this warfare but not removed from it. It is of central importance to the Antiochene conception of religion that the victory must be that of the human will over the temptation to disobedience, for it was this battle of will which Adam fought and in which he was defeated, in which Christ fought and was victorious, and from which the

Christian, whether ascetic or living in the world, is not absolved even by baptism. The joy of victory lies ahead, and during the intervening period of warfare the human will may fail.

> 'We must cherish the remembrance of this profession of faith [made at baptism] and with great care keep what we receive. When we shall have in reality received in their perfection these heavenly blessings in which we rejoice . . ., we cannot lose them any more, but in this world – since it is in hope that we receive them in participating in these mysteries – it is still possible to lose them as a result of our mutable nature. We must therefore with great fear take care to be watchful, in order to hold strongly to the hope lying ahead of us.'[81]

Theodore in no way softens the harshness of his portrayal of the embattled and perilous circumstances of human life. There are moments in his catechetical lectures when it sounds as though he is softening to the extent of allowing that comfort can be received from the holy Spirit. Paraphrasing king David's expression of his struggle in Psalm cxv.2, Theodore says, 'I should have been almost lost if thy wonderful help had not supported me'.[82] But it is no part of the work of the holy Spirit to make life easier for man, for this would interfere with man's moral autonomy: man must face life as it is, unsoftened by divine palliatives. The work of the Spirit is to teach the truth.[83] He is called Paraclete, giver of consolation, 'because he is able to teach what is necessary to them to strengthen them in the manifold trials of this world'.[84] The grace of the Spirit who will be with us always, promised by Christ at John xiv.15f., lies in the fact that 'he will gain for you heavenly blessings' in the future age.[85] He who raised Christ's body will also raise ours.[86]

Theodore's refusal to soften the outlines of man's moral struggle has of course led to the accusation of Pelagianism,[87] an accusation which has been associated with his view of the fall of man and his denial of inherited guilt, and with his christology. Marius Mercator appears to have originated the idea that Theodore's teaching that the fall of Adam and Eve 'harmed none of their posterity . . . but hurt themselves alone'[88] was transmitted to the west by one Rufinus, a Syrian, who in turn influenced Pelagius, and that Theodore had direct contact with Augustine's Pelagian opponent, Julian of Eclanum.[89] It may be that separation of the doctrine of the fall of Adam from that of inherited guilt ought to have led Theodore to Pelagianism, but in fact there is a wide gulf between the optimism of Pelagius that man can achieve perfection on earth and Theodore's reiteration of his view that perfection is only to be achieved in the age to come. There is no hint in Theodore of Pelagius' denial that man needs to pray for help, or of his view that the human soul is perfectible by baptism and retains no trace of sin. The enthusiasm of a popular preacher like Chrysostom, extolling the blessed life of the ascetic, could indeed lead a Pelagian, Anianus of Celeda, to think that he was reading the work of a fellow Pelagian, and could lead him to set about translating Chrysostom's sermons into Latin for the benefit of the west,[90] but this kind of ecstatic utterance, designed to encourage the laity of Antioch to follow the holy man into the desert, is a far cry from the systematic dryness of Theodore's catechetical homilies. For Theodore the Christian is struggling to hold himself worthy of the divine promise made at his baptism, and the struggle derives precisely from the fact that baptism does not confer immutability upon the soul in this present life.[91] God has promised, and will keep his promise to those who can receive it. There is indeed in Theodore little of the formidable subtlety of Augustine's vision of the complexity of the process of choosing and of the spiritual dislocation implied by the very fact that there are choices to be made.[92] R. A. Norris is right in seeing Theodore as neither a Pelagian nor an Augustinian, but as himself.[93]

It is not only in Theodore that we encounter language which could point towards Pelagianism. Theodoret's description of four hundred monks at Apamea, 'lovers of holiness who by their labours have purchased heaven', could sound dangerous to minds not in sympathy with Antiochene thought.[94] John Chrysostom insists that God never overrules the free choice of men: Let us keep watch lest we sleep. It is in our power to stand firm. Even God's will does not overrule our freedom of choice, for if it always did so we would be blameless. We may legitimately talk as though we attribute everything to the One to whom most is attributable, and thus we say that a builder is responsible for a well-built house. But others also were involved in the building, labourers, the man who paid for the materials, and so on. So in any human act most is attributable to God, but not all, though our own small contribution to it must not lead us to pride.[95] Sahdona sings the praise of the grace of Christ, and then qualifies his words with the reminder that Christ does not do everything for us. 'We receive the blessings [of the age to come] as a kind of just reward for our conduct, and we rejoice in them as the labours of our hands without suffering the shame and confusion which would be ours if we had received them by grace without our own effort.' Sahdona cites in evidence scriptural examples of those who worked for their reward, the labourers who bore the heat of the day in Matt. xx.1-16 and the prodigal's elder brother at Luke xv.28. God leaves us to work out our own salvation.[96] This kind of writing could appear dangerously Pelagian if the reader assumes that it implies Pelagius' cardinal point, the perfectibility of man in this life. 'Be ye perfect' was to the Pelagian an end to be achieved here and now: to Theodore and his successors it characterized the achievement of the life to come, towards which we move through God's training school. We have the promise; we have the sacraments; we have the examples of the saints and martyrs to encourage us; we have the holy Spirit to teach us; but in the end we have our own will power, mutable and frail. This is not Pelagianism.

There can be no guarantee of success hung like a label round the neck of the Christian. This is central to Antiochene thought, perhaps its most important single characteristic. It is first manifested in the anti-gnostic insistence upon the reality of Christ's manhood in the letters of Ignatius, and reasserts itself constantly through the centuries to follow, reaching a peak in the controversy aroused by Nestorius and in the integrated theology woven round it by Theodore, and stretching far beyond the fourth century and far beyond the confines of the city of Antioch through Babai Magnus to the middle ages. It creates for itself an appropriate exegesis of Scripture in which the primary concern is to answer the question, 'What, in the context of his own age, did the writer of this passage mean by it?' It attracts to itself the logical and scientific work of Aristotle and the late Platonists to provide itself with a suitable philosophical armoury. The human experience of Christ provides a point with which the struggling Christian can identify himself and which brings within the realm of human capability the daunting words, 'Follow me.' The Antiochene quest of the historical Jesus was rather a function of religion than of antiquarian curiosity, the answer to the human need for a salvation which fits the facts of man's condition and which does not sacrifice facts to the interests of neat abstract patterns. It kept its feet on the ground. Perhaps the late Roman empire did not want such a faith, for at the time when Antiochene Christianity was resisting the danger of gnosticism in its many forms, and the dangers of speculative theological fantasies, other-worldly constructions of myth and allegory and cult, the world was embracing these very dangers as the means of escape from a hostile and uncertain present.[97] It was not in the end Antiochene Christianity which satisfied the needs of the Church. Of the major figures of Antioch whose minds we have been seeking to understand, only John Chrysostom came to be widely known in the west in Latin translation, and he, great though he was as a spiritual and religious force, contributed less than any of them to Antiochene thought. It was John Chrysostom alone of them who received canonization at the hands of Rome.

Appendix 1: Eastern representation at Nicaea

The lists of bishops present at Nicaea are collected in H. Gelzer, H. Hilgenfeld, O. Cuntz, *Patrum Nicaenorum Nomina* (*Script. Sacri et Profani*, ii), Leipzig, 1899. We are here concerned only with the eastern bishops, that is those representing Palestine, Phoenicia, Syria, Arabia and Mesopotamia.

For Palestine most sources (Latin, Greek, Coptic, Syriac, Arabic) are agreed on the following: Macarius of Jerusalem, Germanus of Neapolis, Marianus (or Marinus) of Sebaste, Gaianus of Sebaste, Eusebius of Caesarea, Sabinus of Gadara, Longinus of Askalon, Peter of Nicopolis, Macrinus (or Marianus) of Jamnia, Maximus of Eleutheropolis, Paul (or Paulinus) of Maximianopolis, Januarius of Jericho, Heliodorus of Zabulon, Aetius of Lydda, Silvanus of Azotus, Patrophilus of Scythapolis, Asclepius (or Asclepas) of Gaza, Peter of Aila, Antiochus (or Antipatros) of Capetolias (or Gaza). The Coptic lists add Diodore of Basulon, Aetius of Dintra and Sabinus of Azotus (22 names in all). Marianus and Gaianus of Sebaste are differentiated in the Greek lists, the former being Sebastenos, the latter Sebastes, both Sebastenus in Latin.

For Phoenicia: Zeno of Tyre, Aeneas (or Ananias) of Ptolemais, Magnus of Damascus, Theodore of Sidon, Hellanicus (or Hellaticus) of Tripolis, Philocalus (or Philocanus, Phicas) of Paneas, Gregory of Berytus, Marinus of Palmyra, Thadoneus (or Baddoneus) of Alassos (or Emesa, Agela), Anatolius of Emesa. The Coptic lists add Synodorus (or Zenodorus) of Antaradus, Ballaus of Thersea (12 names in all).

For Syria: Eustathius of Antioch, Zenobius of Seleucia, Theodotus (or Theodorus) of Laodicea, Alphius (or Ulphius) of Apamea, Basianus (or Asienus, Asionus, Sabianus) of Raphanea, Philoxenus of Hierapolis, Salamanes (or Salamias) of Germanicia, Piperius of Samosata, Archelaus of Doliche, Euphration of Balanea (or Daneis), Phaladus (or Baladus, Paulus) chorepiscopus, Zoilus of Gabala, Bassos of Zeugma, Gerontius of Arethusa, Maricius of Epiphaneia (or Hamath), Eustathius of Arethusa (or Ariston), Paul of Neocaesarea, Siricius (or Diricius) of Cyrrhus, Seleucus chorepiscopus, Peter of Gindara (or Cytalus), Pegasius (or Pelagius) of Arbocadama, Bassones of Gabula (or Tabula). The Latin lists add Gerontius (or Leontius)

165

of Larissa; the Coptic lists add Heliconus of Abala (24 names in all). The Greek and Coptic wrongly assign Siricius of Cyrrhus to Cyprus.

For Arabia: Nicomachus (or Nicomas, Nicimus) of Bostra, Cyrian of Philadelphia, Gennadius of Isbounta, Severus of Sodom, Sopater of Beritaneus (or Botanias, Beresatana), Severus of Dionysias (6 names).

For Mesopotamia: Aeithales (or Ethilaos, Ethalas, Aithilaha, Absalom) of Edessa, Jacob of Nisibis, Antiochus of Resaina, Mareas (or Marius, Maras, Maraus) of Macedontopolis, John of Persa. One Syriac list (Ebedjesu) adds Simeon of Amida, Maruthas of Maipherqat, George of Šingara. Barhadbešabba (Pat. Or. xxiii.2, p. 209) adds to these, Nonnus of Circesium, Mara of Doura, John of Goustra, Addai of Arbel. He also names (*Ibid.*, p. 205) John of Arbel and Šahdost the presbyter. John of Persa, a town in the extreme north of Mesopotamia on the Armenian frontier, appears wrongly in the lists as 'Persia', and possibly in Eusebius, *Vita Const.*, iii.7, as 'a Persian bishop' (see Gelzer, p. xxxix, n. 1). O. Braun, *De Sancta Nicaene Synodo*, Münster, 1898, p. 52, gives Jonas of Ciresium and Addai of Agal. (For Mesopotamia 13 names in all.) We may note that Ephrem does not appear in the lists.

Allowing for ambiguities, these lists give us over 70 bishops from the east.

Appendix 2: The feminine element in Syrian Christianity

With the feminine element in the Syrian conception of deity we may associate the importance of the feminine element in semitic *cultus* from earliest times: see S. H. Hooke, *The Seige Perilous*, London, 1956, p. 104, on primitive fertility prostitution rites in Israel; F. Cumont, *Les Religions Orientales dans le Paganisme Romain*, 4th ed., Paris, 1949, p. 106 on prostitution in the Elagabal temple at Emesa; E. S. Bouchier, *Syria as a Roman Province*, Oxford, 1916, p. 261 on the part played by ecstatic women in the worship of Atargatis at Heliopolis. In justifying the destruction of such sites, much use was made by Christians of the prostitution practised there, e.g. Eus., *V.C.*, iii.55; so R. Dussaud, *Mana*, i.2, Paris, 1949, p. 399. The feminine element in the *cultus* is maintained strongly in Simon Magus and his associate Helen, who was variously identified with Helen of Troy; the feminine Sophia of Prov., viii.22ff.; Korê, the daughter of Zeus; Athena; Isis, and other divine figures, exemplifying the complex cross-fertilization of myth underlying accounts of her (R. M. Grant, *Gnosticism and Early Christianity*, New York, 1959, p. 84). Grant suggests (p. 82) that descriptions of Helen as a prostitute may have been hostile inventions. The same may be true of the accusation of unchastity levelled at Paul of Samosata on account of his female choir, who may exemplify not simply the rich Syrian tradition of hymnody but also the Syrian feminine tradition, subjected to denigration by later critics of Paul. On the institution of Daughters of the Covenant at Edessa (*b'nath q'yâmâ*, parallel to the male *b'nai q'yâmâ*) see F. C. Burkitt, *Early Eastern Christianity*, London, 1904, pp. 128ff., many of whose conclusions are questioned by A. Vööbus, *History of Asceticism in the Syrian Orient*, i, C.S.C.O. 184 (Subsid. 14), Louvain, 1958, pp. 184ff. Early anti-feminine severity derived from further east, and was in process of relaxation at about the time of Afrahat, when the indigenous Syrian tradition asserted itself. The *b'nath q'yâmâ*, as brides of Christ, may exhibit characteristics analogous to the women of the Qumran community (*Zadokite Document*, vii. 6-9) and in some Essene communities (Jos., *B.J.*, ii.8.13), though the latter countenanced marriage. The strictness of one *mēmrā* of Narsai against the rôle of women in the Church suggests that in his time at Nisibis (after 471) the question was at least sufficiently important to claim his attention (A. Vööbus, *History of the School of Nisibis*, C.S.C.O. 266 (Subsid. 26), Louvain, 1965, p. 83.

The common factor here seems to be women set apart from the normal affairs of life, dedicated in some capacity to the service of God, the capacity varying according to the current conception of deity. The dedicated woman was peculiarly exposed to misrepresentation and hostility from those who did not share the cultural background; e.g. persecution at Bēt Arāmāiē in 377 by Persians to whom the virginity of the Christian *b'nath* was offensive (Vööbus, *History of Asceticism*, i, p. 255), or Christian hostility to Paul of Samosata's female choir, which suffered the contrary imputation of unchastity.

Notes

Introduction: Survey of the History of Antioch

1 The main sources for this Introduction are: John Malalas, *Chronographia*, books i-viii, xiii-xviii, ed. L. Dindorf, Bonn, 1831, Corp. Script. Hist. Byzant. vol. xv; books ix-xii, ed. A. Schenk von Stauffenberg, *Die römische Kaisergeschichte bei Malalas*, Stuttgart, 1931; Ammianus Marcellinus, *Histories*, ed. J. C. Rolfe, London, 1935-9, Loeb Class. Lib.; Julian, *Works*, ed. W. C. Wright, London, 1949-53, Loeb Class. Lib.; Libanius, *Opera*, ed. R. Foerster, Leipzig, 1903-22. This section of the book is heavily dependent upon G. Downey, *A History of Antioch in Syria from Seleucus to the Arab Conquest*, Princeton, 1961; J. H. W. G. Liebeschuetz, *Antioch. City and imperial administration in the later Roman empire*, Oxford, 1972; R. Devreesse, *Le patriarcat d'Antioche*, Paris, 1945.

2 Polybius, v. 61. J. H. W. G. Liebeschuetz estimates that by the fourth century A.D. the population of the city was about 150,000, and of the administrative region of Antioch about 400,000 (*Antioch*, p. 41).

3 For the further history of the city, see P. K. Hitti, *History of the Arabs*, 6th ed., London and New York, 1956; C. Cahen, *La Syrie du nord à l'époque des croisades et la principauté franque d'Antioche*, Paris, 1940.

1 The religious background to Antiochene Christianity: pagan, jewish, gnostic

1 *Hebrew Lexicon*, Brown, Driver and Briggs, 1906, p. 127.

2 We may in this way understand the term *lithoi empsuchoi*, 'ensouled stones'; Philo of Byblos, ii.20; Hippolytus, *Haeres*. v.7.10.

3 R. Dussaud, *Mana. Introduction à l'histoire de religion*, Paris, 1949, pp. 393ff., cites an inscription from Zendjirli in which Hadad is *ba'al* of the waters.

4 G. A. Cooke, *Text book of North Semitic Inscriptions*, Oxford, 1903, p. 295, no. 135, 'to him whose nature is blessed for ever, the good and the compassionate'. H. Ingholt and J. Starcky, 'Receuil des inscriptions semitiques', *La Palmyrene du Nord-Ouest*, ed. J. Schlumberger, Paris, 1951, p. 152, 'to the djinn, good and rewarding god'; cf. unnamed djinns, pp. 158, 160, etc.

5 A. F. Rainey, *Israel Exploration Journal*, xviii, 1968, 1-14.

6 W. F. Albright, *Archaeology and the Religion of Israel*, 3rd ed., Baltimore, 1953, p. 73; both appear as consorts of El in Sanchuniaton.

7 This translation of the name is defended in detail by S. Ronzevalle, 'Les monnaies de la dynastie de Abd-Hadad et les cultes de Hiérapolis-Bambycé', *Mélanges de l'Université de Saint Joseph*, xxiii, Beyrouth, 1940, 26-39.

8 K. Müller, *Fragmenta Historicorum Graecorum*, 5 vols., Paris, 1841-70, iii, 569.

9 M. Rostovtzeff, *Caravan Cities*, Oxford, 1932, plate xxx. 2, p. 184.

10 G. A. Cooke, *North Semitic Inscriptions*, p. 88, no. 30; cf. pp. 75–8, nos. 24, 25, 27.

11 Müller, *Frag. Hist. Graec.*, iii, 568.

12 M. Rostovtzeff, *Dura Europos and its Art*, Oxford, 1938, p. 44. Cf. p. 64, plate xi.1, for a relief of Zeus Kurios.

13 L. B. Paton, 'Ba'al', ii, *Encyclopaedia of Religion and Ethics*, 1909, p. 294.

14 Dussaud, *Mana*, p. 399.

15 P. K. Hitti, *History of Syria*, London, 1951, p. 310.

16 *Antioch-on-the-Orontes*, iii, Princeton, 1941, the excavations 1937–9, 'Greek and Latin inscriptions', G. Downey, p. 113.

17 Chrysostom, *Ad pop. Ant.*, 19, P.G. 49, 188; cf. P.G. 57, 74; Theodoret, *Hist. Rel.*, P.G. 82, 1352B, 1404C, 1424C, 1441A.

18 A mosaic pavement at Daphne depicts the metamorphosis, Doro Levi, *Antioch Mosaic Pavements*, I, Princeton, 1947, pp. 211–14.

19 E. T. Newell, *Seleucid Mint at Antioch*, New York, 1918, p. 37.

20 G. Downey, *Ancient Antioch*, Princeton, 1963, p. 104. J. H. W. G. Liebeschuetz, *Antioch*, Oxford, 1972, p. 140, sees in the survival of the games till A.D. 520 at Antioch evidence of the 'strength and persistence of the Hellenistic traditions of the city'.

21 *Antioch-on-the-Orontes*, ii, 1938, 'The Shrines of St. Babylas at Antioch and Daphne', G. Downey, pp. 45–8. We learn of the translation from Zonaras, xiii.8. 25–31 and Ammianus Marcellinus, xiv.7.4.

22 Libanius, *Orat.* xv.53.

23 Julian, *Misopogon*, 346BD; Libanius, *Orat.* xv.79.

24 Julian, *Misopogon*, 361D.

25 Philostorgius, *Hist. Eccles.*, vii.8; Socrates, *Hist. Eccles.*, iii.18; Sozomen, *Hist. Eccles.*, v.19.

26 Ammianus Marcellinus, xxii.13.1–5; Libanius, *Orat.* lx; Julian, *Misopogon*, 361BC.

27 Theodoret, *Hist. Eccles.*, iii.12.4.

28 C. N. Cochrane, *Christianity and Classical Culture*, Oxford, 1940, p. 285.

29 G. Downey, *History of Antioch*, pp. 392f.

30 This is presupposed by Chrysostom, *Hom. contra Jul. et gentiles*, 3, P.G. 50, 537; *Hom. in Matt.*, 33f., P.G. 57, 392; so Liebeschuetz, *Antioch*, p. 225.

31 E.g. *Cod. Theod.*, xvi.10.8 (A.D. 382). The main anti-pagan legislation of Theodosius came slightly later: forbidding pagan cults in 392 (*Cod. Theod.* xvi.10. 12); destruction of temples in 399 (xvi.14.16); destruction of altars and confiscation of buildings in 408 (xvi.10.19).

32 Liebeschuetz, *Antioch*, pp. 237ff. Similar action is recorded in Egypt, where Theophilus of Alexandria used an army of fanatical monks for the purpose; D. Chitty, *The Desert a City*, Oxford, 1966, p. 54.

33 Libanius, *Orat.* xxx.51; the temples of Zeus, Athene, Dionysus and Fortuna; Liebeschuetz, *Antioch*, p. 237.

34 *Vita Rabbulae*, ed. J. J. Overbeck, Oxford, 1865.

35 O. Hendricks, 'L'activité apostolique des premiers moines syriens', *Le Proche-Orient Chrétien*, 8, 1958, pp. 18f., argues that the anti-pagan activity of the monks points to an increase of pagan practices in fifth-century Syria.

36 P. N. Ure, *Justinian and his Age*, London, 1951, p. 130; A. H. M. Jones, *The Decline of the Ancient World*, London, 1966, p. 108. To show greater concern for heresy than for paganism does not imply indifference to the latter: Chrysostom treats pagans less harshly than heretics, *Hom. in I Cor.*, iv.6, P.G. 61, 38–40.

37 Downey, *History of Antioch*, p. 483f.

38 An episode characterized by Downey, *Ibid.*, p. 559, as but one of a number of such prosecutions whose records are lost.

39 Downey, *Ibid.*, p. 563f.

40 Michael the Syrian, *Chron.*, x.12, ed. J. B. Chabot, 1901. We may note the account of Zacharias Rhetor (*Hist. Eccles.*, viii.4, C.S.C.O. *Syr.* 3.5, 1924, p. 75f.) of the 'year of disasters' (525?) in which the Ba'albek temple, which he identifies with a foundation of Solomon (1 K.ix.17, 'Solomon built ba'alat'), was struck by lightning and burnt. The three great stones 'on which now stands the oratory of the Virgin Mary', remained undamaged.

41 Elias, *Vita Johannis episc. Tellae*, 43,55.

42 Severus, *Hom.* 123, Pat. Or. xxix. 1, 1960, p. 197.

43 *L'Hist. de Barhad. Arbaia*, Pat. Or. xxiii. 2, 1932, pp. 507f.

44 The brief summary which follows is heavily dependent upon specialist work such as G. F. Moore, *Judaism in the first centuries of the Christian era*, Harvard, 1930–2; Ben Zion Bokser, *Pharisaic Judaism in transition*, New York, 1935; I. Epstein, *Judaism*, (rev. ed.) London, 1945.

45 H. L. Strack, *Introduction to the Talmud and Mishnah* (Jewish Publication Society of America), Philadelphia, 1931.

46 Josephus, *Bell.* vii.3.3.

47 *Cod. Theod.*, xvi.8.22 (A.D. 415).

48 Chrysostom, *Adv. Jud.*, i.3, P.G. 48, 847f.

49 *Ibid.*; cf. Marcel Simon, *Verus Israel. Étude sur les relations entre Chrétiens et Juifs dans l'empire romain, 138-425*, Bibliothèque des écoles français d'Athènes et de Rome (fasc. 166), Paris, 1948, p. 418.

50 Chrysostom mocks Jewish discomfiture when Julian's death left the rebuilding scheme in its infancy. The Jews should have known, he says, that the prophecies forbade its success, *Adv. Jud.*, v.11, col. 900.

51 Rowan A. Greer, *Theodore of Mopsuestia, Exegete and Theologian*, London, 1961, pp. 86ff., 'In great measure Christian exegesis was determined by Jewish ideas on the subject'. On Jewish exegesis, E. Schurer, *Geschichte*, vol.I (3rd ed.), 1901, pp. 330-50.

52 J. Rendel Harris, *The Commentaries of Isho'dad of Merv*, ed. M. D. Gibson (Horae Semiticae V), vol.I, Cambridge, 1911, Introduction, p. xxii; F. X. Funk, *Die Haggadische Elemente in den Homilien des Aphrahats des persischen Weisen*, Wien, 1892, pp. 24ff.; *Aphrahats des pers. Weisen Homilien*, ed. G. Bert, T.U. iii. 3.4, 1888, Einleitung, p. xxxv.

53 Renunciation of property and marriage was not a characteristic of mainstream Judaism, A. Vööbus, *History of Asceticism in the Syrian Orient*, i, C.S.C.O. Subsidia 14, 1958, pp. 14-25.

54 J. Rendel Harris, *The Commentaries of Isho'dad of Merv*, p. xxii.

55 Ignatius, *Ad Magnes.* 8 and 10; *Ad Philad.* 6.

56 *Synazarium eccles. Constantinopol.*, ed. H. Delehaye, Brussels, 1902, p. 138.

57 Chrysostom, *Adv. Jud.*, viii.4, col. 933.

58 *Ibid.*, i.5, cols. 850f.; vi.2, col. 913.

59 *Ibid.*, i.7, col. 853.

60 *Ibid.*, iii.3, col. 865.

61 *Ibid.*, iv.1, col. 875.

62 Malalas, *Chron.*, xv.103. Doubtless the reason for this was political rather than ecclesiastical. The need felt by Jewry to maintain good relations at court may be reflected in Chrysostom's savage reminder that they chose this policy on the

occasion of the crucifixion of Christ: We have no king but Caesar. *Ibid.*, i.2, col. 846.

63 G. Downey, *History of Antioch*, p. 108, on such friction arising from political rivalry between the Seleucid and Ptolemaic factions.

64 Chrysostom, *Adv. Jud.*, iv.4, col. 876f.

65 Athanasius, *Orat.* i, *Contra Arian.*, 78, P.G. 26, 89; Theodoret, *Haeret. fab. compend.*, ii.8, P.G. 83,393.

66 Theodore of Mops., *Comm. in Jn.*, vi.57, ed. Vosté, p. 107.

67 Chrysostom, *De Sacerdot.*, lv.4, P.G. 48, 667.

68 *Cod. Just.*, i.1.8.

69 Zach. Rhetor, *Hist. Eccles.*, vii.8, C.S.C.O. *Syr.* iii. 5, 1924, vol. 2, p. 42.

70 Irenaeus, *Contra Haer.*, iv.21.1.

71 Eusebius, *Dem. Evang.*, i.2.10. The evidence from Eusebius is given more fully in my *Eusebius of Caesarea*, London, 1960, p. 169ff.

72 *Praepar. Evang.*, vii.9.

73 A useful outline of the complexity of the matter is found in R. McL. Wilson, *Gnosis and the New Testament*, Oxford, 1968, ch. 1. Among the more important contributions to the study of gnosticism are W. Bousset, *Hauptprobleme der Gnosis*, Göttingen, 1907; H. Leisegang, *Die Gnosis*, Stuttgart, 1924; H. Jonas, *Gnosis und spätantiker Zeit*, Göttingen, 1934-54; R. McL. Wilson, *The Gnostic Problem*, London, 1958.

74 Irenaeus, *Adv. Haer.*, i.23.

75 R. M. Grant, *Gnosticism and early Christianity*, New York, 1959, ch. 3, examines in detail the problems connected with Helena.

76 Justin, *Apol.*, i.26.

77 Irenaeus, *Adv. Haer.*, i.24.1.

78 Eusebius, *Hist. Eccles.*, iv.30.3.

79 Ephrem, *Contra Haer.*, Hymn 14.7, C.S.C.O. *Syr.* 76, 1957, p. 51. See also C. W. Mitchell, *Ephraim's Prose Refutations of Mani, Marcion and Bardaisan*, I, London, 1912, p. 141, for Ephrem's view of Marcion's denigration of matter.

80 *Contra Haer.*, Hymn 40.1-4, p. 120.

81 Ephrem, *Contra Haer.*, iii.7, C.S.C.O. *Syr.* 76, p. 12.

82 A. Adam, *Texte zum Manichaismus* (*Kleine Texte für Vorlesungen und Übungen*, 175), 1954, no. 56, pp. 82f.; P. Brown, 'The Diffusion of Manichaeism in the Roman Empire', *J.R.S.*, lix, 1969, p. 92.

83 *Chronicum Maroniticum*, C.S.C.O. *Syr.*, iii.4, 1904, p. 59.

84 A. Vööbus, *History of Asceticism in the Syrian Orient*, i, C.S.C.O. Subsid. 14, p. 160, contradicting F. C. Burkitt, *The Religion of the Manichees*, Cambridge, 1925, p. 44, who sees no Buddhist influence in Manichaeism.

85 C.S.C.O. *Syr.* 1, 1903, *Chronica Minora* i, pp. 33f.

86 Pat. Or. xxix. 1, 1930.

87 The last element is doubtful; Augustine, *contra Faust.*, ii.3, designates it *aer*.

88 On the Manichaean conception of salvation, H. C. Puech, 'Der Begriff der Erlösung in Manichaismus', *Eranos Jahrbuch*, 1936, pp. 224ff. The Manichaean myth is set out in detail in F. C. Burkitt, *Religion of the Manichees*, Cambridge, 1925, pp. 17-42.

89 Severus, *Hom.* 223, Pat. Or. xxix, 1, 1930, p. 150.

90 *Ibid.*, p. 152.

91 *Ibid.*, pp. 154-70.

92 *Ibid.*, pp. 174-8.

93 E. G. Browne, *Literary History of Persia*, i, pp. 160ff.

94 Baghdad embraced the pagan Thabit ibn Qurra, Christians like Hunayn ibn Ishaq, Muslim heretics, Jews. There were active persecutions of Manichaeans in A.D. 780, 782 and 786-7; Browne, *Literary History of Persia*, i, pp. 306f.

95 E.g., Chrysostom, *Comm. in Gal.*, P.G. 61, 668.

96 Ephrem, *Contra Haer.*, iii.7, C.S.C.O. *Syr.* 77, p. 12; A. Vööbus, *Hist. of Asceticism*, i, p. 10.

97 On its decline in the west, P. Brown, 'The Diffusion of Manich.', pp. 101f.

98 F. Nau, Pat. Syr. i. 2, 1907, p. 527, warns us that the gnosticism and Manichaeism of Bardaisan's later disciples must not be read back into his own beliefs.

99 Patristic tradition aligns him with Valentinus; *Biographie inédité de Bardesane l'Astrologue*, ed. F. Nau, Paris, 1897, p. 15; so Eusebius, *Hist. Eccles.*, iv.30.3; Jerome, *De vir. ill.*, 33. Philoxenus, Pat. Or. xiii. 2, 1916, p. 248, says that B. held certain doctrines in common with Val.; Epiphanius, *Haeres.*, lvi, B. reverted to Val. from Christianity; Ephrem, *Contra Haer.*, iii.5, C.S.C.O. *Syr.* 76, who says much about B., does not refer to a connection with Val. J. Quasten, *Patrol.*, i, 1950, p. 263, accepts the link with Val., so also F. C. Burkitt, *Early Eastern Christianity*, p. 157, but A. Vööbus, *Hist. of Ascet.*, i, pp. 64f., disputes it. F. Nau, Pat. Syr. i. 2, 1907, p. 535, suggests that B.'s association with Val. was in respect of his astrological knowledge alone.

100 Ephrem was the first to associate the two; H. J. W. Drijvers, *Bardaisan of Edessa*, (Eng. tr. Studia Semitica Neerlandica, 6) Assen, 1966, pp. 42ff.

101 Eusebius, *Praepar. Evang.*, vi.10. De Fato, probably a summary of B.'s teaching assembled by a disciple, Philip, is extant as *Liber Legum Regionum*, Pat. Syr. i. 2, 1907, cols. 536-611.

102 Ephrem, *Contra Haer.*, iii. 5, C.S.C.O. *Syr.* 77, p. 11.

103 The 'Hymn of the Soul', 41f., in *Acts of Thomas*, is attributed to the school of Bardaisan by A. A. Bevan, *Texts and Studies*, v. 3, 1897, but is perhaps rather Manichaean in origin, W. Bousset, *Z.N.T.W.*, xviii, 1917-18, p. 1-39. Bousset, *Hauptprobleme*, p. 71, associates Bardaisan's triad with semitic pagan triads; so F. Cumont, *Les Religions orientales dans le Paganisme romain*, 4th ed., Paris, 1929, p. 262, n. 77.

104 C. W. Mitchell, *S. Ephraim's Prose Refutations of Mani etc.*, vol. ii, p. 5, distinguishes Bardaisan's creation doctrine from that of Mani. Ephrem mentions only four principles, omitting light from the list, F. Nau, *Biographie*, p. 502.

105 *Adamantii Dialogus de Recte in Deum Fide*, P.G. 11, 1796, early fourth century, of the school of Bardaisan, wrongly attributed to Origen.

106 *Ibid.*, col. 1792.

107 Ephrem, *Contra Haer.*, vi.10, p. 24.

108 *Ibid.*, lii, p. 199.

109 *The Discourses of Philoxenus*, XII, ed. E. A. Wallis Budge, 1894, vol. i, p. 512; Introduction, vol. i, p. xiv. So also Akhsenaya in Pat. Or. xiii.2, 1916, p. 248. This is not found in Ephrem, who says that B. taught that Christ received his divine nature from God and his humanity from the virgin; Nau, *Biographie*, pp. 504, 511.

110 F. C. Burkitt, *Early Eastern Christianity*, p. 160; Nau, *Biographie*, pp. 504, 511.

111 Cf. H. E. W. Turner, *The Pattern of Christian Truth*, London, 1954, p. 93.

112 A. Vööbus, *Hist. of Asceticism*, i, p. 61.

2 The interpretation of the biblical record

1 *Commentaire d'Išo'dad de Merv sur l'ancien testament*, C.S.C.O. *Syr.* 75, 1955, p. 30.
2 J. Daniélou, *Origen*, Eng. tr., London, 1955, pp. 178-91; but cf. H. de Lubac, *Histoire et Esprit*, Paris, 1950, pp. 150-66.
3 *Ibid.*, p. 140.
4 The inconsistencies between the Synoptics and the fourth gospel are raised from the level of literal contradiction to that of spiritual agreement in *Comm. Jn*, x.5. 20.
5 So the narrative of the garden of Eden is 'stories of things that never really happened', but figuratively they refer to hidden truths, *Hom. in Gen.*, vi.1.
6 *Hom. in Ezek.*, ii.2, 'the Holy Spirit is the true exegete'. *Ibid.*, iv.3, 'We always need the Holy Spirit in order to understand the Scriptures'.
7 The authority of St Paul for spiritual interpretation is derived in *de Princ.*, iv.1. 12f. from I Cor. ix.9f. and Gal. iv.21ff.
8 Often it is no more than this. The Old Testament could lead to unchastity, for example, if the polygamy of the patriarchs was followed literally; *de Princ.*, iv.6.
9 The particular application of this to the text of Exodus is discussed by H. de Lubac, *Origène, Homélies sur l'Exode*, S.C. 16, Paris, 1947, Introduction. On the liturgical importance of allegorizing, see de Lubac, *Hist. et Esprit*, pp. 131ff.
10 J. Daniélou, *Origen*, p. 161, sums up his extended study of Origen's exegesis by saying that in Origen there are only two meanings to Scripture, the literal and the christological, and that the threefold scheme was a complication from Plato.
11 *Hom. in Levit.*, v.1; *Select. in psalmos*, i.4.
12 'He was always consorting with Plato', said Porphyry of Origen, Eus. *Hist. Eccles.*, vi.19.8. But the identification of this Origen is in doubt.
13 *Hom. in Josh.*, viii.4, 'These things are now given to us in outline . . . the outline will be filled in at the second coming, and what we now grasp in anticipation by faith and hope we shall then grasp bodily in its reality'.
14 *Hom. in Exod.*, v.2.
15 *Hom. in Gen.*, ii.6.
16 Gregory Thaumaturgos, *Paneg. in Origen*, 16, writes of Origen's long struggles and meditations to arrive at the truth; cf. Pamphilus, *Apol.*, P.G. 17, 543.
17 Origen urges would-be exegetes to exercise caution: 'There are so many mysteries that we cannot hope to explain them', *Hom. in Gen.*, x.5. He claimed no originality in his method of exegesis: 'I will attempt to show what the accepted methods are . . . the rule which has always been used', *de Princ.*, iv.2.2.
18 H. de Lubac, *Origène, Homélies sur l'Exode*, S.C. 16, Introduction, p. 47.
19 Porphyry in Eusebius, *Hist. Eccles.*, vi.19.4.
20 We are warned against this by J. Daniélou, *Origen*, p. 164: both schools used typology, 'but at Antioch theologians concentrated on the catechetical traditions . . . while the Alexandrians concentrated on what tradition had to say about the spiritual life'.
21 I. Epstein, *Judaism*, London, 1945, p. 198. 'Whilst Talmudic teachers did occasionally employ allegory in their interpretation of the Bible, they never lost sight of the fact that the Bible is primarily a revelation of God's will, and not a guide for ecstatic contemplation of the divine'. For haggadic treatment of the Scriptures by gnostics - e.g. Saturninus - see R. M. Grant, *Gnosticism and Early Christianity*, New York, 1959, p. 114.

22 Rowan A. Greer, *Theodore of Mopsuestia, Exegete and Theologian*, London, 1961, pp. 86-8, relates Jewish exegetical practice to Antiochene.
23 Lucian's recension of the Bible has received much attention: see H. B. Swete, *Introduction to the Old Testament in Greek*, Cambridge, 1900, pp. 80ff.; G. Bardy, *Recherches sur Saint Lucien d'Antioche et son École*, Paris, 1936, pp. 164ff.; on the transmission of the recension to become the received text see F. G. Kenyon, *The Text of the Greek Bible*, London, 2nd ed., 1949, pp. 197ff.
24 Jerome, *Ep.* 106 *ad Sunniam*, ii.
25 P.G. 84, 29ff.
26 This version was used by Theodore of Mopsuestia and corrected by him still further in the direction of intelligibility (R. Devreesse, *Essai sur Théodore de Mopsueste*, Vatican, 1938, pp. 55ff.), omitting or rejecting certain passages such as psalm titles which appeared to him to have no relevance. Rejection of difficult passages was according to Origen (*Comm. in Matt.*, xv.3) one of the inevitable results of the Antiochene rejection of allegorization. Origen was writing with special reference to Marcion's rejection of the Old Testament.
27 Origen, *Hom. in Jeremiah*, 39: like botanists, Christians 'gather all the letters they find in Scripture, even the iotas; they ascertain the peculiar virtue of each and what it is useful for, and they see that nothing in Scripture is unnecessary'.
28 Eustathius, *De engastrymutho contra Origenem*, P.G. 18, 613-74.
29 *De engastr.*, 16.
30 *Ibid.*, 28f.
31 Greg. Nyssa, *de pythonissa*, P.G. 45, 107-14.
32 Orig., *Hom. in Gen.*, vi.1.
33 Orig., *Hom. in Levit.*, i.1.
34 Eusebius, *Hist. Eccles.*, vi. 37, describes Origen's invitation to correct the doctrinal errors arising from their literalism. Extreme literalism seems to have remained a characteristic of Arab exegesis. Cf. the disputation between the 8-9th century Mar Timothy I and Caliph Mahdi (A. Mingana, *Kitab ad Dīu wad Daula*, ed. and tr., Manchester, 1923-4, p. 17): if Christ is the Son, whom did God marry? pp. 21f., how could God beget without genital organs? pp. 47ff. Mahdi assumes that the Christian gospels were given by God to Christ as the Qur'an was given to Muhammad. But Mahdi by no means always has the worst of the argument: he rejects Timothy's 'similes and comparisons', p. 79.
35 On this point, see A. Vaccari, 'La *theoria* nella scuola esegetica di Antiocha', *Biblica* i, 1920, pp. 3ff.
36 Cyril Alex., *Comm. in Hos.*, ii.23, P.G. 71, 100.
37 Theodoret, *Comm. in Hos.*, ii.23, P.G. 81, 1568.
38 Theodore Mops. *Comm. in Hos.* ii.23, P.G. 66, 144.
39 Cyril Alex., *Comm. in Hos.* xiii.14, P.G. 71, 312.
40 Theodoret, *Comm. in Hos.*, xiii.14, P.G. 81, 1628.
41 Theodore Mops., *Comm. in Hos.*, xiii.14, P.G. 66, 205.
42 Cyril Alex., *Comm. in Zech.*, ix.9, P.G. 72, 145.
43 Theodoret, *Comm. in Zech.*, ix.9, P.G. 81, 1921.
44 Theo. Mops., *Comm. in Zech.*, ix.9, P.G. 66, 556-60.
45 Cyril Alex., *Comm. in Mic.*, iv.2, P.G. 71, 693-5.
46 Theodoret, *Comm. in Mic.*, iv.2, P.G. 81, 1760f.
47 Theo. Mops., *Comm. in Mic.*, iv.2, P.G. 66, 364f.
48 G. W. Ashby, *Theodoret of Cyrrhus as Exegete of the Old Testament*, Grahamstown, 1972, pp. 40-4.
49 The term *theoria* only came to be distinguished from allegorization in the late

4th century, prior to which it had denoted any kind of contemplation of the truth including allegorization. Diodore of Tarsus makes the distinction in the *Prooemium* to his Commentary on ps.118 (L. Mariès, 'Extraits du Commentaire de Diodore de Tarse sur les Psaumes', *Recherches Sc. Relig.*, 10 (1919), p. 96).

50 Facundus of Hermiana, *Pro defensione Trium Capitulum*, iii.6, P.L. 67, 602: 'unde et odium Origenianorum incurrit'.

51 Theo. Mops., *Comm. in Mic.*, v.5f., P.G. 66, 377.

52 Theo. Mops., *Comm. in Nahum*, iii.8, P.G. 66, 420.

53 Gal. iv.24. H. B. Swete, *Theodori Episcopi Mopsuesteni in Epistolas B. Pauli Commentarii*, Cambridge, 1880, vol. i, pp. 73ff.

54 *Ibid.*, p. 79.

55 Below, ch. 3 pp. 61f.

56 Theo. Mops., *Hom. Cat.*, xiv.14, ed Tonneau, pp. 431f.

57 *Comm. in Joel*, P.G. 66, 212.

58 *Ibid.*, P.G. 66, 229–33.

59 *Comm. in Mal.*, P.G. 66, 620f.

60 *Ibid.* 560.

61 R. Devreesse, *Essai sur Théodore de Mopsueste*, Vatican, 1948, pp. 70f.

62 C. Sant, *The Old Testament Interpretation of Eusebius of Caesarea*, Malta, 1967. Professor Sant has kindly put at my disposal the whole of his doctoral thesis of which the published book comprises Part II.

63 C. Sant, unpublished thesis, 1964, pp. 681ff.

64 This is very close to Theodore's insistence upon establishing the regulating idea of each psalm, and interpreting the details in the light of that idea.

65 G. W. Ashby, *Theodoret of Cyrrhus as Exegete of the Old Testament*, Grahamstown, 1972, p. 55.

66 *The Commentaries of Isho'dad of Merv, bishop of Hadatha*, Cambridge, 1911 (*Horae Semiticae* V) vol. i, p. xxxi.

67 Ps. cxviii.22; Afr. Hom. i, *Aphraat's des persischen Weisen Homilien ans dem Syrischen übersetzt und erläutert* von Georg Bert, T.U., iii.3, 4, 1888, p. 6.

68 *Ibid.*, p. 8. Afrahat's insistence that Christ is the rock, following the lead of I Cor. x.4, 'and that rock was Christ', and the absence of reference to Peter as the rock (Matt. xvi.18, 'upon this rock'), may have a parallel in Afrahat's consistent treatment of Christ rather than Peter as 'chief shepherd', noted by C. S. C. Williams, 'Aphraat on St. Peter', *J.T.S.*, l, nos. 197–8, 1949, pp. 71f., against D. J. Parisot, Pat. Syr. i. 1, 1894, Introduction, p. liii. It signifies perhaps an unawareness of Roman claims rather than opposition to them.

69 Gen. xlix.10, 'When he comes, the heathen will hope in him'; Ps. ii.7, 'thou art my son'; Ps. xxii.16, 'they pierced my hands and my feet'; Ps. xvi.10, 'thou wilt not suffer thy holy one to see corruption'; Ps. xviii.44, 'a strange people will hear me'; Ps. lxix.21, 'they gave me gall'; Ps. cx.3, 'from the womb thou hast endowed me with princely gifts'; Is. vii.14, 'a virgin shall conceive'; Is. ix.6, 'to us a child is born'; Is. lii and liii *passim*; Dan. ix.26f., 'after sixty two weeks will the anointed come and will be killed'; Zech. xiii.7, 'a spear will slay the shepherd'; Zech. xiv.7, 'the Lord will declare a day when the day will be as night'; Afrahat, *Homily 17*, pp. 285–8.

70 *Saint Ephrem, Commentaire de l'Evangile Concordant*, texte syriaque (MS Chester Beatty 709), ed. and tr. Dom Louis Leloir, O.S.B. (*Chester Beatty Monographs*, 8), Dublin 1963, p. 234–5.

71 *Sancti Ephraem Syri in Genesim et in Exodum Commentarii*, C.S.C.O. Syr. 71, p. 25.

72 *Ibid.*, xix.3, p. 84.
73 *Ibid.*, xxvi.2f.; p. 89.
74 *Ibid.*, xxxiv.5, p. 97.
75 *Ibid.*, xli.4, p. 110.
76 *Comm. in Exod.*, xii.2f., p. 141.
77 *Ibid.*, xxiv.1, p. 151.
78 *Comm. in Gen.*, ii.9, p. 30.
79 *Ibid.*, i.1, p. 8.
80 *Ibid.*, ii.34, p. 45.
81 *Ibid.*, xiii.1-5, pp. 72f.; cf. Galatians iv.21ff.
82 *Afrahat*, ed. G. Bert, T.U. iii. 3, 4, 1888, p. 8.
83 *Ibid.*, p. 9.
84 Ephrem, *Comm. de l'Évangile*, ed. Leloir, p. 42.
85 *Ibid.*, pp. 160-1.
86 *Ibid.*, p. 164.
87 *Ibid.*, p. 124.
88 *Ibid.*, p. 70.
89 *Ibid.*, p. 216.
90 *Afrahat*, ed. G. Bert, pp. 336-45. His enthusiasm for detailed parallelism may be thought to defeat its purpose when he sees a typological connection between the facts that Joseph was buried in Egypt and Christ in Jerusalem.
91 Ephrem, ed. Leloir, p. 168.
92 *Ibid.*, p. 118.
93 *Ibid.*, pp. 126-7.
94 *Ad Autol.*, iv.24.
95 T. Jansma, 'L'Hexaméron de Jacques de Sarûg', *L'Orient Syrien*, iv.2, 1959, pp. 135-42. The idea appears as late as the ninth century in Išoʻdad of Merv; C. van den Eynde, C.S.C.O. *Syr.* 75, Preface, p. xiv.
96 *Homélies de Narsai sur la Création*, (Pat. Or. xxxiv. 3, 4, 1968, pp. 461f., especially p. 462 n. 10.
97 *Ibid.*, p. 514.
98 'Theophilus of Antioch to Autolycus', *H.T.R.* 40, 1947, p. 237; cf. *H.T.R.* 43, 1950, p. 196. We may note that the idea that Adam was created neither mortal nor immortal but neutral (*ad Autol.*, i. 27) is described by Nemesius of Emesa as what 'the Hebrews say', *de nat. hom.*, P.G. 40, 514B.
99 *Art. cit.*, p. 235.
100 F. L. Cross, *The Early Christian Fathers*, London, 1960, p. 57.
101 *Ad Autolycum*, ii.15, P.G. 6.
102 *Ibid.*, ii.14.
103 *Ibid.*, ii.17.
104 *Ibid.*, ii.16.
105 *Ibid.*, ii.13.
106 *De opif.*, vii(26f.).
107 *Ad Autol.*, ii.13.
108 *De opif.*, xi(38).
109 *Ad Autol.*, ii.15.
110 *De opif.*, xiv(45).
111 *Ad Autol.*, ii.16.
112 *De opif.*, xx(63).
113 *Leg. alleg.*, ii.15.53.
114 *Ad Autol.*, ii.25.

178   *Notes*

115 *Leg. alleg.*, i.19.63f.
116 *Ad Autol.*, ii.24.
117 A. Vööbus, *History of the School of Nisibis*, C.S.C.O., Subsidia 26, Louvain, 1965, p. 20. What is written here is heavily dependent upon the work of Prof. Vööbus.
118 Translated by A. Vööbus, *Nisibis*, p. 17, from Cod.B.M. Add. 12, 138.
119 Andreas of Samosata, *Ep.* to Alex. of Hierapolis, P.G. 84, 649.
120 Facundus, *Pro defens. trium capit.*, vi.1, P.L. 67, 655f.
121 A. Vööbus, *Nisibis*, pp. 57–89.
122 *Homélie de Narsai sur les trois docteurs nestoriennes*, ed. A. Mingana, Mausilii, 1905, the three doctors being Diodore, Theodore and Nestorius.
123 P. Gignoux, Pat. Or. xxxiv, 3–4, 1968, p. 425. For an extended study of Narsai's doctrinal position, see pp. 459–516.
124 F. Martin, 'Homélie de Narsès sur les trois docteurs nestoriennes', *Journal Asiatique*, sér.ix, t.xiv, 1899, p. 475.
125 T. Jansma, *Étude sur la pensée de Narsai: l'homélie xxxiv, Essai d'interprétation*, *Oriens Syr.*, xi, 1966, p. 168. P. Gignoux, *op. cit.*, pp. 461–5, shows Narsai's use of Afrahat's *Demonstrations*; and p. 470, that Ephrem exercised 'possible' influence, but not of importance.
126 P. Gignoux, *op. cit.*, p. 425.
127 *Hom.* iii.119f., Pat. Or. xxxiv.3/4, p. 590.
128 *Hom.* iii.183–7, p. 594.
129 *Hom.* iv. 71–9, p. 614.
130 A. Vööbus, *Nisibis*, pp. 125f.
131 *Ibid.*, p. 140.
132 Paulos, *de partibus divinae legis*, in Procopius, *Anecdota*, ed. J. Haury, *Opera* xx.17, Leipzig, 1905–13, p. 127.
133 A. Vööbus, *Nisibis*, pp. 179–85.
134 *Synodicon orientale ou receuil de synodes nestoriens*, ed J. B. Chabot, *Notices et extraits des MSS de la Bib. Nat. . . .*, 37, Paris, 1902, pp. 136ff.
135 A. Vööbus, *Nisibis*, p. 235; cf. Assemani, *Bib. Orient.* iii.1, pp. 81ff.
136 Išo'dad quotes his work, and there are possible extracts in the tenth century *Gannat Bussamē*, the standard commentary on the Nestorian lectionary.
137 The term of abuse is from *Histoire de Mar Jabalaha*, P. Bedjan, Paris, 1893, p. 477. A. Vööbus, *Nisibis*, p. 264, notes the general affinity of Henana with Origen, Neo-Platonism and mysticism. Cf. also Hoffmann, *Auszügen aus syrischen Akten persischer Märtyrer*, Leipzig, 1880, pp. 102ff.
138 Assemani, *Bib. Orient.*, iii.1, p. 84. Ibn at Tayyib's report is confirmed by Išo'dad's *Prooemium* to Job. The sentence of anathema is recorded in *Synodicon orientale*, ed. Chabot, p. 138.
139 *The Commentaries of Išo'dad of Merv*, Cambridge, 1911, (*Horae Semiticae V*), vol. 2, pp. 131, 135.
140 *Traités d'Isaï le docteur et de Henana d'Adiabene sur les Martyrs, le Vendredi d'or et les Rogations*, Pat. Or. vii.1, 1911, pp. 58f.
141 *Histoire nestorienne*, Pat. Or. xiii. 4, p. 534.
142 *Synodicon orientale*, p. 198, quoted by Vööbus, *Nisibis*, p. 303.
143 *Histoire nestorienne*, xiii.4, p. 511; Vööbus, *Nisibis*, p. 312.
144 J. Rendel Harris, in his Introduction to M. D. Gibson's text of Išo'dad's Commentaries (Cambridge, 1911, vol. i, pp. xxxiii–vi) identifies over 150 quotations of Theodore in the Commentary on John alone.
145 G. Diettrich, 'Isho'dadh's Stellung in der Auslegungsgeschichte des Alten Testaments an seinem Commentaren zu Hosea, Joel, Jona, Sacharja 9–14 und einigen

angehängten Psalmen', *Z.A.T.W.*, Beiheft vi, Giessen, 1902, pp. lxif.
146 *Comm. on Matt.*, ed. M. D. Gibson, p. 4.
147 *Commentaire d'Isho'dad de Merv sur l'ancien testament*, vol. i. Genèse, 1955 (C.S.C.O. *Syr.* 75, p. vii. The Syriac text appears in C.S.C.O. *Syr.* 67, 1950).
148 *Comm. on Matt.*, ed. M. D. Gibson, p. 55.
149 *Ibid.*, p. 57. The reader may wonder whether in this instance Išo'dad improves much upon Origen.
150 *Comm. on Genesis*, ed. van der Eynde, p. 30.
151 G. Diettrich, *Isho'dad's Stellung . . .*, *Z.A.T.W.*, vi, 1902.
152 *Comm. on Matt.*, ed. M. D. Gibson, p. 6.
153 *Comm. on John*, ed. M. D. Gibson, p. 211.
154 *Comm. on Mark*, ed. M. D. Gibson, p. 143; *Comm. on John*, pp. 224, 283, etc.
155 *Comm. on John*, pp. 289f.
156 *Comm. on Luke*, ed. M. D. Gibson, p. 153.
157 *Ibid.*, p. 163.
158 *Ibid.*, p. 168.
159 *Comm. on Matt.*, p. 24.
160 *Ibid.*, p. 42.
161 *Ibid.*, p. 80.
162 C.S.C.O. *Syr.* 75, p. x.
163 Canon viii, Assemani, *Bib. Orient.*, iii. 2, p. 188.

3 Historiography in the Eastern Church

1 Cf. R. L. P. Milburn, *Early Christian interpretations of history*, London, 1954, ch. 3; L. G. Patterson, *God and history in early Christian thought*, London, 1967, ch. 2, and bibliography on p. 158.
2 This is documented in my *Eusebius of Caesarea*, London, 1960, ch. ix.
3 Eus., *Laus Const.*, xvi.4f.
4 F. Jacoby, *Frag. Gr. Hist.*, p. 260. Cf. Fergus Millar, 'P. Herennius Dexippus: the Greek world and the third century invasions', *J.R.S.* lix, 1969, pp. 14f., summarizes the development of pagan and Christian historiography and sees Porphyry as the only pagan writer to compose comparative chronology of this kind.
5 'Pagan and Christian historiography in the fourth century', in *The Conflict between Paganism and Christianity in the fourth century*, ed. A. Momigliano, Oxford, 1963, p. 85.
6 G.C.S., *Eusebius Werke* V, ed J. Karst, 1911 (Armenian version), pp. 2, 127, 40.
7 A. Momigliano, *Conflict*, p. 85.
8 Zacharias Rhetor, *Hist. Eccles.*, i.1, C.S.C.O. *Syr.* iii. 5, 1924, p. 5.
9 C.S.C.O. *Syr.* ii. 91, 92, 1913, 1915.
10 *Ibid.*, i. 2, C.S.C.O. *Syr.* ii. 91, pp. 22f.
11 *Ibid.*, i. 3, pp. 24f.
12 *Ibid.*, i. 4, pp. 25-8.
13 C.S.C.O. *Syr.* iii. 4, part 3 section 2, 1905.
14 *Ibid.*, pp. 265ff.
15 C.S.C.O. *Syr.* iii. 7, 1910.
16 *Ibid.*, p. 9.
17 *Ibid.*, p. 20.
18 *Incerti auctoris Chronicon ps.-Dionysianum vulgo dictum*, C.S.C.O. *Syr.* iii. 1/2, 1927/33.

19 Long acquaintance with Eusebius' work persuades me that the charge that Eusebius was a careless and unscrupulous user of sources is a serious exaggeration; e.g. Lawlor and Oulton, *Eus. Eccles. History*, 1927, vol. 2, intro., sect. iii; R. M. Grant, 'Early Alexandrian Christianity', *Church History* 40, 1971, no. 2, p. 142, 'Eusebius can never be trusted if contradicted by a more reliable witness, hardly ever even if not contradicted'.

20 Eus., *Prae. Evang.* vii.8.23.

21 *Vita Const.*, i.1; cf. also i.8.

22 *Laus Const.*, i.4ff. The theme returns at iii.5, 'the emperor frames his earthly government after the pattern of the divine original'; and iv.3, 'the Word expresses by the similitude of an earthly kingdom that heavenly one to which he earnestly invites all mankind'.

23 *Theophany*, ii.65ff.

24 I accept the analysis of the structure of the *Hist. Eccles.* in R. Laqueur, *Eusebius als Historiker seiner Zeit*, Berlin and Leipzig, 1929.

25 E.g. the Huns, Zacharias Rhetor, *Hist. Eccles.*, vii, C.S.C.O. *Syr.* iii. 5, 1924, part i; *Edessene Chronicle* xl, C.S.C.O. *Syr.* iii. 4, part 1 section 1, 1903.

26 Zacharias Rhetor, *Hist. Eccles.* xii.15, one of the fragments of which is part of an account of barbarian attacks upon the city of Rome.

27 For the rebuilding of the city, Procop., *de aedif.*, ii.10.2-25, on which see G. Downey, 'Procopius of Antioch: a study of method in *De Aedificiis*', *Byzantion* xiv, 1939, pp. 361-79.

28 *Chron. Edess.* xl, C.S.C.O. *Syr.* iii. 4, part 1 section 1, 1903.

29 Pat. Or. xxiii.2, 1932.

30 *The Histories of Rabban Hormizd the Persian and Rabban Bar-'Idta*, ed. E. A. Wallis Budge, London 1902, vol. i, 882-94, p. 150.

31 *Ibid.*, 1271-1316, pp. 166-8.

32 *Chron. Anon.*, C.S.C.O. *Syr.* iii. 4, part 1 section 2, 1903, pp. 21, 23.

33 *Chron. Miscell. ad 724*, C.S.C.O. *Syr.* iii. 4, 1904, p. 145.

34 *Chron. ad 846*, C.S.C.O., *Syr.* iii. 4, 1904, p. 229.

35 *Chron. Jacobi Edess.*, C.S.C.O. *Syr.* iii. 4, 1905, p. 326.

36 *Histoires d'Aboudemmeh et de Marouta*, Pat. Or. iii. 1, 1909, pp. 77f.

37 *Ibid.*, p. 55.

38 *Chron. Maroniticum*, C.S.C.O. *Syr.* iii. 4 part 2, 1904, pp. 71f.

39 *Eliae Metropolitae Nisibeni Opus chronologicum*, C.S.C.O. *Syr.* iii. 7, 1910, pp. 126-33.

40 A. Vööbus, *op. cit.*, pp. 15, 105, secular history was taught at the school of Edessa and perhaps also at Nisibis.

41 *Incerti auctoris Chronicon ps.-Dionysianum vulgo dictum*, C.S.C.O. *Syr.* iii. 1/2, 1927/33, is an exception. Its later chapters, dealing with the sixth century, are a telling narrative, giving us glimpses of real people carrying on their lives in the midst of a battlefield, e.g. pp. 296-313.

42 Theod., *Hist. Eccles.*, i.1.

43 Eus., *Theophany*, iv.36 on Matt. xxiv.14. So also his *Commentary on the Psalms* constantly interprets the psalm-heading 'For the end' as referring to the earthly rule of Christ.

44 Theod., *Hist. Eccles.*, i.2.9.

45 A. J. Festugière, *Antioch païenne et chrétienne*, Paris, 1959, p. 293.

46 P.G. 82, 1283ff.

47 Theod. *Hist. Eccles.*, iv.23; *H. Rel.*, viii,1373AB.

48 P.G. 82, 1377B.

49 A. Vööbus, *History of Asceticism in the Syrian Orient* i, C.S.C.O. Subsidia 14, Louvain 1958, discusses the ascetic, dualist elements in early Syrian Christianity and suggests eastern roots, possibly Indian (pp. 166f.). In the early fourth century the Church tried to sever its connections with this eastern link carrying gnostic implications, and the transition is to be observed in Aphrahat's *Homilies* (*op. cit.*, pp. 173–8).

50 P.G. 47, 623–92.

51 See R. A. Norris, *Manhood and Christ*, Oxford 1963, pp. 160–72, on the concealed Platonism of Theodore. The quasi-Platonist terminology may be the fourth century expression of the same pre-philosophical dualism that is so strong an element in Syrian monasticism.

52 P.G. 66, 317C. Something of this twofold division may appear in the lectures delivered soon after 551 by Paulos, *De Partibus divinae legis*, in which he divides his subject matter into two after his initial treatment of the nature of God (*de part.*, i.12-20): the first, the present age (ii.1-13), followed by the age to come (ii.14-25).

53 Cf. Theo. *Comm. in I Thess.*, v.4, Swete, ii, p. 33; *Hom. Cat.*, xiv.10, ed. Tonneau, p. 423; *Comm. in Ephes.*, ed. Swete, p. 128f. Christ, 'by his union with our nature, became to us a pledge of our participation in the event', that is, the ascension to immortality, *Comm. on the Lord's Prayer and on the Sacraments*, ed. A. Mingana, *Woodbrooke Studies* 6, Cambridge, 1933, p. 147. Notice also the imagery of the seed sown for future germination: 'When [the sacramental bread] receives the Holy Spirit and his grace, it is enabled to be sown for its eater to [bear fruit in] the happiness of immortality', *Ibid.*, p. 213.

54 R. A. Norris, *Manhood and Christ*, p. 175.

55 Cf. R. A. Greer, *Theodore of Mopsuestia. Exegete and Theologian*, London, 1961, p. 23.

56 The primary importance of human freedom finds constant expression in Theodore's work; for example, *Paulus kommentare aus dem griechischen Kirche*, ed. K. Staab, Munster, 1933, p. 119. The question is treated by A. Vööbus, 'Regarding the theological anthropology of Theodore of Mopsuestia', *Church History* 33, 1964, pp. 118ff.

57 A. Vööbus, *History of the School of Nisibis*, C.S.C.O. Subsidia 26, 1965, p. 259, draws attention to Aphrahat *Demonstrationes* vii.313, (Pat. Syr. i.1-2, Paris, 1898-1907) and xiv.685; Ephrem, *Contra Haereses*, xviii.3, C.S.C.O. Syr. 76, 1957 and *De Virginitate* iii.8 (*Hymni de virg.*, ed. i.e. Rahmani, Scharfeh, 1907, p. 9). At a later date, Henana's purge of Theodore's influence brought upon him from Babai the accusation of deterministic denial of free will.

58 Theo. Mop., *Comm. in Galat.*, ii.15f., ed. Swete, i, p. 26.

59 Theo. Mop., *Comm. in Coloss.*, ii.11, ed. Swete, i, p. 287.

60 Assemani, *Bibl. Or.*, iii.1, pp. 71, 148, 169f.

61 Pat. Or. iv. 4, 1908, ed. A. Scher.

62 The eclectic and heterogeneous nature of the material lends colour to J. B. Chabot's belief that the work is a conflation of diverse documents, but this view is disputed by A. Scher, Pat. Or. iv. 4, Introduction, pp. 323f.

63 *Ibid.*, pp. 329-31.

64 On the importance to Theodore of the theme of man as *microcosm*, the bond holding together the two orders of creation, see R. A. Norris, *Manhood and Christ*, pp. 143f., and his extended note, pp. 146-8.

65 Barhadbešabba, Pat. Or. iv. 4, p. 341.

66 *Ibid.*, pp. 341-8.

67 *Ibid.*, pp. 348–52.
68 *Ibid.*, pp. 356–9.
69 *Ibid.*, pp. 363–7.
70 *Ibid.*, pp. 368–72.
71 *Ibid.*, p. 375.
72 *Ibid.*, p. 378.
73 K. Brockelmann, *Lexicon Syriacum*, Berlin, 1895, p. 280.
74 Barhadbešabba, Pat. Or. iv. 4, p. 379.
75 *Ibid.*, p. 380.
76 *Ibid.*, pp. 380f.
77 *Ibid.*, pp. 382f.
78 *Ibid.*, pp. 383–6.
79 *Ibid.*, pp. 390–2.
80 Scher, Pat. Or. iv. 4, p. 323, suggests that the present work may have been composed in order that its author might regain his place in the Nestorian congregation. If so, we might expect a more forthright disavowal of allegiance to Henana.
81 *L'Histoire de Barhadbešabba 'Arbaia*, part 2, ed. F. Nau, Pat. Or. ix. 5, 1913, pp. 615, 630.
82 F. Nau, Pat. Or. xxiii. 2, 1932, *Avant-propos*, gives his opinion that the *Hist. Eccles.* of Theodoret is 'une collection de monographies'. It seems to me a good deal more homogeneous than this.
83 Barhadbešabba, *Hist. Eccles.*, xiii, Patr. Or. xxiii. 2, 1932, p. 271.
84 C.S.C.O. *Syr.* iii. 1, p. 239.

4 The doctrine of the nature of God

1 The dating is that of F. Nau, Pat. Or. ix. 5, Paris, 1913, p. 493, correcting Assemani, who probably places Barhadbešabba a century too late.
2 *L'Histoire de Barhadbešabba 'Arbaia*, part i, Pat. Or. xxiii. 2, 1932, p. 199.
3 See ch. 6 below for treatment of the weight of Nestorian opposition to the Monophysites.
4 *Ad Autolycum*, ii.15.
5 W. L. Knox, *St. Paul and the Church of the Gentiles*, Cambridge, 1939, pp. 57ff.
6 R. M. Grant, 'Theophilus of Antioch to Autolycus', *H.T.R.*, 40, 1947.
7 *Ad Autolycum*, i.7, i.13, ii.9.
8 *Ibid.*, ii.10.
9 *Ibid.*, ii.22.
10 *Ibid.*, i.3.
11 *Ibid.*, ii.22.
12 For the reconstruction of his views, see F. Loofs, 'Paulus von Samosata', T.U. xl. 5, Leipzig, 1924; G. Bardy, *Paul de Samosate*, 2nd ed., Louvain, 1929; H. de Riedmatten, *Les Actes du procès de Paul de Samosate* (*Paradosis* 6), Fribourg, 1952, on which see the review by H. Chadwick, *J.T.S.*, 4, 1953, pp. 91–4.
13 J. Starcky, *Palmyre*, Paris, 1952, pp. 53f.
14 Fergus Millar, 'Paul of Samosata, Zenobia and Aurelian: the Church, local culture and political allegiance in third-century Syria', *J.R.S.*, lxi, 1971, pp. 8f.
15 The Jewish element in Paul's teaching is emphasized by opponents of later date: Filastrius, *Divers. haeres. liber* 36/64 (C.S.E.L., 38, p. 33); John Chrysost., *Hom. 8 in Joannem*, (P.G. 59, 66); Theodoret, *Haeret. fab. compend.*, ii.8 (P.G. 38, 393); Photius, *Bibl.*, 265 (ed. Bekker, p. 492) on Zenobia.

16 G. Bardy, *Paul de Samosate*, p. 260. Cf. Bardy's section on the social and political background of Syria, pp. 239ff.

17 Fergus Millar, pp. 13ff.

18 These points of criticism are cited from the synodal letters of the Council of 268 by Eusebius, *Hist. Eccles.*, vii.30.6-16; cf. Socrates, *Hist. Eccles.*, i.24.

19 A. Harnack, *Lehrbuch der Dogmengeschichte*, 4th ed., vol.1, p. 722.

20 Eus., *Hist. Eccles.*, vii.27.2.

21 *Ibid.*

22 G. Bardy, *Paul de Samosate*, p. 285.

23 Synodal letter of 268, Eus., *Hist. Eccles.*, vii.30.4.

24 Eus., *Hist. Eccles.*, vii.29.2. Cf. M. Richard, 'Malchion et Paul de Samosate. Le témoignage d'Eusèbe de Césarée', *Eph. Theol. Louvaniensis* xxxv, 1959, p. 325.

25 Fergus Millar, pp. 14f. suggests that this may be analogous to the house-church at Dura Europos, that is a domestic building in which Paul continued to hold services, perhaps under the shield of Gallienus' edict of toleration of ten years earlier.

26 Eus., *Hist. Eccles.*, vii.30.19. F. Loofs, 'Paulus von Samosata', p. 59, questions the likelihood of imperial intervention of this kind; the account by Eus., is defended by H. Grégoire, 'Les persecutions dans l'empire romain', *Acad. R. de Belgique*, 46, fasc. 1, 1951.

27 *Serm. de Fide*, C.S.C.O. *Syr.* 88, 1961, p. 58.

28 *Contra Haer.*, C.S.C.O. *Syr.* 76, 1957, p. 79.

29 *Eranistes*, Dialogue iii.316, ed. G. H. Ettlinger, Oxford, 1975, p. 252.

30 Theod., *Ep.*, civ.

31 *Ep.*, cli.

32 *Philalethes*, C.S.C.O. *Syr.* 67, 1952, p. 147. Cf. Loofs, *Nestoriana*, Halle, 1905, p. 192.

33 *Philalethes*, p. 151.

34 Philox., *Discourses*, ed. E. A. Wallis Budge, vol. i, London, 1894, pp. cxxi, cxxxviii.

35 *Chron. Minora*, part 2, C.S.C.O., *Syr.* iii. 4, 1904, p. 58.

36 *Ibid.*, p. 126. A chronicle to the year 846, in the same volume of *Chron. Minora*, p. 189, unfortunately exhibits a *lacuna* in the codex at the point at which Paul would appear.

37 *Documentum Nestorianum*, C.S.C.O. *Syr.* iii. 4, 1904, p. 377.

38 *L'Histoire de Barhad.*, Pat. Or. xxiii. 2, 1932, p. 199.

39 *Ibid.*, Pat. Or. xxxi, p. 600.

40 H. de Riedmatten, *Les Actes du procès de Paul de Samosate*, Fribourg, 1952, pp. 57ff., analyses the Origenist basis of the doctrine underlying the *Acta* of the Antioch Council.

41 Origen, *Contra Celsum*, v. 39; *Comm. in Joann.*, xiii.25.

42 H. Chadwick, *Early Christian thought and the classical tradition*, Oxford, 1966, pp. 72f., shows that one of Origen's primary aims in *de Principiis* was to refute the gnosticism of Valentinus and Basilides, and that he follows the polemical method of St John and St Paul by incorporating and absorbing as much as possible of his opponents' systems within his own. But see J. Daniélou, *Origen*, Eng. tr. London, 1955, pp. 45f., on the gnostic *didaskalos* as Origen's ideal. For Origen's refutation of the gnostic idea that matter is evil, *Contra Cels.*, iv. 66.

43 Origen, *De Princ.*, i.2.6.

44 *Comm. in Hebr.*, frag. 24. Cf. the account of Origen's theology in J. Daniélou, *Origen*, pp. 251-75, linking it to the middle Platonism of his day.

45 Hilary of Poitiers, writing a century later, says that Paul used the term *homoousios* against Malchion and the Origenists at the trial, and that his judges rejected this as turning the Father and the Son into a single unit. Hil., *De synodis*, 81.
46 Epiph., *Haeres.*, 65.1.
47 Leontius of Byzant., *De sectis*, iii.3 (Riedmatten, frag. 25).
48 Severus, *Contra Grammaticum*, iii.25 (Riedmatten, frag. 14).
49 Leontius, *Adv. Nest. et Eutych.*, iii, P.G. 86, 1 (Riedmatten, frag. 26).
50 Riedmatten, frags. 25, 29.
51 Riedmatten, frag. 22.
52 Leontius, *Adv. Nest. et Eutych.*, iii, P.G. 86. 1; Riedmatten, frag. 36.
53 Riedmatten, frag. 30.
54 Dion. Rom., letter in Athanasius, *de decret. Nic.*, 26.
55 Eus., *Contra Marcellum*, i.1.
56 G. L. Prestige, *God in Patristic Thought*, London, 1936, p. 113, 'No ancient Father until Basil uses the word *prosopon* in this sense of mask.'
57 Leontius, *De sectis*, iii.3, distinguishes between Paul and Sabellius. Such care in definition is rare in patristic exposition of heresy.
58 *Chron. Miscell. ad 724*, C.S.C.O. *Syr.* iii. 4, part 2 section 3, 1904, p. 150. G. L. Prestige, *op. cit.*, p. 114, suggests that the origins of Sabellius' view lie in Simon Magus, who held that he was himself God who had appeared at three different places in three different guises.
59 F. Loofs, 'Paulus von Samosata', pp. 301f., speculates on the possibility that the intermediary between Paul and the later generation of Antiochene theologians may have been Philogonius.
60 Eus., *Contra Marcell.*, i.1.
61 *De Eccles. Theod.*, i.1.
62 *Ibid.*, i.7.
63 *Ibid.*, i.16. In the Maronite *Chronicle* (C.S.C.O. *Syr.* iii. 4, part 2 section 1, 1904, p. 64) Marcellus is 'given to the doctrine of Paul of Samosata'. The continuation of the passage in cod. B.M. Add 17, 216 is unfortunately disfigured by a *lacuna*.
64 H. Gwatkin, *Studies in Arianism*, 2nd ed., 1900, p. 81, describes Marcellus' system as 'an appeal from Origen to St John, a defence of the simplicity of Scripture from philosophical refinement and corruption'.
65 *Contra Marcell.*, i.1, 'He has not followed accurately the plain sense of the divine Scriptures'; *Ibid.*, i.2, He quotes Zechariah, Matthew and Galatians but misunderstands them; he adds to the text of psalm 109 to enable him to make his point.
66 *Contra Marcell.*, i.4.
67 Cf., Marcellan fragments, G.C.S., Eusebius Werke 4, Berlin, 1906, nos. 66, 76ff.
68 *Contra Marcell.*, ii.2.
69 J. N. D. Kelly, *Early Christian Creeds*, London, 1950, pp. 103f. The creed is transmitted by Epiphanius, *Haeres.*, 72.3.1.
70 Klostermann, frags. 10f.
71 Klostermann, frag. 121.
72 Marcellus claims scriptural support in his letter to Julius, in Epiph., *Haeres.*, 72.2. His claim is defended by T. Zahn, *Marcellus von Ancyra*, Gotha, 1867, p. 164. Cf., G. W. H. Lampe, 'The Exegesis of some Biblical texts by Marcellus of Ancyra', *J.T.S.*, 49, 1948, pp. 169-75.
73 F. Loofs, 'Paulus von Samosata', p. 301, thinks that Eustathius was an avowed Paulian early in his life, but G. Bardy, *Paul de Samosate*, p. 506, refutes this on

the ground of the absence of any patristic rehabilitation of Eustathius, which would have been probable in such a case.

74 The most recent collection of the extant fragments of his work is by F. Scheidweiler, 'Die Fragmente des Eustathios von Antiocheia', *Byz. Zeitschr.*, 48, Leipzig, 1955, pp. 73-85.

75 H. Chadwick, 'The Fall of Eustathius of Antioch', *J.T.S.*, 49, 1948, pp. 27-35, correcting the previously-accepted date, 330.

76 Eus., *Vita Const.*, iii.59. The trouble may have been fanned by Eusebius of Nicomedia's party.

77 Described by Hilary, *Hist. frag.*, ii.22, as 'liber quam de subiectione Domini Christi ediderat'. This work may have been occasioned by a letter of Asterius in defence of Eus. of Nicomedia; so Schwartz, 'Zur Geschichte der Athanasius', viii, *Nachrichten*, Göttingen, 1911, p. 403.

78 Cf., Marcellus fragments ed. E. Klostermann, G.C.S., *Eus. Werke*, 4, Berlin, 1906; especially frag. 87, p. 204, where Marcellus is concerned with Asterius' letter in defence of Eusebius of Nicomedia.

79 The letter appears in Epiphanius, *Haeres.*, 72.2f.; Eng. tr. in J. Stevenson, *Creeds, Councils and Controversies*, London, 1966, pp. 9f.

80 Soc., *Hist. Eccles.*, ii.8; Soz., *Hist. Eccles.*, iii.5.

81 These words conclude the so-called third creed of Antioch, which was a self-justificatory document presented by Theophronius of Tyana; Athan., *de synod.*, 24.

82 This is Socrates' account, *Hist. Eccles.*, ii.18; Athanasius, *de synod.*, 25, attributes the continued activity to the eastern bishops.

83 Soc., *Hist. Eccles.*, ii.20.7-11.

84 Theod., *Hist. Eccles.*, ii.8.38-43 and 45-8, Eng. tr. in Stevenson, *Creeds*, pp. 16ff. Cf., J. N. D. Kelly, *Early Christian Creeds*, p. 278.

85 Epiphanius, *Pan. haeres.*, 71.1ff.

86 Hilary, *Hist. frag.*, ii.21.

87 Cf., Zahn, *Marcellus von Ancyra*, pp. 88-94.

88 Epiph., *Haeres.*, 72.10-12.

89 Basil, *Epp.* 265, 266.

90 Soc., *Hist. Eccles.*, vii.15; Theod., *Hist. Eccles.*, v. 23.

91 Theod., *Hist. Eccles.*, v.35.

92 Origen's most sustained exposition of his conception of the divine nature is *de princ.*, i.1.

93 *De princ.*, ii.6.1.

94 *Contra Celsum*, iii.34.

95 *De princ.*, i.2.2.

96 *Contra Cels.*, v.39; cf., *Comm. in Joann.*, vi.39.

97 *Comm. in Joann.*, xiii.25. But *Comm. in Matt.*, xv.10, 'the analogy between God's goodness and the goodness of the Saviour, who is the image of that goodness, is closer than the analogy between the Saviour and a good man'.

98 *Comm. in Matt.*, xv.10; *Comm. in Joann.*, xiii.25; *de princ.*, i.2.5f.

99 *De princ.*, i.2.4, 9; *Comm. in Jer.*, ix.4; *de Orat.*, xv.1.

100 *De princ.*, i.3.1.

101 See above, p. 30.

102 B. H. Streeter, *The Four Gospels*, London, 1936, p. 116, quoting F. C. Burkitt. Lucian's recension is nonetheless independent of Origen's. On its pre-hexaplar characteristics, see A. Rahlfs, *Septuagintastudien* 3, 1911.

103 Jer., *de vir. ill.*, 77.

104 On the creeds issuing from the Dedication Council of 341, see J. N. D. Kelly, *Early Christian Creeds*, ch. ix, and his short bibliography on p. x.

105 Transmitted by Athanasius, *de synod.*, 23, and Hilary, *de synod.*, 29. See G. Bardy, *Recherches sur Saint Lucien et son école*, Paris, 1936, pp. 85-132.

106 Eng. tr., J. Stevenson, *Creeds, Councils and Controversies*, pp. 12f.

107 Soz., *Hist. Eccles.*, iii.5.

108 H. Lietzmann's account of the creed's teaching, *History of the Early Church*, iii, London, 1950, p. 197.

109 Transmitted by Theod., *Hist. Eccles.*, i.11f. Cf., G. Bardy, *Recherches*, pp. 122f.

110 Theod., *Hist. Eccles.*, i.4.46; J. Stevenson, *A New Eusebius*, London, 1957, p. 349. See also the reference to a Lucian in Eusebius, *Hist. Eccles.*, vii.9.6.

111 C. E. Raven, *Apollinarianism*, Cambridge, 1923, pp. 72ff.

112 Ruf., *Hist. Eccles.*, ix.6.

113 Epiph., *Ancoratus*, 33; *Haeres.*, 43.1.

114 G. Bardy, *Recherches*, pp. 47-58, surveys the evidence in detail, and concludes that the Lucian of Alexander's letter was not Lucian of Antioch but some other: the name was common.

115 So Tillemont, but Bardy, *Recherches*, p. 49, rejects this hypothesis.

116 Philost., *Hist. Eccles.*, ii.14.

117 Arius, letter to Eusebius of Nicomedia, in Theod., *Hist. Eccles.*, i.5.4; Epiph., *Haeres.*, 69.6.

118 W. Telfer, 'When did the Arian controversy begin?' *J.T.S.*, xlvii, 1946, pp. 129-42, argues for 323, against H.-G. Opitz, 'Die Zeitfolge des arianischen Streites', *Z.N.T.W.*, xxxiii, 1934, pp. 131-59. Telfer has little following for his view.

119 Eus., *Hist. Eccles.*, vii.32.4, 'We have heard him expound the scriptures in the church.'

120 No longer extant, but fragments in Philost., *Hist. Eccles.*, ii.13, 14; iii.21, edited from the Arian side. Cf., J. Bidez, *Philostorgius Kirchengeschichte*, G.C.S., 21 (1913), pp. lxxxviii ff. A number of later references to the *Vita Luc.* exist, e.g. Suidas, *Lexicon*. An anonymous fourth century Commentary on Job (P.G. 17, 470) gives some details of his martyrdom. See also *pass. Luciani* (P.G. 104), on which P. Batiffol, 'Le passion de St. Lucien d'Ant.' (*Comptes rendues du 2e congrès scient.*, Paris, 1891, vol. 2).

121 Athan., *de synod.*, 22; Soc., *Hist. Eccles.*, ii.10.4; Eng. tr. by J. Stevenson, *Creeds, Councils and Controv.*, p. 11.

122 Epiph. *Ancorat.*, 33.

123 Important recent studies of Arianism include T. E. Pollard, 'The origins of Arianism', *J.T.S.*, ix. 1, 1958, pp. 103-11, and *Johannine Christology and the early Church*, Cambridge, 1970; M. T. Wiles, 'In defence of Arius', *J.T.S.*, xiii. 2, 1962, pp. 339-47; G. C. Stead, 'The Platonism of Arius', *J.T.S.*, xv. 1, 1964, pp. 16-31; 'The *Thalia* of Arius and the Testimony of Athanasius', *J.T.S.*, xxix. 1, 1968, pp. 20-52; *Divine Substance*, 1977; E. P. Meijering, *Orthodoxy and Platonism in Athanasius. Synthesis or Antithesis*, Leiden, 1968.

124 Ath., *De Syn.*, 15 attributes 'beget' to Arius; *Contra Ar.*, i.5f. attributes to him 'create'. There is scriptural authority for 'create' at Prov. viii.22, and it is possible that Arius would have defended his use of the term on this ground.

125 Cf. the letter of Alexander in Theodoret, *Hist. Eccles.* i.4.

126 Theod., *Hist. Eccles.*, i.6.

127 Athan., *de decret. Nic. syn.*, 8; Philost., *Hist. Eccles.*, ii.14, writing from the Arian position, excuses Asterius on the ground that he sacrificed under duress.

128 Athan., *de decret. Nic. syn.*, 8.

129 Athan., *de synod.*, 17ff.
130 Fragments in Eus., *Contra Marc.*, i.4.9f., 17f., 22.
131 *Hom.* 123, Pat. Or. xxix, 1960, pp. 202f.
132 *Chron. ad 724*, C.S.C.O. *Syr.* iii. 4, 1904, p. 129.
133 *Ibid.*, p. 130.
134 *Chron. Minora*, part 2, C.S.C.O. *Syr.* iii. 4, p. 61.
135 *Chron. Jacobi Edesseni*, C.S.C.O. *Syr.* iii. 4, pp. 263f.
136 *Chron. Minora*, part 2, C.S.C.O. *Syr.* iii. 4, pp. 192f.
137 *Histoire Nestorienne (Chron. de Séert)*, part 1, Pat. Or. iv. 3, 1907, p. 245. A. Scher speculates whether Ourighanis is Gregory of Berytus or Theognis, but elsewhere, e.g. p. 293, Ourighanis is Origen.
138 *L'Hist. de Barhad. 'Arbaia*, part 1, Pat. Or. xxiii. 2, 1932, p. 207.
139 Greg. Nyss., *Vita Ephr. Syri.*, P.G. 46, 825 C.
140 *L'Hist. de Barhad. 'Arbaia*, part 1, p. 205f.
141 *Ibid.*, part 2, F. Nau, *Intro.*, p. 493, correcting the dating of Assemani, *Bibl. Or.*, iii.1, 169, who places Barhad. too late.
142 *L'Hist. de Barhad. 'Arbaia*, part 1, p. 209. Perhaps a confused memory of Epiphanius, *Haer.*, lxviii.8, where Eus., is accused at Tyre by Potammon of apostasy during the persecution by Diocletian.
143 On the eastern bishops present at Nicaea, see Appendix 1.
144 Ed. G. Bert, T.U., iii. 3/4, 1888, pp. 206ff.
145 *Ibid.*, pp. 285ff.
146 Theod., *Hist. Eccles.*, iv.26.1–6; *H. Rel.*, P.G. 82, 1373 AB.
147 Theod., *H. Rel.*, P.G. 82, 1776 A–C.
148 A. J. Festugière, O.P., *Antioche païenne et chrétienne*, Paris, 1959, p. 274, treats the narrative with reserve.
149 *Chron. Edess.*, *Chron. Minora*, part 1, C.S.C.O. *Syr.* iii. 4, part 1 section 1, Louvain, 1903, p. 5. J. B. Segal, *Edessa, 'the blessed city'*, Oxford, 1970, p. 175, dates the event 'about 372'.
150 Zosimus, iv.13.
151 Theod., *Hist. Eccles.*, iv.15.
152 *Ibid.*, ii.19.
153 *Ibid.*, ii.25.
154 *Ibid.*, ii.27.
155 *Ibid.*, iii.1.
156 *Ibid.*, iv.11.
157 Julian, *Ep.*, 26. Under cover of the toleration of the Edict of Milan, Julian aimed at creating ecclesiastical confusion. Theodoret, *Hist. Eccles.*, iv.12, describing Valens' restoration of the *status quo*, places this after Valens' baptism in 367.
158 The legislation in *Cod. Theod.*, xvi.5.3 is directed towards Manichaeism, and is concerned with the west rather than the east.
159 Valens' legislation against the practice of magic (*Cod. Theod.*, ix.16.8) and his expulsion of Julian's pagan court were counterbalanced by his toleration of pagan practices (Theod., *Hist. Eccles.*, iv.21, 24).
160 Theod., *Hist. Eccles.*, iv.13.
161 *Ibid.*, iv.15.
162 *Ibid.*, iv.22f.
163 *Ibid.*, iv.25.
164 *Ibid.*, v.7.
165 *Cod. Theod.*, xvi.1.2 (Feb. 380) commending allegiance to Nicaea; xvi.5.6 (Jan. 381) forbidding heretical assemblies in cities; confirmed by the Council

of Constantinople in May 381 (Soz., *Hist. Eccles.*, iv.27); xvi.5.7 (July 381) forbidding Arian assemblies outside cities, and the standard of orthodoxy defined
as allegiance to Constantinople, Alexandria and the main eastern sees.

166 *H. Rel.*, xxvi.12. Cf., A. J. Festugière, *Antioche païenne et chrétienne*, pp. 347ff.

167 J. N. Schofield, *The Religious Background of the Bible*, London, 1944, pp. 71f.,
describes pillars as marking ancestral tombs and sacrificial sites, citing Dhorme,
L'Évolution religieuse d'Israel, 1937.

168 Keret, i.3.53ff. A. R. Millard, in *Peoples of Old Testament Times*, ed. D. J. Wise-
man, Oxford, 1973, p. 44, cites similar practices at Shechem and Megiddo. See
also Tyre (Herodotus, ii.41) and Emesa (Herodian, v.3.5).

169 Lucian, *De Dea Syria*, xvi. His designation of the pillars as *phalli* is probably a
mistaken Greek interpretation of their significance; so W. Robertson Smith,
Religion of the Semites, 3rd ed., London, 1927, p. 456f.; H. Lietzmann, 'Des
Leben des Heiligen Symeon Stylites', T.U. xxxii. 4, 1908, p. 243; A. J. Festugière, *Antioche païenne et chrétienne*, Paris, 1959, p. 310, n.1.

170 Lucian, *De Dea Syria*, xxviii f.

171 Afrahat, *Hom.*, 23.63.

172 Cited by F. C. Burkitt, *Early Eastern Christianity*, London, 1904, p. 90. See also
Or., *Hom. on Jeremiah*, xv. 4. Cf., M. R. James, *The Apocryphal New Testament*,
Oxford, 1924, p. 2.

173 Cited by J. W. Sweetman, *Islam and Christian Theology. A Study of the Interaction of Theological Ideas*, i. 1, London, 1945, p. 69. John of Damascus, *De
Haeresibus*, P.G. 94, 764f., says that Muhammad learnt about Christianity from
an Arian monk.

174 See Appendix 2.

175 F. C. Burkitt, *op. cit.*, pp. 26-8, suggests that the story that Palut of Edessa went
to Antioch for ordination means not that Edessa was subject to Antioch but
that Palut was trying to forge closer contact with the west, hence the term
'Palutians' to denote orthodox Christians in Edessa. Barhadbešabba however
suggests a firmer ecclesiastical link than this between Seleucia-Ctesiphon and
Antioch at the time of Nicaea (*L'Hist. de Barhad.*, part 1, p. 205) in that his
clergy had to receive ordination from Antioch.

176 Text in *Oecumenical Documents of the Faith*, ed. T. H. Bindley, London, 1899,
4th ed. revised by R. W. Green, London, 1950, pp. 191-3.

177 Evagrius, *Hist. Eccles.*, iii.14, P.G. 86, 2620-5.

178 *Cod. Just.*, i.1.6f.

179 E.g., *Novel* xlii, in which Justinian condemns those who depart from 'the four
sacred councils [Nicaea, Constantinople, Ephesus and Chalcedon], while pretending to subscribe to them'.

180 Evagrius, *Hist. Eccles.*, v.4.

181 *Cat.*, v.3b.

182 Nic. Kall., *Hist. Eccles.*, xvii, P.G. 147, 424f. See also Zacharias Rhetor, *Hist.
Eccles.*, x, C.S.C.O. *Syr.* iii. 5, 1924, pp. 163f.

183 *Documenta ad Origines Monophysitorum Illustrandas*, C.S.C.O. *Syr.* ii. 37, 1908,
p. 156.

184 *Ibid.*, p. 161.

185 *Ibid.*, p. 35.

186 *Ibid.*, p. 37.

187 Severus, *Contra Imp. Grammat.*, C.S.C.O. *Syr.* iv. 4, ed. J. Lebon, 1938, *Prae-
fatio*, p. i.

188 *Ibid.*, ii.1, p. 56.

189 *Ibid.*, p. 57.

190 *Ibid.*, pp. 58–61.

191 *Ibid.*, pp. 62–5.

192 For the place of the 6th century tritheist heresy in the history of the Mono-physite movement, see W. H. C. Frend, *The Rise of the Monophysite Movement*, Cambridge, 1972, pp. 289–91.

5 The use of Greek philosophy by the Eastern Church

1 R. Walzer, 'Arabic Transmission of Greek Thought to Medieval Europe', *Bulletin of John Rylands Library*, Manchester, 29. 1, 1945, pp. 166ff.

2 R. Walzer, 'Aristutalis', *Encyclopaedia of Islam*, vol. i, p. 630.

3 I. P. Sheldon-Williams in *Cambridge History of later Greek and early Medieval Philosophy*, part vi, pp. 478ff., on Ammonius, John Philoponus, Olympiodorus, Elias, David and Stephanus, all of whom were actively concerned with the study of Aristotle in the fifth and sixth centuries.

4 'An intelligent and observant observer of notoriously difficult texts', H. J. Dros-saart Lulofs, *Nicolaus of Damascus on the Philosophy of Aristotle* (*Philosophia Antiqua* xiii) Leiden, 1965, p. viii.

5 R. T. Wallis, *Neoplatonism*, London, 1972, p. 32.

6 Porphyry, *Vita Plotini* witnesses to his influence on Plotinus; for his bearing upon Christian thought, J. Daniélou, *Origen* (Eng. tr. London, 1955) pp. 89ff.; H. C. Puech in *Mélanges Bidez*, ii, pp. 746–78.

7 R. T. Wallis, *Neoplatonism*, pp. 97–116 summarizes Porphyry's position.

8 R. T. Wallis, *Neoplatonism*, p. 123.

9 Agathias, *Hist.*, ii.30; R. T. Wallis, *Neoplatonism*, p. 13. It is tempting to include Syrianus in this list, but he was Alexandrian by birth; *ibid.*, p. 13, n. 2.

10 H. Chadwick, 'Philo', *Cambridge History of later Greek and early Medieval Philo-sophy*, part vi, pp. 155f.

11 R. E. Witt, *Albinus and the History of Middle Platonism*, Cambridge, 1937, pp. 10ff., 64f.; I. P. Sheldon-Williams in *Cambridge History of later Greek and early Medieval Philosophy*, pp. 314–20.

12 *Parmenides* 132d.

13 *Phaedo* 78c–d.

14 *Cratylus* 389a–c.

15 *Symposium* 210c–211b.

16 *Republic* 596a.

17 *Republic* 509d.

18 *Republic* 511b.

19 *Phaedrus* 265d.

20 *Laws* 534e. Cf., *Laws* 965b on the 'guardians' being able to see beyond pheno-mena to take a general view and arrange particulars in the state in relation to the Idea.

21 *Phaedo* 72b.

22 On the theory of Ideas especially *Anal. Post.*, 77a; *Met.*, 991a–b, 1033b, 1079b, 1086b.

23 The transcendental element is particularly prominent from the *Symposium* on-wards, reaching its most sustained statement in the *Timaeus*.

24 The matter is presented fully in R. A. Norris, *Manhood and Christ*, Oxford, 1963, ch. 14.

25 Theodore, *Comm. in Galat.*, i.3ff., ed. Swete, vol. i, p. 7, 'When man was first

made, if he had remained immortal, there would have been no existence of the sort which is now come upon us.' (Norris' trans., *Manhood and Christ*, p. 174).

26 *Comm. in Rom.*, vii.14, ed. Staab, p. 131.
27 Norris, *Manhood and Christ*, pp. 182–4.
28 *Phaedo* 66c–68b.
29 Numenius, *Testimonium* 30.
30 Plotinus, *Enn.*, i.1.7; iv.4.14; vi.4.15.
31 *Ibid.*, iii.6.2.
32 Iamblichus, *De anima*, 370.5ff.
33 H. de Riedmatten, *Les Actes du procès de Paul de Samosate* (*Paradosis* vi), Fribourg en Suisse, 1952.
34 So Numenius and Plotinus; cf., *Enn.*, iii.4.2; iv.3.12; v.2.2; vi.7.6f.
35 *Enn.* iii.4.2.
36 Apollinarius, frag. 34.
37 *Ibid.*, frag. 25.
38 In *Apodeixis*. The tripartite soul is expressly denied by Theodoret, *Eranistes* ii, ed. G. H. Ettlinger, Oxford, 1975, p. 112.
39 Plotinus, *Enn.* iii.4.2; iv.9.3; v.2.2; vi.7.5f.
40 *Phaedrus* 247c.
41 Albinus, *Epitome* xxiv.1.
42 Apollinarius, *Comm. in Rom.*, vii.7, ed. K. Staab, Munster, 1933, p. 64.
43 Plotinus, *Enn.*, iv.8.2.; iv.4.17ff.
44 *Ibid.*, iv.3.12, 15.
45 *Ibid.*, iv.8.6; v.4.1. The emanation from the One is 'natural' in so far as it could not have not happened, which is not quite analogous to the Christian concept of the love of God.
46 *Enn.*, iii.8.7.
47 Theodoret, *Graec. Affect. Cur.*, i.36.
48 i.9. Cf., ii.6; Plato, 'the best of the philosophers', would have exiled Homer from his state, referring to *Rep.*, ii.377e–378d, which Eus., *Prae. Ev.*, ii.7.4ff., and xiii. 3.3ff., quotes in full.
49 i.17f., quoting *Sophist* 242c–d, 246a from Eus., *Prae. Ev.*, xiv.4.8f.
50 iii.7, quoting *Cratylus* 397c–d from Eus., *Prae. Ev.*, i.9–12.
51 iv.23, quoting *Timaeus* 29d–e from Eus., *Prae. Ev.*, xi.21.2.
52 iv.34; an untraced passage of Plato quoted by Theodoret from Clem. Alex., *Strom.*, v.11.75.
53 iv.36; *Rep.*, vi.509b, quoted from Eus., *Prae. Ev.*, xi.21.5.
54 iv.37; *Tim.*, 28b–c, quoted from Eus., *Prae. Ev.*, xi.29.3f.
55 iv.39; *Tim.*, 38c, quoted from Eus., *Prae. Ev.*, xi.30.2.
56 iv.41f.; *Tim.*, 29a, quoted from Eus., *Prae. Ev.*, xi.31.
57 vi.26; *Laws* iv.715–716b, quoted from Clem. Alex., *Protrept.*, vi.69.4, Eus., *Prae. Ev.*, xi.13.5.
58 vi.28f.; *Gorgias* 525a–c, quoted from Eus., *Prae. Ev.*, xii.6.9–11.
59 viii.42; *Phaedo* 114b, quoted from Clem. Alex., *Strom.*, iii.3.19.
60 i.90; quoted from Clem. Alex., *Strom.* ii.4.15.
61 v.25, quoted from Clem. Alex., *Strom.*, viii.4.10.
62 xi.13; xii.53; quoted from Clem. Alex., *Strom.*, ii.21.128.
63 xii.61ff.; Aristox., frag. 17–28 Müller, 54b Wehrli. Aristox., is also mentioned in passing at i.24.
64 viii.34; xii.51; quoted from Eus., *Prae. Ev.*, xv.2.8.

65 i.47f.; Porph., *Ep. ad Aneb.*, xxix (ed. Parthey), xlv; *Ep. ad Boeth.*; quoted from Eus., *Prae. Ev.*, xiv.10.1-3.

66 iii.60; Porph. *de Abstin.*, ii.41f. Theod., iii.62; Porph., *de Phil. ex Orac.*, 147. Theod., iii.63; Porph. *de Phil. ex Orac.*, 150. All quoted from Eus., *Prae. Ev.*, iv. 22f.

67 vii.36ff.; Porph., *de Abstin.*, ii.5; quoted from Eus., *Prae. Ev.*, i.9.7f.

68 x.11; Porph., *de Phil. ex Orac.*; quoted from Eus., *Prae. Ev.*, vi.5.1. Theod., x. 17f.; Porph., *op. cit.*, quoted from Eus., *Prae. Ev.*, iv.20.1; Theod., x.22; Porph., *op. cit.*; quoted from Eus., *Prae. Ev.*, v.8.5ff.

69 vi.59-72; Plot., *Enn.*, iii; Theod., v.1.6f.; Plot., v, quoted from Eus., *Prae. Ev.*, xi.17.

70 i.14; ii.81; ii.84f.; ii.114; Numen. *frags.* 7, 9, 10 (ed. Leemans); quoted from Clem. Alex., *Strom.*, i.22.150.

71 ii.44; Porph. *Contra Christ.*, iv, quoted from Eus., *Prae. Ev.*, i.9.21.

72 The view of G. H. Ettlinger, *Theodoret of Cyrus Eranistes*, Oxford, 1975, p. 26, that turning hostile witnesses to good account in this way is peculiar to the *Eranistes* needs widening to include the *Curatio Graec. Affect.* In the *Eranistes* it is of course heretical Christian opponents who are in question.

73 *Cur. Gr. Affect.*, ii.28; iii.36.

74 *Ibid.*, ii.33.

75 *Ibid.*, ii.38, 42, 73; iii.34.

76 *Ibid.*, ii.77.

77 One cannot be certain even of these. If Theodoret quoted *Enn.*, iii from the original, why did he need to take *Enn.*, v from Eus., *Prae. Ev.*, xi? P. Canivet makes the best case that can be made for Theodoret's independence (*Sources chrétiennes* 57, Paris, 1958, pp. 55-9). On the patristic *florilegia* concerning the Monophysite dispute see M. Richard, 'Les florilèges diphysites du ve et vi^e siècle', *Chalkedon* i, 721-48.

78 Text in G. H. Ettlinger, *Theodoret of Cyrus Eranistes*, Oxford, 1975, pp. 254-65.

79 Cf., R. Walzer, 'Arabic transmission of Greek thought to Medieval Europe', *Bulletin of John Rylands Library*, 29. 1, 1945, p. 169, who says that the eastern Church as a whole abandoned philosophy during the fourth and fifth centuries. W. Jaeger, *Humanism and Theology*, Milwaukee, 1943, traces the survival of Platonist elements in Christian education in the east.

80 H. E. W. Turner, *The Pattern of Christian Truth*, London, 1954, pp. 448-56, gives a summary of Stoic influence upon patristic thought in general.

81 R. M. Grant, 'Theophilus of Antioch to Autolycus', *H.T.R.*, 40, 1947, p. 230.

82 Theophilus, *ad Autol.*, ii.10; 22.

83 *Ibid.*, i.3.

84 Parallels to his ideas are to be found, for example, in Chrysippus, but Theophilus seems to be more constantly in touch with Hellenistic ideas through Philo Judaeus.

85 *Ad Autol.*, iii.6.

86 Cf., W. Jaeger, *Nemesios von Emesa*, Berlin, 1914, p. 103; E. Skard, *Nemesios-Studien* (Symbolae Osloenses, xv/xvi), 1936, pp. 23-43; K. Reinhardt, 'Posidonios von Apamea', Pauly-Wissowa, *Realencycl.*, xxii.1.9.

87 *De Nat. Hom.*, xx.40; cf., E. Skard, *Symbol. Oslo.*, xxii, 1942, pp. 40-8. The direct influence of Galen is disputed by F. Lammert, 'Hellenistische Medizin bei Ptolemaios und Nemesios', *Philologus* xciv, 1940, pp. 125-41.

88 *De Nat. Hom.*, xxxv.51.

89 *Ibid.*, v.25; xxviii.44, 54.

90 *Ibid.*, i.3; iv.23.
91 *Ibid.*, v.24.
92 *Ibid.*, viii.30; xxvii.43; xxviii.44.
93 *Ibid.*, xv.34f.
94 *Ibid.*, xxx.46. The intermediary source may be Galen in the view of E. Skard, but this is disputed by W. Telfer, *Nemesius of Emesa on the Nature of Man* (Lib. Christian Classics iv) London, 1955, p. 305.
95 Aeneas of Gaza, *Theophrastus*, P.G. 85, 872-1004.
96 Zacharias Rhetor, *De mundi opificio contra philosophos disputatio*, P.G. 85, 1012-1144.
97 *Theophrastus*, col. 881.
98 *Ibid.*, cols. 888-97.
99 *Ibid.*, col. 909f.
100 *Ibid.*, col. 916.
101 *Ibid.*, col. 920.
102 *Ibid.*, col. 945.
103 *Ibid.*, col. 953.
104 *Ibid.*, col. 961.
105 *Ibid.*, col. 964.
106 *Ibid.*, col. 965.
107 *Ibid.*, cols. 981-3.
108 *Disputatio*, col. 1113.
109 *Ibid.*, col. 1081.
110 *Ibid.*, col. 1100f.
111 *Ibid.*, col. 1105.
112 Severus, *Liber contra impium grammaticum*, C.S.C.O. *Syr.* iv. 4, ed. J. Lebon, 1938.
113 *Ibid.*, ii. 1, pp. 56-61.
114 *Ibid.*, ii. 8, p. 96ff.
115 *Ibid.*, ii. 17, p. 144.
116 *Ibid.*, pp. 148-50.
117 *Ibid.*, ii. 17, pp. 150-4. Cf., the Plotinian doctrine of the interpenetration of all by the One, and hence of all by all others, modified by Iamblichus (Proclus, *Elements of Theol.*, 103, 195).
118 *Ibid.*, p. 165.
119 *Ibid.*, p. 167.
120 A. Vööbus, *History of the School of Nisibis* (C.S.C.O., Subsid. 26), Louvain, 1965, p. 15. The ready adoption of Aristotelianism in eastern Syria and Mesopotamia may have its deepest roots in the Hellenizing policy of Alexander the Great during the fourth century B.C. That interest in western philosophy and science was not confined to Christians is seen in the foundation in about A.D. 550 by Khosrau of a university at Jundishapur for the study of mathematics and astronomy; E. G. Browne, *A Literary History of Persia*, i, London and Leipzig, 1909, p. 305; C. Brockelmann, *Geschichte der arabische Literatur*, i, 1898, p. 201ff. On the medical teaching at Jundishapur, S. H. Nasr, *Islamic Science* (World of Islam Festival Publishing Co. Ltd.), 1976, pp. 11, 155.
121 A. Baumstark, *Geschichte der syrischen Literatur*, Bonn, 1922, p. 59. The binding up of Aristotle with this codex is of later date.
122 A. Baumstark, *Aristoteles bei den Syrern*, i, Leipzig, 1900, pp. 4ff.
123 P.L. 68, 15-42.
124 The influence of Theodore of Mopsuestia may be felt in this arrangement into

two 'ages', as well as in details concerning christology, exegetical method and
the books to be regarded as canonical.
125 Junilius included the work of Paulos in his *Instituta Regularia Divinae Legis*; cf.,
O. Bardenhewer, *Patrologie*, 3rd ed., 1910, p. 552. Junilius introduces the work
(P.L. 68, 15): '... ad haec ego respondi, vidisse me quemdam Paulum nomine,
Persam genere, qui in Syrorum schola in Nisibi urbe est edoctus, ubi divina lex
per magistros publicos, sicut apud nos in mundanis studiis grammatica et rhet-
orica, ordine ac regulariter traditur'.
126 A. Baumstark, *Geschichte der syrischen Literatur*, Bonn, 1922, p. 167.
127 Assemani, *Bibliotheca Orientalis*, iii.1, p. 87.
128 A. Vööbus, *History of the School of Nisibis* (C.S.C.O., Subsid. 26), p. 21.
129 Assemani, *Bibliotheca Orientalis*, iii.1, pp. 154f.
130 Pat. Or. iv. 4, 1908.
131 *Ibid.*, pp. 333-44.
132 *Histoires d'Ahoudemmeh et de Marouta*, Pat. Or. iii. 1, 1909, pp. 97ff.
133 Cf., Aristotle, *Eth.*, i.21.
134 Cf., Aristotle, *Eth. Eud.*, iii.1.
135 Ahoudemmeh, ii. 2f., pp. 103-5.
136 *Ibid.*, ii.4, p. 106.
137 *Ibid.*, iii.1, p. 108.
138 *Ibid.*, iii.3, pp. 110f.
139 *Ibid.*, iii.6, p. 112.
140 *Ibid.*, iii.8, pp. 113f.
141 *Ibid.*, iv, p. 114.
142 Babai Magnus, *Liber de Unione*, i.2, C.S.C.O. *Syr.* ii. 60, 1915, p. 8.
143 Babai's cautious use of trinitarian and christological analogies is noted in the
next chapter.
144 *Liber de Unione*, vi.20, p. 202.
145 So F. Nau, *Histoires d'Ahoudemmeh et de Marouta*, Pat. Or. iii. 1, 1909, Intro.,
p. 98.
146 A. Vööbus, *Hist. of the School of Nisibis*, C.S.C.O., Subsidia 26, pp. 323ff.
147 A. Baumstark, *Gesch. der syr. Lit.*, Bonn, 1922, p. 246.
148 Assemani, *Bibliotheca Orientalis*, iii.1, p. 154.
149 *Ibid.*, p. 194f.; Baumstark, *Gesch. der syr. Lit.*, pp. 215f.
150 Pat. Or., xxix. 1, 1960, p. 34.
151 Baumstark, *Gesch. der syr. Lit.*, p. 197.
152 *Ibid.*, pp. 214f., 272, 341.
153 Cf., O. Bardenhewer, *Patrologie*, 3rd ed., 1910, p. 504. Text in P.G. 94, 518-
675.
154 Porphyry's order is not followed precisely, e.g. in the reversal of the order of
property and accident, P.G. 94, 576f. John follows these categories with non-
Porphyrian material.
155 Baumstark, *Gesch. der syr. Lit.*, pp. 227-31.
156 R. Walzer, 'Arabic transmission . . .', *Bulletin of the John Rylands Library*, 29. 1,
1945, p. 167.
157 R. Walzer, 'Aflatun', *Encycl. of Islam*, i, 1960, p. 234.
158 For Arab understanding of Plato and Aristotle and transmission of their work to
the west, see P. Moraux, *Les listes anciennes des ouvrages d'Aristotle*, Louvain,
1951; F. Rosenthal, 'On the knowledge of Plato's philosophy in the Islamic
world', *Islamic Culture*, 14, 1940, pp. 387ff.
159 The Monophysite schools paid more attention to secular studies, especially to

Peripatetic thought, than did the Nestorians; J. B. Chabot, 'L'école de Nisibe, son histoire ses statutes', *Journal Asiatique*, 9ᵉ série, viii, 1896, p. 65.

160 A. Vööbus, *History of the School of Nisibis* (C.S.C.O., Subsid. 26), p. 15.

161 Assemani, *Bibliotheca Orientalis*, iii.1, pp. 154f.

162 A. Baumstark, *Gesch. der syr. Lit.*, Bonn, 1922, p. 197.

163 F. Nau, *Le traité de Sévère Sebokt sur l'astrolabe plan*, Paris, 1899.

164 *Ibid.*, pp. 239–45.

165 Assemani, *Bibliotheca Orientalis*, iii.2, p. 428.

166 Text and tr., E. A. Wallis Budge, *Syrian Anatomy, Pathology and Therapeutics*, Oxford, 1913.

167 A. Baumstark, *Gesch. der syr. Lit.*, p. 230, n. 2; p. 352 add. notes. See also H. Gollancz, *The Book of Protections*, London, 1912.

168 *Acta Martyrum et Sanctorum*, ed. P. Bedjan, Paris, 1890-7; *Les Versions grecques des Actes des Martyrs persans sous Sapor II*, ed. H. Delehaye, Pat. Or. ii. 4, 1905.

169 Cf., *Acta Mart.*, ii, pp. 260-74, 278ff., 291ff., 297ff., etc.; *Les Versions grecques . . .*, p. 233.

170 A. Vööbus, *History of Asceticism in the Syrian Orient*, i, C.S.C.O., Subsid. 14, 1958, pp. 237f.

171 Cf., F. Cumont, *Les Religions orientales dans le Paganisme romain*, 4th ed., 1929, ch. 6, pp. 125ff., on Persian religion; ch. 7, pp. 151ff., on astrology. A. Vööbus, *History of Asceticism*, i, pp. 145f., suggests that Syrian monasticism owed its early third-century beginning in part to the hostility of the Magians.

172 Photius, *Bibl.*, 223. Christians were not the only opponents of fatalism; cf., Alex. Aphrodis., *De Fato*, attacking the dishonesty of astrologers.

173 Magic was also attacked by imperial opposition; Dion., lii.34.3; Manilius, ii.108.

174 Zacharius Scholasticus, *Vita Severi*, Pat. Or. ii, pp. 57ff.

175 Photius, *Bibl.*, 81.

176 Barhadbešabba, *Hist. Eccles.*, Pat. Or. ix. 5, 1913, p. 620.

177 A. Vööbus, *History of the School of Nisibis*, p. 215.

178 Christians who defended the Stoic conception of order and unity could oppose its associated fatalism with vigour; cf., Nemesius, *De Natura Hom.*, xxv.51ff.

179 Codex Univ. Cambr. Gg. 2.14.

180 H. J. Drossaart Lulofs, *Nicolaus Damasc. on the Philosophy of Aristotle*, Leiden, 1965, p. 35. But note the evidence of the late tenth century *Kitab al-Fihrist*, whose list of Aristotle's work gives eight logical works first, then seven physical works of which *De Meteor.*, is fourth, suggesting a change of emphasis in Arabia; I. Düring, *Aristotle in the Ancient Biographical Tradition* (*Studia Graeca et Latina Gothoburgensia* V), Göteborg, 1957, pp. 191-4.

181 Plotinus, *Enn.*, ii.9.

182 *Ibid.*, ii.9.4, 8.

183 *Ibid.*, ii.9.18.

184 *Ibid.*, ii.9.6.

185 Pat. Or. xxix. 1, 1960.

186 *Ibid.*, p. 150.

187 *Ibid.*

188 In the concept of darkness as substantial, Mani is close to Bardaisan; so F. C. Burkitt, *The Religion of the Manichees*, Cambridge, 1925, p. 78, citing Ephraim in support.

189 Severus, *Hom.* cxxiii, p. 152.

190 *Ibid.*, pp. 176-8.

191 *Ibid.*, p. 178.
192 The popularity of this work in Syriac-speaking regions is attested by the survival of two slightly differing Syriac translations; see A. Guillaumont, *Les six centuries des Kephalaia Gnostica d'Évagre le Pontique*, Pat. Or. xxviii. 1, 1958, Intro., p. 5.
193 Evagrius, *Kephalaia Gnostica* i.1-3, p. 16.
194 *Ibid.*, vi.10, 13, pp. 220-2.
195 *Ibid.*, i.14, p. 22, citing psalm ciii.22.
196 *Ibid.*, iv.62, p. 162; cf., iv.66, p. 166.
197 *Ibid.*, i.41, p. 36.
198 *Ibid.*, i.59, p. 44.
199 *Ibid.*, ii.8, p. 62f.
200 Plato, *Parmenides* 134d.
201 Aristotle, *Met.*, 991a develops all these objections to Plato's Idealism.
202 *Met.*, 992a.
203 *Met.*, 1037b; 1045a.
204 *Met.*, 1066b.
205 *Met.*, 1028a.
206 *Met.*, 1031b.
207 *Met.*, 1033b.
208 *Met.*, 1034a.
209 The relation of potentiality to actuality is treated in *Met.*, ix.
210 *Met.*, 1049a.
211 *Met.*, 1066b.
212 Philip Sherrard, 'Christian Theology and the Eclipse of Man', in *Sobornost* (The Journal of the Fellowship of St Alban and St Sergius) Ser. 7, no. 3, 1976, pp. 166-79, makes this point well in a different connection.

6 The human experience of Christ and the salvation of man

1 B. H. Streeter, *The Primitive Church*, London, 1929, pp. 163-78.
2 Eustathius *apud* Theod. *Eranistes* i (89), ed. G. H. Ettlinger, 1975, p. 100.
3 *Ibid.*, p. 101.
4 *Ibid.*, ii (177), p. 159.
5 *Ibid.*, iii (285), p. 231.
6 C. P. Caspari, *Alte und neue Quellen zur Geschichte des Taufsymbols*, Christiania, 1879, pp. 176ff.
7 Eustath., *apud* Theod. *Eran.*, i (88), Ettlinger, p. 100.
8 *Ibid.*, iii (288), p. 232.
9 Basil, *Ep.*, 244.3; Jerome, *De vir. ill.*, 119.
10 Julian *apud* Facundus, *Pro defens. trium. capit.*, iv.2.
11 Socrates, *Hist. Eccles.*, vi.3; Sozomen, *Hist. Eccles.*, viii.2.
12 *Cod. Theodos.*, xvi.1,3.
13 The fragments of Diodore are edited by R. Abramowski, 'Der theologische Nachlass des Diodor von Tarsus', *Z.N.T.W.*, 42, 1949, pp. 19-69.
14 *Syriac fragment* 4, Abramowski, p. 25. I accept the argument of Rowan A. Greer that when Diodore appears to distinguish between 'body' and 'humanity' he is using two interchangeable terms to refer to the same human subject; 'The Antiochene Christology of Diodore of Tarsus', *J.T.S.*, n.s. xvii. 2, 1966, pp. 327-41, disputing the distinction between 'body' and 'humanity' made by A. Grillmeier, *Christ in Christian Tradition*, Eng. tr. London, 1965.
15 *Frag.*, 6, p. 27.

16 *Frag.*, 11, p. 31.
17 *Frag.*, 13, p. 31.
18 *Frag.*, 20, p. 39.
19 *Frag.*, 24, p. 43.
20 *Frag.*, 30, p. 47.
21 *Frag.*, 33, p. 49.
22 *Frag.*, 48, p. 58.
23 *Frags.*, 26, p. 43; 2, p. 23.
24 *Frag.*, 16, p. 33.
25 *Frag.*, 18, p. 37.
26 *Frag.*, 19, p. 38f.
27 Syriac fragment from Severus of Antioch, quoting Cyril, Abramowski, p. 63.
28 This was not the later Syrian view. Babai Magnus, *Liber de Unione*, iii.10, C.S.C.O. *Syr.* ii. 60, 1915, pp. 113f., says that Christ received the divine Word at conception and a human soul in the normal way 40 days after conception.
29 R. V. Sellers, *Two Ancient Christologies*, London, 1940, p. 162.
30 Theodore, *De Incarn.*, xii, Swete, vol. ii, p. 303.
31 E.g., M. Jugie, 'Le "liber ad baptizandos" de Theodore de Mopsueste', *Échos d'Orient*, xxxv, 1935, pp. 257ff.; W. de Vries, 'Der "Nestorianismus" Theodors von Mopsuestia', *Orientalia Christiana Periodica*, vii, 1941, pp. 91ff.; F. A. Sullivan, *The Christology of Theodore of Mopsuestia*, Vatican City, 1956.
32 *Comm. in Joh.*, v.30, Vosté, p. 86.
33 *Comm. in Pss.*, viii.5, Devréesse, p. 47.
34 Swete, vol. i, p. 62.
35 *Comm. in Joh.*, xii.30, Vosté, p. 174.
36 *De Incarn.*, Swete, vol. ii, p. 298.
37 *De Incarn.*, xv, frag. 3; Swete, vol. ii, p. 311.
38 Language specifically refuted by Theodore, *De Incarn.*, ix, frag. 1, Swete, vol. ii, p. 300.
39 *Ad Baptizandos*, ed. A. Mingana, 'The Commentary of Theodore of Mopsuestia on the Nicene Creed', *Woodbrooke Studies* 5, 1932, p. 54.
40 *Comm. in Joh.*, x.17, Vosté, p. 148.
41 *Hom. Catech.*, v.19, Tonneau, p. 127.
42 *Ibid.*, v.10, p. 115.
43 *Ibid.*, viii.5, p. 193.
44 *Comm. in Joh.*, viii.16, Vosté, pp. 119f. Later Nestorians were to reject these analogies on philosophical grounds, e.g. Babai Magnus, *Liber de Unione*, iii.9, C.S.C.O. *Syr.* ii. 60, ed. A. Vaschalde, 1924, pp. 80f.
45 *De Incarn.*, ed. Swete, vol. ii, p. 300.
46 *Ad Baptizandos*, ed. Mingana, p. 87.
47 *Ibid.*, p. 89.
48 *De Incarn.*, Swete, vol. ii, p. 295.
49 Developed fully by Babai Magnus, *Liber de Unione*, iii.10, pp. 89ff.: the Word inhabited the body from its conception; the human soul entered the body forty days after conception.
50 *Hom. Catech.*, vi.3, Tonneau, p. 135.
51 *De Incarn.*, frag. 2, Swete, vol. ii, p. 310.
52 *Relatione, anaphora.*
53 Named, through the mistake of the Syriac translator, the *Bazaar of Heracleides*.
54 Nestorius, *the Bazaar of Heracleides*, newly translated from the Syriac, G. R. Driver and L. Hodgson, Oxford, 1925.

55 Gennadius, *de vir. ill.*, 33. He is described by Socrates as a fluent and vain speaker anxious for applause; Socrates, *Hist. Eccles.*, vii.29.
56 The Pelagian connection aroused great hostility in the west to Antiochene doctrine. Cf., the opposition of Rome to Theodore in 423; Marius Mercator in Schwartz, *A.C.O.*, i.v, p. 5. See below, ch. 7.
57 *Cod. Theod.*, xvi.5.66.
58 This was Cyril's estimate of the matter in a letter to John of Antioch, P.G. 77, 177; cf., J. N. D. Kelly, *Early Christian Doctrines*, pp. 311f.
59 Loofs, *Nestoriana*, pp. 166f., *Ep. i ad Caelest.*
60 Loofs, *Nestoriana*, p. 353.
61 Loofs, *Nestoriana*, p. 303, *Sermo* xviii. Nestorius follows Theodore in allowing *communicatio idiomatum*. 'He who had a beginning and grew and was perfected is not God, though he is so called on account of the manifestation that took place gradually', *Ep. ci ad Cledonium*.
62 Loofs, *Nestoriana*, p. 177, *Ep. ii ad Cyrill.*
63 Loofs, *Nestoriana*, p. 177, *Ep. i ad Caelest.*; a qualification insisted on in other letters, e.g. Loofs, pp. 181, 184f.
64 *Heracl.*, i.3, Driver and Hodgson, p. 99.
65 Nestorius *apud* Socrates, *Hist. Eccles.*, vii.34.
66 *Heracl.*, ii.1, Driver and Hodgson, p. 137.
67 Socrates, *Hist. Eccles.*, vii.29.
68 *Heracl.*, i.1.20, Driver and Hodgson, p. 16.
69 Loofs, p. 166, *Ep. i ad Caelest.*
70 *Heracl.*, i.1.49, Driver and Hodgson, pp. 40f.
71 *Heracl.*, i.2, Driver and Hodgson, pp. 92f.
72 *Sermo* x, Loofs, pp. 265ff.
73 *Contra Theopaschitas seu Cyrillianos*, fragments in Loofs, pp. 209ff.
74 *Heracl.*, ii.1, Driver and Hodgson, p. 183.
75 *Ibid.*, i.1; p. 9.
76 *Ibid.*, ii.1; p. 179.
77 *Ibid.*, i.1.57; p. 53.
78 *Ibid.*, i.1.58; p. 54.
79 *Ibid.*, p. 55.
80 *Ibid.*, ii.1; p. 181.
81 *Ibid.*, ii.1; p. 168.
82 Theod., *Ep.*, 157.
83 R. V. Sellers, *Two Ancient Christologies*, pp. 143, 189, 202, etc.
84 Cyril, *Apol. contra Theod.*, xii.
85 R. A. Norris, *Manhood and Christ*, pp. 127ff.
86 Theodore, *Comm. in Rom.*, xi.15, P.G. 66, 853; 'Rational creatures distinguish good from evil and they choose what seems best by the power of the will'.
87 *Heracl.*, ii.1, Driver and Hodgson, p. 181.
88 H. Chadwick, 'Eucharist and Christology in the Nestorian Controversy', *J.T.S.*, n.s., ii. 2, 1951, pp. 145-64.
89 The reply to Cyril's eucharistic teaching by later Nestorians, especially Babai Magnus, will be considered later in this chapter.
90 Chalcedon, Def. iv. Text in Schwartz, *A.C.O.*, ii.1.2 (1933), pp. 126-30. Cf., R. V. Sellers, *The Council of Chalcedon*, London, 1961, pp. 207-28.
91 Nest., *Heracl.*, ii.2, Driver and Hodgson, p. 374.
92 Chalcedon, Def. iii, iv.
93 Apollinarius, *Ad Diocaes.*, ii, ed. H. Lietzmann, Berlin, 1904, p. 256.

94 He was born between 312 and 315 and died about 392.

95 Jerome, *Ep.*, lxxiv.3.1. Even after Apollinarius' death Jerome was by no means hostile; *Ep.*, lxi.1.1 (A.D. 396), ed. C. Favez (*Collect. Latomus* iv), 1950, pp. 38f., 'non quo omnia dicam esse damnanda quae in illorum voluminibus continentur sed quo quaedam reprehendenda confitear'. *Ep.*, lxx.3.1 (A.D. 397-8), p. 45, speaks appreciatively of Apollinarius' defence of the faith against Celsus and Porphyry.

96 The sentence was ratified two years later at Constantinople and followed in 383 by a declaration of the illegality of his heresy by Theodosius.

97 The main sources of his life are Socrates, *Hist. Eccles.*, ii.46; Sozomen, *Hist. Eccles.*, v.18; Theod., *Hist. Eccles.*, v.10f.; Jerome, *De vir. illust.*, civ. The fragments of his work are collected in H. Lietzmann, *Apollinaris von Laodicea und sein Schule*, Tübingen, 1904.

98 *Apodeixis*, Lietzmann, frag. 70.

99 *De Unit.*, Lietzmann, frag. 2.

100 *Ad Diocaes.*, Lietzmann, p. 256.

101 *Anac.*, 23, Lietzmann, p. 245.

102 Lietzmann, frag. 87.

103 Lietzmann, frag. 126.

104 Cf., Plotinus, *Enn.*, iv.3.4., pp. 27ff., on the division of soul from spirit.

105 Lietzmann, frag. 81.

106 *Contra Diod.*, Lietzmann, frag. 138.

107 The early sixth century *Adversus fraudes Apollinaristarum*, possibly by Leontius of Byzantium, puts the worse interpretation on the matter, that the Monophysites had deliberately adopted fraudulent attributions of Apollinarius's work to Gregory Thaumaturgos, Athanasius and Julius of Rome. Cf., H. de Riedmatten, 'Les fragments d'Apollinaire à l'Éranistes', *Das Konzil von Chalkedon Geschichte und Gegenwart*, ed. A. Grillmeier and H. Bacht, i, 1951, pp. 203-12.

108 E.g. Greg. Nyssa, *Antirrheticus*: in Christ there was a fully human mind, but it was emptied of sin before the Word took it – the worst of both worlds.

109 Theodore, *De Incarn.*, xv, Swete, vol. ii, frag. 3, p. 311.

110 Later Nestorians could conflate Ap. with Eutyches; e.g. Babai Magnus, *Liber de Unione*, iii.9, C.S.C.O. *Syr.* ii. 60, 1915, p. 74: Ap. taught that the Word 'brought down a body from heaven'. But Babai's real answer to Apollinarius is that his Christ is a mixture of God and man, and that the infinite is not susceptible of mixing.

111 Theodore, *De Pecc. Orig.*, iii, Swete, vol. ii, p. 332.

112 Theodore, *De Incarn.*, xv, Swete, vol. ii, frag. 3, p. 311.

113 Theodore, *Comm. in Galat.*, v.9, Swete, vol. i, p. 91.

114 Theodoret, *Ep.*, 104. The numbering of Theod.'s letters used here is that of Migne, P.G. 83, 1173-1409.

115 *Ep.*, 145.

116 *Hist. Eccles.*, v.3.

117 *Ep.*, 151.

118 *Ep.*, 162.

119 *Eranistes*, ii, ed. G. H. Ettlinger, 1975, p. 113.

120 *Ep.*, 109.

121 E.g. Cyril Alex., *Ep.*, 4: 'If we reject this hypostatic union [of divine and human in Christ] as either impossible or unfitting, we fall into the error of making two sons.'

122 Theodoret, *Ep.*, 145.

123 The text of these works is in Migne, P.G. 76, 9–248 and in Schwartz, *A.C.O.*,
     i.1.6, 1914.
124 Theodoret, *Ep.*, 112.
125 *Ep.*, 151.
126 *Ep.*, 169.
127 Text in Migne, P.G. 76, 385–452, and Schwartz, *A.C.O.*, i, 1914.
128 Cyril, *Ep.*, 39.
129 Cyril, *Ep.*, 40.
130 Theod., *Ep.*, 125.
131 Theod., *Ep.*, 130.
132 Theod., *Ep.*, 162.
133 Cyril, *Ep.*, 39, P.G. 77. The part that Rabbula of Edessa may have played in the
     reconciliation is discussed by G. G. Blum, *Rabbula von Edessa*, C.S.C.O., Subsidia
     34, 1969, p. 180.
134 Theod., *Ep.*, 172.
135 *Ep.*, 176. Later Syrian opinion made no such allowances for John's betrayal. In
     the late sixth century, Barhadbešabba (*L'Histoire de Barhadbešabba 'Arbaia*,
     part 1, Pat. Or. xxiii. 2, ed. F. Nau, 1932), xxvii, p. 564, accuses John of being
     jealous of Nestorius' popularity. The anonymous *Expositio Officiorum Ecclesiae*
     (C.S.C.O. *Syr.* ii. 91, ed. R. H. Connolly, 1913), ii.6, p. 144, says 'After Cyril and
     John and the other westerners had wickedly anathematized the blessed Nestorius
     and driven him into exile, then the Orient turned its back on the patriarch of
     Antioch and ignored him because he had fallen into error, and withdrew recog-
     nition from him'.
136 *Ep.*, 180.
137 *Eranistes, prolog.* 28, Ettlinger, pp. 61f.
138 The gnostic antecedents of contemporary heresy are emphasized again in Theod.,
     Ep., 145, to the monks of Constantinople. Gnostic denial of Christ's true
     humanity is seen as the source of all error, hypothetical opinion masquerading
     as doctrine.
139 E.g. Severus of Antioch, *Ad Nephalium*, C.S.C.O. *Syr.* iv. 7, 1949.
140 *Chron. Edessenum*, C.S.C.O. *Syr.* iii. 4, 1903, p. 7.
141 A. Vööbus, *History of the School of Nisibis*, p. 11.
142 On the disputed dating of the move from Edessa to Nisibis, see A. Vööbus, *His-
     tory of the School of Nisibis*, pp. 32ff.
143 *Hist. Nestorienne*, Pat. Or. vii. 2, 1911, p. 187.
144 W. H. C. Frend, *The Rise of the Monophysite Movement*, pp. 260ff., identifies
     this activity, from about 530, as the beginning of the permanent separation of
     the Monophysites from the Imperial Church. Imperial reaction took the form of
     savage repression, including the exile of Severus of Antioch and the martyrdom
     of John of Tella.
145 *The Histories of Rabban Hormizd the Persian and Rabban Bar 'Idta*, ed. E. A.
     Wallis Budge, 1902, vol. ix, pp. 119f.
146 A. Vööbus, *History of the School of Nisibis*, p. 156.
147 The Monophysites adapted the name 'Jacobites' from James Bar'adai.
148 On Henana, see Vööbus, *History of the School of Nisibis*, pp. 300ff. The School
     was left with about twenty scholars who supported Henana; *ibid.*, p. 312.
149 Michael the Syrian, *Chron.*, x.25, ed. Chabot, vol. 2, p. 379.
150 On Severus, J. Lebon, *Le Monophysisme séverien. Étude historique littéraire et
     théologique*, Louvain, 1909; W. H. C. Frend, *The Rise of the Monophysite Move-
     ment*, Cambridge, 1972, for Severus' historical setting; Roberta C. Chesnut,

Three Monophysite Christologies, Oxford, 1976, part 1, for his theology. In this section, I have drawn gratefully on Professor Chesnut's analysis.

151 Severus, *Ep.*, ii, Pat. Or. xii, 1919, pp. 189f.

152 *Ep.*, xv, *ibid.*, p. 210.

153 For the Aristotelian and Stoic treatment of this in relation to christology, see Chesnut, *Three Monophysite Christologies*, pp. 18f.

154 Severus, *Ep.*, x, ed. E. W. Brooks, p. 203.

155 Chesnut, *Three Monophysite Christologies*, pp. 20ff.

156 *Ibid.*, p. 27.

157 Severus, *First Ep. to Sergius*, C.S.C.O. Syr. iv. 7, 1949, p. 82.

158 Chesnut, *Three Monophysite Christologies*, p. 33.

159 *Ibid.*, pp. 35f.

160 Severus, *Philalethes*, C.S.C.O. Syr. 67, 1952, p. 232f. Cf., *Hom.* 83 on the Nativity and Epiphany, Pat. Or. xx. 2, 1928, p. 416.

161 Severus, *Ep.*, xxv, cited by Chesnut, *Three Monophysite Christologies*, p. 19, n. 4.

162 *Hom.* 66, on the Epiphany, Pat. Or. viii. 2, 1911, p. 347; *Hom.* 46, on Pentecost, Pat. Or. xxxv. 3, 1969, p. 294.

163 *First Ep. to Sergius*, C.S.C.O. Syr. iv.7, 1949, pp. 82f.

164 Cf., Babai Magnus, *Liber de Unione*, C.S.C.O. Syr. ii. 61, 1915, pp. 96f.: a composite being is limited by its component parts. A composite man-God is neither man nor God but a 'peculiar and unique hypothesis'. This peculiarity and uniqueness of Christ, so distasteful to Babai, was what the Monophysites were defending as vital to man's salvation.

165 Leo could appear Nestorian to Monophysite minds. Cf., the Monophysite document in Pat. Or. xiii. 2, 1916, pp. 183f., which identifies Leo and Diodore of Tarsus point by point.

166 Cyril, *Ep.*, 72 to Proclus, P.G. 77, 345.

167 *Colloquium cum Severianis*, Pat. Or. xiii. 2, 1916, pp. 194f.

168 F. C. Burkitt, *Early Eastern Christianity*, 1904, p. 155.

169 How much more there may yet be to come appears in A. Vööbus' valuable use of unpublished material.

170 *Six Explanations of the Liturgical Feasts*, C.S.C.O. Syr. 155, 1974.

171 This freedom is found especially in Cyrus' *Explanation of the Passion*, vii. He has the authority of Galatians iv for treating Abraham's bondwoman and free woman typologically, but extends the same treatment to Abraham's offerings of animals and birds in Gen. xv.9 (*Passion*, vii.6, p. 94); to the prophecy of a prince in Judah in Gen. xlix.10 (*Passion*, vii.7, p. 95); to the binding of the colt to the vine in Gen. xlix.11, typifying the conjunction of man and Word in Christ (*Ibid.*, vii.8, p. 95); to the translation of Enoch, the ascension of Elijah and Abel's blood, typifying the Resurrection (*Res.*, vii.4–6, pp. 119f.); and to the ascensions of Enoch and Elijah typifying the Ascension of Christ (*Asc.*, v.6, p. 153).

172 *Passion*, iii.7, p. 76, Macomber's tr., C.S.C.O. Syr. 156.

173 *Fast*, iv.21, p. 20.

174 *Ibid.*, vi.3, p. 24.

175 In distinction not only from the gnostic fasts but also from the obligatory Jewish fasts, *Ibid.*, viii.3, p. 37.

176 *Ibid.*, i.5, p. 8.

177 *Res.*, ii.4, pp. 103f.

178 *Ibid.*, ii.8, p. 106.

179 Martyrius (Sahdona), *Oeuvres spirituelles, i, Livre de la perfection*, C.S.C.O. part i, *Syr.* 86 (1960); part ii, *Syr.* 90 (1961) and 110 (1965); ed. André de Halleux.
180 *Liber perfect.*, part i, iii.12f., p. 32. We may note here also Sahdona's characteristically Semitic emphasis upon the feminine gender of the Holy Spirit in his describing the Spirit protecting us 'in motherly fashion', *Ibid.*, iii.13.
181 A. de Halleux, 'La christologie de Martyrios-Sahdona dans l'évolution de Nestorianisme', *Orientalia Christiana Periodica* 23, 1957, pp. 5-32.
182 Babai Magnus, *Liber de Unione*, i.3, C.S.C.O. *Syr.* ii. 60, 1915, p. 24.
183 *Ibid.*, iii.9, p. 96. So iv.12, p. 138, Cyril and Henana alike hold that the Word was subjected to human limitation, the infinite made finite; v.19, pp. 183, 186f., Henana is accused with Origen of compromising the reality of Christ's human body.
184 Sahdona, *Liber perfect.*, ii.21, C.S.C.O. *Syr.* 90, 1961, p. 16.
185 Babai, *Liber de Unione*, iv.17, pp. 159-71.
186 *Liber perfect.*, ii.28, p. 18.
187 *Ibid.*, ii.30, p. 19.
188 *Ibid.*, ii.24, p. 17. John i.14 was always a hard text for Nestorians. Cf., Dadišo (7th cent.): the Word is said to 'become' flesh in the same sense that a king is said to have 'become' a labourer if he assumes the outer clothing of a labourer. We cannot attribute real 'becoming' to the Godhead; *Commentaire du livre d'Abba Isaïe (logoi i-xv) par Dadišo Qatraya*, vii.12, C.S.C.O. *Syr.* 144, 1972, pp. 122f.
189 *Ibid.*, ii.23, p. 16.
190 *Ibid.*, ii.36, p. 21.
191 *Ibid.*, xi.4-7, vol. 3, *Syr.* 110, 1965, pp. 82f.
192 *Ibid.*, part i, *Syr.* 86, 1960, iv.2.35, p. 97.
193 Babai, *Liber de Unione*, ii.7, pp. 51f. See above pp. 109f.
194 *Ibid.*, p. 52.
195 Cf., Roberta C. Chesnut, *Three Monophysite Christologies*, pp. 33f.
196 *Ibid.*, pp. 52-5.
197 *Ibid.*, p. 56.
198 *Ibid.*, iii.9, pp. 80f.
199 *Ibid.*, i.2, p. 12.
200 *Ibid.*, i.3, p. 20.
201 *Ibid.*, iii.9, p. 97.
202 H. Chadwick in *J.T.S.*, n.s. ii.2, 1951, pp. 145-64.
203 Cyrus of Edessa, *Six Explanations of the Liturgical Feasts*, C.S.C.O. *Syr.* 155, 1974, 'Expl. of the Fast', v.4, p. 21: 'By means of that which is near we would be guided towards that which is in heaven' - concerning the eucharistic bread.
204 *Liber de Unione*, iii.9, pp. 105f.
205 *Ibid.*, iii.10, p. 95.
206 *Ibid.*, iv.16, p. 154.
207 *Ibid.*, vi.20, p. 223.
208 *Ibid.*, vi.21, p. 238.
209 As William G. Macomber suggests of the passage quoted above from Cyrus of Edessa, C.S.C.O. *Syr.* 156, 1974, p. 18, n. 8.
210 *Liber de Unione*, iii.10, p. 109.
211 *Ibid.*, vi.20, pp. 202f.
212 *Ibid.*, p. 203.
213 *Ibid.*, pp. 228f.
214 *Ibid.*, p. 231.

215 *Ibid.*, p. 234.
216 *Ibid.*, p. 240.
217 *Ibid.*, p. 243.
218 W. H. C. Frend, *The Rise of the Monophysite Movement*, pp. 61f., 212.
219 Zach. Rhetor, *Hist. Eccles.*, iii.5, C.S.C.O. *Syr.* iii. 5, 1924, p. 159.
220 W. H. C. Frend, *The Rise of the Monophysite Movement*, pp. 10f., 16. On the
     Jewish influence in Antioch, J. H. W. G. Liebeschuetz, *Antioch*, Oxford, 1972,
     pp. 34f., 225, 232ff. On gnostic influence upon the monks, A. Vööbus, *History of Asceticism in the Syrian Orient*, i, C.S.C.O., Subsidia 14, 1958.
221 J. H. W. G. Liebeschütz, *Antioch*, pp. 226-31.

7 Antiochene theology and the religious life

 1 John Chrysostom, *Hom. in Heb.*, iv.3, 4, P.G. 63, 40f.
 2 Zacharias Rhetor, *Hist. Eccles.*, iii, C.S.C.O. *Syr.* iii. 5, 1924, p. 151.
 3 Sahdona (Martyrius), *Liber Perfectionis*, i.3.12f., C.S.C.O. *Syr.* 86, 1960, p. 32.
 4 Cyrus of Edessa, *Six Explanations of the Liturgical Feasts*, The Resurrection
     ii.8, C.S.C.O. *Syr.* 155, 1974, p. 106.
 5 *Ibid.*, ii.4, pp. 103f.
 6 Babai Magnus, *Liber de Unione*, iv.15, C.S.C.O. *Syr.* ii. 60, 1915, pp. 142-6.
 7 Sahdona, *Liber Perfectionis*, ii.10.26f., C.S.C.O. *Syr.* 110, p. 60f.
 8 *Ibid.*, xiii.24, p. 156.
 9 *L'histoire de Barhadbešabba*, part ii, xxvi, Pat. Or. ix.5, 1913, pp. 561f.
10 John Chrysostom, *Hom. in Heb.*, v.2, P.G. 63, 47.
11 *Ibid.*, v.4f., col. 51f.
12 *Ibid.*, xxviii.2, col. 194.
13 *Ibid.*, xxviii.3, col. 196.
14 *Ibid.*, xxix.1, col. 203f.
15 *Ibid.*, xxxiii.4, col. 229.
16 *The Discourses of Philoxenus*, vol.i, 'On poverty', London, 1894, pp. 237f.
17 *Ibid.*, pp. 335-49.
18 Sahdona, *Liber Perfect.*, ii.8.55, C.S.C.O. *Syr.* 86, 1960, p. 22.
19 *Ibid.*, ii.8.58, p. 23.
20 *Ibid.*, ii.8.69, p. 26.
21 *Ibid.*, iv.3.2, p. 109.
22 *Ibid.*, iv.3.25, pp. 111f.
23 *Ibid.*, iv.3.34, p. 115.
24 *Ibid.*, xii.22, C.S.C.O. *Syr.* 110, 1965, p. 109.
25 *Ibid.*, xii.43, p. 114.
26 Theodoret, *Hist. Relig.*, iv, P.G. 82, 1341. The term appears elsewhere in the
     literature of Syrian asceticism, e.g. Afrahat, *Demonstrationes*, 'de monachis', Pat.
     Syr. i. 1, 1894, p. 248, 'He who receives the likeness of angels will be strange to
     men'; *Vita Rabbulae*, ed. J. J. Overbeck, Oxford, 1865, p. 169, 'The monk lives,
     body and soul, after the manner of the angels'. Sahdona uses the term to refer
     to the life to come, *Liber perfect.*, part 1, ii.8.21, C.S.C.O. *Syr.* 86, 1960, p. 13:
     Perfection, the transcending of all that pertains to the age of mortality, is the
     angelic life, reserved for the life after the resurrection (Matt. xxii.30 is quoted in
     support: 'For in the resurrection [men and women] neither marry, nor are given
     in marriage, but are as angels in heaven'). Cf., A. Vööbus, *History of Asceticism*,
     i, pp. 97ff.

27 Jerome, *Ep.*, xvii.3 (the numbering of the letter as in P. Cavallera, *Saint Jérôme*, i.2, 1922, pp. 12ff.) on the monks of Chalcis, suspicious, hostile, clamouring for Jerome to leave them. 'Very well, I go. Let them go to heaven by themselves, since Christ died for them alone!'

28 John Chrysostom, *De Sacerdotio*, vi.5, contrasts the life of the ascetic with that of the bishop on the ground that the former has at least eliminated bodily needs: 'if their body be not strong, their zeal is confined and has no outlet in practice; for prolonged fasting, lying on the ground, vigils, abstention from washing, severe toil and all other exercises which tend towards the mortification of the flesh are impossible' [for the bishop].

29 John Chrysostom, *Hom. in Matt.*, 55, 68, P.G. 58, 560, 673, 675.

30 *Les cinq recensions de l'Ascéticon Syriaque d'Abba Isaïe*, i.2a, C.S.C.O. *Syr.* 120, 1968, p. 2; i. 3a, p. 4; etc. Cf., also Theodore of Mops., *Comm. on the Lord's Prayer*, ed. A. Mingana (*Woodbrooke Studies* 6), 1933, p. 128: 'Because those who strive after perfection have unceasing molestation from the urges of nature, from the promptings of demons and from daily happenings which often cause many to stumble and deviate from the path of duty, they have a constant struggle in this world' (Mingana's tr., p. 4).

31 Eusebius, *Mart. Palest.*, i.5 (Alphaeus); ii.1ff. (Romanus); iii.3 (six young men at Caesarea); iv.8ff. (Apphianus); v.2ff. (Aedesius); ix.4f. (Antoninus, Zebinas, Germanus).

32 *Vita Rabbulae*, ed. Overbeck, pp. 164f.

33 G. G. Blum, *Rabbula von Edessa*, C.S.C.O., Subsidia 34, 1969, p. 22.

34 *Vita Rabb.*, p. 169f. This was not an isolated incident. Cf., Libanius, *Pro Templis*, xxx.8 (between A.D. 381-91) describing attacks on temples by monks, 'hurling themselves on the temples, carrying as weapons, wood, stone, iron or for lack of these even using hands and feet ... smashing roofs, walls, statues, altars. The priests must remain silent or die.' All this Libanius holds to be in defiance of imperial law. It is perhaps associated with the fourth-century conception of the monk as a 'soldier of Christ'; cf., K. Holl, *Die Geschichte des Wortes Beruf* (*Gesamm. Aufsätze*, iii, pp. 193, 196, Tübingen, 1928).

35 *Vita Rabb.*, p. 170.

36 His opposition to Nestorianism, in particular to Theodore, began after his consecration to the see of Edessa in 412; cf., G. C. Blum, *Rabbula von Edessa*, p. 54f.

37 E. Schürer, *Geschichte des jüdischen Volkes im Zeitalter Jesu Christ*, ii (4th ed., 1907), pp. 267ff.; G. Schrenk, *Theologisches Wörterbuch zum Neuen Testament*, ed. G. Kittel, iii, 1918, pp. 265-84.

38 For a discussion of the letter, see T. W. Manson, 'The Problem of the Epistle to the Hebrews', *Bulletin of the John Rylands Library*, 32, Manchester, 1950, pp. 1-17, reprinted in *Studies in the Gospels and Epistles*, ed. M. Black, Manchester, 1962, pp. 242-58.

39 Cyril Alex., *Comm. in Heb.*, ii.17, P.G. 74, 963. There are Armenian fragments of Cyril's Commentary, J. Lebon, 'Fragments arméniens du Comm. sur l'Épître aux Hebreux de saint Cyrille d'Alexandrie', *Le Muséon. Revue d'études orientales*, 44, 1931, pp. 69-114; 46, 1933, pp. 237-46; and a Syriac fragment, A. Mingana, *Woodbrooke Studies* 4, Cambridge 1931, p. 47.

40 P.G. 74, 968.

41 *Ibid.*, ii.18, col. 968.

42 *Ibid.*, iv.14, col. 972.

43 John Chrysostom, *Comm. in Heb.*, vii.2, P.G. 63, 64.

44 *Ibid.*, viii.1, col. 68. So Theodore, *Les homélies catéchetiques*, vi. 8, ed. R. Tonneau, p. 144; Christ lived a life 'with much weariness and sweat, and showed his great patience towards us who were sinful'.

45 Chrysostom, *Hom. in Heb.*, xiv.1, col. 111.

46 *Ibid.*, xv.3, cols. 120f.

47 *Ibid.*, xvii.3f., col. 131. Chrysostom's treatment of Hebrews constantly runs parallel to that of Theodore, *Homilies on Baptism and the Liturgy*, ed. A. Mingana, *Woodbrooke Studies* 6. Cf., the need for the high priest to be one with those for whom he intercedes, *Homily on Baptism*, p. 145, 'Men would only have entered the heavenly places after a man from us had been assumed'; *Ibid.*, p. 148, 'From the fact that the man who was assumed from us had such a confidence [with God], he became a messenger on behalf of all the [human] race so that the rest of the human race might participate with him' (Mingana's tr., p. 22).

48 Babai, *Liber de Unione*, iii.10, C.S.C.O. *Syr.* 60, 1915, pp. 113f.

49 Theodore, *Homs. on the Liturgy*, v, ed. A. Mingana, makes considerable use of the idea of the high priesthood of Christ and quotes Hebrews in this connection, but not the Melchizedek verses, Heb., v.10, vi.20ff. Melch. is referred to in *Hom. on Bapt.*, ii, ed. Mingana, p. 144, quoting Heb., vi.20 without comment on the typology. Ephrem, in treating Gen., xiv.18, does not make any mention of Melch. as a type of Christ (*Sancti Ephrem Syri in Gen. et in Exod. Comm.*, C.S.C.O. *Syr.* 71, 1955, p. 55). In the extant fragment of Eustathius' Commentary (P.G. 18, 696) the writer allows Melch. to be a type of Christ's divinity in that Melch. had no genealogy: Christ's humanity is given a genealogy in the gospels, but his divinity belongs to a more sublime order in which genealogies are not appropriate. To Cyrus of Edessa the eucharistic bread is an image of the body hidden from our sight in heaven, 'where Christ has entered ahead of us, having become a high priest for ever after the order of Melchizedek (*Six explanations of the liturgical feasts*, C.S.C.O. *Syr.* 155, 1974, 'On the pasch', p. 49). Babai Magnus sees Melch. as prefiguring Christ's human birth from a mother and no human father, (*Liber de Unione*, iii.9, C.S.C.O. *Syr.* 60, 1915, p. 83); he was born 'in his humanity, in time and by union [with the Word] from his mother without a father, as the scriptures show through the mystery of Melch.'. Cf., also iii.10, p. 122.

50 *Liber de Unione*, pp. 118, 122f.

51 *Ibid.*, vi.20, pp. 215f.

52 *Liber perfectionis*, part ii, iii.6, C.S.C.O. *Syr.* 110, 1965, p. 27.

53 Martyrius (Sahdona), *Lettres à ses amis solitaires*, C.S.C.O. *Syr.* 112, 1965, p. 60.

54 The identity of Abba Isaias remains in dispute. The generally accepted view that the *Asceticon* was written by Isaias of Gaza (d. 488) is challenged by R. Draguet (*Les cinq recensions de l'Ascéticon syriaque*, C.S.C.O. *Syr.* 122, 1968, 'Introduction au problème isaïen', p. 115), who concludes that the author is Isaias who lived at Scete at the end of the fourth century.

55 *Ascet.*, Logos i.2a, p. 2.

56 *Ibid.*, p. 3.

57 *Ibid.*, i.4b, p. 6.

58 *Ibid.*, ii.4, p. 10.

59 *Ibid.*, vii.11, pp. 66f.

60 *Ibid.*, vii.18, p. 74.

61 *Ibid.*, vii.25, pp. 86f.

62 *Ibid.*, xi.75, pp. 145f.

63 *Ibid.*, vii.17, p. 73; ix.2, p. 98.
64 *Anonymi auctoris Expositio officiorum Ecclesiae*, C.S.C.O. *Syr.* ii. 91, 92, 1913/15.
65 *Ibid.*, iv.1, vol. 92, pp. 2f. Cf., Theodore, *Homily on Baptism*, ed. A. Mingana, pp. 144f., contrasting Jewish ceremonies as 'shadows' of reality with Christian ceremonies, which are 'images' of reality. 'When we look at an image we recognize the person who is represented in it . . . but we are never able to recognize a man represented only by his shadow, since this shadow has no likeness to the real body from which it emanates.'
66 *Ibid.*, ii.12, vol. 91, pp. 178f.
67 *Ibid.*, iv.2, vol. 92, p. 3.
68 Theodore, *Homily on Baptism*, ii, ed. A. Mingana, pp. 144f. The distinction between image and shadow is repeated from Theodore by Cyrus of Edessa, *Six explanations of the liturgical feasts*, 'Pasch', i.3, C.S.C.O. *Syr.* 155, 1974, p. 44.
69 *Ibid.*, iv, p. 184.
70 *Ibid.*, p. 187.
71 *Ibid.*, *Homily on the Eucharist*, v, p. 210. Consecration of the bread and wine by the descent upon them of the holy Spirit does not reflect the primitive liturgical tradition of Syria. It first appears in the third century, Syrian *Didascalia Apostolorum* (ed. R. H. Connolly, 1929, p. 244), and is found a century later in Cyril of Jerusalem, *Catechesis*, xxiii.7, 'We entreat God . . . to send forth the holy Spirit . . . that he may make the bread the body of Christ'. The same teaching is implied by John Chrysostom, *De Sacerdotio*, iii.4, 'The priest stands bringing down not fire but the holy Spirit', and is explicit in later Syrian texts, e.g. Babai Magnus, *Liber de Unione*, i.3, C.S.C.O. *Syr.* 60, 1915, p. 22, 'The holy Spirit descends incomprehensibly and performs these mysteries on the altars in every place and makes them the body of Christ' (cf., iv.16, p. 153); *Ibid.*, iii.10, p. 95, 'The grace of the holy Spirit descends and makes perfect the mystery of our salvation'; vi.20, p. 223, the consecrated bread 'through the prayer of the priest and the descent of the holy Spirit receives virtue and becomes the body of our Lord'. The more primitive Syrian tradition followed the Epistle to the Hebrews in seeing Christ as the agent of consecration, since he is both sacrifice and sacrificer; so Afrahat, *Demonstratio*, xii.6, Pat. Syr. i.1, 1907, pp. 516f.; xxi.9, p. 957; xxi.10, p. 960; Ephrem, *Sermon in Holy Week*, iv.4. The *epiclesis* of the Spirit derives not from the Syrian liturgy but from that of Jerusalem, influenced at this point by the Egyptian rite, G. Dix, *The Shape of the Liturgy*, 2nd ed., London, 1945, p. 280.
72 Theodore, *Homily on Baptism*, ii, ed. A. Mingana, p. 146.
73 *Ibid.*, p. 147.
74 *Ibid.*, iv, p. 184; Mingana's tr., pp. 52f.
75 *Hom. Catech.*, ed. R. Tonneau, vii.4, p. 166; vii.7, p. 170. In Tonneau's words, paraphrasing Theodore, 'L'homme sauvé en espérance, est encore ici-bas dans la maison terrestre, avec son lot entier de misères et le poids de sa déchéance initiale', Introduction, p. xxviii.
76 *Hom. on Bapt.*, iv, ed. A. Mingana, p. 181.
77 John Chrysostom, *Hom. in Heb.*, xxx.1, P.G. 63, 209, 'discipline is training'.
78 Cyrus of Edessa, *Six explanations*, 'Resurrection', viii.5, C.S.C.O. *Syr.* 155, 1974, p. 122; we have to live in this life 'as though in a training school'.
79 Barhadbešabba, *Cause de la fondation des écoles*, Pat. Or. iv.4, 1908, pp. 351ff.
80 John Chrysostom, *De Sacerdotio*, vi.13.
81 Theodore, *Hom.* i.6, ed. R. Tonneau, p. 11. Cf., John Chrysostom, *Hom. in Heb.*,

vi.1, P.G. 63, 56f., on Heb., iii.7ff., gives repeated warnings against losing the kingdom of God through faithlessness after Christ has won it for us. *Ibid.*, xx.1, cols. 143f., 'You are pure after baptism but are still free to slide backwards.' Sahdona, *Liber perfect.*, part i, iii.35f., C.S.C.O. *Syr.* 86, p. 37. 'It is impossible to avoid preoccupation with the body and its lusts.'

82 Theodore, *Hom.*, x.4, p. 250.

83 *Ibid.*, x.3, p. 248.

84 *Ibid.*, x.7, p. 256.

85 *Ibid.*, x.3, p. 248.

86 *Ibid.*, x.11f., pp. 262, 264. John Chrysostom's pastoral care leads him to advise his flock in the matter of finding comfort in tribulation: there are two ways to do so - by remembering the fortitude of others and by reducing the impact of bodily suffering through quietness of mind, *Hom. in Heb.*, xxix.1, P.G. 63, 203.

87 On Pelagius, see G. de Plinval, *Pélage: ses écrits, sa vie et sa réforme*, Lausanne, 1943; on the alleged Pelagianism of Theodore, the useful summary in R. A. Norris, *Manhood and Christ*, Oxford, 1963, pp. 184-6, 240f., 259-62.

88 Schwartz, *A.C.O.*, i.5 (Collectio Palatina), 1924, pp. 5f.

89 See P. Brown, *Augustine of Hippo*, London, 1967, chs. 29-31.

90 P.L. 48, 626-30; P. Brown, *Augustine*, p. 371.

91 See above, n. 89.

92 P. Brown, *Augustine*, pp. 373f.

93 R. A. Norris, *Manhood and Christ*, p. 184.

94 Theod., *Hist. Rel.*, iii.1325.

95 John Chrysostom, *Hom. in Heb.*, xii.3, P.G. 63, 99f.

96 Sahdona (Martyrius), *Liber perfect.*, part i, iv.2.35f., p. 97; iv.2.39, pp. 97f.

97 See the accounts of the religious currents in the empire in A. D. Nock, *Conversion*, Oxford, 1933; E. R. Dodds, *Pagan and Christian in an age of Anxiety*, Cambridge, 1965; F. Cumont, *Les Religions orientales dans le Paganisme romain*, 4th ed., Paris, 1929.

Bibliography

I Primary Sources

Acta Martyrum et sanctorum, ed. P. Bedjan, Paris (1890-7).

Acta - Les versions grecques des Actes des martyrs persans sous Sapor II, ed. H. Delahaye, Pat. Or. ii. 4 (1905).

Adamantii Dialogus de recte in Deum fide, P.G. 11, 1711-1884.

Aeneas of Gaza, *Theophrastus*, P.G. 85, 872-1004.

Afrahat (Aphraat), *Demonstrationes*, ed. D. J. Parisot, Pat. Syr. i. 1, 1-1050 (1894) and 2, 1-489 (1907).

Georg Bert, *Aphrahats des persischen Weisen Homilien aus dem Syrischen übersetzt und erläutert*, T.U. iii. 3, 4 (1888).

Agathias, *Historia*, in *Historici Graeci Minores*, Teubner series, vol. 2 (1871).

Akhsenaya, *see* Philoxenos

Anonymi auctoris Expositio Officiorum Ecclesiae Georgio Arbelensi vulgo adscripta, ed. R. H. Connolly, C.S.C.O. *Syr*. ii. 91/92 (1913/15).

Apollinarius, *Apodeixis* (fragments); *De Unione Corporis et Divinitatis in Christo*; *Contra Diodorum*; *Recapitulatio*, in *Apollinaris von Laodicea und seine Schule*, ed. H. Lietzmann, T.U. 1 (1904).

K. Staab, *Pauluskommentare aus der griechischen Kirche*, 57-81, Münster (1933).

J. Reuss, *Matthäus-Kommentare aus der griechischen Kirche*, 1-54, T.U. 61 (1957).

J. Flemming and H. Lietzmann, *Apollinaristische Schriften. Syrisch, mit den griechischen Texten* (Abhandlung der Gesellschaft der Wissenschaften zu Göttingen, N.F. 7. 4) Berlin (1904).

Babai Magnus, *Liber de Unione*, ed. A. Vaschalde, C.S.C.O. *Syr*. ii. 60/61 (1915).

Bardaisan (Bardesanes), *Liber Legum Regionum*, ed. F. Nau, Pat. Syr. i. 2, 490-657 (1907).

Barhadbešabba 'Arbaia, *Cause de la fondation des écoles*, ed. A. Scher, Pat. Or. iv. 4, 319-404 (1908).

Historia Ecclesiastica, ed. F. Nau, part 2, Pat. Or. ix. 5 (1913); part 1, Pat. Or. xxiii. 2 (1932).

Chronicon Anonymum, ed. I. Guidi, C.S.C.O. *Syr*. iii. 4, part 1 section 2 (1903).

Chronicon ad annum domini 846 pertinens, ed. E. W. Brooks, C.S.C.O. *Syr*. iii. 4, part 2 section 4 (1904).

Chronicon Edessenum, ed. I. Guidi, C.S.C.O. *Syr*. iii. 4, part 1 section 1 (1903).

Chronicon Maroniticum, ed. E. W. Brooks, C.S.C.O. *Syr*. iii. 4, part 2 section 1 (1904).

Chronicon Miscellaneum ad annum domini 724 pertinens, ed. E. W. Brooks, C.S.C.O. *Syr*. iii. 4, part 2 section 3 (1904).

Incerti auctoris Chronicon ps.-Dionysianum vulgo dictum, ed. J. B. Chabot, C.S.C.O. *Syr*. iii. 1/2 (1927/33).

Chrysostom, *see* John Chrysostom.
Colloquium cum Severianis, ed. F. Nau, Pat. Or. xiii. 2 (1916).
Cyril of Alexandria, *Explanatio in Epistolam ad Hebraeos* (fragments), P.G. 74, 953–1005.
 Commentarii in Prophetas Minores, P.G. 71.
 Contra Theodorum Mopsuestenum et Diodorum Tarsensem, P.G. 76, 1437–1452.
 J. Lebon, 'Fragments arméniens du commentaire sur l'Épître aux Hébreux de S. Cyrille d'Alexandrie', *Le Muséon, Revue d'études orientales*, 44, 69–114, Louvain (1931); 46, 237–46 (1933).
 Adversus Nestorii Blasphemias, P.G. 76, 9–248; *A.C.O.* i.1.6, 13–106.
 De Recta Fide, P.G. 76, 1133–1200; *A.C.O.* i.1.1, 42–72.
 Epistolae, P.G. 77, 9–390.
 Twelve Chapters against Nestorius: (a) *Explicatio duodecim Capitum Ephesii pronunciata*, P.G. 76, 293–312; (b) *Apologeticus pro duodecim Capitibus adversus orientales episcopos*, P.G. 76, 315–385; (c) *Epistola ad Euoptium adversus impugnationem duodecim Capitum a Theodorato editam*, P.G. 76, 385–452; all these are in *A.C.O.* i.1.7.
Cyrus of Edessa, *Six Explanations of the Liturgical Feasts*, ed. William F. Macomber S.J., C.S.C.O. *Syr.* 155/156 (1974).
Dadišo Qatraya, *Commentaire du livre d'Abba Isaïe (logoi i–xv)*, ed. René Draguet, C.S.C.O. *Syr.* 144/145 (1972).
Didascalia Apostolorum, the Syriac version translated and accompanied by the Verona Latin fragments, R. H. Connolly, Oxford (1929).
 J. V. Bartlet, 'Fragments of the *Didasc. Apost.*' (Greek fragments), *J.T.S.* xviii, 301–9 (1916–17).
Diodore of Tarsus, 'Der theologische Nachlass des Diodor von Tarsus', ed. R. Abramowski, *Z.N.T.W.* 42 (1949).
Doctrine of Addai, the Apostle, now first edited in a complete state in the original Syriac, ed. G. Phillips, London (1876).
Documenta ad origines Monophysitorum illustrandas, ed. J. B. Chabot, C.S.C.O. *Syr.* ii. 37 (1908/33).
Documentum Monophysitanum, ed. F. Nau, Pat. Or. xiii. 2 (1916).
Documentum Nestorianum, ed. J. B. Chabot, C.S.C.O. *Syr.* iii. 4 (1904).
Elias of Nisibis, *Opus Chronologicum*, ed. E. W. Brooks and J. B. Chabot, C.S.C.O. *Syr.* iii. 7/8 (1910).
Ephrem, *Sancti Ephrem Syri in Genesim et in Exodum Commentarii*, ed. R. M. Tonneau, C.S.C.O. *Syr.* 71/72 (1955).
 Saint Éphrem, Commentaire de l'Évangile concordant, text syriaque (MS Chester Beatty 709), ed. Dom Louis Leloir O.S.B., *Chester Beatty Monographs* 8, Dublin (1963).
 Des heiligen Ephraem des Syrers Hymnen Contra Haereses, ed. E. Beck, C.S.C.O. *Syr.* 76/77 (1957).
 Des heiligen Ephraem des Syrers Sermones de Fide, ed. E. Beck, C.S.C.O. *Syr.* 88/89 (1961).
Eusebius of Caesarea, *Chronicle*, ed. R. Helm, G.C.S., *Eus. Werke* (Latin text), vii. 1, 2, Leipzig (1913, 1926). Both volumes together (1956).
 Chronicle, ed. J. Karst, G.C.S., *Eus. Werke* (German translation of Armenian text), v, Leipzig (1911).
 Historia Ecclesiastica, ed. E. Schwartz and Th. Mommsen, G.C.S., *Eus. Werke*, ii. 1, 2, 3, Leipzig (1903–9).

Eustathius of Antioch, 'Die Fragmente des Eustathios von Antiocheia', ed. F. Scheid-weiler, *Byzantinische Zeitschrift*, 48, 73–85 (1955).
Fragments, P.G. 18, 675–704.
De Engastrimutho contra Originem, P.G. 18, 613–674.
Evagrius Ponticus, *Les six centuries des Kephalaia Gnostica d'Évagre le Pontique*, ed. A. Guillaumont, Pat. Or. xxviii. 1 (1958).
George of Arbela, *Expositio Officiorum Ecclesiae*, ed. R. H. Connolly, C.S.C.O. Syr. ii. 91/92 (1913–15).
Gregentius of Zafar (Tapharensis), *Disputatio cum Herbano Judaeo*, P.G. 86 (i), 621–784.
Henana of Hadiab, *Traités d'Isaï le docteur et de Hnena d'Adiabène sur les martyrs, le vendredi d'or et les rogations*, ed. A. Scher, Pat. Or. vii (1911).
Histoires d'Aboudemmeh et de Marouta, métropolitains jacobites de Tagrit et de l'Orient, ed. F. Nau, Pat. Or. iii. 1 (1909).
Histoire Nestorienne (Chronique de Séert), ed. A. Scher, Pat. Or. iv. 3 (1907); vii. 2 (1911); xiii. 4 (1919).
The Histories of Rabban Hormizd the Persian and Rabban Bar 'Idta, ed. E. A. Wallis Budge, London (1902).
Hunain ibn Ishaq, *Syrian Anatomy, Pathology and Therapeutics*, ed. E. A. Wallis Budge, Oxford (1913).
Ignatius of Antioch, *Letters*, ed. J. B. Lightfoot, *The Apostolic Fathers* ii, 2nd ed. London (1889).
Irenaeus of Lyons, *Adversus Haereses*, P.G. 7, 433–1224.
Išai, *Les cinq recensions de l'Ascéticon syriaque d'Abba Isaïe*, ed. René Draquet, C.S.C.O. Syr. 120–123 (1968).
Išo'dad of Merv, *Commentaire d'Išo'dad de Merv sur l'ancien testament*, ed. Ceslas van den Eynde O.P., C.S.C.O. Syr. 75, Genèse (1955); 80/81, Exode, Deut. (1958); 96/97, Livre des Sessions (1962–3); 120/123, Isaïe et les douze (1969).
The Commentaries of Isho'dad of Merv, bishop of Hadatha, ed. M. D. Gibson with introduction by J. Rendel Harris, *Horae Semiticae* v (3 vols), Cambridge (1911).
G. Dietrich, *Išo'dads Stellung in der Auslegungsgeschichte des alten Testaments, an seinen Commentaren zu Hosea, Joel, Jona, Sacharja 9–14 und einigen ange-hängten Psalmen*, Z.A.T.W., Beihefte vi (1902).
Jacob of Edessa, *Chronicon Jacobi Edesseni*, ed. G. W. Brooks, C.S.C.O. Syr. iii. 4, part 3 section 2 (1905).
Hexameron, ed. A. Vaschalde, C.S.C.O. Syr. ii. 56 (1928–32).
John Chrysostom, *Homiliae*, P.G. 51–56 (Old Testament); P.G. 57–59 (Gospels); *Homiliae in Epistolam ad Hebraeos*, P.G. 63, 13–226.
Adversus Judaeos, P.G. 48, 844–942.
John of Damascus, *Dialectica*, P.G. 94, 518–675.
De Fide Orthodoxa, P.G. 94, 784–1228.
Disceptatio Christiani et Saraceni, P.G. 94, 1586–1598.
John Philoponus, *Documenta ad origines Monophysitorum illustrandas*, ed. J. B. Chabot, C.S.C.O. Syr. ii. 37 (1907).
Martyrius (Sahdona), *Oeuvres spirituelles i, Livre de la perfection*, ed. André de Halleux, C.S.C.O. Syr. 86 (1960); 90 (1961); 110 (1965).
Michael the Syrian, *Chronicon*, ed. J. B. Chabot, Paris (1899–1905).
Narsai, *Homélies de Narsai sur la création*, ed. P. Gignoux, Pat. Or. xxxiv. 3, 4 (1968).
Nemesius of Emesa, *De Natura Hominis*, P.G. 40, 508–818.

Nestorius, *The Bazaar of Heracleides, newly translated from the Syriac*, by G. R. Driver and L. Hodgson, Oxford (1925).

J. Lebon, 'Fragments syriaques de Nestorius dans le *Contra Grammaticum* de Sévère d'Antioche', *Le Muséon. Revue d'études orientales*, 36, 47–65, Louvain (1923).

F. Loofs, *Nestoriana, Die Fragmente des Nestorius gesammelt, untersucht und herausgegeben, mit Beiträgen von S. A. Cook und G. Kampffmeyer*, Halle (1905).

F. Nau, *Nestorius, le livre d'Héracleide de Damas* (French translation), Paris (1910).

Nicolaus of Damascus, *Nicolaus Damascenus on the Philosophy of Aristotle. Fragments of the first five books translated from the Syriac with Introduction and Comments*, Philosophia Antiqua xiii, ed. H. J. Drossaart Lulofs, Leiden (1965).

Paulos of Nisibis (Paul the Persian), *Instituta Regularia Divinae Legis*, in Junilius, *De Partibus Divinae Legis*, P.L. 68, 15–42.

Philoxenus of Mabboug (Akhsenaya), *The Discourses of Philoxenos*, ed. E. A. Wallis Budge, 2 volumes, London (1894).

Philostorgius, *Historia Ecclesiastica*, ed. J. Bidez, G.C.S. 21 (1913).

Procopius of Caesarea, *De Bellis*, ed. J. Haury, Loeb Classical Library, 7 volumes (1914–40).

Profession of Faith made by Nestorian bishops, ed. A. Scher, Pat. Or. vii. 1, 82–87 (1911).

Sahdona, *see* Martyrius.

Severus of Antioch, *Homiliae Cathedrales*: *Homs.* 46–51, ed. M. Brière and F. Graffin, Pat. Or. xxxv. 3 (1969); *Homs.* 52–57, ed. R. Duval, Pat. Or. iv. 1 (1908); *Homs.* 58–69, ed. M. Brière, Pat. Or. viii. 2 (1911); *Homs.* 70–76, ed. M. Brière, Pat. Or. xii. 1 (no date); *Hom.* 77, ed. M. A. Kugener and E. Triffaux, Pat. Or. xvi. 5 (1922); *Homs.* 78–83, ed. M. Brière, Pat. Or. xx. 2 (1928); *Homs.* 84–90, ed. M. Brière, Pat. Or. xxiii. 1 (1932); *Homs.* 91–98, ed. M. Brière, Pat. Or. xxv. 1 (1935); *Homs.* 99–103, ed. I. Guidi, Pat. Or. xxii. 2 (1929); *Homs.* 104–112, ed. M. Brière, Pat. Or. xxv. 4 (1943); *Homs.* 113–119, ed. M. Brière, Pat. Or. xxvi. 3 (1947); *Homs.* 120–125, ed. M. Brière, Pat. Or. xxix. 1 (1960).

Liber contra impium grammaticum, ed. J. Lebon, C.S.C.O. Syr. iv. 4 (1938).

La Philalèthe, ed. R. Hespel, C.S.C.O. Syr. 67/68 (1952).

Socrates Scholasticus, *Historia Ecclesiastica*, P.G. 67, 28–852.

Sozomen, *Historia Ecclesiastica*, P.G. 67, 853–1630.

Synodicon Orientale ou receuil de synodes nestoriennes, ed. J. B. Chabot, *Notices et extraits de la Bibliothèque Nationale*, 37, Paris (1902).

Theodore of Mopsuestia, *Fragmenta in Genesin*, P.G. 66, 633–646.

Theodori Mopsuesteni fragmenta Syriaca (Genesis), ed. E. Sachau, 1–21, Leipzig (1879).

Théodore de Mopsueste Interprétation de la Genèse (fragments), ed. R. M. Tonneau, *Le Muséon. Revue d'études orientales*, 66, 45–61, Louvain (1953).

Le Commentaire de Théodore de Mopsueste sur les Psaumes, ed. R. Devréesse, Studi e Testi 93, Vatican City (1939).

Commentarius in duodecim prophetas minores, P.G. 66, 105–632; E. Sachau, *op. cit.*, 22–7.

In Evangelium Johannis Commentarii Fragmenta, P.G. 66, 728–765.

Commentary on John, ed. J. M. Vosté O.P., C.S.C.O. Syr. iv. 3 (1940).

Theodori episc. Mopsuesteni in Epistolas Beati Pauli Commentarii, ed. H. B. Swete, 2 volumes, Cambridge (1880–2).

K. Staab, *Pauluskommentare aus der griechischen Kirche* (fragments: Romans,

113-72; 1 Corinthians, 172-96; 2 Corinthians, 196-200; Hebrews, 200-12), Münster (1933).

Commentary of Theodore of Mopsuestia on the Nicene Creed, ed. A. Mingana, *Woodbrooke Studies* 5, Cambridge (1932).

Commentary of Theodore of Mopsuestia on the Lord's Prayer and on the Sacraments of Baptism and the Eucharist, ed. A. Mingana, *Woodbrooke Studies* 6, Cambridge (1933).

Les Homélies catéchetiques de Théodore de Mopsueste, ed. R. Tonneau, *Studi e Testi* 145, Vatican City (1949).

De Incarnatione, ed. H. B. Swete, *op. cit.*, vol. 2, 290-312 (fragments); E. Sachau, *op. cit.*, 28-57 (Syriac fragments).

Theodoret of Cyrrhus, *Epistolae*, P.G. 83, 1173-1409.

Eranistes, ed. G. H. Ettlinger, Oxford (1975).

Graecarum Affectionum Curatio, ed. R. P. Canivet, *Théodoret de Cyr Thérapeutique des maladies helléniques*, 2 volumes, *S.C.* 57, Paris (1958).

Historia Ecclesiastica, ed. L. Parmentier, G.C.S. 19 (1911); 2nd ed. revised by F. Scheidweiler (1954).

Historia Religiosa, P.G. 82, 1283-1496.

Interpretatio in duodecim Prophetas Minores, P.G. 81, 1545-1988.

Reprehensio Duodecim Capitum, ed. E. Schwartz, *A.C.O.* i.1.6, 107-46.

Theophilus of Antioch, *Libri tres ad Autolycum*, P.G. 6, 1023-1167.

Zacharias Rhetor, *Historia Ecclesiastica*, ed. E. W. Brooks, C.S.C.O. *Syr.* iii. 5, 2 volumes (1924).

De Mundi Opificio contra Philosophos Disputatio, P.G. 85, 1012-1144.

II Secondary Sources

Albright, W. F. , *Archeology and the Religion of Israel*, 3rd ed, Baltimore, 1953-4.

Antioch-on-the-Orontes. Publications of the Committee for the Excavation of Antioch and its Vicinity, vols. i-iv. 2, Princeton, 1934-52.

Ashby, G. W., *Theodoret of Cyrrhus as Exegete of the Old Testament*, Grahamstown, 1972.

Assemani, J. S., *Bibliotheca Orientalis*, 4 vols., 1719-28.

Bardy, G., *Paul de Samosate*, 2nd ed, Louvain, 1929.

Recherches sur Saint Lucien d'Antioche et son école, Paris, 1936.

Bartsch, H. W., *Gnostisches Gut und Gemeindetradition bei Ignatius von Antiochen*, Gütersloh, 1940.

Batiffol, P., 'Le passion de St. Lucien d'Antioche', *Comptes rendues du 2e congrès scientifique*, vol. 2, Paris, 1891.

Baumstark, A., *Aristoteles bei den Syrern*, Leipzig, 1900.

Geschichte der syrischen Literatur, Bonn, 1922.

Bindley, T. H., *Oecumenical Documents of the Faith*, London, 1899, revised F. W. Green.

Blum, G. G., *Rabbula von Edessa*, C.S.C.O., Subsidia 34, 1969.

Bokser, Ben Zion, *Pharisaic Judaism in Transition*, New York, 1935.

Bousset, W., *Hauptprobleme der Gnosis*, Göttingen, 1907.

Brown, P., 'The Diffusion of Manichaeism in the Roman Empire', *J.R.S.*, lix, 1969.

Browne, E. G., *A Literary History of Persia*, London and Leipzig, 1909.

Burkitt, F. C., *Early Eastern Christianity*, London, 1904.

The Religion of the Manichees, Cambridge, 1925.

Chabot, J. B., 'L'école de Nisibe, son histoire et ses statutes', *Journal Asiatique*, 9ᵉ série, viii, 1896.

Littérature syriaque, Paris, 1934.

Chadwick, H., 'The Fall of Eustathius of Antioch', *J.T.S.* 49, 1948.

'The Silence of Bishops in Ignatius', *H.T.R.* 43, 1950.

'Eucharist and Christology in the Nestorian Controversy', *J.T.S.*, N.S., ii. 2, 1951, pp. 145-64.

Chesnut, Roberta C., *Three Monophysite Christologies*, Oxford, 1976.

Chitty, D., *The Desert a City*, Oxford, 1966.

Corwin, V., *St. Ignatius and Christianity in Antioch* (*Yale Publications in Religion*, i), New Haven, 1960.

Cross, F. L., *The Early Christian Fathers*, London, 1960.

Crowfoot, J. W., *Early Christian Churches in Palestine*, London, 1941.

Cumont, F., *Les Religions orientales dans le Paganisme romain*, 4th ed., Paris, 1929.

Devréesse, R., *Essai sur Théodore de Mopsueste* (*Studi e Testi*, 141), Vatican City, 1938.

Downey, Glanville, 'The Shrines of St. Babylas at Antioch and Daphne', *Antioch-on-the-Orontes*, ii, Princeton, 1938, pp. 45-8.

'Personification of abstract ideas in the Antioch mosaics', *Transactions of the American Philological Association*, lxix, 1938, pp. 349-63.

'Julian the Apostate at Antioch', *Church History*, viii, 1939, pp. 303-15.

'Procopius of Antioch, a study of method in *De Aedificiis*', *Byzantion*, xiv, 1939.

'Ethical themes in the Antioch mosaics', *Church History*, x, 1941, pp. 367-76.

'Greek and Latin inscriptions', *Antioch-on-the-Orontes*, iii, 1941, pp. 83-115.

Dussaud, R., *Mana. Introduction à l'histoire de religion*, i. 2, Paris, 1949.

Eger, H., 'Kaiser und Kirche in der Geschichtstheologie Eusebs von Cäsarea', *Z.N.T.W.*, xxxviii, 1939, pp. 97-115.

Epstein, I., *Judaism*, London, 1945, (revised ed.).

Festugière, A. J., *Antioche païenne et chrétienne* (*Bibliothèque des écoles françaises d'Athènes et de Rome*, fasc. 194) Paris, 1959.

Frend, W. H. C., *The Rise of the Monophysite Movement*, Cambridge, 1972.

Galtier, P., 'Théodore de Mopsueste: sa vraie pensée sur l'Incarnation', *Recherches de science religieuse*, 45, 1957, pp. 161-86, 338-60.

Grant, R. M., 'Theophilus of Antioch to Autolycus', *H.T.R.* 40, 1947.

The Letter and the Spirit, London, 1957.

Greer, Rowan A., *Theodore of Mopsuestia, Exegete and Theologian*, London, 1961.

'The Antiochene Christology of Diodore of Tarsus', *J.T.S.*, N.S., xvii. 2, 1966, pp. 327-41.

Grillmeier, A., *Christ in Christian Tradition*, London, 1965 (Eng. trans. of *Das Konzil von Chalkedon*, i, pp. 5-202, Würzburg, 1951).

Guillet, J., 'Les exégèses d'Alexandrie et d'Antioch. Conflit ou malentendu?', *Recherches des sciences religieuses*, 34, 1945.

Gwatkin, H., *Studies in Arianism*, 2nd ed., 1900.

Halleux, A. de, 'La christologie de Martyrius-Sahdona dans l'évolution de Nestorianisme', *Orientalia Christiana Periodica*, 23, 1957.

Hendriks, O., 'L'activité apostolique des premiers moines syriens', *Le Proche-Orient Chrétien*, 8, 1958.

Hitti, P. K., *History of Syria, including Lebanon and Palestine*, London, 1951.

Hoffman, J. G. E., *Auszügen aus syrischen Akten persischer Märtyren*, Leipzig, 1880.

Jaeger, W., *Nemesios von Emesa*, Berlin, 1914.
Jansma, T., 'L'Hexaméron de Jacques de Sarûg', *L'Orient Syrien*, iv.2, 1959, pp. 3–42; 129–62; 253–84.
'Investigations in the early Syrian Fathers on Genesis. An Approach to the Exegesis of the Nestorian Church and Comparison of Nestorian and Jewish Exegesis', *Oud Testamentische Studien*, Deel xii, Leiden, 1958.
Jones, A. H. M., *The Decline of the Ancient World*, London, 1966.
Jugie, M., 'Le "liber ad baptizandos" de Théodore de Mopsueste', *Échos d'Orient*, xxxv, 1935.
Laistner, M. W. L., 'Antiochene exegesis in Western Europe', *H.T.R.* 40, 1947.
Lampe, G. W. H., 'The exegesis of some biblical texts by Marcellus of Ancyra', *J.T.S.* 49, 1948.
Lebon, J., *Le monophysisme séverian. Étude historique, littéraire et théologique*, Louvain, 1909.
Liebeschuetz, J. H. W. G., *Antioch. City and Imperial Administration in the later Roman Empire*, Oxford, 1972.
Lietzmann, H., *Apollinaris von Laodicea und seine Schule*, Tübingen, 1904.
'Das Leben des heiligen Symeon Stylites', T.U. xxxii. 4, 1908.
Loofs, F., *Nestorius and his place in the history of Christian doctrine*, Cambridge, 1914.
'Paulus von Samosata', T.U. xl. 5, 1924.
Mariès, L., 'Extraits du Commentaire de Diodore de Tarse sur les Psaumes', *Recherches des sciences religieuses*, 10, 1919.
Martin, F., 'Homélie de Narsès sur les trois docteurs nestoriens', *Journal Asiatique*, ser. 9, vol. xiv, 1899.
Millar, F., 'Paul of Samosata, Zenobia and Aurelian: the Church, local culture and political allegiance in third-century Syria', *J.R.S.*, lxi, 1971, pp. 1–17.
Mitchell, C. W., *Ephrem's prose refutations of Mani, Marcion and Bardaisan*, London, 1912.
Nau, F., 'Scriptorum testimonia de Bardesanis vita, scripta doctrina', Pat. Syr. i. 2, 1907, pp. 492–535.
Opitz, H. G., 'Die Zeitfolge des arianischen Streites', *Z.N.T.W.* xxxiii, 1934.
Puech, H. C., 'Der Begriff der Erlösung in Manichäismus', *Eranos Jahrbuch*, 1936, pp. 183–286.
Le Manichéisme: son fondateur, sa doctrine (Musée Guimet. Bibliothèque de diffusion, lvi) Paris, 1949.
Rabin, B., *Prokopius von Kaisareia*, Stuttgart, 1954.
Raven, C. E., *Apollinarianism*, Cambridge, 1923.
Richard, M., 'Malchion et Paul de Samosate. Le témoignage d'Eusèbe de Césarée', *Ephemera Theol. Louvaniensis*, xxxv, 1959.
Sant, C., *The Old Testament interpretation of Eusebius of Caesarea*, Malta, 1967.
Schilling, F. A., *The Mysticism of Ignatius of Antioch*, Philadelphia, 1932.
Schlier, H., 'Religionsgeschichtliche Untersuchungen zu den Ignatienbriefen', *Z.N.T.W.*, Beiheft viii, 1929.
Sellers, R. V., *Two ancient Christologies*, London, 1940.
The Council of Chalcedon: a historical and doctrinal survey, London, 1961.
Sheldon-Williams, I. P., 'The Greek-Christian Platonist tradition from the Cappadocians to Maximus and Eriugena', *Cambridge History of late Greek and early Medieval Philosophy*, ed. A. H. Armstrong, Cambridge, 1967, pp. 425ff.
Skard, E., *Nemesios-Studien* (Symbolae Osloenses, xv–xvi), 1936.

Sullivan, F. A., *The Christology of Theodore of Mopsuestia*, Vatican City, 1956.

Sweetman, J. W., *Islam and Christian theology. A study of the interaction of theological ideas*, London, 1945.

Vaccari, A., 'La *theoria* nella scuola esegetica di Antiocha', *Biblica*, i, 1920.

Vööbus, A., 'Celibacy, a requirement of admission to Baptism in the early Syrian Church', *Papers of the Estonian Theological Society in Exile*, 1, Stockholm, 1951.

'Manichaeism and Christianity in Persia under the Sassanides. Some notes on the Manichaean ecclesiology and its background', *Yearbook of the Estonian Learned Society in America*, i, New York, 1951-3.

'The Origin of Monasticism in Mesopotamia', *Church History*, xx, 1951.

'Literary, critical and historical studies in Ephrem the Syrian', *Papers of the Estonian Theological Society in Exile*, 10, Stockholm, 1958.

History of Asceticism in the Syrian Orient, vol. 1, C.S.C.O., Subsidia 14, 1958; vol. 2, Subsidia 17, 1960.

History of the School of Nisibis, C.S.C.O., Subsidia 26, 1965.

Wallace-Hadrill, D. S., *Eusebius of Caesarea*, London, 1960.

Wallis, R. T., *Neoplatonism*, London, 1972.

Walzer, R., 'Arabic transmission of Greek thought to medieval Europe', *Bulletin of the John Rylands Library*, Manchester, 29. 1, 1945.

'Aristutalis', *Encyclopaedia of Islam*, i, 1960.

'Aflatun', *Ibid.*

Index

Abraham de-bet Rabban 47, 62, 65, 140
Adam, Mortality and Moral Responsi-
    bility 37, 44, 98f., 145, 161f.
Addai 64
Aeneas of Gaza 104f.
Aetius 67
Afrahat 39-43, 61f., 89, 91f.
Africanus, Sextus Julius 53
Agathius 57
Ahoudemmeh 109, 140
Akhsenaya (Philoxenus of Mabboug)
    26, 64, 71, 87, 154
Alexander of Alexandria 64, 82f., 88
Alexandria 14, 21, 22, 24, 30, 39, 50,
    58, 70, 72, 81, 86, 92f., 107, 149
Alexandrian Exegesis 29-35, 37-45,
    49-51
Allegorical Exegesis 35-45, 47, 49f.,
    64, 75
Al Kindi 92
Ammianus Marcellinus 57
Anastasius, Emperor 10
Andrew of Samosata 138
Antioch, City of 1-12, 58, 77f., 91
Antioch
    Council A.D. 264: 69
    Council A.D. 268: 70, 72-5
    Council A.D. 341: 81-4, 86
    Council A.D. 513: 93
Apollinarius of Laodicea 71, 88, 92,
    100f., 118f., 126, 131-7, 142,
    146f.
Arab Invasion of Syria 12, 59
Arianism 7-9, 60f., 82-4, 87-92, 94,
    118f., 128
Aristobulus 68
Aristotelianism 96, 102f., 107, 110f.
Aristotle 47, 63, 93-6, 98, 101, 104,
    106-12, 114-16, 142, 164
Arius 20, 60, 82-5, 87f., 94f., 118,
    126, 139
Artemon 67, 71
Ascetic Life 25, 153-6, 162
Asterius the Sophist 77, 84, 86f.

Athanasius of Alexandria 64, 78f.,
    84-6, 88, 92, 95, 134, 139
Aurelian, Emperor 70

Ba'al 15, 17
Ba'albek 15, 17, 155
Ba'albek, Oracle of 17
Babai Magnus 109f., 144-9, 152, 158,
    164
Babylas of Antioch, Saint 8, 16
Baghdad 25, 110
Bahram, King of Persia 58
Bardaisan 21f., 25f., 112, 114, 139,
    143
Barhadbešabba of 'Arbaya 17, 58, 63-7,
    72, 88f., 108, 153, 161
Bar-'Idta, History of 58f., 140
Barsai, Bishop of Edessa 90
Barsauma 64, 140
Basil of Caesarea 49, 64, 79, 81, 95,
    134, 140
Basilides 21, 67
Bible, Exegesis 19, 22, 27-51, 64, 164

Carrhae 17
Celestine, Pope 126f.
Cerdo 67, 139
Cerinthus 67
Chalcedon, Council A.D. 451: 10, 19,
    46, 93, 111, 131, 140, 142, 149,
    151
Christ, Divinity and Humanity 9, 26,
    67, 69, 70-2, 74f., 77, 82, 89, 92,
    96, 106f., 115, 117-50, 152-64
Chrysostom, John, of Constantinople
    18-20, 29f., 38, 46, 48f., 51, 61,
    64, 94f., 117, 119, 130, 151,
    153-5, 157, 161-4
Clement of Alexandria 101f.
Collucianists 83f., 86
Communicatio Idiomatum 124, 127
Conon 94
Constans, Emperor 81

215

Constantine the Great, Emperor 6f., 53, 87
Constantinople 12, 14, 17, 61, 126, 131, 140f., 149
Constantinople, Council A.D. 381: 93
Constantius II, Emperor 7f., 78, 90f.
Cyril of Alexandria 29f., 33–5, 39, 49, 95, 110, 119, 121, 126–31, 134–42, 144f., 147, 150, 153, 157
Cyrus of Edessa 143f., 147, 152, 161

Dani'el of Edessa 45
Daphne, Suburb of Antioch 1f., 8f., 16f., 21
Dea Syria, Atargatis 92
Denba 59
Diatessaron 39, 43
Diodore of Tarsus 38f., 45, 64, 71, 87, 91f., 112, 117, 119, 120f., 132, 143, 149
Dionysius of Alexandria 69f., 73, 84f.
Dioscorus of Alexandria 139f., 151f.
Docetism 118, 150
Domnus of Antioch 17, 138, 151
Dorotheus of Antioch 38, 83

Edessa 12, 15, 17, 25, 43, 45f., 58, 64, 89, 91f., 107, 111, 140
Elias of Nisibis 55, 59
Elisha bar Quzbaie 47, 62, 112
Ephesus
    Council A.D. 431: 93, 139
    Council A.D. 449: 140
Ephrem Syrus 22, 25f., 39–43, 45, 49, 62, 64, 71, 87f.
Epiphanius 73, 82
Eucharist 75, 131, 147f., 160f.
Eudoxius of Constantinople 90, 118
Eugenius 94
Eunomius 67, 139
Eusebius of Caesarea 7, 20, 25, 29, 38f., 45, 51–7, 59–61, 65, 70f., 75–8, 81, 83f., 86–9, 102, 105, 107, 155
Eusebius of Nicomedia 77, 83f., 86, 88f.
Eusebius of Samosata 90
Eustathius of Antioch 7, 29, 31f., 39, 45, 64, 77, 83, 88, 118
Eutyches 118, 131, 143, 150f.
Evagrius 64, 113f., 140
Expositio Officiorum Ecclesiae 54, 159f.

Facundus 35
Firmilian 70
Flavian of Antioch 9, 91

Gnosticism 14, 20–6, 67, 72, 110, 113f., 118, 164
God
    Father: 76f., 80–5, 90, 92, 102, 126, 137f., 148
    Son: 72f., 75f., 79, 82, 84–6, 90, 118, 122f., 131, 144, 152, 155
    Word (*Logos*): 67–9, 72–4, 76f., 79f., 82, 84f., 90, 102, 118–25, 128f., 133, 135f., 139, 142–4, 146, 148f., 152, 158
    Holy Spirit: 27f., 31, 69, 72, 75f., 80, 92, 135, 147, 152, 162, 164
Gratian, Emperor 17
Gregory of Nyssa 32, 49, 81, 88, 134
Gregory Thaumaturgos 28

Hebrews, Epistle to 150, 151–8
Henana of Hadiab 47–9, 50f., 64f., 110, 140, 143f., 147
Henotikon 93
Heracleitus 104
Heraclius, Emperor 11, 59
Hībā of Edessa (Ibas) 45f., 107, 117, 140, 142f., 152
Hierapolis 89, 91f.
Historical Method of Exegesis 29–51, 64, 66, 75, 119, 164
Historiography 52–66
Homoousios 77, 81f., 90
Hunain ibn Ishaq 110f.
Hypostasis 94f., 106, 130f., 137, 141, 143f., 147, 149

Iamblichus 97, 104, 111
Ibas, see Hiba
Ignatius of Antioch 5, 19, 21, 117f., 164
Irenaeus 20
Isaias, Abba 155, 159
Isha'ia of Tahal 48
Ishaq ibn Hunain 110f.
Islam 25, 59, 92
Išo'dad of Merv 27, 47–50, 87
Išo'yabh 54f., 143, 160

Jacob of Edessa 55, 58, 87
James Bar'adai 43, 140f., 150
Jerome 30f., 81, 132, 155
Jerusalem 18, 58f.
Jews, Judaism 4f., 8, 10, 14, 18–20, 43, 71, 76, 150, 156–8
John of Antioch 137f.
John of Damascus 110
John of Tella 140, 150
Jovian, Emperor 17

Julian, Emperor 8, 9, 16, 19, 60, 90, 119
Justin Martyr 21
Justin I, Emperor 10
Justin II, Emperor 11, 93
Justinian, Emperor 10, 17, 93, 97, 110, 140, 143

Khosrau I, King of Persia 11, 57f., 140f.
Khosrau II, King of Persia 58f.
Kūmī of Edessa 45, 107

Leo I, Emperor 10
Leo I, Pope 131, 142, 151
Leontius of Antioch 74, 84, 90
Libanius 9, 16
Liber Perfectionis 154f.
Literal Exegesis 27, 29, 31-51
Lucian of Antioch 19, 30, 38, 81-4, 86-8, 135
Lucian of Samosata 91

Macedonius 20, 67
Magianism, Persian 59, 111f., 116
Malchion 70, 73
Mā'nā of Shiraz 45
Mani 22-6, 67, 112-14, 118f., 143, 150
Manichaeism 23-5, 71, 151
Marcellus of Ancyra 38f., 71, 75-83, 86, 107, 135
Marcian, Emperor 131
Marcion of Pontus 22, 25f., 67, 139, 143, 150
Maris of Chalcedon 83f., 88
Marouta, History of 59
Mary, Virgin 71, 73, 76, 92, 119-25, 131
Maurice, Emperor 11, 58
Megas, Bishop of Beroea 57
Meletian Heresy 83
Melkites 57
Menander 21, 67
Menophantius of Ephesus 84
Methodius 84
Mohammad 58f.
Monophysitism 9, 17, 45, 56, 61, 65, 67, 93, 100, 106-8, 111, 116, 131f., 140-4, 148-52

Narsai 43, 45-7, 62, 64f., 72, 140
Nemesius of Emesa 103f.
Nestorianism 27, 47f., 56, 64-7, 87, 92f., 111, 115f., 119, 122, 131f., 134f., 140-5, 147, 149-52, 155, 158f.

Nestorius 20, 45, 64, 71f., 92, 117, 125, 126-31, 136, 138f., 140, 142f., 145, 149, 153, 164
Nicaea, Council A.D. 325: 64f., 68, 71, 74, 77, 79, 82, 85-9, 91, 93f., 118, 129
Nicolaus of Damascus 96, 112
Nisibis 43, 46-9, 64, 107, 110, 140
Numenius of Apamea 96, 102

Odeinath, Prince of Palmyra 6, 69
Origen 27-32, 49, 52, 70, 72-4, 76-85, 92, 114, 139
Ousia 94, 106f.

Paganism at Antioch 8-10, 14-18, 60f.
Palmyra 6, 69-71
Pamphilus of Caesarea 28, 87
Parthia 2f., 5
Paul of Samosata 20, 69-76, 78, 80-3, 87, 92, 99f., 119, 125, 135, 148
Paulos of Nisibis (Paul the Persian) 47, 49, 107f.
Pelagianism 126, 145, 162-4
Persia 5-7, 10-12, 16, 57-9, 63f., 93, 111, 140f.
Persona, Prosopon, Parsupa 75, 124f., 128-32, 141, 144
Peter of Alexandria 84
Philo Judaeus 27, 30, 44f., 52, 64, 68, 97
Philoponus, John, the Grammarian 93-5, 106f., 111
Philostorgius 83
Philoxenus, see Akhsenaya
Phocas, Emperor 11
Photinus 67, 71, 78
Pillars, sacred 91
Plato 96-9, 101, 104f., 111, 113-15
Platonism 31, 61, 63, 72, 96-104, 107, 109, 111, 115f., 130, 132-5, 145, 164
Plotinus 97, 102, 104f., 112f.
Porphyry 97, 102, 104f., 107f., 110f.
Posidonius 103
Prōbā of Edessa 45, 107
Procopius of Caesarea 57
Pythagoras 96, 104

Qiiōrē of Edessa 45, 64, 140

Rabbula of Edessa 16, 45, 51, 64, 155f.
'raza, Mystery 159f.
Recognitions, Clementine 45

Sabellius 20, 75-9, 83, 88, 107, 135, 148

Sabrišo 48
Sahdona 144f., 152f., 155, 158
Sargis of Rišʿaina 108
Satornilus (Saturninus) 21
Seleucia-Ctesiphon 47, 89, 110, 140
Serdica, Council A.D. 342/3: 78
Severus of Antioch 17, 23-5, 71, 73,
    87, 92, 95, 106f., 113, 141-3,
    145-7, 150
Shahpur I, King of Persia 6, 8, 69
Simeon Stylites 91
Simon Magus 21, 67, 139
Sirmium, Council A.D. 351: 78
Socrates Scholasticus 54f., 57
Sozomen 57, 82
Spiritual Exegesis 28, 30-45, 48-51
Stoicism 68, 97, 103f., 116, 131

Tarsus 10, 14, 119
Theodore of Mopsuestia 17, 29, 33-8,
    40, 42f., 45-52, 61-5, 72, 74, 87,
    92, 98f., 106f., 112, 115, 117,
    119, 122-4, 126, 130, 134, 139f.,
    142-5, 149f., 160-4
Theodoret of Cyrrhus 15, 20, 29f.,
    33-5, 39, 45, 48, 54, 57, 60f.,
    65, 70f., 87, 89, 90-2, 101f.,
    104-6, 117-19, 129, 134-43,
    152, 155, 161, 163

Theodosius of Alexandria 94f.
Theodosius I, Emperor 9, 16f., 91, 119
Theodosius II, Emperor 126
Theodotion 67
Theodotus of Ancyra 127, 137
Theodulos 64
Theognis of Nicaea 83f., 88
Theophilus of Antioch 43-5, 67-9,
    72f., 103
Theophronius of Tyana 81
Theotokos 71, 92, 124, 126f., 131,
    137, 157
Titus of Bostra 45
Trinity, Christian Doctrine 26, 67,
    72-8, 81f., 84, 92-5, 106, 109,
    114, 144, 146, 148
Typology 33-45, 157, 159f.
Tyre, Council A.D. 514: 93

Valens, Emperor 9, 17, 61, 89-92, 119
Valentinus 21, 67, 139

Wahballath, Prince of Palmyra 69
Wisdom of God 67f., 72f., 80, 84

Zacharias Rhetor 54, 58, 65, 104, 149
Zeno, Emperor 10, 17, 93
Zenobia 6, 19, 69-71
Zosimus 57